AND MAN CREATED GOD

'Expansive and intelligent... O'Grady's book should be read by both believers and non-believers in the open and enquiring spirit it exemplifies' *Guardian*

'In a panoramic survey, [O'Grady] shows the intimacy of the relationship between the way that people lived and the gods they worshipped... Vivid and learned' Tom Holland, *Mail on Sunday*

'A sweeping account of relations between faith and power at the dawn of the Christian era... the result is an enjoyable, informative romp through the subject of comparative religion' *Economist*

'Compulsively good history... Selina O'Grady is also a first-rate storyteller with a finely tuned ear for character and an impressive eye for atmosphere and the telling detail.' *Country Life*

'A dazzling, dizzying, compelling panorama of the world that Jesus knew and the worlds he had never heard of... a remarkable book... I cannot think of anyone who will not learn a huge amount from reading this book' *Tablet*

Isis and Horus. Wellcome Library, London

AND MAN CREATED GOD

KINGS, CULTS, AND CONQUESTS AT THE TIME OF JESUS

SELINA O'GRADY

Atlantic Books
London

First published in Great Britain in 2012 by
Atlantic Books, an imprint of Atlantic Books Ltd.

This paperback edition published in Great Britain
in 2013 by Atlantic Books

9 8 7 6 5 4 3 2 1

A CIP catalogue record for this book is available from the British Library.

Paperback ISBN: 978 1 84354 697 9
E-book ISBN: 978 0 85789 876 0

Printed in Great Britain by CPI Group (UK) Ltd, Croydon, CR0 4YY

Atlantic Books
An imprint of Atlantic Books Ltd
Ormond House
26-27 Boswell Street
London WC1N 3JZ

www.atlantic-books.co.uk

To my darling Anna and Sibby
who put up with my obsession

And to Tony who was and is invaluable

Acknowledgements

Thanks to my ebullient and constantly helpful agent, Ivan Mulcahy; to Toby Mundy, who got me thinking about this book; to all those who read and commented – Claudia Fitzherbert, Daniel Jeffreys, Lucy Lethbridge, Kathy O'Shaughnessy, Graeme and Terrence Mitchison, Oliver Ramsbotham and Victoria Curzon Price; to my academic readers – Dr Lindsay Allen, Nell Aubrey, Professor Timothy Barrett, Professor Paul Morris, Dr Tadeusz Skorupski, and William Fitzgerald – who saved me from at least some of the oversimplifications which drive experts mad; to Rebecca Fraser, Anthony Grayling and Malise Ruthven for their incredibly generous comments; to my brother Jeremy for his titles and masterly editorial eye; to my ever-supportive sister Jane; to Caroline Law; to my daughters; to Richard Milbank for being a learned and wonderful editor; to Sarah Norman and Margaret Stead, who were my editors for all too short a time; to my copyeditor Helen Gray; and above all, to Tony Curzon Price.

Contents

Illustrations

Map 1. The 'known world' around the time of Jesus

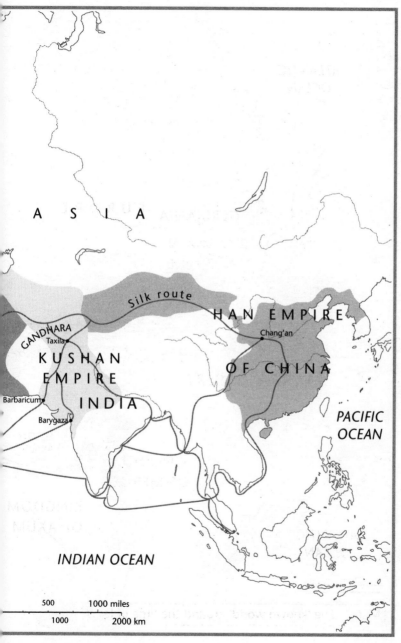

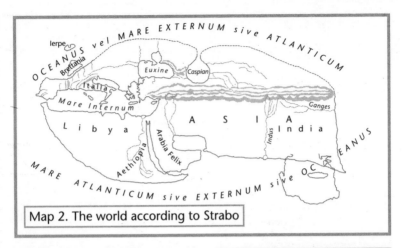

Map 2. The world according to Strabo

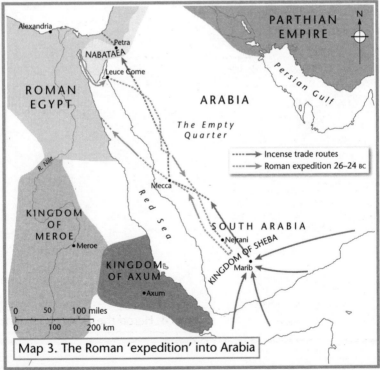

Map 3. The Roman 'expedition' into Arabia

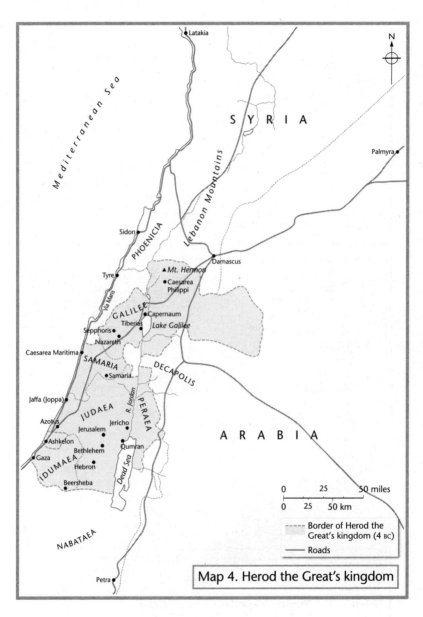

Map 4. Herod the Great's kingdom

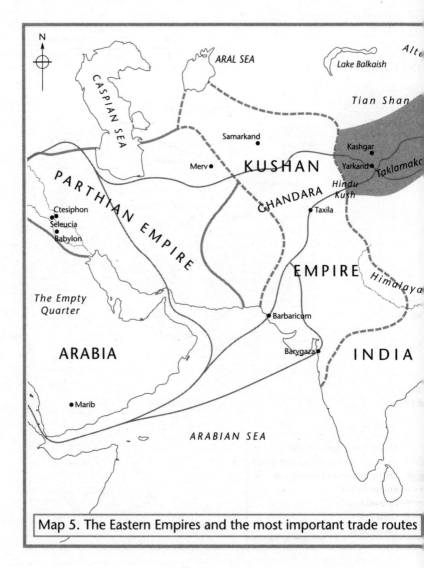

Map 5. The Eastern Empires and the most important trade routes

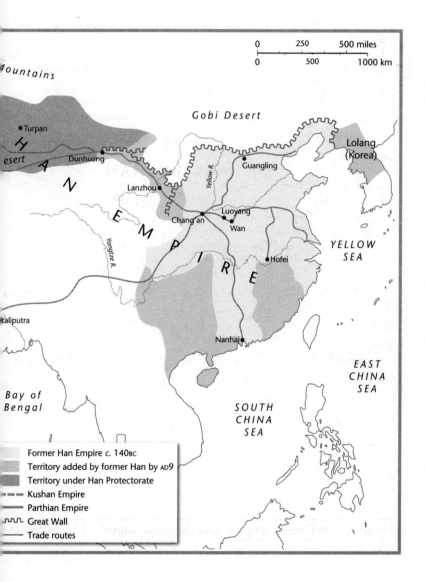

0   250   500 miles

0   500   1000 km

Gobi Desert

Mountains

• Turpan

Lolang
(Korea)

esert   Dunhuang •

Yellow R.

Guangling •

Lanzhou •

H A N   E M P I R E

Chang'an •   Luoyang •
      • Wan

Yangtze R.

YELLOW
SEA

• Hofei

taliputra

Nanhai •

EAST
CHINA
SEA

*Bay of
Bengal*

SOUTH
CHINA
SEA

Former Han Empire *c.* 140BC
Territory added by former Han by AD9
Territory under Han Protectorate
--- Kushan Empire
—— Parthian Empire
ᴨᴨ Great Wall
—— Trade routes

Timeline

Note: Many of these dates are approximate

BC

1500–1000 Aryan (Indo-Iranian) tribesmen from the steppes of southern Russia move into the Indus Valley – in present-day Pakistan and north-west India – and begin to compile the hymns of the *Rig Veda*, the oldest sacred text of Hinduism

1200 The Aryan priest Zoroaster has a vision of the first supreme god Ahura Mazda and begins preaching in ancient Iran

1070 Egypt loses control of Meroe – present-day southern Egypt and Sudan – and it becomes an independent kingdom

1070–AD 350 EMPIRE OF MEROE

753 Legendary date for the founding of the city of Rome by Romulus and Remus

744–609 ASSYRIAN (NEO-ASSYRIAN) EMPIRE
—Originally a kingdom of northern Mesopotamia – modern-day northern Iraq – Assyria acquires a vast territory and has its capital at Nineveh on the banks of the Tigris River

727 Meroite King Pye invades Egypt and founds the twenty-fifth dynasty of pharaohs which rules Egypt 727–653

727–653 Twenty-fifth dynasty of Egypt

722 Assyria conquers northern Israel and Jews are deported

700 Construction of Marib Dam in South Arabia
—Towards the end of the 7th century Rome becomes an organized city-state

626 The kingdom of Babylonia in southern Mesopotamia – part of modern Iraq – defeats Assyria

626–539 BABYLONIAN (NEO-BABYLONIAN) EMPIRE

587–537 Captivity of the Jews in the city of Babylon – near present-day Baghdad – under Nebuchadnezzar

586 Babylonia conquers southern Israel (the kingdom of Judah)

563–483 The life of Siddhārtha Gautama, the Buddha

558–479 The life of Confucius

540 Babylonian (Neo-Babylonian) Empire falls to the Persian King Cyrus

540–331 PERSIAN (ACHAEMENID) EMPIRE

539 Cyrus allows the Jews to return home

510 The last king of Rome is expelled; Etruscan rule ends and the Republic is established at Rome

510–27 Roman Republic

497–425 Vardhamana Mahavira, the son of a chieftain in the Indian kingdom of Magadha, in north-east India, establishes the central tenets of Jainism

396 Rome begins its conquest of Italy

341–270 Life of Epicurus, founder of Epicureanism

335–263 Life of Zeno, founder of Stoicism

334–328 Alexander of Macedonia defeats Darius and conquers the Persian Empire

334–328 EMPIRE OF ALEXANDER THE GREAT

328 At Alexander's death his general Seleucus 'inherits' the eastern part of the Persian Empire

312–204 SELEUCID EMPIRE

321 Chandragupta Maurya founds India's first and greatest empire; his chief minister Kautilya writes the *Arthashastra*

321–185 BC MAURYAN EMPIRE

269–232 Reign of Ashoka Maurya, first Buddhist emperor of the Indian subcontinent

264 The first of the Punic Wars between Carthage – in present-day Tunisia – and Rome; Rome's conquest of Sicily signals the beginning of its imperial expansion beyond the borders of peninsular Italy

250 Parni nomads from Central Asia settle in Parthia – in present-day Iran – and begin their conquest of the Seleucid Empire

250 BC–AD 224 PARTHIAN (ARSACID) EMPIRE

220 Qín Shi Huáng, king of the state of Qin in western China, defeats rival warring states and becomes the first emperor of a unified China; he extends the Great Wall, begun in the 4th century BC, to keep out invading nomads

220–AD 1912 CHINESE EMPIRE

218–202 The Carthaginian general Hannibal invades Italy but is eventually defeated by Scipio

206–AD 9 FORMER (WESTERN) HAN DYNASTY (CHINA)

146 Greece reduced to a Roman province

135–132 Slave revolt in Sicily led by Eunus, a Syrian slave inspired by the mystery cult of Atargatis

63 Pompey captures Jerusalem; Palestine becomes a client state of Rome

53 Parthians defeat the Romans at the Battle of Carrhae

50 Yuezhi/Kushan tribesmen from western China push into India

44 Julius Caesar is assassinated

37–4 Reign of Herod the Great

31 Octavian/Augustus, great-nephew of Julius Caesar, defeats Mark Antony and Cleopatra at the Battle of Actium

27 The Senate bestow on Octavian the title of 'Augustus', the revered one

27–AD 14 Reign of Augustus, the first Roman emperor

27–AD 476/1453 ROMAN EMPIRE
The Western part of the empire collapses in AD 476 and the Eastern part – the Byzantine Empire – with the fall of Constantinople in AD 1453

26 Aelius Gallus leads disastrous Roman 'expedition' into South Arabia

25 Juba installed as King of Mauretania – part of present-day Algeria and Morocco

—Queen Amanirenas of Meroe leads her army against Roman-controlled Egypt

20 Peace treaty between Augustus and Queen Amanirenas settles the border disputes between Roman Egypt and Meroe – present-day southern Egypt and Sudan

4 Jewish students in Jerusalem smash the golden eagle erected by Herod the Great on one of the Temple gates

—Death of Herod the Great

—Most likely date for the birth of Jesus

4/2 Former slave-girl Musa murders her husband and becomes co-ruler of Parthia with her son/new husband Phraataces

3 Cult of the Queen Mother of the West sweeps through China

2 Augustus is proclaimed *pater patriae* ('father of the fatherland')

AD

2 Parthians and Romans celebrate their peace agreement on the banks of the Euphrates

6 Rome takes direct control of Judaea and orders a census so that the province can be assessed for tax; Judas the Galilean and Zadok call for a mass boycott – this marks the birth of the Zealots, the radical wing of Pharisaism

9 Battle of Teutoburg Forest; German tribesmen, led by Arminius, wipe out almost the whole Roman army of the Rhine

—China's acting emperor Wang Mang seizes the throne and proclaims the Xin ('new') dynasty

9–23 Rule of Wang Mang

14 Augustus dies and is declared to be a god by the Senate

14–37 Tiberius, Augustus' thirty-year-old stepson, becomes emperor

20–46 Gondophares rules over the kingdom of Gandhara – a vast region in present-day eastern Afghanistan, northern Pakistan and northern India – within the Parthian Empire; whether he rules as a loyal client king or has broken away from Parthia is unclear; his capital city is Taxila, near present-day Islamabad in Pakistan

23 Wang Mang, the usurper of the Han throne, is defeated and killed

24 Pontius Pilate is appointed procurator (governor) of Judaea

25 Emperor Guangwu restores the Chinese Han Dynasty

25–220 LATER (EASTERN) HAN DYNASTY

28/29 John the Baptist baptizes his cousin Jesus

—Jesus begins his mission

—John the Baptist is beheaded

—Many of John's disciples become followers of Jesus

30–80 Kujula Kadphises, chief of the Yuezhi tribesmen from Central Asia, becomes the first Kushan emperor

First–Third centuries KUSHAN EMPIRE (present-day Central Asia and northern India)

—Kujula and his successors are patrons of a more populist form of Buddhism, Mahayana Buddhism, which they export to China

30 Rome takes control of Palmyra

31/33 Jesus is crucified

32 Paul's conversion on the road to Damascus

37 Death of Tiberius; his nephew Caligula becomes emperor

38 Pogrom inflicted on the Jewish community of Alexandria; the Roman prefect Aulus Avillius Flaccus forces Jews to live in one area – the world's first ghetto

—Apollonius, the wandering holy man and miracle worker, visits the Parthian province of Mesopotamia, where the Parthian King Vardanes I is embroiled in a civil war

40 Paul begins his missionary work in the Near East (modern Turkey and the Middle East) and Greece

41 Caligula is assassinated; his uncle, Claudius, becomes emperor

43 Claudius conquers Britain

48 Paul and Barnabas set off on their first missionary journey

—Paul preaches his first recorded sermon at 'Psidian Antioch' (in modern Turkey)

49 Claudius imposes martial law on an increasingly violent Palestine, and expels the Jewish community from Rome

—Paul travels to Jerusalem for a conference to try to heal the differences between the 'party of the circumcision', led by Jesus' brother James, and the 'party of the uncircumcision', led by Paul

54 Death of Claudius; his stepson Nero becomes emperor

58 Paul returns to Jerusalem, where he is arrested in the Temple; he demands to be tried as a Roman citizen under Roman law and is taken to Rome

60/61 Boudicca, queen of the Iceni, leads a rebellion in Britain against the

Romans, but is defeated and commits suicide

64 Great fire of Rome; Nero blames the Christians who are rounded up to be crucified, torn apart by wild beasts, or burned alive; Paul and Peter may have been among the victims

65 Kujula Kadphises and his Central Asian nomadic army conquer Gondophares' Indo-Parthian kingdom in Gandhara (today's northern Pakistan and eastern Afghanistan)

66–73/4 First Jewish Revolt/War against the Romans

68 Nero commits suicide; his death marks the end of the Julio-Claudian dynasty; he is succeeded by Galba

70 The Temple and Jerusalem are razed to the ground by the victorious armies of the Emperor Vespasian's son Titus

79 Eruption of Vesuvius overwhelms Pompeii

132–135 Second Jewish Revolt / War against the Romans. After the Jews' defeat Hadrian expels them from Jerusalem and the rest of Judaea

—Jerusalem is renamed Aelia Capitolina

224 The last of the Parthian kings is killed in battle; the succeeding Sasanian dynasty imposes its authority over the empire, adopting Zoroastrianism as the state religion

312 Conversion of Constantine to Christianity

—Constantine defeats Maxentius, his rival as emperor, at the Milvian Bridge in Rome

335 Emperor Ezana of Aksum converts to Christianity, and makes Christianity the official state religion

391 Theodosius bans all non-Christian rites and orders the destruction of all temples, cult images and ancient festivals

—Christianity is established as the official religion of the Roman Empire

395 After the death of Theodosius the Roman Empire is irrevocably split into the Western and Eastern (Byzantine) Empires

INTRODUCTION

At the end of the first century BC, the world was full of gods. Thousands of them jostled, competed and merged with one another. Many of them flourished briefly before vanishing from view. In Syria ecstatic devotees castrated themselves in the streets so as to become priests of Atargatis – goddess of love and war, of fertility and virginity – the contradictory, but for pagans entirely unproblematic, result of a fusion of Syrian, Phoenician, Babylonian and Canaanite goddesses. In the Galilee of Jesus' time, a region that had been forcibly converted to Judaism only a century earlier, holy men turned oil into wine, healed the sick, drove out devils, and claimed to be the Messiah. One of the most famous preachers of his day, a neo-Pythagorean from Tarsus in modern-day Turkey, who raised a girl from the dead and – according to his disciples – came back to life shortly after his death, preached to the Parthian emperor in Babylon. And he preached further away still – to the ruler of the rising Kushan Empire in what is now Afghanistan and Pakistan, where images of the Buddha dressed in a toga, and standing in the attitude of a Greek god, were being carved into the mountainsides.

Kings, queens and emperors were riding on the back of religion as they had always done. Augustus, the first emperor of Rome, though he never dared use the title in the sense of a permanent supreme authority, was manoeuvring his way to becoming worshipped as a god; the creation of the Roman cult of emperor-worship formed part of one of the most brilliant makeovers ever undertaken by a state. But what for Augustus was a delicate matter was effortless for the stout, one-eyed warrior-queen Amanirenas of the empire of Meroe in north-east Africa: divinity was her inheritance. In China an administrator named Wang Mang, who like Augustus wore platform shoes to enhance his less than impressive height, usurped the imperial throne by manufacturing Confucian omens to prove he had Heaven's backing. But though he began his rise to power by cynically using Confucianism he lost both his throne and his life as a result of his obsession with it.

Gods were getting bigger – small divinities were coalescing with others to become more powerful. But all of them – except, to the amused bewilderment of the pagan observers, the jealous God of the Jews – tolerated the existence of other gods. In the cities that were springing up around the Roman world, under the relative peace that Rome had established, temples were built to the Greek/Roman god Jupiter, to the Turkish goddess Cybele, to the Babylonian god Bel, and to the myriad gods in their numberless forms that populated the ancient world.

This great churn of gods and religions was powered by trade and the city. Cities and towns were booming along the trade routes that threaded together four empires – Roman, Parthian (formerly Persian), Kushan and Chinese. To the cities came merchants, artisans and peasants from every part of the trading world, thousands of immigrants trying to make a home for themselves, all bringing their gods with them. Alexandria, the Roman Empire's greatest commercial city, was home to a notoriously aggressive and turbulent population of 600,000 people, rivalled by the equally tumultuous and vast city of Seleucia in the Parthian Empire and China's twelve-gated city of Chang'an with its nine heavily regulated markets. People were on the move as they had never been before, and as they would never be again until Victorian times.[1] A babble of languages rose up from the quaysides and marketplaces of these booming cities, where the poor built makeshift homes on derelict sites or jammed themselves into tenement blocks.

In the absence of constant warfare, there was money to spend. And so, like small cities on the march, merchants – protected by armed guards if they were lucky – struggled over mountains, plodded with thousands of heavily laden camels through deserts, or risked shipwreck and pirates to bring silk from China, frankincense and myrrh from Southern Arabia, spices and pearls from India, and pomegranates and rugs from Parthia to people who were discovering the delights of luxury goods.

Trade and the cities it created are at the heart of this book. Pockmarked with building sites, crammed with strangers – all with their own distinctive customs, languages, foods, clothes and religious practices – the cities ripped apart the old ties to tribe and neighbour, the old traditions and certainties. They magnified old needs and gave birth to new ones.

A large measure of peace was essential for the growth of cities, yet peace, paradoxically, was hugely disruptive. The trade it brought created a bewildering, potentially incendiary mix of peoples and ideas and an increasingly wealthy group of merchants who were struggling for status against the entrenched interests of the landed aristocracy. The ancient world* was undergoing a period of globalization every bit as dislocating and traumatic as our own.

And much as they do today, people looked for ways to build new communities as they left their old ones behind or saw them disintegrating. Surrounded by strangers, living in splintered ethnic groups which periodically exploded in violence, they needed to find comfort and reassurance in a new community, a new set of shared beliefs and rituals that took account of the complexity of their new urban world. Having lost the traditions and customs laid down by the family, village or tribe, they needed to find a new sense of meaning, a new guide to behaviour, to find a moral system under which the Samaritan would treat a stranger – even his historic enemy, the Judaean Jew – as a neighbour to be cared for rather than an outsider to be reviled.

---

* By 'world', I mean what the ancient Romans meant by it, that is, one which stretched from China in the East to Britain in the West and from Ireland in the North to Ethiopia in the South. (See Map XX, Strabo's Map of the World.)

For the rulers, peace posed a different sort of problem: a problem of legitimacy. How could they secure loyalty to their rule now that they could no longer command it by military might? The bargain between ruler and ruled that the English political philosopher Thomas Hobbes would describe some 1,650 years later – that is, the gift of stability in exchange for the people's obedience – no longer worked in a time of relative peace. Rulers required a different form of legitimation and a new way of binding together disparate peoples. Force, of course, was always available if persuasion did not work. But persuasion was cheaper and ultimately more efficient – willing subjects are far more faithful than coerced ones; and force was anyway not always successful. Rome's expedition to seize the incense-rich kingdoms of Southern Arabia in 26 BC ended in disaster thanks to a bungling leader who failed to see through the clever tactics of an 'unscrupulously ambitious and cruel' Arabian minister; around 21 BC the one-eyed African Queen Amanirenas successfully invaded Rome's province of Egypt, though she was eventually beaten back; and, most catastrophic of all, in AD 9 Rome's army of the Rhine was wiped out by German tribesmen in the Teutoburg Forest.

Each of the four great empires of the Eurasian landmass used religion, to varying degrees, as a means of establishing and strengthening a centralized grip on its territory and peoples. Rulers needed religions to keep them on their thrones, just as religions needed rulers to help spread their message and protect their followers.

Empire and religion often used each other, but it was not always possible. In Palestine the violent opposition of the Pharisees to Herod the Great, most loyal of all Rome's 'vassal' kings, proved that Judaism was incapable of allying itself to an invading imperial power: the nationalism that lay at the heart of Judaism – and that had kept the Jews together as a nation without a land during the 'Babylonian Captivity' of the sixth century BC – inevitably put it at odds with foreign rule.

Nor could all religions adapt to the changing conditions created by trade. Cities killed off most of the old pagan gods. It is not for nothing that the early Christians called non-Christians *pagani*: the Latin *paganus* means 'country-dweller'. The pagan gods offered insurance against disaster, as long as they received an appropriate bribe in the form of sacrifice. But they did not provide what the mystery cults such as Isis and certain other religions were beginning to offer: a way to live one's earthly life, the promise of an afterlife and a personal relationship with god. Such comforts as these, which today are seen as defining elements of what constitutes a religion, were increasingly necessary in the alien world of the cities of the late first century BC.

The grand causal chain of history is, of course, always twisted by the randomness of the individual. Perhaps Confucianism would never have become so essential to the Chinese Empire had it not been for the usurper Wang Mang's ineptness as a politician, his indecisiveness and belief in magic. The Jesus cult was lucky to have the bandy-legged, touchy, obsessive, brilliant galvanizer, theologian and letter-writer Saul/Paul – the best creative thinker and marketer any religion has probably ever had. Paul's remoulding of Jesus, whom he had never even met, transformed a minor Jewish cult into a religion fit for an empire.* The wandering philosopher and holy man Apollonius, on the other hand – a near contemporary of Jesus but in his lifetime much more famous – did not find in his biographer Philostratus as passionate and subtle a champion and theologian as Jesus would find in Paul.

Under the forcing house of globalization, pagan gods rose and fell and fluid sets of beliefs and practice coalesced into what we now think of as the 'world religions' – Judaism, Christianity, Brahmanism, or Hinduism as it came to be called, and Buddhism. The fifth world

---

* In modern usage 'cult' has become a pejorative term for groups with strange or distasteful ideas under the control of a strong leader. Religious historians, however, tend to use 'cult' in its traditional sense of *cultus*, literally 'care', referring to the ritual practice involved in worshipping a god. The difference between a cult, in this sense, and a religion is a difficult one, but hinges on the relative importance of beliefs. I try to use the word 'cult' in its academic, neutral sense, concentrating on ritual practice. I use the word 'religion' for a set of beliefs which would include all or some of the following: an explanation for the origin of the universe and mankind, some sort of deity, a goal for humans to reach involving some kind of afterlife, and a moral code for living.

religion, Islam, would not of course emerge and go on its journey with empire for another six centuries.

Why amongst the countless religious options available did empire and religion make the particular pairings they did? Why was the tiny Jesus cult, rather than the Isis cult, eventually adopted by Rome's emperors? Isiacism was a religion far more popular and widespread, which also promised some sort of afterlife, believed in some sort of resurrection and had a compassionate goddess. Why did China's rulers hitch their fate to Confucianism, a philosophy more than a religion, which almost uniquely made no attempt to popularize itself and spread its appeal beyond the elite? How religion uses empire and empire uses religion is the subject of this book.

1

THE REBRANDING
OF ROME

What race is so distant from us, what race is so barbarous, O Caesar,
that from it no spectator is present in your city! The cultivator of
Rhodope [in Thrace] is here from Haemus, sacred to Orpheus. The
Scythian who drinks the blood of his horses is here; he, too, who
quaffs the waters of the Nile nearest their springing; and he also
whose shore is laved by the most distant ocean. The Arabian has
hastened hither; the Sabaeans have hastened; and here the Cilicians
have anointed themselves with their own native perfume. Here
come the Sicambrians with their hair all twisted into a knot, and
here the frizzled Ethiopians. Yet though their speech is all so
different, they all speak together hailing you, O Emperor, as the true
father of your country.

Martial, *Epigrams*, IX.3, *c*.AD 81–96

But it were a difficult thing to administer so great a dominion
otherwise than by turning it over to one man, as to a father.

Strabo, *Geographia*, VI.4, *c*.20 BC–AD 23

In the life of Augustus, we behold the tyrant of the republic,
converted, almost by imperceptible degrees, into the father of his
country, and of human kind.

Gibbon, *Decline and Fall of the Roman Empire*, vol. II, ch. 18, 1781

Roman, remember by your strength to rule
Earth's peoples – for your arts are to be these:
To pacify, to impose the rule of law,
To spare the conquered, battle down the proud.

Virgil, *Aeneid*, VI, 1151–54 29–19 BC

Zero AD in Rome, the largest city in the world. Nearly one million people lived there, packed into its stinking tenement blocks or squatting in its vacant lots and abandoned buildings. Among them were more than 30,000 Jews, many of whom had been brought back as slaves by Pompey after his capture of Jerusalem in 63 BC.

At night, wagons rumbled through the narrow streets, bringing huge pine trunks, stone and marble blocks for the new imperial buildings which were rising up out of the wooden city, where old tenement blocks either constantly collapsed because of their height, burned down or were knocked down and rebuilt (though according to the new building regulations they could not be more than 21 metres high). The alleyways were dark and deserted – the haunts of muggers and gangs of well-born youths out to beat up passers-by, manhandle women or smash up shops. Flaming torches or horn-covered lanterns occasionally lit up the four-storey apartment buildings as a troop of slaves ran by bearing a litter, its perfumed occupant reclining inside behind drawn silken curtains. At major crossroads, lamps flickered behind stone masks with gaping holes for eyes and mouth. Only the wide boulevards were fully lit by oil lamps burning in every shop.

Out on the streets during the day the butcher cut up meat, the barber shaved his customers. Drink-sellers and cake-sellers hawked their custom. At countless bars and cafes men ate hot sausages, pastries and olives or drank wine mixed with water. From the new public baths came the sounds that would infuriate neighbours like the Stoic philosopher Seneca: men grunting over their weights, people singing, the splash of swimmers and the 'thin screech' of the hair-removal expert, who was only silent 'when he's plucking a customer's armpits and can make someone else do the yelling for him'.

In the Subura, to the south of what is today Rome's main railway station – a red-light district then as it still is now – water boys waited outside the brothel doors with bidets; in the classier establishments hairdressers repaired the ravaged locks of the vainer, more fastidious clients. A 33-metre-high fire-resistant wall separated the crumbling alleyways and lath-and-plaster houses of the Subura from the vast new Forum Augustum.

In 2 BC, when Jesus was about two years old, Augustus – 'the revered one' – formerly known as Octavian Caesar, marked the dedication of his new Forum by treating Rome's inhabitants to a celebration of their empire and their ruler. The lavish games and spectacles that Augustus laid on were also his thank you to the Senate and the people for bestowing on him the title of *pater patriae* ('father of the fatherland'). The title was confirmation that they had – officially at least – accepted the magnificent charade that Augustus was father and moral leader of the nation, and not the autocrat that his less politically adept great-uncle and adopted father Julius Caesar had so nakedly been, and for which he had been assassinated only forty-two years earlier.

The Forum was imperial Rome incarnate – brute force backed by divinity embodied in glittering white marble, bronze and gold. Ranged around its vast paved open space were the temple to Vesta, goddess of the hearth, guarantor of Rome's permanence, whose cult was said to have been introduced by Rome's deified founder Romulus, and the gleaming snow-white marble temple to Augustus' ancestor the war-god Mars, its entrance heaped with the standards and arms of the peoples Rome had conquered.

Augustus had vowed to build the temple to Mars after defeating Julius Caesar's assassins Brutus and Cassius in 42 BC at Philippi in Macedonia, where ninety-one years later Paul would found his first

Christian church. Steep steps led up to a dense row of huge Corinthian columns. Inside the temple were great gold and ivory statues to another of Augustus' ancestors, the goddess Venus, and to Julius Caesar, who had been deified at the prompting of Augustus. Outside were two colonnades; ranged along the left were yet more statues to Augustus' ancestors, to Venus' son Aeneas, to Mars' sons Romulus and Remus; and to the founding kings of Rome. Flanking them on the right-hand colonnade were statues to other great men of Rome.

This was Rome as conceived by Augustus, his coolly beautiful wife Livia and his right-hand men, Agrippa and Maecenas.

Noble-born Maecenas, the effete and bisexual 'soft comforter of adulteresses', as Augustus called him, was patron to a circle of writers who would prove to be the most successful propagandists for a regime that the world has ever seen. 'That stern man' Agrippa, in Pliny's admiring phrase – plebeian populist, military strongman and builder of a monumental new Rome of white, pink and greeny-blue marble standing alongside the tiny streets and flammable wooden houses – became the most powerful man in the empire after Augustus. Livia – 'Ulysses in petticoats' as her great-grandson Caligula called her – was the most powerful woman in the Roman Empire: dignified consort and alleged murderess, she would later be co-ruler of the empire with her son Tiberius. The ruthless and politically brilliant Augustus was, at the age of sixty-one, still remarkably handsome and his curly hair was still yellow – even if he was beginning to lose his teeth; he was so proud of the 'divine radiance' of his eyes that 'it gave him profound pleasure if anyone at whom he glanced keenly dropped his head as though dazzled by looking into the sun'.[1] He claimed to be 5 feet 7 inches tall, but, like the Chinese usurper Wang Mang, who had just begun to manipulate his way to the imperial throne nearly 5,000 miles to the east, he wore platform shoes to reach even that height. Together Augustus and his three strategists were constructing an entirely new type of regime.

As always in the attempt to create a stable state, it required persuasion more than force. Military might was both too expensive and too unreliable. The people must *want* to belong to the new, wider entity of the empire, or that empire would never stay together. But the Augustan strategists had the additional task of stage-managing the transformation from republic – in effect an oligarchy – to empire after nearly sixty years of civil war. Augustus was viewed with deep suspicion by powerful families, by cities and provinces, and by kings and local elites who had fought for the Republic or later sided with Mark Antony against him. King Herod of Judaea, who would become one of Agrippa's closest friends, had been one of Mark Antony's supporters.

Augustus had to reconcile his enemies to each other and to himself, and that meant attracting the loyalty of many different recalcitrant elements. He and his strategists were trying to persuade a Roman elite, accustomed to 500 years of ruling as an oligarchy, to accept submission to an emperor in the sense of a hereditary supreme ruler; only forty-two years earlier many of them had supported the assassination of Julius Caesar precisely because of his autocratic ambitions. Julius Caesar, like all successful Roman generals, had used the title *imperator* (emperor). Originating probably in the second century BC as a title used by every military commander (*imperare* means 'to command'), it had evolved into a special title bestowed on victorious generals and those elected to positions of great military authority. But it was a temporary title the commander relinquished at his triumph or at the end of his time in office. Julius Caesar, however, assumed it permanently. Augustus was much more tactful in asking for annual re-election and by using *imperator* as a first name, rather than as an official title. It was not, in fact, until Vespasian, successor to Nero in AD 69 that *imperator* became the title by which Roman rulers were known.

As well as mollifying the elite, the new Augustan regime also needed to keep the army on its side. Beyond Rome and Italy's borders, it needed to turn the elites of Rome's conquered provinces from potentially resentful humiliated enemies into loyal defenders of the empire. And from Spain to Syria, from modern-day Romania to

Egypt, from city-dweller to peasant to nomad tribesman, the regime needed to mould its eighty million ordinary subjects – all to varying degrees ready to revolt against the imposition of Roman power and Roman taxation in particular – into faithful subjects united in a sense of Romanness. Such a task required not just the inducements of the material but of the divine as well. Augustus was being transformed from the thug who tore out the eyes of a praetor suspected of hiding a sword underneath his robe (though in reality it was only a set of writing tablets), into a clement, moral, semi-divine if not divine, ruler. Such a transformation would not, however, convince all his subjects.

The Forum Augustum represented the Augustan vision of Rome. Augustus himself had written the eulogies below the statues of his ancestors and the other noble Romans ranged in its colonnades. But, above all, the Forum embodied the triumphalist Rome of Maecenas's protégé Virgil. In the *Aeneid* – the story of Aeneas's founding of Rome after the fall of Troy – Virgil wrote one of the greatest foundation myths that any nation has ever had. Aeneas leaves a Troy destroyed by war, survives shipwreck and despair, resists the love of Carthage's Queen Dido, and descends to the underworld to be shown the future great men of Rome – including 'Caesar Augustus, son of the deified, who shall bring once again an Age of Gold'[2] – before conquering the small kingdom of Alba Longa in Italy, from where his heirs will 'win the mastery of the world'. The *Aeneid* rests self-consciously on its great Homeric predecessors. But unlike the *Iliad* and the *Odyssey*, the *Aeneid* is not just a celebration of military glory and heroic virtue. It is an attempt to create the moral foundations of an empire. The *Iliad* and the *Odyssey* celebrated the way of life of a warrior class. Aeneas, however, is both mighty warrior and also clement, 'duty-bound', rational ruler, the 'son of gods and sire of gods to come'. His mission in founding Rome is to 'bring the whole world under law's dominion'.

Like the eponymous hero of *Beowulf*, written at least eight centuries later, Aeneas is a hero on the cusp between old pagan military virtues and the new 'softer' virtues of mercy, pity and charity. Aeneas represents the beginning of a change in ideal from the self-assertive to the self-denying man. Odysseus was dedicated to love and family; his journey was a journey home. Aeneas, on the other hand, gives up the siren charms of Dido in order to fulfil his destiny of founding an empire. His final enemy is the wild bull-like Turnus, the warrior incarnate, who laughs with joy at sight of his charging horses, and who is in many ways a more sympathetic and better-drawn character than the upright Aeneas. Aeneas represents the new world not of the passion-driven Turnus, the military hero, but of rationality, law and order.

But whether the new world should triumph is left superbly ambiguous at the end of the *Aeneid*, when Turnus is defeated by Aeneas in a sword fight to the death. His knees buckling under him, the groans of his watching soldiers echoing in the surrounding mountains and forests, Turnus asks but does not beg for mercy. Aeneas is faced with a choice of sparing Turnus or exacting vengeance; he chooses vengeance. The Christian virtues, the non-noble virtues of the weak as Nietzsche sneeringly called them, had not yet conquered the old Roman ones. Such a surprising ending, given the whole trajectory of the *Aeneid*, may have arisen simply because Virgil died in 19 BC before he had had a chance to revise it – Augustus in fact ignored his wish that the poem should be destroyed. But it may have been an accurate reflection of Rome's and Augustus's increasingly divided loyalties – to the old noble virtues associated with might and conquest, and the non-heroic virtues associated with peace.

Having built its empire over the previous centuries, Rome in the late first century BC ruled 'the length of land between the sunset and the dawn', in the words of Maecenas' great friend Horace. Its writ extended from Spain in the west to Syria in the east, and from Egypt in the south to the borders of Germany in the north. Rome had been an empire territorially long before it became an empire politically under Augustus. But its aim now was to consolidate rather than expand (see chapter 5). Law and order were taking over from the spoils of conquest as the *raison d'être* of empire. True, Augustus wore a steel corselet under his toga, and he was always accompanied by 500 Praetorian Guards to protect him from assassination, though in deference to Republican feelings they did not wear military uniform but togas, under the folds of which they kept their weapons concealed. Military might was still the foundation stone of the empire, but it was no longer given the value and pre-eminence it had once enjoyed.

When the Senate, whether prompted or not, proclaimed Augustus *pater patriae*, they were honouring him not for his military prowess but for being the supreme father of the empire. Augustus was fulfilling Aeneas' mission to create an empire ruled through law and order and only as a last resort by force. This shift in value goes some way to explain the popularity of gladiatorial combats. They provided a vicarious way for the elite to enjoy the warrior's glory that they were now deprived of.

And so tens of thousands of discerning spectators packed the Campus Martius, the Field of Mars – north of the Forum Augustum – where Julius Caesar had been assassinated, and where Augustus' strategist Agrippa had built a huge pleasure park for the people. There they watched gladiators fighting to 'cut-off point', to the death. The gladiators had been fattened up with barley porridge, to give them the maximum protection and weight. The semi-naked gladiators wore visored helmets whose anonymity made it easier to injure or kill an opponent with whom they had been living and training for months if not years. During the midday lunch-break crowds could stay if they wanted to watch condemned criminals tied to stakes being eaten by lions, or – a less expensive form of execution – being crucified. The great geographer Strabo had watched Selouros, a famous bandit who had terrorized the area around Mount Etna, 'torn to pieces by the beasts in the Forum while a contest of gladiators was being performed. He had been put on a high platform, as though on Mount Etna, and when the platform suddenly broke up and collapsed, he himself crashed down into wild-beast cages which easily broke open.'

Ranged in their respective ranks around the arena were the social strata of Rome that Augustus had to appease. In the front fourteen rows, the Orchestra, were the senators, their white togas gashed with a broad purple stripe, so that in their supremely status-conscious world everyone would know that they belonged to the tiny elite of the richest and most privileged perched on top of the steep pyramid of Roman society. Once they had been the most powerful social and political figures in Rome, but their power and status were slowly being undermined by Augustus, who was both turning the Senate into a rubber-stamping body and controlling entry into it. Beside the senators sat the *equites* – the knights, or equestrians – gold rings on their fingers. Though senatorial and equestrian families were often related, equestrians were marginally below senators in wealth and status, reflected in the slightly thinner purple stripe on equestrian togas. Hitherto equestrians had formed the non-political section of the aristocracy.[3] But Augustus had begun to promote them to positions formerly reserved for senators, and equestrian prestige was growing as a result.

Augustus had decreed that soldiers (though probably not the high-ranking officers who were appointed from the senatorial and increasingly from the equestrian orders) should sit separately from civilians.[4] These middle- and lower-ranking soldiers, the centurions and ordinary legionaries, formed part of the vast body of 'plebeians'. Over the course of the Early Republic from the fifth to the third century BC the plebeians had fought for political equality with the patricians, the hereditary nobility. By the time of Augustus that battle was over: the plebs had acquired the rights and privileges of full citizens, and the old patrician families had anyway virtually died out. 'Plebeians' had come to mean simply the ordinary, non-aristocratic Roman citizens who were neither senators nor equestrians. They were the professionals: the schoolmasters, architects and physicians, as well as the merchants, shopkeepers, traders and artisans – beneficiaries of the booming trade which the *pax Augusta* had brought.

Watching the gladiatorial contests from the back rows were non-citizens, foreigners and slaves (slaves made up about 10 per cent of the empire's population[5]). Ex-slaves, the freedmen, were also forced to sit there. Though some of the freedmen had become fabulously wealthy as merchants and traders or as officers in the imperial household, they were despised by the elite. Hence the popularity amongst aristocratic readers of the *Satyricon*, a mid-first century AD work of fiction, with its savage portrait of Trimalchio, the nouveau-riche vulgarian ex-slave, drying his hands on a slave's head and weeping, along with his guests, at the thought of his own death.

Under Augustus, women found themselves confined to the back rows, but as a group apart. In the interests of his moral 'restoration' campaign, he had proclaimed that women and men could no longer sit together. Only women of the imperial family and the six vestal virgins, the only female priests in Rome, could sit in the better seats. Servants of Vesta, goddess of the hearth, the vestal virgins had sworn a thirty-year vow of chastity and were buried alive if they broke it. Four centuries later, the Christian poet and ascetic Prudentius would fulminate against their quasi-sexual delight in the gladiator as they 'looked closely at the bronze-covered face, smashed by repeated casts of the trident, and at the part of the arena which a bleeding gladiator stains with his gaping wounds as he tries to flee, and at how many steps he can manage, marked by his blood'. Christians would object to gladiatorial contests because they were sexually titillating, not out of concern for the gladiator. Successful gladiators could indeed have their pick of elite women. Crescens the *retiarius* was so successful with his trident and net that he became notoriously desirable, described in a piece of graffiti in Pompeii as 'the netter of girls by night'. Since he had about a one in seven chance of living into an extremely comfortable retirement, the gladiator's life might be worth the risks in a world where three persons out of five would die before they reached their twenties.

Augustus had laid on the combats as a triumphant celebration of

Romanness for 'the lords of the world, the toga-bearing Romans', as his favourite line from the *Aeneid* called them,[6] though in reality togas had become so unpopular that Augustus had to legislate that senators and anyone entering his Forum wore a toga rather than the more practical tunic.

By a specially constructed lake on the Campus Martius 50,000 baying spectators watched 3,000 slaves and condemned criminals fighting for their lives; rowing in warships and triremes, they refought the fifth-century BC naval battle of Salamis, when the Greeks defeated Xerxes and his invading Persian army; and like the original combatants they were wounded or killed.

This staged naval battle was designed specifically to remind the spectators of the battle of Actium, fought off the western coast of Greece in 31 BC. Actium was the battle in which Octavian (as Augustus was then known) defeated Mark Antony, his rival since the assassination of Julius Caesar, and put an end to the long-running series of civil wars over the future of the Roman Republic. Augustus' victory made him sole ruler of Rome. But for all its historical importance, the battle had been an inglorious affair: it is unlikely that much blood was shed, and, as in all civil war battles, loyalties were uncertain and contingents changed sides at the last moment.[7] But in the *Aeneid* Virgil had transformed this unheroic encounter into the moment when Rome reclaimed its *virtus* (that sum of manly virtues including valour, required of the true Roman) and defeated the barbaric and decadent East where Mark Antony and Cleopatra had ruled, presenting themselves to the people as the resurrected god Osiris and his wife-sister Isis. It was the moment when Egypt's queen with her 'monster forms of gods of every race, and the dog-god Anubis barking' were defeated by 'our Neptune, Venus, and Minerva' and 'Mars, engraved in steel'. Noble, plain, rugged Rome in the shape of Augustus had prevailed.

In Virgil's heroic reimagining of the battle, Augustus Caesar leads the senators and people, along with the household gods and great gods, to victory. Agrippa, 'favoured by winds and gods', plays – as he would throughout his life – the part of second in command. In reality he was much the better general, and it was his tactics that won the battle for Augustus. Agrippa and Maecenas had been amongst Augustus' earliest backers and at Actium their gamble paid off. Once that battle was won, however, the struggle between them for Augustus' favour began in earnest.

Maecenas and Agrippa probably loathed each other. They were totally different in background, temperament and taste. A naked statue of Agrippa at about the time of his victory at Actium when he was thirty-one, the same age as Augustus, shows brute force personified. Square-faced, with a boxer's slightly squashed nose and vast thighs, he stands frowning, his whole body proclaiming that what he lacked in refinement – his father was a plebeian, a non-aristocrat – he made up for in power and energy. For Pliny, he was the ideal Roman: soldier-statesman and practical man of letters. Agrippa embodied the strength and virility of Rome, though even Pliny admitted that he was 'a man more accustomed to rustic pursuits than to culture'. Agrippa was and consciously remained a man of the people, despised, feared and disliked by the old Roman aristocrats for being a 'new man', a *novus homo* (the derogatory term for the first man of a family to reach the Senate).

Stern, ruthlessly ambitious and morally upstanding, Agrippa stood in total contrast to the louche, aristocratic Maecenas, the descendant of Etruscan kings. Lean-faced, his thin lips poised for a witticism, and with slightly bulging eyes, he maliciously enjoyed emphasizing Agrippa's humble origins, just as Mark Antony had sneered at those of Augustus. Like Agrippa, Augustus was of plebeian, non-noble stock. Augustus' great-grandfather had been a freedman, an ex-slave and ropemaker. His grandfather had become a wealthy usurer and it was thanks to that wealth that Augustus' father had entered the top ranks of the aristocracy and become a senator: money had always ensured some social mobility. But as the first member of the family to become a senator, Augustus' father would always be considered a *novus homo* by the old nobility, even if he had married the niece of Julius Caesar. The age of their lineage was often the only measure of superiority the old noble families had left to them.

Maecenas made an aristocratic show of indolence and lack of ambition, though in reality he must have been as eager as Agrippa to profit from his friendship with Augustus. According to Velleius Paterculus, admittedly an historian with a tendency to flatter, Maecenas 'lived thoroughly content with the narrow stripe of the equestrian order', rather than striving to acquire the broad purple band of a senator.

Many – including the Stoic philosopher Seneca – distrusted Maecenas for his effeminacy and decadence. Even his admirer Velleius Paterculus conceded that though he was 'a man who was literally sleepless when occasion demanded... when any relaxation was allowed him from business cares [he] would almost outdo a woman in giving himself up to indolence and soft luxury'. Maecenas had, like Agrippa, fought with Augustus against Sextus Pompeius in Sicily, against Brutus and Cassius at Philippi, and against Antony and Cleopatra at Actium, though he had never equalled Agrippa in military success. But he excelled as ideologue/ propagandist. An appalling writer himself, ridiculed by Augustus for his florid style, and sneered at by Seneca who compared 'the looseness of his speech' to his 'ungirt attire', Maecenas had not only a superb eye for discerning literary talent in others but also the ability to encourage or channel that talent into eulogizing the ideals of the new imperial regime. Chief among the writers who enjoyed his patronage were Livy, the historian who defined for Romans the greatness of their national character; the shy and taciturn Virgil, who laid out Rome's moral destiny; and the poet Horace, who – though he had fought for the Republicans with Brutus and Cassius at Philippi – went on to celebrate Augustus as the epitome of 'the just and steady-purposed man', a man who was on his way to godhead. Amongst the great writers of the period, only Ovid seems to have been outside Maecenas' influence. Ovid only became an 'Augustan' poet when he was exiled to Tomis in modern Romania and, heartsick for Rome, desperately tried to flatter his way back into Augustus' and Livia's favour; he never succeeded.

To his detractors Agrippa represented the aggressive coarseness of an earlier militaristic age; to his admirers he was, in a sense, Virgil's Turnus – exemplar of the old military Roman virtues and symbol of Rome's strength and virility. On the other hand 'the soft Maecenas', as the satirist Juvenal called him, was, for his enemies, the antithesis of the noble, upright Roman. His love of the good life (he was said to have had the first heated baths in Rome), his love affair with the actor Bathyllus and his seduction of other men's wives (although he loved his own beautiful and unfaithful wife Terentia) embodied the weakness and decadence of the new Rome. But to his supporters Maecenas symbolized the new civilized Rome of thought and beauty, which could only be created by honouring the gentler virtues of peace.

Maecenas was known for restraining Augustus' rages. Augustus had been the most vengeful member of the triumvirate in dealing with the supporters of Julius Caesar's assassins. But after the defeat of Brutus and Cassius, Maecenas had counselled mercy for the defeated. And Augustus had followed Maecenas' advice. 'Great clemency was shown in the victory; no one was put to death, and but few banished who could not bring themselves even to become suppliants,' wrote Augustus in the *Res Gestae Divi Augustae* (*The Achievements of the Divine Augustus*), the only account written by an emperor of his own career, which was inscribed on pillars outside Augustus' Mausoleum on the Campus Martius. Maecenas, from this perspective, did not exactly represent Aeneas – he was far too decadent for that – but he did represent a newer world that valued rationality and law more than military glory.

Following in the tradition of Thucydides who put into the mouths of his historical subjects oratorical set pieces, the Greek senator and historian Cassius Dio, writing in the early third century AD, imagines

Agrippa and Maecenas arguing before Augustus about what direction the new regime should take.*

Agrippa, the plebeian, not surprisingly takes a more populist approach and argues for the restoration of the Republic, by which he really meant oligarchic rule: in such a system each member of the oligarchy works for the benefit of the whole because they share an equality before the law; in a 'tyranny', the majority 'exert themselves only in their own interests and hate their fellow citizens' and the ruler dare not promote talented men to be his advisers because they would then pose a threat to him.

Maecenas, the elitist aristocrat, argues that 'the supposed freedom of the mob proves in reality to be the bitterest servitude, under which the better elements suffer at the hands of the worse, until in the end both are destroyed'; much better (as Brahmin priests, the upholders of the caste system on the Indian subcontinent, would agree) that each class of citizens 'zealously discharge the duties which devolve upon them'. Monarchical rule ensures better government for all. More tellingly, perhaps, Maecenas argues that a 'republic' might work in a homogeneous society but cannot work in an empire as diverse as Rome's:

> while we were but... few in number and differed in no important respect from our neighbours, we got along well with our government... but ever since we were led outside the peninsula and crossed over to many continents and many islands, filling the whole sea and the whole earth with our name and power..., like a great merchantman manned with a crew of every race and

* In this and the following chapter, I have based my own account of the ideological construction of the Augustan regime on Dio's schematic rendering (Cassius Dio, Book 52). Dio was writing 200 years after the events he describes and, given the turbulent times he was living through, was far more sympathetic to an imperial form of government than the nostalgic Republican Tacitus who was writing 100 years earlier. Nonetheless, Dio is surprisingly balanced. Dressed up in fictionalized speeches though his account is, he is quite prepared to reveal the brutal side of Augustus and the illusory nature of his regime – the difference between the reality and the spin which Augustus and his strategists put on it.

lacking a pilot, [Rome] has now for many generations been rolling and plunging as it has drifted this way and that in a heavy sea, a ship as it were without ballast.[8]

Maecenas was right. Over the previous three centuries Rome had created a territorial empire roughly the same size as China's, but without imposing on it the same centralized governmental control. Rome's empire was far more heterogeneous, partly because it was fundamentally a trading empire, based round the Mediterranean, but also because it was culturally and linguistically divided between its Eastern half which had been Hellenized thanks to Alexander the Great's conquests, and its Western non-Hellenized half. At the time of Augustus, the Eastern part of the empire consisted of what is now Greece, Asia Minor (that is, modern-day Turkey east of the Bosphorus), Egypt, Syria and Judaea. The Western part of the empire consisted of Spain, Gaul, Italy, parts of Germany – Rome never managed to subdue all of Germany, though Augustus was beginning to control Central Europe – and North Africa along the Mediterranean coast, that is, parts of modern Tunisia, Algeria and Libya. Britain had not yet been conquered despite invasions by Julius Caesar and three planned invasions by Augustus, which, however, were called off.

At the end of the first century BC, the empire was a mosaic of semi-autonomous cities run by local wealthy landowners and loosely bound together into provinces under Roman control. Roman imperial government was in fact minimal: even by the end of the second century AD there was still only one Roman administrator for every 400,000 people.[9] Routine administration was predicated on the co-operation of the local elites of the provinces, just as the defence of the empire was largely dependent on client kings (rulers who were given nominal independence and the protection of the Roman Empire in return for their loyalty) and their troops.

Augustus would use the city as an essential element in the Romanization of his empire. The residents of the cities of the empire, and certainly their wealthier members, would become the most reliable supporters of the imperial regime, and it was on them – and on the army – that the emperor's power would rest.[10] But the cities themselves remained collections of diverse peoples who brought their differences with them from all over the empire: they came with their distinctive clothes and customs, and they brought their gods. And they spoke a bewildering array of languages. Although there were the linguae francae of Latin in the Western and Greek in the Eastern parts of the empire, Celtic dialects and Iberian were spoken in the West; a Libyan-Punic dialect was used in the Roman province of Africa, that is, North Africa; Coptic dialects were spoken in Egypt; Syriac, Armenian, Phoenician and Aramaic were spoken in the Near East (modern Turkey and the Middle East), along with Hebrew in Palestine, and all the cities of the Jewish Diaspora.*

According to Cassius Dio, the Augustan task was to construct a political system that would be acceptable to both Agrippa and Maecenas – to the populist and to the elitist. The problem was how to satisfy both the politically powerful in Rome and the numerous Roman subjects throughout the empire. The political solution was to disguise the emperor in the Republican garb of *primus inter pares*; the religious solution was the imperial cult.

In engineering the sea-change from republic to empire Augustus paid careful attention to the sensitivities of the elite. Almost every noble family had some members who had fought against Augustus. They might have greeted the end of the civil wars with relief, but any overt sign that they had lost their power risked provoking violent resentment. And so Augustus played out a long charade in which he never formally took on authoritarian powers or the 'perpetual dictatorship'** which had been conferred on Julius Caesar.

Instead, he ruled through an ad hoc system of prolonged extraordinary powers and special privileges all 'voted' him by the Senate, and through the Plebeian Council, which elected those who

---

* Jesus would have spoken Aramaic, but may also have spoken Hebrew and Greek.
** The 'dictator' was an elected official, a magistrate, granted extraordinary, but temporary, powers to deal with a military or domestic crisis.

qualified by birth or by Augustus' favour for magistracies and priesthoods. Augustus was, according to this consciously constructed fiction, merely first amongst his aristocratic equals. He greeted each senator by name (though Augustus' *nomenclator*, a slave employed by the wealthy to remind them of the names of people they met, was said to be rather forgetful) and kissed them, probably lightly on the mouth. This mode of greeting was a sign of equality, unlike kissing the hand, which the client did when he begged a favour of his patron, or, worse still, kissing the feet, which the Emperor Caligula would later demand. Kissing on the mouth would become such a common form of greeting amongst the Roman elite that Augustus' successor Tiberius had to ban it in order to stop a serious outbreak of herpes.

In 28 BC Augustus entered the Senate wearing a sword and steel corselet hidden under his tunic, 'with ten burly senatorial friends crowding around him';[11] they would only allow senators to approach Augustus' chair 'singly and after the folds of their robes had been carefully searched', according to the imperial biographer Suetonius whose biographies are filled with gossipy details, making him delightful to read though he is not nearly as perceptive a historian as Tacitus, who saw the big issues of cause and effect behind the detail. Augustus read out a list of the senators who had been selected for a new purged Senate. Over 300 of the old Senate's 1,000 members had supported Mark Antony and the Republic, though some had quickly swapped sides before the final battle of Actium. Augustus now purged 140 senators. At the head of the new list of senators Augustus had entered himself as *princeps*, a title that had been bestowed on the leading citizens of the state from the early days of the Republic. From this moment on, the Augustan regime effectively took over control of the Senate and increasingly of the elite in general.

Partly to counter the power of the senators, Augustus deliberately increased the status and numbers of equestrians and increasingly relied on them to run the empire. He promoted equestrians to senatorial rank – not just in Rome but amongst the local elites in the provinces as well. Formerly senators had had a virtual monopoly on high office. Augustus now appointed equestrians instead, above all in the vital task of overseeing taxation.

Augustus in effect nationalized the collection of direct taxes. Taxation from the provinces financed the empire. It took the form of a property tax on land, houses, slaves and ships, and a head tax, which was levied on all adults between the ages of twelve or fourteen and sixty-five regardless of income. Tax farming had been a way for the Roman aristocracy and local elites to recoup the expenses of public life and finance their own systems of patronage. In 27 BC Augustus introduced a regular census on which calculations of tax could be based – Jesus' family, according to the Gospel of Luke, had to travel to Bethlehem to be registered in the Judaean census of AD 6.* The head count gave the imperial treasury a good idea of what it could expect in tax revenue so that neither senatorial governors nor *publicani* – the corporations of Roman businessmen with whom senators had often collaborated in financial sharp practice – could milk the provinces as they had done so spectacularly in the past. Augustus appointed equestrians to collect the taxes, with strict instructions not to 'exact money beyond the amount appointed'.[12] These tax collectors, and even the equestrian governors he appointed to run the less important provinces, were for the first time paid a fixed salary. The Augustan regime was, it could claim, freeing the provinces from the worst effects of Roman extortion. By allowing them to bask in prosperity, the *pax Augusta* was also giving the provinces an incentive to stay loyal – although not all would do so.

In January 27 BC, before a Senate now packed with his supporters, Augustus formally renounced the consulship (the highest office of state and the crown of a senatorial career), which had been bestowed on him by the Senate. As Augustus himself put it in the *Res Gestae*, his own triumphal summary of his reign, which he wrote at the age of seventy-six: 'When I had extinguished the flames of civil war, after

---

* The Gospel of Luke gives this as the reason Jesus was born in Bethlehem, although it is wrong both in saying that the family had to travel to Bethlehem at all and in even linking the Nativity to the census; see chapter 7.

receiving by universal consent the absolute control of affairs, I transferred the republic from my own control to the will of the senate and the Roman people.'

In return, the grateful Senate promptly made him proconsul of the provinces of Gaul, Spain, Syria and Egypt. In theory, the proconsulship simply made Augustus the equal of any other proconsul ruling a province, but he had been given control of the most strategically important Roman provinces, where the great bulk of the legions were stationed to guard the empire's vulnerable borders from attack. In Gaul the threat came from Germanic tribesmen on the Rhine frontier; in Syria from the Parthians on the Euphrates; and in Egypt from the Meroites of sub-Saharan Africa whose Queen Amanirenas was about to invade (see chapter 4). Thanks to the power formally granted him by the Senate, Augustus now directly controlled twenty-three of Rome's twenty-seven legions: military power was in his hands.

Augustus had reduced the size of the army to about 300,000 men, barely 2 per cent of all adult males in the empire, compared to 13 per cent in its aggressive heyday during the previous two centuries BC.[13] Although its primary role was now not territorial conquest but defence of Rome's 4,000 miles of frontier and maintenance of order in the provinces, the Augustan regime depended as much as any on the threat of force. And Augustus well understood the necessity of maintaining the army's loyalty. As Plutarch, the Greek historian, philosopher and biographer of the late first century AD, would remark in his *Precepts of Statecraft*: 'do not have great pride or confidence in your crown, for you see the soldier's boot just above your head'.

Augustus made sure to keep the soldiers sweet. He turned what had been an army of conscripts into a professional standing army of volunteers and rewarded them well. They received fixed salaries, plus cash rewards and allotments of land (admittedly often on poor soil far from home) on retirement – a package that made them better off than most of their civilian peers. He also increased their chances of promotion: under the Republic an ordinary soldier, however talented, could rise no higher than the rank of centurion (commanding a century, that is, a company of about 80 to 100 men), but under Augustus he could rise to a senior command. And Augustus further boosted the status of the equestrians, who became in effect the junior officer corps of the army. He even appointed equestrians instead of senators as heads, *praefecti*, of the Praetorian Guard, and doubled their pay, a wise move given that they would play such a determining role in the life and death of succeeding emperors. Augustus' stepson and immediate successor, Tiberius, was probably murdered by the head of the Praetorian Guard; his nephew Caligula would be trapped in a narrow exit from the arena by his Praetorian Guard and assassinated; Caligula's cruel, stammering uncle Claudius owed his throne to the Praetorian cohorts, as did Claudius' stepson, Nero, who later lost his throne when they deserted him in favour of Galba.

Unlike some of his successors, Augustus never underestimated the importance of his army. Promotion in the army became increasingly dependent on him. Rather than swearing an oath of loyalty to their own general, soldiers now swore an oath of loyalty to Augustus, who became the sole head of a permanent army.

Augustus was creating a compliant elite. His regime kept the Republican institutions – the Senate and the plebeian assemblies – in place, but it simply sidestepped them or transformed them into instruments of patronage. 'From this time there was, strictly speaking, a monarch,' wrote Cassius Dio. 'The Senate as a body, it is true, continued to sit in judgment as before, and in certain cases transacted business with embassies and heralds, from both peoples and kings; and the people and the plebs, moreover, continued to meet for the elections; but nothing was done that did not please Caesar.'

Augustus, however, proclaimed that the Republic had been restored. When in 22 BC plague and famine hit Rome, and the people shut the senators up in their meeting place and threatened to burn the building down if they did not elect Augustus dictator, he 'fell on his knee and, throwing back his gown to expose his naked breast, implored their silence'.[14] But Augustus did accept the *cura annonae* (charge of the corn supply, including the distribution of free corn to an allocated number of Roman citizens), a hugely important route to popularity, since it enabled him to alleviate the starvation that threatened Rome's people.

Four days after the Senate had in effect handed over control of the army to their *princeps*, they bestowed on him the novel title 'Augustus' – 'the revered one'. Augustus, formerly known as Octavian Caesar, had together with his strategists put in place the political framework of the new imperial regime. They had dressed up an empire in the clothes of a republic; they had given the Roman elite and those other potentially dangerous elements of the empire – the conquered elites, the army and the ordinary people – good material reasons to support the new regime.

Augustus had established himself by military force. Now, like every successful ruler, he had to find something beyond the threat of arms to command the obedience of his subjects. The Hobbesian contract between ruler and ruled of stability and protection in return for obedience, had been made redundant by the *pax Augusta*. Though ultimately he would always rely on brute force, Augustus increasingly needed to wield power by manipulating the beliefs and behaviour of his subjects. In doing so, he would discover the great power of religion in capturing hearts and minds. Augustus was on his way to becoming a god.

2

AUGUSTUS: GOD AND FIRST CITIZEN

The poets were not alone in sanctioning myths, for long before the poets the states and the lawmakers had sanctioned them as a useful expedient. They needed to control the people by superstitious fears, and these cannot be aroused without myths and marvels.

Strabo, *Geographia*, I.2.8, *c*.20 BC–AD 23

The various modes of worship, which prevailed in the Roman world, were all considered by the people, as equally true; by the philosopher, as equally false; and by the magistrate, as equally useful.

Gibbon, *Decline and Fall of the Roman Empire*, vol. I, ch. 2, 1776

. . . religion has been the historically most widespread and effective instrumentality of legitimation.

Berger, *The Sacred Canopy*, 1967

The Senate's 'decision' in 27 BC that their *princeps* (their leading citizen) should become 'Augustus' marked the beginning of the imperial cult. Within a few decades, the divine or semi-divine Augustus dominated the physical and mental landscape of the empire. Altars and temples to him were built in the highest and most prominent places in hundreds of cities; great carnivalesque festivals, with sacred processions, public banquets and games celebrating events in the life of Augustus and his family, were added to the monthly round of festivals dedicated to the gods.

The worship of a divine man was not new, but under Augustus and his fellow strategists it was moulded into a unifying political force. Thanks to them, worship of the divine man reached unparalleled heights.[1] By the end of the first century AD, the idea of the divine emperor would be so well entrenched that Vespasian was acknowledged as *soter* (saviour), and his son Domitian demanded to be called *dominus et deus* (lord and god). The imperial cult, which was actually a much looser practice than the term implies, encompassing any type of worship of an emperor living or dead, lasted into the fourth century AD when the Emperor Theodosius finally did away with all the gods, including the divine emperors, in favour of the one Christian God. Worship of the emperor had prepared the mental and emotional ground for the worship of one supreme ruler.

The founding of the imperial cult, like the founding of the political regime, had to be very carefully tailored to the more or less resistant constituents of the empire: both the Eastern and Western parts of the empire which were culturally so distinct, the one Hellenized, the other not; and within that basic division, the elite of Rome and Italy, the local elites of the conquered provinces East and West, and the ordinary people of the empire both within Italy and beyond.

Augustus had, according to Cassius Dio, been

> exceedingly desirous of being called Romulus, but when he perceived that this caused him to be suspected of desiring the kingship, he desisted from his efforts to obtain it, and took the title of 'Augustus', signifying that he was more than human; for all the most precious and sacred objects are termed augusta. Therefore they addressed him also in Greek as Sebastos, meaning an august personage, from the passive of the verb sebazo, 'to revere'.[2]

The new title of 'Augustus' had strong associations with divinity – it was a synonym for *sanctus* (holy) and *divinus* (divine). Its advantage was that while indicating Augustus' superiority over the rest of humanity, and hinting at his divinity, it avoided any overt reference to his autocratic rule.

The Augustan strategists were playing a delicate game. A cult that glorifies the individual ruler will almost inevitably antagonize the elite whose own status and power is correspondingly degraded. The assertion of Augustus' divinity would enhance his majesty and authority in the eyes of the people, but it could also fatally antagonize a Roman elite brought up to humble themselves to no one, not even their gods. Julius Caesar had made the fatal mistake of 'accepting' divine honours in his lifetime: it only served to make his dictatorship that much more unpalatable to his supposed peers. The regime had to balance the Agrippan populist strategy of appealing to the people with the Maecenas one of appealing to the elite.

Yet again Cassius Dio makes Maecenas a determining voice. The interdependence of religion and state was an integral and unquestioned feature of every empire in the ancient world. Political power naturally had a religious dimension. And Maecenas was well aware of the crucial role religion could play in shaping the nature of both ruler and ruled and moulding resistant peoples into loyal subjects. 'You must worship the divine everywhere and in every way according to ancestral custom and force everyone else to honour it', Maecenas counsels, 'since anyone despising them [the gods] will not honour anyone else.'[3] It was commonly believed that Rome had nearly destroyed itself in civil war because the old Roman piety had been neglected.

Inevitably, the elite were likely to be more sceptical than the majority. By virtue of their wealth, they had less need of the divine. Amongst this elite were some of the richest men in the world. Living in their airy villas, waited on by hundreds of slaves, they were comparatively cushioned from the vagaries of fate, unlike the majority of people who struggled more or less desperately to survive in a world where famine constantly threatened, where half the babies born in a city would die before they were five years old and those that survived would lose at least one of their parents before gaining adulthood. Ordinary people needed their gods as insurance policies; the elite less so. For the elite, the gap between them and the gods was smaller than for ordinary people and allowed less room for awe, fear and gratitude. Like elites throughout the ancient as in the modern world, they liked to make a distinction between their 'rational' belief and the superstitious, irrational belief of the common and not so common people.

But, as Seneca delighted in pointing out, they were on the same spectrum of belief, magic and superstition as everybody else. 'Go into the Capitol and you will be ashamed of the madness on display,' he wrote in a polemic against superstitious worship, now lost but quoted in the early fifth century by Augustine, the North African bishop of Hippo, in his *City of God*.

One is suggesting divine commands to a god; another is telling the hours to Jupiter; one is his bather, another his anointer – at least he makes an empty gesture with his arms to imitate anointing... There are women who arrange the hair of Juno and Minerva, standing far away not only from her image, but even from her temple. These move their fingers in the manner of hairdressers. There are some women who hold a mirror. There are some who are calling the gods to assist them in court. There are some who are holding up documents to them, and are explaining to them their cases.[4]

Augustus himself 'had absolute faith' in premonitions and dreams. He wore a sealskin amulet for protection against thunder and lightning, of which he was terrified. Many people wore as amulets bits of the bodies of those who had suffered a violent death such as gladiators, or executed criminals. Prominent Romans listened to the voice of god speaking through an oracle and were as hoodwinked as everyone else by the gifted faker Alexander, who rigged up a talking serpent as an oracle for which he charged high prices. Cato the Elder joked that when two *haruspices* (diviners who interpreted the entrails of sacrificed animals) passed one another in the street they could not help but grin at one another.

Rich and poor celebrated the same festivals, and performed the same rites. The difference between them turned more on the nature of their belief. Ordinary people still believed in the individual gods who haphazardly affected humanity according to their own self-indulgent whims. But the elite's gods were turning from flawed superhumans into something more abstract and moral, according to the historian of ancient Rome, Paul Veyne.[5] When the Romans began their conquest of Greece in the second century BC, Zeus, the sexually uncontrolled, self-indulgent but most powerful of all the gods, merged with the Roman god Jupiter to become 'the supremely just, powerful, and even benevolent protector of the Roman empire'.[6] But whereas most people continued to worship Zeus/Jupiter as an individual, in the eyes of the elite he was shedding his individual identity and becoming part of an amorphous collective identity – 'the gods' or even 'god' – a sort of divine providence or Fate which loved virtuous men and would ensure the victory of the just cause. The amoral individual gods were combining to become a moral force. Augustus had embarked on the same moral journey, though the elite may have known him too well to have been convinced that he would ever reach his destination (see chapter 8 for more on the coalescing of the gods).

Augustus and Livia had in fact scandalized the more devout citizens of Rome with their 'Feast of the Divine Twelve', a private banquet in which guests came dressed as the twelve Olympian deities; 'impious Caesar', as an anonymous lampoon about the banquet called Augustus, had appeared as Apollo. Now Augustus made a point of restoring Rome's temples which were crumbling away from neglect. They were rebuilt in the traditional style with limestone, heavy wooden roofs and terracotta decoration, while alongside them armies of architects and artisans from the East, who had been schooled in the Greek style, built shining new temples to the gods associated with the imperial house. Senators were no longer allowed to build temples in Rome, though they could do so in the provinces. The grandiose temples rising up in Rome could only be built by members of the imperial family; every marble and bronze facade was associated with an Augustan god and with the great builder Augustus himself. But when it came to Augustus' own divinity, Maecenas advocated caution. 'No man ever became a god by popular vote,' Cassius Dio makes him say.

'Hence, if you are upright as a man and honourable as a ruler, the whole earth will be your hallowed precinct, all cities your temples, and all men your statues'; as to those rulers who too overtly took on the mantle of divinity, 'such honours not only do not lend holiness to them, even though shrines are set apart for them in all their cities, but even bring a greater reproach upon them, becoming, as it were, trophies of their baseness and memorials of their injustice'.[7]

Agrippa did not agree with Maecenas. He wanted to build a temple to Augustus which would form the centrepiece of the great building scheme he was undertaking on the Campus Martius, the vast open space on the Tiber flood plain, where part of the 2 BC games to celebrate Augustus would be held. Augustus, however, declined the honour of a temple. It would have been too direct an attribution of divinity. Instead the temple was dedicated to Augustus' ancestors – Venus, Mars and the deified Julius Caesar – and the temple was named the Pantheon, meaning 'all the gods' (though it was not until the second century AD, during the reign of Emperor Hadrian, that it was remodelled into the Pantheon we know today). A statue to Augustus was placed not inside the temple, as Agrippa had wished, but on one side of the entrance; on the other was that of Augustus' faithful helpmeet, Agrippa himself.

Paradoxical though it might seem, it was perhaps not surprising that Maecenas, who in Cassius Dio's schematic rendering of the creation of the Augustan regime advocated one-man rule, was more cautious about the imperial cult than the populist Agrippa. Maecenas, the aristocrat, was far more sensitive to how Augustus' deification would be perceived by the elite. For the old Roman nobleman, brought up in a tradition of Republicanism and struggling to come to terms with the new regime, it might well have been intolerable to accept that one of them – a man not even as good as many of them since his father had been a *novus homo*, the first member of the family to become a senator – had been elevated to divinity.

It was not that the idea of a man becoming god was inconceivable. Egypt had worshipped its pharaohs for centuries. Throughout the Hellenized east, the ruler had been worshipped as divine since at least the fourth century BC, when Alexander the Great brought the tradition from Greece to his conquered lands. Rome had its deified founder Romulus. Only the monotheistic Jews made a clear-cut distinction between the divine and the human. For Philo, the first-century AD Jewish philosopher from Alexandria, the change from man to god 'was not a small one but an absolutely fundamental one, namely the apparent transformation of the created, destructible nature of man into the uncreated, indestructible nature of God, which the Jewish nation judged to be the most horrible of blasphemies; for God would change into man sooner than man into God'. But for the non-monotheists, the pagans, the divine nature was not something totally perfect or therefore totally different from the flawed human: gods and humans were on a continuum, not two distinct species.

The gods were jealous, lustful, capricious and touchy; they were humans but on a more magnificent scale – and they were immortal. Man's relationship with them reflected the relationship which patterned the Roman world – that of client and patron. The gods were super-patrons and Augustus fitted easily into that mould. His rule rested on patronage as the whole of Roman society did. Rome was governed through webs of personal relationships, unlike China where, despite the rise of an inner court of the emperor's favourites, there was always the outer court, the meritocratic civil service, to contend with. In Rome there was no clear distinction between the personal and the political, just as there was no clear cut-off between the political and the religious, or the divine and the human. It would take Saul/Paul, the zealous Pharisee who would transform a small Jewish cult into a world religion, to sever the connections by demarcating a personal spiritual domain that was superior to the physical world (see chapter 19).

In Rome in the early mornings, while the public slaves were cleaning the pathways or repairing the aqueducts, and cafes were selling rolls and cheese, the alleys and lanes were filled with 'clients' walking or being carried in litters and chairs to their patrons' houses for the morning *salutatio*.[8] In return for performing small favours, poor clients could virtually eke out an existence on gifts from their patrons. They might be given *tesserae* or tokens entitling them to admission to the games, a small sum of money or even a pot of hot food carried on a portable barbecue by 'a poor little slave', wrote Juvenal, 'with head erect, fanning the flame as he runs along'. Wealthier clients might hope to get an appointment through their patron's influence – *testimonia* were routinely sent to the emperor, recommending officials.

But as far as the Roman elite were concerned, it was essential that the power imbalance inherent in the relationship of client and patron should be disguised. Patronage for them had to be more an exchange of favours between equals, not a bestowal of favours by the powerful on the less powerful. Though satirists like Juvenal and Martial took delight in exposing the true nature of the relationship between the 'voluntary slave', as Juvenal called the client, and the arrogant patron, the fiction of equality was maintained by each addressing the other as *amicus* (friend).

The Confucian civil servant's kowtowing to his emperor in China would have been unthinkable to a member of the Roman elite. It was too demeaning, too antithetical to their sense of all that was virtuous and noble about being a man. Only the common people worshipped, placated and begged for favours from their patrons, just as they did from their gods. The Roman elite preferred to treat their gods as partners with whom they could offer *quid pro quos* – sacrifices in return for favours. When they passed a statue of their god in the streets they blew him a kiss with their fingers: this was no reverential genuflection.

Deference was the attitude of the slave to his master. Humility was not a virtue, merely a sign of inferiority. But for the non-elite, and for many of Rome's conquered peoples, elite and non-elite alike, the experience of being humbled was always with them. It was Paul's triumph to transform the ever-present discomfort of humiliation into a spiritual exercise. He turned humility from something shameful into a supreme virtue. What better way to reconcile the ordinary people of the empire to their status as subjects? As Nietzsche commented, it was the elevation of the everyday reality of submission into an ideal.[9]

But this could not – yet – be an ideal for an elite for whom any sign of submission could be seen as an acknowledgement of defeat. Which was why Augustus, the super-patron of the empire, played the game of equality. He too had his *salutatio*, his morning greeting, though he had instituted the requirement that when he was resident in Rome every senator and prominent equestrian had to attend him, unless they were specifically excused. To control the numbers, the visitors to his palace on the Palatine Hill were divided up into groups. But the emperor made sure to kiss each one in greeting and to address them by name, at the prompting of his *nomenclator* (who was, unfortunately for Augustus, rather forgetful). Beneath the velvet glove of apparent approachability, however, there lurked the iron fist of imperial power. One *amicus* was unwise enough to have been overheard talking about the imperial succession to his wife. When it was his turn to greet the emperor, Augustus replied: 'Farewell, Fulvius.' His meaning was all too clear. Fulvius went home and committed suicide, along with his wife.[10]

It was the increasing dominance of Augustus and the erosion of their own political power, however well disguised by the Augustans, that perhaps explained the appeal of Stoicism for the elite. The goal of Stoicism – founded in the early fourth century BC in Athens by Zeno – was autonomy and mastery, rather like that of the aristocrat in control of his estate. The Stoic's mastery, however, was not of the external world, but of his private interior world, the inner space which certain religions were beginning to create, or colonize, and where many – especially city-dwellers (see chapter 3) – would find solace. Stoicism carved out for the individual an internal realm where he could reign supreme as sovereign of the self, 'not being a slave to any circumstance, to any constraint, to any chance', in the words of the Spanish Stoic Seneca who would become tutor and then political adviser to Nero, the fifth and last emperor of the Julio-Claudian dynasty that Augustus had founded. Stoicism offered a form of mastery that compensated for the political mastery the Roman elite were losing. By the time Paul began preaching his own Judaic version in which the powerless found solace in an inner realm created by God, Stoicism had overtaken Epicureanism as the religion of the elite and was hugely popular.

Epicureanism (founded, like Stoicisim, in Athens in the early fourth century BC) also offered its solace to the elite for its loss of power: but Epicureanism's solution was a retreat from the world, a withdrawal from competition. Horace, who described himself as 'fat and sleek, a hog from Epicurus's herd', proclaimed in all his letters and poems the Epicurean message that the happiest life was the life of retreat, the simple rural life, free from the distresses of the world of ambition, of its jealousies, failures, unfulfilled longings for luxuries, and satiety when luxuries were obtained. A sort of Buddhism for Romans, the Epicurean goal was pleasure, but a pleasure that was more serenity than hedonism, a freedom from pain and anxiety. And a freedom from fear, including fear of the gods who did not care about people and had absolutely no effect on their lives. Though Maecenas was thought to be a sympathizer, Epicureanism was inevitably less popular with members of the elite who wanted to engage with the world and make their mark in it, even if Augustus was giving them less scope to do so.

In theory the slave, as much as the Roman senator, could be ruler of his own internal universe since according to Stoicism every human shared a spark of the divine *logos*, the principle of reason or soul of the universe, which permeated and activated all reality. 'One may leap to Heaven from the very slums,' wrote the enormously wealthy Seneca.[11] In practice, however, Stoicism's brotherhood of man was too rational and comfortless a religion to appeal much beyond the elite. Stoicism was suspicious of the emotions; man's aim was to detach himself from the vagaries of passion rather than enjoy them, because only then could he achieve his true nature as a free individual, guided by the spark of *logos* within him.

Self-control was an essential virtue for the Stoic and its perceived lack was one of the reasons why Seneca considered Maecenas a contemptible example of a man whose 'uncontrolled, passionate, and effeminate soul' was under the tyrannical sway of his emotions. The Roman elite were always torn between their desire to portray themselves in busts and statues as self-restrained Stoics, immune to the temptations of the world, and their desire for display and the histrionic gesture. Augustus and his heirs were constantly baring their breasts to be stabbed as a gesture of sincerity; Suetonius and Cassius Dio describe Augustus tearing open his gown and falling to his knees in order to convince the people that he did not want the office of dictator that they were offering him;[12] an advocate or senator would enhance the effectiveness of his speech with the occasional sob to which the audience was expected to respond in kind; mourners keened in sackcloth and ashes. Exaggerated passion and extravagant displays of emotion were signs of sincerity, though they were opposed by the true Stoics.

Far more attractive than Stoicism to ordinary people were the mystery cults of Isis, Cybele and Atargatis – respectively Egyptian, Phrygian (Turkish) and Syrian deities whose worship had spread throughout the Graeco-Roman world (I will be looking in more detail at the cult of Isis in chapter 3 and the cult of Atargatis in chapter 8). They were also carving out an inner realm of the individual, but their appeal was emotional, not rational; they provided ecstasy, comfort and a sense of belonging. From the state's point of view the mystery cults were dangerously anarchic and periodically had to be suppressed. When Augustus was absent in Italy, in 21 BC, Agrippa, no doubt with

Augustus' approval if not at his suggestion, had forbidden anyone to practise the Isis cult within the city of Rome and within one mile beyond its city walls. The mystery cults were antithetical to everything the imperial cult would try to achieve: they engendered private ecstasy, and a passionate focus of loyalty to a goddess and an organization which was beyond the confines of the state; the mystery cults would not create good Roman subjects and could create subversive ones. Stoicism, on the other hand, promoted the disciplined well-ordered individual, who guided himself by *logos*, reason; it was hardly surprising that Augustus and Livia were Stoic sympathizers.

Augustus successfully presented himself both as Stoic and as embodiment of the tough, courageous countryman idealized by Horace and Virgil. He made a point of living simply. His mansion on the Palatine Hill (known as *palatium*, hence 'palace') was where the elite of Rome lived and also where the augurs, the priests who specialized in interpreting the flight of birds, had their observation posts. But it was modest at least by later emperors' standards, and probably even by Maecenas'. It had no marble decorations; Augustus used the same bedroom in summer and winter for more than forty years and slept on a simply furnished bed. Unlike the vulgarly ostentatious Trimalchio of *Satyricon*, with his never-ending banquet, each course more elaborate than the last, Augustus 'preferred the food of the common people: the coarser sort of bread, small fishes, fresh hand-pressed cheese, and green figs'.[13] He wore simple clothes supposedly made by his wife who spun and wove as all good Roman matrons were meant to do.

Livia, whom Augustus genuinely loved according to Suetonius, played her part well. Her head modestly covered by a shawl, she maintained an appearance of simplicity – with the help of her staff of more than 1,000 slaves and freed slaves who dressed her hair, attended to her clothes, made her shoes and jewellery, and gave her massages. Livia was politically extremely competent: Augustus took her opinions so seriously that he would come into her bedroom at night, notebook in hand, to consult her. She was extremely ambitious for her family, resorting to murder if her enemy Tacitus is to be believed; she had divorced her first husband Tiberius Claudius Nero when she was pregnant with their second child, in order to marry Augustus. Yet she always appeared as the model pious, modest wife of nostalgic Republican memory.

Under the guise of a return to the golden age – the propagandist myth of the new regime – Augustus brought about the imperial revolution. The regime was built on the illusion that it was not ruled by an emperor (in the sense of a supreme hereditary monarch), that it was in fact not creating a monarchical form of government but restoring all that was great in pre-civil war Republican Rome, a Rome which had become mythically glorious in its remodelling by Virgil and the other protégés of Maecenas.

Into this 'restored' moral order Agrippa, 'a great-souled man', according to Seneca, fitted easily. Agrippa was, more naturally than Augustus, the embodiment of the straight, true and unadorned Roman of the golden age before the civil wars. But for Maecenas the moral world that he had done so much to create was a disaster. He either could not, or thought he was powerful enough not to have to be seen to, conform to its precepts. Seneca considered him to be 'equally unusual, unsound, and eccentric'. Maecenas represented all that was decadent, luxury-loving, and soft – those vices of the East that might have destroyed Rome had Augustus not defeated Mark Antony and Cleopatra at Actium. Maecenas seduced other men's wives – including at one dinner party the wife of his host who tactfully pretended to be asleep – but he also loved men: in later life he was infatuated with the star mime-actor Bathyllus. He raced through the crowded streets of Rome in a two-wheeled chariot, a new style imported from Britain. He introduced Romans to a new delicacy of young donkey. He feasted with his friends, careless of the social status of his guests as long as they were talented, according to his friend Horace, himself the son of a freedman.

Initially Augustus treated the dissolute Maecenas indulgently, laughing at his 'myrrh-distilled ringlets' and mocking the ornateness of both his way of life and his literary style by addressing him extravagantly as 'my ebony of Medullia, ivory from Etruria, lasar of Arretium, diamond of the upper sea, Tiberine pearl, emerald of the Cilnii, jasper of the Iguvians, Porsenna's beryl, ruby of the Adriatic'.[14] Whenever he was ill, Augustus would stay at Maecenas' magnificent villa on the Esquiline Hill in Rome.

But in 23 BC Augustus' great friend and adviser fell from grace. Maecenas, who was according to Tacitus the 'pre-eminent repository of imperial secrets', was indiscreet enough to warn his wife Terentia that her brother Murena was implicated in a conspiracy to assassinate Augustus. Murena, a hunchback who as consul occupied the most important senatorial position, had been openly critical of the authoritarianism of the Augustan regime. He was put to death without trial. Maecenas was effectively frozen out of the inner circle, for his 'inability to hold his tongue'.

But what Seneca found particularly despicable was Maecenas' horror of death, a fear that was as antithetical to the Epicureans as it was to the Stoics. 'Torture my body, rack me with gout; break and distort my limbs; nail me to a cross; grant me but Life and it is well,' Seneca quotes Maecenas as saying. For Seneca, the ideal way to face death was that displayed by the best gladiators.

The gladiator occupied an extraordinarily ambivalent position in Roman society. He was despised as a social outcast: gladiators were slaves, often prisoners of war, or convicted criminals classified in Roman law along with prostitutes. Yet gladiators were also honoured as exemplars of courage and military skill. Rome might be basking in the *pax Augusta*, but it was still too new for Romans to have accommodated themselves fully to it. The gladiators were Rome's warriors and the warrior was still the ideal man.

For Seneca, the wise Stoic and the brave gladiator were at one in understanding that their life was temporary and that they must surrender it without reluctance in accordance with the contract they had signed – with their divine master in the case of the Stoic; with their trainer in the case of the gladiator. Such carelessness in the face of death made the Stoic free, just as it ennobled the gladiator and freed him from his status of slave or condemned criminal. 'For no man is free who is a slave to his body,' Seneca wrote, ten years after Paul too had advocated rejection of what he considered to be the debasing demands of the body, though for Paul it was not freedom but God that was the goal: 'Meats for the belly, and the belly for meats: but God shall destroy both it and them. Now [is] not for fornication, but for the Lord; and the Lord for the body.'[15]

Maecenas had signally failed to subdue or distance himself from worldly things. For the last fourteen years of his life he tried hard to regain his footing with Augustus but remained in a sort of exile in Rome, becoming increasingly valetudinarian and burdening those friends who stuck by him, like Horace, with his complaints. In the last three years of his life, he suffered from such acute insomnia that, according to Pliny the Elder, he 'never enjoyed a moment's sleep' and though he 'drugged himself with wine, the sound of falling waters, the choicest wines, the music of symphonies gently rising and falling in the distance – all were vain'.

In the battle for Augustus' favour Maecenas had lost to Agrippa. 'You have made him so great that he must either become your son-in-law or be slain,' Maecenas remarked bitterly to Augustus.[16] Agrippa duly divorced Augustus' niece to marry Augustus' daughter, the witty, lascivious, independent-minded sixteen-year-old Julia.

In 15 BC Agrippa set off on a loyalty-building tour of the East. When he visited his – and Rome's – great friend Herod the Great in the semi-independent kingdom of Judaea, temples to Augustus were going up in Panias, Samaria and Herod's newly renamed city of Caesarea Maritima, as they were in cities throughout the Eastern part of the empire.

Augustus still refused to allow overt worship of himself within Italy, though he would soon introduce the imperial cult in disguised form. But outside Rome and Italy, in the Eastern part of the empire, it was a different matter. When Bithynia and what was called Asia, two provinces in Asia Minor (most of modern Turkey), requested permission to build a temple to the god Augustus in their capital cities, Augustus agreed, though on condition that the goddess Roma, the personification of Rome, would also be worshipped in the temple.

It was not surprising that these two provinces should have been first to erect temples to the god Augustus. The imperial cult grew there naturally out of a centuries-old tradition of ruler worship. Asia Minor contained hundreds of cities. Most of them had been founded after the Macedonian Greek Alexander the Great's conquests in the fourth century BC. The Greeks' own tradition of deifying their kings probably began with him; he certainly actively encouraged belief in his own divinity. By the time of Augustus, Asia Minor's cities had overtaken the decaying cities of mainland Greece in brilliance.[17] Asia Minor was the most enthusiastic supporter of the imperial cult, as it would later be of Christianity.

Ephesus (on Asia Minor's Mediterranean coast), where Paul would proclaim a new god, was one of the first cities to build a temple to Augustus. It was the commercial centre of Asia Minor, straddling the East–West trade route through the region. It was home to hundreds of cults, and possible final resting place, though his death was a matter of doubt amongst his followers, of the 'pagan Christ' Apollonius (see chapter 10). The peoples of Asia Minor were no strangers to the idea of worshipping a man who became a god.

Provincial assemblies (their members drawn from the elite of the province's cities) eagerly petitioned Augustus to found an imperial cult. Individual cities desperately competed for the privilege of building a temple to him, though the final decision as to which city should have that honour ostensibly lay in the hands of the Senate, to save Augustus the embarrassment.

The imperial cult was one of the crucial ways by which local elites could signal their loyalty to Rome, and gain the privileges and benefits that Rome could bestow – citizenship for themselves or even for the whole city, which meant the full protection of Roman law, the right to stand for office and to vote in provincial assemblies, as well as exemption from most taxes. To be a priest of the imperial cult meant securing a place within the patronage network of the local Roman governor. A word from the governor might help the priest's sons enter the Roman administration as equestrians. The holding of an office connected with the imperial cult rapidly came to be seen as the pinnacle of a local career and a passport to success for the whole family.

For a city to gain the right to build a temple to Augustus and found an imperial cult enhanced its importance, and firmly embedded it within an increasingly stable and ordered empire. It was at the altar of Augustus or before the temple of Augustus that Rome's new subjects swore their allegiance. Cities like Halicarnassus, on the Mediterranean coast of Asia Minor, dedicated their new temples to 'Caesar Augustus, Father of his own Fatherland, divine Rome, Zeus Paternal, and Saviour of the whole human race, in whom Providence has not only fulfilled but even surpassed the prayers of all men: land and sea are at peace, cities flourish under the reign of law, in mutual harmony and prosperity.'

Was the request to found the imperial cult expedient flattery, or the expression of genuine homage and gratitude? The fact that it did the local elites no harm to be generous upholders of the imperial cult did not automatically mean that they were cynical. Expediency and belief are not necessarily incompatible. Augustus had indeed brought peace, prosperity, and law and order.*

The willing participation of the local elite in the imperial cult signalled their compliance with Roman rule. For certain groups within Rome's conquered provinces – even, sometimes, for members of the local elites themselves – this subordination to Rome and to

---

* The problem for the elites of the Eastern part of the empire was more one of etiquette. The citizens of the city of Mytilene on the Aegean island of Lesbos, for instance, were unsure what was the most suitable animal to sacrifice to a living emperor – should it be a dark animal which was usually sacrificed at night to the gods of the earth and underworld, or a light-coloured animal which was usually burned in honour of other gods? In the end they plumped for neither but went for spotted animals.

Roman mores was a source of disquiet. But it would never create such tensions as it did for the Jews of Palestine.

That Agrippa was aware of the sensitive nature of the imperial cult for Herod's Jewish subjects was clear from his remarkably conciliatory attitude when he visited Judaea in 15 BC. He visibly showed his delight in walking around one of the biggest building sites in the ancient world, the Temple in Jerusalem, on one of whose gates Herod had inscribed Agrippa's name, and offered 100 oxen, a hecatomb, to the God of the Jews. He 'feasted the people, without omitting any of the greatest dainties that could be gotten', according to the Jewish historian Josephus.* When he left the city, Agrippa was so popular that he was escorted to the harbour 'not by one city only but by the whole country, having branches strewed in his road, and being greatly admired and respected for his piety'.[18]

About a year after his trip East, Agrippa, suffering badly from gout which he tried in vain to conceal, was dispatched to Pannonia, in central Europe, to put down a serious rebellion. It was his last campaign. He died the following year, in 12 BC, at the age of fifty-one. Augustus honoured his faithful deputy by interring Agrippa's ashes in his own mausoleum and organizing funeral games, including gladiatorial combats. But, according to Cassius Dio, 'none of the prominent men wished to attend the festivals'. Though Augustus 'felt his loss for a long time', the Roman elite were unmoved by the death of the upstart who had become the second most powerful man in the empire and who would be grandfather of Caligula and great-grandfather of Nero. But Herod, the loyal Roman, mourned the loss of his friend. He named his grandson, the future king of Judaea, after him and gave the harbour city of Anthedon the new name of Agrippias. How the Roman elite felt five years later, when Maecenas died after his fifteen years of 'exile' in Rome, we do not know, though Cassius Dio noted that Augustus 'regretted his loss exceedingly'. No doubt that was partly because Maecenas had bequeathed almost all

---

* Josephus is the only near-contemporary writer to mention Jesus apart from Tacitus and, of course, the Apostles.

his vast wealth to Augustus, despite his fall from grace. Maecenas was buried beside his friend Horace who died the same year.

On 1 August 12 BC, five months after Agrippa's death, Augustus' stepson Drusus officially founded the imperial cult in the Western part of the empire. Together with the most prominent men of Gaul, Drusus processed up one of two monumental ramps leading to a large terrace set across the river from the city of Lugdunum (today's Lyons). There he dedicated a marble altar to the gods Roma and Augustus. With him was the *sacerdos*, the chief priest of the new cult, whose name, C. Julius Vercondaridubno, reflected his potentially dual allegiance as both Roman citizen and tribesman. The altar was flanked by sixty statues, each representing one of the tribes of Gaul.

The province of Gaul had just recently risen in revolt against Rome. The cause of the unrest, as so often in the empire, was taxation. Rome had imposed a tax census to fund its expansion into German territory and Gaul had erupted in protest. Drusus, Livia's second son from her first marriage, and a far more attractive personality than his elder brother and future emperor, Tiberius, marched in to restore order. The new altar dedicated by Drusus at Lugdunum had carved on it the names of all the tribal chiefs. The restless tribesmen were now enmarbled with Rome and its leader.

More than the East, the relatively new, unsettled provinces of Gaul, Germany and Spain in the Western part of the empire needed to enlist the imperial cult in the task of Romanizing its peoples and securing their loyalty. Gaul had only been fully conquered in 51 BC by Julius Caesar, though southern France (Gallia Narbonensis as it became under Augustus) had been a province of Rome since about 121 BC. Spain, birthplace of the Stoic Seneca and the poet Martial, had only finally been subjugated by Agrippa, who put down the last of the Spanish tribes to resist Rome in 19 BC; Augustus had tried six years earlier, with the help of the North African King Juba (Rome's most loyal client king apart from Herod). Agrippa, the better general, succeeded.

But whereas in the Eastern part of the empire, emperor worship appeared to be a spontaneous extension of existing forms of worship and flourished without the necessity of much prompting from the centre, in the Western provinces the imperial cult had to be actively promoted by the regime. The West had never been Hellenized, and had no long tradition of ruler worship; it was less civilized, literally, in that it had few cities and therefore lacked the administrative machinery that made the propagation of the imperial cult so relatively easy in the East. And so Augustus and his family had to deliberately install the imperial cult in the Western part of the empire. Drusus went on to dedicate a further temple to Augustus in Gaul and may well have presided over the establishment of the imperial cult on the German frontier at Ara Ubiorum (Cologne), though it was probably not Drusus but the Roman governor who established three altars to Augustus in the north-west of Spain.

The same year that Drusus founded the imperial cult in Gaul, Augustus officially took control of Rome's religion. Lepidus, the ineffectual third triumvir who had once ruled Rome with Mark Antony and Augustus, died, leaving the office of *pontifex maximus* vacant. The *pontifex maximus* had had general oversight over religious law and practice in Rome, but had always decided matters collegiately with his fellow priests in the college of Pontifices. (Catholic bishops of Rome would assume the title for themselves in the fifth century.) Augustus was voted in overwhelmingly as *pontifex maximus* but transformed the position by making himself uniquely responsible for Rome's relationship with the gods. He had become, or had made himself, officially head of the 'church' as well as head of state, though, of course, the Romans themselves would not have recognized such a distinction.

Augustus now introduced the imperial cult to Rome itself, but of course veiled in tradition. In effect, he remodelled the ancient practice of ancestral worship into the worship of himself and his family, rather as Confucianism had moulded the age-old ancestor worship of China into a doctrine of devotion to the emperor.

For centuries, Roman families had worshipped the *lares* of their household, the spirits of their ancestors who lived in the underworld but could influence the lives of their descendants. Along with shrines in their own homes, there had traditionally been shrines to the *lares* at every crossroads in every ward (district) in Rome, though these *lares* had been generalized spirits of the dead rather than the ancestors of a particular family. But the shrines fell into disuse when Julius Caesar suppressed the associations responsible for running the cult, along with all other guilds – any association of people was a potential focus for rebellion.

In 12 BC Augustus 'restored' the shrines and had new statues placed in them, only now they were statues of the *lares Augusti*, the ancestors of his own family. The statue of the *Liber Pater*, a phallic divinity that had previously stood with the *lares*, was replaced by a statue of the *Genius Augusti*, usually dressed in a toga and with Augustus' features. Just as every family worshipped the spirits of their dead ancestors, so they also worshipped the Genius – the spirit – of the living head of the household. Henceforth Rome and all Italy could worship the Genius of their imperial father who benignly ruled over his super-household.

As with all the cults, to be an office holder was highly prized; it was a badge of success and harbinger of more success to come. And to be one of the *Augustales* offered a stake in the empire to a group whose position was becoming increasingly problematic.

Freedmen were becoming wealthy in growing numbers as they handled the trade that their former masters did not want to dirty their hands with. Many of them had looked after their masters' business interests when they were slaves and had then either become rich enough to buy their freedom or been manumitted (that is, freed by their owner).

But if the freedman was becoming richer, his status did not reflect his new position. Though freedmen automatically became Roman citizens when they were manumitted, and were therefore theoretically entitled to stand in elections for public office, they could not be elected to the Senate in Rome or the city councils in the rest of Italy.

At the games, they were relegated to the back rows; when the freedman Sarmentus – a beautiful, witty favourite of Maecenas who had bought Sarmentus as a slave and manumitted him – presumed to sit with the equestrians at the theatre, he was booed out of his seat.[19] At private dinners freedmen were given the least honoured seats on the couches; at public banquets their whole rank might be excluded or they might be segregated and offered a lesser share of the feast. They were forbidden to serve in the legions.

Their sons could escape the legal restrictions of the freedman as long as they were born after their fathers' manumission – but they could not escape 'the chalk of the slave market still on their heel', as Juvenal, the son of a freedman, put it. Horace, another son of a freedman, was well aware what the aristocrat thought: 'Although you strut around in all the pride of wealth, good fortune cannot change your breed.'

Augustus mollified the old aristocracy by enforcing this strict demarcation in status between the freedmen and the aristocrats. He forbade them to marry any woman of senatorial rank (the penalty could be execution). But, at the same time, he was increasingly making wealth the passport for entry into the aristocracy: potential senators had to own property worth at least 1 million sesterces, that is, about 250,000 times the day's wage of a labourer, and equestrians had to have an estate worth about 400,000 sesterces. Horace had been elevated to the higher ranks of the equestrian order, thanks to the wealth he derived from the Sabine farm given to him by Maecenas.

The old landed aristocracy were uncomfortably aware that in the competition for material wealth they might lose out to the freedman. So they fell back on the intangible – on ancestry, taste, good breeding, manners – which was why they loved the savage portrait of the vulgarian freedman Trimalchio in the *Satyricon*. Trimalchio had been left a fortune by his master, and with the money had founded a hugely profitable business, shipping wine, bacon, beans, perfume and slaves. He had built one of the vast villas in the Bay of Naples – then, as now, the haunt of the rich, but also of the not-so-rich, who were criticized for their drunkenness, for bathing naked in the lakes at night and singing too loudly.

Trimalchio was probably richer than most of his aristocratic readers but to his creator Petronius he was ineffably vulgar, and absurd in his pretensions. His balding head sticking out of his scarlet coat (a close crop was a sign of the slave or ex-slave), Trimalchio is carried to his dining room on a litter with his 'favourite boy' perched in front, and deposited on his cushions. Slaves rub perfumed cream into the guests' feet. The courses get increasingly elaborate and obscene – hounds dash round the dining room, followed by the carcase of a vast wild boar from which a flock of thrushes fly when it is carved by a bearded slave; the guests reach out to grab apples and grapes from a Priapus made of pastry; the panels of the coffered ceiling open to let down presents of gold crowns and alabaster jars of perfume. The drunken, overfed men, leaning on their left elbows, eating with their right hands, boast of their self-made wealth, and sneer at their host while drinking from his Corinthian bronze goblets and kissing his slave boys; their wives show off their jewellery, giggling and kissing each other as they get progressively drunker (the women of better-class families drank sparingly if they drank at all).

But if Trimalchio was fatally vulgar in the eyes of the aristocrat, he and the 'class' he represented were nonetheless becoming a force that needed to be appeased. The imperial cult offered freedmen a way of obtaining status while at the same time binding them to the emperor himself. Trimalchio was a 'priest of the Augustan college', as an inscription on the doorpost to his dining room announced and as he never tired of telling his guests. Membership of one of the colleges that tended the cult of the emperor offered prominent freedmen a position in Roman society, which the aristocracy was so keen to deprive them of. Denied public office and the honours associated with it, they were now entitled to virtually equivalent privileges as *Augustales*. In return for funding the cult, its festivals, banquets and sacrifices – a pig for the *lares Augusti* and a bull for the Genius of the emperor – they could make public appearances dressed in senatorial purple. Trimalchio ostentatiously wears a napkin round his neck with purple tassels and a broad purple stripe, the distinguishing mark of the senator's toga; like other important office holders he could be preceded down the street by lectors, freedmen of lesser standing than himself, who processed in single file, carrying 5-foot-long bundles of elm or birch rods over their left shoulder, and shouting *animadvertite* ('take note') to clear the path of obstacles, human or otherwise.

Just as the Augustan regime was capturing the Senate by appointing its own men, and trying to secure the loyalty of the equestrians by promoting them to higher office, so through the imperial cult it was trying to gain the support of prominent freedmen, of local elites and also of ordinary people.

The cult spread quickly. Not only was it in the interests of so many, but it also had the right environment in which it could flourish – the rapidly expanding cities, home to vast and ethnically diverse populations. Augustus and his family were a constant physical presence to city-dwellers. His temple dominated the skyline. Athens built a temple to Augustus on the Acropolis near the Parthenon. King Juba's great Roman city of Iol in today's Algeria had its sacred grove dedicated to Augustus. No Roman or Italian townsman could pass a crossroads without seeing a shrine to the *lares Augusti* and the Genius of Augustus.

The great public places of the city had their statue of Augustus, and often of Livia, who became the first woman in Roman history to be honoured on a major scale by sculpted portraits. Roman sculptors were unsurpassed – and still are – in their ability to capture the individual: the anxious old man with overhanging eyebrows, the plain middle-aged woman gazing unselfconsciously downwards. Above all, they could convey sheer power in the often unlovely faces of the Roman elite, benignly or malignantly plump, creased in thought, sensuous or grim-faced with determination. But in portraying Augustus, the sculptors adopted the classical, rather impersonal, Greek style. An idealized Augustus bestrode the cities, looking far more imposing than he did in real life. Under his sculptors' hands, Augustus had become physically perfect; all human frailty and flaws had disappeared. He was a noble, austere visionary. A toga covered his head, signifying the humble attitude the priest adopted when he performed a sacrifice (Romans covered their heads for the gods, but uncovered them in the presence of a superior in order not to make the gods jealous). The menacing power that oozed from the statues of Agrippa and his ilk was absent. The sculptors had sidestepped the sensitive issue of Augustus' political position by emphasizing his piety. This was not the warrior king, but the guardian of peace and order, Virgil's 'duty-bound' Aeneas, bearing with dignity the burden of destiny. Passers-by made sacrifices before Augustus' statue; runaway slaves or suspected criminals could claim the right of asylum beside it. As Augustus grew older, and his teeth decayed and began to fall out, he remained forever young and perfect in his statues, as did his wife Livia.

Augustus' and Livia's images were so ubiquitous that their clothing and hairstyles became the fashionable models for every aspiring man and woman. Spreading via the cities, the imperial cult contributed to the globalization of Roman culture across the empire. Temples with the same steps mounting up to the same huge portico of high Corinthian pillars, topped by a steep, richly decorated portico, were going up from Rome to North Africa. The rich in Egypt as in Syria ate off the same type of silverware, placed their sandalled feet on the same mosaic decorations; schoolboys from Turkey to Gaul studied the same books of rhetoric.[20]

At the heart of this Romanization was the emperor himself, the focal point of the physical and mental lives of his subjects. Roman families had always poured a libation of wine or offered flowers and incense to their ancestors during their meal at the end of the day. Now they offered a libation to the Genius of Augustus as well, thanks to the Senate who had decreed that 'at all banquets, not only public but private as well, everybody was to pour a libation to him'.[21] Every holder of public office, however minor, had to swear an oath of loyalty which included an invocation to the *Genius Augusti*.

Families placed statuettes of Augustus and members of his family in their household shrines and burned incense to him; Ovid made great play of doing the same. And they now celebrated him in the festivals which regularly punctuated the Roman year and which were all dedicated to the gods.

Festivals were great for trade. Pimps, prostitutes and more reputable traders and craftsmen from around the empire flocked to the city to take advantage of the huge crowds, who had sometimes to be kept in order by attendants lashing out with whips and staves. The city's inhabitants hung lamps and garlands on the doors of their shops and homes. They performed sacrifices at altars outside their houses and lined the streets to watch the processants filing past in their clean white robes. (Towards the end of the first century AD, Jesus' Apostle John registered his disapproval of a festival in honour of Artemis in Ephesus by wearing black, for which he was nearly killed by her worshippers.[22]) Crowds packed the theatres to cheer and boo the athletes, boxers, wrestlers, charioteers and gladiators, and to watch the venations (*venationes*), when starving panthers, lions, tigers, crocodiles, hippos, rhinos, elephants – the more exotic the animal the better – were let out of their cages to chase and be chased by gladiators. The venations, like the whole of the games, were a celebration not just of Augustus but of Rome and Romanness, its manliness and bravery, its conquest over raw nature, the extent of its dominions (since it could command animals from such distant lands) and its wealth.

Festivals were an extremely effective way of buying affection and Augustus made sure to control this route to the people's hearts. He put his praetors (imperial administrators) in charge of the festivals and provided money from the public treasury, to some extent indistinguishable from his own vast wealth, to fund them. And so that the praetors did not become too popular, the amount of their own money they could contribute to the festivals was restricted. They were also forbidden to hold more than two gladiatorial combats a year, each of which was to be limited to no more than 120 men.

In Rome no one had ever provided so many and such splendid festivals as Augustus, according to Suetonius. Augustus gave the people what, in the hackneyed phrase of Juvenal, was all they wanted in exchange for their political independence – bread in the shape of the corn dole, which he was now in charge of distributing, and circuses (the circus was traditionally where the games, especially chariot races, were held). The corn dole and the festivals were nothing new; citizens had been getting free corn at times of food shortage and famine since 123 BC, and Romans had been honouring their gods with festivals since time immemorial. The difference was that now the bounty was under the control of one man. In the bitter words of Tacitus:

> He [Augustus] seduced the army with gifts, the common people with a constant supply of cheap food, and everyone by the siren song of peace. Step by step he increased his powers, taking over those of the Senate, the magistrates and their laws. The aristocracy received wealth and position in proportion to their readiness to accept servitude, and they preferred the existing security to the dangers and uncertainties of the past... how many remained who remembered the Republic? The state had been transformed, and the old Roman character was gone forever. Equality among the citizens was completely abandoned, all waited for the imperial command.[23]

The restored regime which was in fact a new regime, the reformed Republic which was in fact an empire, the *primus inter pares* who was in reality an emperor, were in place. A few months before Augustus' birth in 63 BC the Senate had ordered that all baby boys should be killed because signs portended that 'a king of the Romans' was about to be born. It was a testament to the success of the Augustan regime and its ideologues that the Senate was now prepared to acknowledge

Augustus as their supreme father, their *pater patriae,* just as the Chinese did their emperor. Augustus had metamorphosed from Turnus to Aeneas, though, like Aeneas, he would still revert to the old warrior mores. Suetonius describes how Augustus broke the legs of his secretary for having disclosed the contents of a letter; and forced one of his favourite freedmen to commit suicide for seducing married women. He was not yet the supreme, beneficent father-ruler to whom was owed all love and obedience.

Of course, the Augustan spin could never be completely successful. Tacitus exaggerated the success of the Augustan regime in moulding its people: no state can ever suborn its subjects as much as it would like to. Augustus met resistance, not just from those who refused to accept with gratitude the reality of their conquest, but even from within his own family. Like Maecenas, Augustus' daughter Julia could not or would not submit to the new moral order so carefully constructed by her father. Augustus himself was notoriously unfaithful, but he maintained the charade of rectitude; Julia did not.

During her marriage to Agrippa Julia had acquired a reputation for infidelity, according to the only character sketch we have of her, written four centuries later by Macrobius. When a close friend asked her how despite her numerous affairs she managed to bear children who unmistakably resembled Agrippa, Julia replied, 'I never let passengers board ship until the cargo is in the hold.' After Agrippa's death, she had been married off to Livia's son Tiberius, a dour character, though probably made more so by his marriage to Julia. He had been happily married to Agrippa's daughter Vipsania until he was forced to divorce her for Julia. And Julia for her part allegedly compensated for her own boredom and unhappiness by going to wild parties and having drunken sex everywhere, even in the Forum.

Julia was thirty-seven. Her hair was beginning to go grey. 'She possessed great charm,' according to Macrobius, but she was also the spoilt child of dynastic privilege. 'Time and again, with a mixture of indulgence and seriousness, her father had suggested that she should behave less extravagantly and choose quieter friends', but Julia's response was that if 'he could forget that he was Augustus, she could not forget that she was Augustus' daughter.'

That relationship did not save her. In 2 BC, the same year that Augustus became *pater patriae* and dedicated his new Forum Augustum, he was told by informers of the scandalous behaviour of his daughter. The moral father of the empire had fathered an immoral child and must punish her. Augustus exiled Julia to Pandateria (modern Ventotene), a windy volcanic island within tantalizing sight of the western coast of Italy. Deprived of all the luxuries she had been used to, forbidden wine and all male company, Julia had only her mother, Scribonia, Augustus' first wife whom he had divorced to marry Livia, to keep her company. Ten years later, Augustus exiled Julia's daughter on the same grounds of adultery. Her illegitimate baby, Augustus' great-granddaughter, was left on a mountainside to die on Augustus' orders. Exposure was the standard way to get rid of unwanted babies; the Romans, like the Greeks, thought it odd that the Egyptians, Germans and Jews did not do the same.[24] In AD 14, the elder Julia died 'by slow starvation', according to Tacitus, under the stern eyes of her guards.

Tacitus believed Livia had concocted libellous rumours against the two women in order to further the succession prospects of her own child Tiberius. Tacitus also claimed to have seen 'the secret hand' of Livia behind the early deaths of the two 'princes', the elder Julia's sons by Agrippa, but then as a Republican sympathizer Tacitus was particularly antagonistic to Livia for the part she played in perpetuating the imperial regime. It is, however, possible that Julia and her daughter had become involved with conspirators. Certainly, the elder Julia misguidedly linked herself to men with dangerous names, including Sempronius Gracchus (descendant of the originator of the civil wars in 133 BC) and Mark Antony's son, Iullus Antonius. But, perhaps as serious, the louche behaviour of mother and daughter threatened to destroy the image of the perfect family so carefully crafted by Augustus and Livia. The empire was created in the image of Augustus. That image had better be good.

In reality, Augustus was unrestrainedly lascivious (perhaps his daughter and granddaughter took after him). 'Not even his friends could deny that he often committed adultery', though according to Suetonius they said it was 'for reasons of state, not simple passion'. At one banquet, Augustus retired with his host's wife who returned later flushed and tousled. Suetonius claimed that Augustus 'harboured a passion for deflowering girls – who were collected for him from every quarter, even by his wife'.[25]

But it was part of the regime's elaborate construction of itself that Augustus should be seen as the guardian of moral order; he was restoring to Rome the decorum and restraint whose loss many believed had precipitated the civil wars. Augustus the adulterer made adultery a crime against the state: the decay of good family values was contributing to the low birth rate amongst the elite. Though Livia and he had managed to produce only one child who had died at birth, Augustus introduced increasingly ferocious penalties against the adulterer and financial incentives for the philoprogenitive: a father could kill his adulterous daughter and her partner; a husband could kill the man who had cuckolded him; or both guilty parties could be exiled to separate islands and most of their fortunes confiscated. Augustus imposed heavier taxes on childless couples and rewarded parents who produced three children and more – fathers of a third child would get accelerated promotion; mothers could acquire full legal independence, including the right to receive and bequeath money. Whether Augustus' morality laws, the *Lex Julia de Adulteriis*, applied to homosexual acts, or at least 'passive' homosexual acts – the only type of same-sex behaviour the Romans thought shameful – is not clear. But it is no wonder that Maecenas did not survive in such a moralistic climate.

Ovid too fell foul of the new morality. Like Maecenas, like Julia, he could not be moulded by the Augustan ideology. Though he was one of Rome's leading poets, Ovid had never been part of Maecenas' circle. His poems concentrated on love rather than Rome. On his third marriage, irreligious, irreverent about traditional moral attitudes, Ovid was banished from his beloved Rome in AD 8 for 'a poem and a mistake'. He never dared reveal what the mistake was. The poem was probably *Ars Amatoria* ('The Art of Love') – a lighthearted manual on how men and women should seduce each other. Ovid was exiled to what he called 'the farthest land of the icy world', the harsh, monotonous steppelands of Pontus in modern Romania where 'the land is merely the sea in disguise'.

Far worse than the geography and climate were the people who 'barely deserve the name'. They were literally 'barely civilized', Ovid wrote from Tomis, one of the province's few cities. For a man who passionately loved Rome, Tomis did not merit the title of city, though scholars take his descriptions of Tomis with a slight pinch of salt.[26] It was perched on a hill defended by fragile walls, but even when the gates were shut, Ovid and the other townsmen would gather arrows that fell in the middle of the streets, shot by enemy tribesmen. 'They think it's a disgrace to exist without pillage,' Ovid wrote in 'Tristia' ('Sorrows'), part of a series of poems lamenting his exile, which were also an impassioned plea for a reconsideration of his sentence. When they weren't attacking the town, great hordes of Sarmatians and Getae, their 'shaggy faces hidden in long hair' which in the freezing, foggy winters tinkled with hanging icicles, rode by on trails outside the town, each one carrying bow and quiver, and arrows pale yellow with viper's gall, hands at the ready on the knife strapped to their side. 'They fear no law: justice yields to force, and right is overturned by the sword's aggression.' Augustus had still not brought law and order to this outpost of the Roman Empire.

Perhaps most unbearable of all for Ovid was that no one spoke Latin. 'Here I'm the barbarian no one comprehends,' he wrote. Ovid in fact became so desperate to find an audience for his poems that he learned the native language in order to read them aloud. Pining for the civilized world of Rome, Ovid resorted to ever more fulsome flattery and ever more heartfelt pleas to the imperial family to be allowed home, or at least nearer home.

Please spare me, undying glory of our age, lord of the earth that
you make your care,
In the name of the fatherland, dearer to you than yourself,
and the gods who œare never deaf to your prayers,
and your bed-mate who alone is equal to you,
...
and your son, like you the model of virtue,
...
and your grandsons, worthy of their father and grandfather.[27]

But Augustus and Livia, the woman Ovid later described as having
'the beauty of Venus' though she was by then in her seventies, refused
to forgive him. Ovid died in his barren exile in AD 17.

Augustus' attempt to control the sexual lives of his elite was not
popular. He was barracked in the Senate. Once, when he attended a
public entertainment, equestrians protested against the imposition
of a law penalizing anyone who failed to marry again. Augustus
responded by calling for his family. With his grandchildren beside
him and his great-grandchildren perched on his knee, Augustus
showed the spectators the image of the model Roman family that
they should emulate, though he did in fact later withdraw the
penalties the equestrians had objected to.

Moulding people into compliant subjects is never easy. But the
creation of willing subjects was all the more important in a trading
empire whose cities were a melting pot – or rather a simmering pot
– of heterogeneous peoples. And just as Augustus, like all successful
rulers, turned to religion to mould his subjects, so his subjects would
also look to religion to answer their new spiritual needs, needs that
were changing as Rome shifted from being a militaristic and
plundering empire to a tax and trading one.

3

ALEXANDRIA: GODS IN THE CITY

Civilization is the art of living in towns of such size that everyone does not know everyone else.

Julian Jaynes, *The Origin of Consciousness in the Breakdown of the Bicameral Mind*, 1976

Among the many things… that our ancestors created and established under divine inspiration, nothing is more renowned than their decision to entrust the worship of the gods and the highest interests of the state to the same men – so that the most eminent and illustrious citizens might ensure the maintenance of religion by the proper administration of the state, and the maintenance of the state by the prudent interpretation of religion.

Cicero, *On His House*, 57 BC

In about 24 BC, some twenty years before the birth of Christ, Strabo, a cross-eyed, Greek-speaking intellectual from Asia Minor, sailed to what he called 'the greatest emporium in the inhabited world', the port city of Alexandria, in Rome's newly acquired province of Egypt.

As the grain ship* carrying 300 passengers, many of them tourists flocking to see the ancient pyramids, neared shore, Strabo caught his first glimpse of one of the tallest structures on earth. Rearing out of the water was Alexandria's white marble lighthouse, already listed as one of the Seven Wonders of the World. With its massive square base, octagonal centre and rounded top, it probably looked rather like

---

* This would have been Strabo's most likely form of transport.

a forty-storey version of the Empire State Building. A bronze mirror at its tip reflected a great beam of sunlight; at night a fire blazed to guide ships safely into Alexandria's Grand Harbour. Beside it was a temple to one of the most popular deities of the ancient world – the Egyptian goddess Isis, whose countless roles included that of protector of the seafarer. It was probably in gratitude to her that the captain of Strabo's ship sprinkled a libation of milk on the harbour waters. A tug, manned by rowers pulling extra long oars, towed the ship towards the massive harbour walls of limestone, pink marble and purple granite.

Only about six years before Strabo's arrival, Mark Antony and Cleopatra had committed suicide in Alexandria as the warrior mores of the time dictated, after being defeated by Augustus at Actium. Augustus' victory had brought an end to fifty years of civil war, but, paradoxically, the *pax Augusta* was hugely disruptive. Peace meant prosperity and prosperity meant trade. People had money to spend and they wanted goods, especially exotic ones. Trade routes to the East opened up to meet that demand. Never before had people travelled as much; nor would they do so again until the nineteenth century.[1] Trade by sea had never been faster or safer: the imperial fleet had nearly eliminated the threat of pirates and the Romans had finally discovered how to use the monsoon winds which gust eastwards to India during the summer and westwards towards Africa during the winter. Roman ships could now set off for India in June and be back in Alexandria within twelve months. Strabo noted that the number of ships making the journey had risen from twenty-one a year in the pre-Augustus days to about 200.

Strabo, like the city itself, was the product of a great cultural mix. In Alexandria, as in most cities, the mix would periodically break down into clashes between different groups – most notably between the Greeks and the Jews. Strabo had resolved his own multicultural tensions by becoming a thoroughly assimilated subject. He had been brought up in the port city of Amasya (in modern Turkey), on the outermost limits of the empire, where his family had been closely connected with the local King Mithridates, Rome's most dangerous enemy since Hannibal. But Strabo had become a proud embodiment of the triumphant new Roman Empire and was utterly convinced of its superiority: 'the Romans', he said, 'occupy the best and the best known portions of ["our inhabited world"], having surpassed all former rulers of whom we have record.' An Asiatic, he was Greek-speaking and Greek-educated and had moved to Rome to study grammar under the Phoenician ex-slave Tyrannio. He was a loyal supporter of the empire and of its emperor, Augustus. Indeed, Augustus probably commissioned Strabo's great work on geography and sent him to Alexandria.

The *Geographia* was written with the needs of the empire and its ruler in mind. It was an account of 'the known parts of the inhabited world' that in Strabo's view stretched north to Ireland and Britain – though he did not think Britain worth conquering – south to Ethiopia, east to India, and west to Spain and Morocco. Beyond that was unknown territory, not because the sea was unnavigable – Strabo thought the Atlantic Ocean 'runs round the earth in one unbroken circle' – but because 'the navigators who sailed in opposite directions towards each other never met', or were driven back by 'destitution and loneliness'. Besides, he thought there were only three continents: Europe, Asia and Africa. No word from the Americas ever reached him, or anyone else at the time. So he never knew of the great Mayan cities that were exploding in the tropical rainforests of Guatemala, or of Teotihuacán, the sprawling urban centre near modern Mexico City. And he gave only a passing nod to China, which the Romans called Serica, meaning silk – the precious material that was beginning to bind the two empires together. Serica, he said, was a country that produced 'everything in abundance', whose people were 'temperate' and 'long-lived'. And that is Strabo's only reference to the world's oldest and best-governed empire.[2]

Strabo was in the middle of writing his great work when he arrived in Alexandria.[3] Like so many cities it was booming under the new peace, producing paper, linen, perfumes, carved ivories, gold ornaments and glassware. Alexandria was the quintessence of what made urban life so heady and so disturbing for the peasants, craftsmen and merchants who were trying to make a living in the city. No city except Rome could rival Alexandria. It was raucous, argumentative and magnificent,[4] home to 500,000 people from all corners of Strabo's known world, and the intellectual and commercial hub of the Roman Empire. Its harbours were filled with the scents of cinnamon, pepper and incense. Slaves unloaded silk from China, spices, pearls and parrots from India, frankincense and myrrh from Arabia, ivory, ebony and gold from the increasingly rich African kingdoms of Meroe (today's southern Egypt and Sudan) and Axum (Ethiopia and Eritrea).

Young Egyptian men in pigtails haggled, hustled and traded with Gauls in their trousers, Greeks in their tunics, with Syrians, Spaniards, Indians, Arabians, 'Ethiopians' (as the Greeks and Romans called all black Africans); and even with Britons who, though they towered half a foot above the tallest people in Rome, were not very prepossessing, according to Strabo; 'they were', he wrote, 'bandy-legged and presented no fair lines anywhere else in their figure.'[5]

Alexandria was a mix of the well ordered, the chaotically diverse and the violent, as were most of the empire's expanding cities. Thousands of people poured into the city every day. The poor made their homes in abandoned buildings or crammed themselves into jerry-built tenement blocks, which regularly collapsed or burned down, while the rich lived in their cool mosaic-tiled villas nearby. Geometrically planned monumental streets resounded with a babel of languages, the blare of trumpets and chants from religious processants.

Climbing the hill to the temple of Pan, Strabo could see the whole of the city stretched below him, sandwiched between the Mediterranean and Lake Mareotis. Canals connected the lake to the River Nile. In the balmy evenings, crowds of revellers headed off by canal to resorts that were springing up along the waterways and becoming notorious for their 'shamelessness', Strabo noted. 'Every day and every night is crowded with people on the boats who play the flute and dance without restraint and with extreme licentiousness, both men and women.'

The granite and marble city – the public face of Alexandria – was laid out as a grid of parallel streets, and had probably the most sophisticated water system in the ancient world. Almost every house and shop had its own supply thanks to a vast underground system of canals that brought water from the Nile. Sacred ibises scavenged with their long curved bills around the meat shops and bakeries, where according to Strabo bakers kneaded bread with their feet. Outside on the streets, music lovers sat listening to cithara concerts.

In the centre of the city, near where two vast boulevards met, clustered the monuments that had already made Alexandria famous. There was the Serapeum Temple elevated on a great platform, over 100 steps high, dedicated to the Greek-Egyptian god Serapis – husband/brother of Isis. All that Strabo saw of Alexandria's once unsurpassed library was probably just its blackened ruins – a casualty of the battle for the city between Julius Caesar and Pompey. But for the tourist strolling down the 100-foot-wide Canopic Boulevard, the most famous monument of all was the walled citadel enclosing the tomb of Alexander the Great, empire-builder of the fourth century BC and founder of the city.

It was because of Alexander that Greek culture was dominant in so much of the Eastern world. After inheriting the throne of Macedon (in today's northern Greece) from his father Philip in 336 BC, Alexander brought most of the Greek city-states under Macedonian hegemony and went on to create an empire stretching from Greece to India in just ten years of military campaigning. At the end of the first century BC that empire had split into three – Roman, Parthian (Persian) and Kushan (what is now northern Afghanistan, Pakistan and northern India). But the influence of Greece was evident everywhere in the architecture of the cities, the gods, the language and the people.

Greeks still ruled Alexandria, as they did so many of the major cities of the eastern part of the empire, but they were often a source of resentment. The 'flattering, cringing, treacherous, artful race' of Greeks, as the satirist Juvenal called them, were privileged citizens who excluded other races from power. They were just one element of Alexandria's potentially incendiary mix of inhabitants: each multi-ethnic wave of newcomers to the city either became thoroughly Romanized or fragmented into separate cultural identities.

Alexandrians were, according to Cassius Dio, particularly aggressive, despite, or because of, the presence of approximately 6,000 Roman soldiers stationed in the city (there were about 15,000 stationed around the whole province, supplemented by auxiliary troops stationed at its borders). Alexandrian Greeks deeply resented Roman rule. An Alexandrian slave of rank and a Roman foot soldier 'would quarrel over the value of their respective slippers'. Chariot races often ended with a stabbing in the crowd. The prefect (governor) of Egypt, Petronius, was almost stoned to death by an Alexandrian mob, while the wife of the later prefect Galerius never dared to set foot outside the official residence or admit a local into it. 'In war and its terrors their conduct is cowardly,' wrote Cassius Dio, 'but in tumults, which with them are very frequent and very serious they without scruple come to mortal blows, and for the sake of the success of the moment account their life nothing, nay they go to their destruction as if the highest things were at stake.'[6] City-dwellers were rubbing up constantly against strangers who inspired the sort of vicious hatred that the satirist Juvenal clearly felt for 'the dregs of Greece', and for 'the scum' from Syria and all the other 'starving myriads ... [that] come and batten on the genial soil of Rome'.

For millions of people, the city meant coming to terms with an entirely new way of living. It was indeed a civilizer, a place where new ideas could fructify, as people left the constraints of tribe and village behind them. But it was also a terrifying and lawless place – of disease, death and violence, of fear and hatred of the stranger, of loneliness and incomprehension. Cut from their roots, appalled by the skyscraper tenement blocks, the noise, the stink and the 'barbarity' of their alien neighbours, the newcomers wanted the reassurance of the old and familiar. So they brought their gods from their homeland and built temples to them in the cities. But few of these gods adapted to the new conditions; they did not solve the problem of how to get on with the stranger next door. The presence of so many gods only added to the chaotic diversity of city life.

Jostling together in the booming new cities of the empire were temples to the Roman god Jupiter, the Syrian goddess Atargatis, the Phrygian (Turkish) Cybele, the Babylonian Bell, and all the other gods in their numberless forms that were worshipped in every field and city street around the Mediterranean. The stench of blood and burning flesh from constant sacrifices was overwhelming. Clouds of flies swarmed over great piles of offal – the bloody remains of the sacrifices performed by a priest who, wrote the satirist Lucian in the second century AD, stood 'wallowing in gore; handling his knife like a very Cyclops, drawing out entrails and heart, sprinkling the altar with blood'. Stray dogs foraged. Beggars were permanently camped in the temple grounds along with exiles, cripples and groups of craftsmen making little shrines and statues. Every temple was half lumber-room, half museum, crammed with fabulous booty brought back by victorious generals, and votive offerings from the ordinary worshipper. Locks of hair, models of ears (symbolizing the worshippers' hopes that the god would listen to their prayers) and model feet (meaning 'I stood and worshipped here') were heaped alongside precious statues, gold cups and jewel-encrusted weapons. In a temple to Apollo, one of Helen of Troy's sandals, the egg from which she was hatched and Orpheus' lyre were displayed alongside an Indian coconut, snakeskins and dental forceps.

Every day at dawn shaven-headed Egyptian priests in white robes opened and cleaned their temples, offered food to the gods' statues and wailed their laments. The Greeks sang to their gods. They kept their temples shut for most of the year and worshipped with heads uncovered. Roman men, on the other hand, covered their heads with their togas, and the women with their veils. Worshippers of Apollo favoured the harp-like cithara; while the followers of the goddess Cybele, whose eunuch priests howled like dogs, had to put up with squealing reed pipes.

To Strabo, most of the foreign gods and the religious beliefs that he encountered (or else described using the accounts of earlier geographers) were absurd. He mocked the Egyptian worship of the shrewmouse, sheep, fish and other 'irrational animals'. He watched with patronizing amusement a sacred crocodile called Suchus, which had become tame from being fed so often by tourists.

> We found the animal lying on the edge of the lake; and when the priests went up to it, some of them opened its mouth and another put in the cake, and again the meat, and then poured down the honey mixture. The animal then leaped into the lake and rushed across to the far side; but when another foreigner arrived, likewise carrying an offering of first-fruits, the priests took it, went around the lake in a run, took hold of the animal, and in the same manner fed it what had been brought.[7]

The feeding of Suchus was for Strabo no more than a rather tacky tourist attraction. But then he was a Stoic, like an increasing number of Rome's political and intellectual elite.

Stoicism, the religion of the rational, of self-mastery, seemed totally at odds with the religion that was becoming the most popular in the Roman Empire: worship of the Egyptian goddess Isis.* Isiacism was the Pentecostalism of its day, a showy, hard-hitting religion, appealing to the emotions, while Stoicism was the sober philosophy of establishment individualism. Yet, despite their superficial differences, there was an underlying similarity between them. Both placed value on the individual and in doing so created universal religions, religions that could appeal to everyone no matter what

---

* I use 'cult' and 'religion' interchangeably when referring to Isiacism, because it seems to be on the cusp between the two: it was a body of ritual practices, which was developing a set of beliefs. Though unfortunately we know all too little about these beliefs, they are recognizably religious in that they concern a deity, moral precepts and an afterlife.

their tribe or where they came from. Devotees were not Greeks, Romans or Jews. They were not defined by their place in a particular group; they were individuals – the characteristic which both made them preciously unique and also united everyone into the universal fold of humanity. Isiacism, however, was a religion of ecstasy and passion and had a mass appeal that the far more aristocratic Stoicism did not attempt.

In *The Golden Ass* (also known as the *Metamorphoses*), one of the world's first novels, written in the second century AD by the North African Apuleius, the hero Lucius stands in the crowd as an Isis procession lurches by.[8] He watches shaven-headed initiates yelling, howling and shaking bronze, gold and silver rattles as they danced themselves into a frenzy to demonstrate their grief at the death of Isis' husband/brother Osiris (Serapis was his Hellenized name), and then their joy at his resurrection by Isis. Accompanied by the thump of drums and the off-key wailing of horns, women dressed in white linen robes with lotus blossoms in their hair scattered flowers or sprinkled the streets with perfumes; a choir of boys sang hymns, followed by more initiates – men and women, of every social class and of all ages. Some had shining mirrors on their backs, while others held ivory combs with which they pretended to comb Isis' hair; behind them swayed the priests, their uplifted faces hidden behind the black and gold masks of Anubis, and other Egyptian animal gods, and of Isis herself.

After the procession, priests and priestesses brought back the statue of Isis to the inner sanctum of the temple, took off her jewels and vulture's feathers, then drew the curtains around her for the night, while her worshippers kissed the temple steps, passed through a series of colossal gateways, crossed the huge paved entrance lined with sphinxes and stepped back into the everyday world.

It was a world that both the Isis cult and Stoicism were beginning to separate off from the sublime spiritual world where the individual took part in a personal communion with god.

Most traditional pagan cults were, in a sense, cults of the group.

For the Romans, worship of the gods was part of a citizen's duties; senators or city officials also served as priests. The function of the priest and the state official, the magistrate, was, after all, the same: to promote the welfare of the state. The Senate had to meet in a temple so that the auspices – divine indications usually from the sky, from thunder or lightning, from the flight, cries or number of birds – could be taken. It was through the auspices that the gods expressed their approval or disapproval of any proposal. No public event, no election, census or military expedition could be undertaken unless the auspices had been consulted and considered favourable. Worship was therefore part of the mundane business of living. The farmer who placed a daisy chain on a turf altar to the gods of his field considered this was as much a practical matter of farming as ploughing.[9] Temples were places to flirt, to do business and to study, as well as to beg for favours from the gods.[10]

In contrast to Isis' festivals, which were frenzied, intense and deeply serious, the monthly round of Roman religious festivals were drunken carnivals. Images of the gods were borne for miles around the countryside or paraded around the city. But there were also riotous all-night banquets in the temple precincts and the streets, with musicians playing on their flutes and pipes, while revellers danced by the light of flaming torches; by day, the amphitheatres were packed with crowds watching enactments of the gods' stories or gladiatorial combats and chariot races, and families picnicked in the fields and suburbs. Certainly, under Augustus the function of the festivals was more to inculcate a sense of Romanness, patriotism and solidarity amongst the disparate peoples of the empire than to honour the gods, though, if Ovid's description of the Roman festivals is anything to go by, pleasure and sex were as much essential components as the rituals of civic duty.

At the end of December, the social order was turned upside down in Rome's equivalent of Twelfth Night, the Saturnalia, a week of present-giving and orgiastic delight, when slaves took off their felt bonnets and were waited on by their masters. In February, for the festival of Lupercalia, young men ran naked, except for a goatskin, through the streets of Rome, striking the young women bystanders with goatskin thongs to induce fertility. In March, Rome's inhabitants left the city to picnic on the banks of the Tiber in celebration of Anna Perenna, goddess of the year. 'Warmed by sun and wine,' they pray 'for as many years as cups, as many as they drink', until they stagger home in the evening, 'a tipsy old woman dragging a tipsy old man.'[11] In the same month, at the Liberalia, in honour of Liber, the ancient rural god of agricultural and human fertility, a phallus was paraded around the fields and cities. Old women dressed up as priests of Bacchus; crowned with ivy, they set up portable altars and sold little cakes of oil and honey to customers for sacrifice, and on the same day sixteen-year-old Roman boys put on the *toga virilis* for the first time and stepped into manhood.

On the whole, the Romans had a prosaic attitude to their gods. Theirs was a religion felt at the fingertips, not in the heart, as Lactantius the North African Christian apologist put it in the third century. Roman relations with their gods were more like a business contract, summarized so clearheadedly in the phrase *do ut des* ('I give so that you may give'). It was a religion concerned with form rather than passion. The gods were addressed in the language of law rather than reverence, as in the prayer that the foremost Roman orator of his age, Cato the Elder, recommended to landowners when they thinned a grove of trees:

Whether you are a god or goddess to whom this grove is sacred, as it is proper to sacrifice to you a pig as a propitiatory offering for the disturbance of this sacred place, and therefore for these reasons whether I or someone I have appointed performs the sacrifice, provided that it be performed correctly, for all this reason, in sacrificing this pig, I pray in good faith that you will be benevolent and well disposed to me, my home, my family [including slaves] and my children.[12]

Cato's prayer admittedly comes from the extreme end of Roman religious pedantry.* But it reflects the Romans' belief that it was not because they were bad that the gods might refuse to grant their prayers, but because they had not accurately followed the rules[13] – hence Pliny's jibe about the pedantic recital of prayers which were read out by one magistrate/priest, closely monitored by a second priest to ensure they were read correctly, while a third enforced silence. If one syllable or ritual gesture was performed incorrectly the prayer might be invalid.[14]

In general, the Roman gods were wayward, cold and not that interested in humans. The worshipper might sacrifice his most precious animal, recite his prayers exactly as instructed – for the life of his child, a safe journey, a cure for baldness or, in the poet Horace's case, 'a goodly supply of books and of food to last the year' – but he knew the gods to be capricious, with little concern for him.

Unlike the Roman gods, however, Isis cared for her devotees. She offered what few other gods did – a personal, loving relationship with her worshippers. Although Christianity may have been the first religion to put love at its centre, and create not just a loving God but a God who urged his worshippers to love each other, Isiacism was in some ways its forerunner as a religion of comfort and kindness. Isis was, according to Isis historian R. E. Witt, unique amongst pagan deities in her affection and compassion. 'Moved by your prayer I come to you,' she says to Lucius in *The Golden Ass*. Isis was a loving wife and mother. Statues showing her son Horus suckling at her breast directly influenced later images of Jesus and Mary.[15]

Isis not only cared for her devotees, but also gave them a sense of belonging that was all the more precious in the increasingly atomized world of the metropolis. Anyone could worship the Roman gods just by virtue of being born within the empire; indeed, it was part of the Roman subject's duty to worship them. Devotees of the mystery religions, on the other hand, had to choose to belong. The mystery

---

* The prayer might also reflect an earlier, more austere, attitude to the gods as Cato recorded this prayer in the second century BC.

cults were what the classicist Mary Beard calls 'elective religions' and inspired that much more loyalty as a result.

Each of the cults struggling for prominence in the crowded city had its own rituals: everyday activities like eating a meal became sacralized, that is, endowed with supra-mundane significance. As the sociologist Durkheim pointed out, ritual is fundamental to the creation of a society and the social groups within it. The shared experience of performing a ritual, the commitment it implies to future participation, binds its performers into a group. The ritual both moulds the behaviour and personality of its participants and inevitably reflects and responds to the society from which it originates.

The rituals of pagan cults were often mundane affairs, however, sometimes involving no more than meeting six times a year for ritual sacrifice and dinner. But worshippers of Isis, along with the other 'mystery religions' of Eleusis, Dionysus, Atargatis, Cybele, and later Mithras, had to perform extraordinarily elaborate initiation rites. They were washed clean and purified so that they were in a fit state to enter a new world where the secrets of life and death would be revealed to them, hence the term 'mystery'.

For Isis worshippers, the very intricacy of their initiation ceremonies, combined with the secrets which were revealed to them and which they could not betray to an outsider, made them feel members of a supremely select group.

In *The Golden Ass*, Lucius described the preparations for his own initiation into the cult of Isis. He was bathed by an old priest who entrusted him with secrets 'too sacred to tell' and ordered him to fast for ten days. On the tenth day, at dusk, a multitude of priests presented him with gifts, dressed him in a white linen robe and took him to 'the most secret and sacred place of all, the temple'. There he stayed all night, but what went on there, said Lucius, he is not allowed to reveal. Only a couple of sentences later, though, Lucius spills the beans. 'I approached the borders of death... I was borne along with the elements. At midnight I saw the sun blazing with bright light. I came into the presence of the gods.' In the morning he left the inner sanctum 'adorned like the sun', carrying a flaming torch, a garland of flowers and palm leaves on his head, his shoulders covered with a 'celestial stole' decorated with brilliantly coloured dragons and gryphons, and stood before the image of Isis. The ceremony ended, inevitably, with a great banquet – the feast that was at the heart of almost every religion.

Lucius had been given the supremely comforting message that he could, for a while at least, outwit death. Isis held out to her adherents the promise of a longer life, though whether she actually offered life beyond death is not clear. If she did, it was a new and wonderful prospect. Even many Jews did not believe in an afterlife. For most pagans, everlasting life was not part of the deal with their gods. The epitaph 'I was not, I was, I am not, I care not' was so often inscribed on Roman tombstones that it had been boiled down to its initial letters – NFFNSNC (*non fui, fui, non sum, non curo*). Isis, however, had brought her murdered husband/brother Osiris back to life by gathering together his dismembered body. As with many mystery religions, death and resurrection were at the heart of her cult.

The Isis cult created a private world where the individual found fulfilment in a relationship with god; other gods offered services or provided insurance against disaster, but they were not concerned with the flourishing of the individual. Paradoxically, by addressing the individual not the group, the Isis cult could now appeal to everyone: the individualist religion was in fact a universalizing one.

The religions that addressed themselves to the group, on the other hand, by definition drew boundaries round a specific set of people. Judaism was almost exclusively a religion for the Jews, though it was possible for a Gentile to convert. Outside the Roman Empire, Hinduism was ineluctably tied to caste, to the group you were born into, and therefore excluded the foreigner who was not born into the caste system. By contrast, the individualist religion embraced diverse peoples because it was precisely their individuality that they shared in common. Buddhism, born out of opposition to the caste system, focused on each individual's ability to achieve nirvana, spiritual freedom, and would spread throughout the East. Stoicism, that other individualist 'religion' of the Roman Empire, believed in the brotherhood of man because each person had a spark of the divine *logos* within them, though as a far more rationalist, less comfortable 'religion', it would never have the popular appeal of Isis. A universalist religion can unite peoples from a multiplicity of cultures, religions and languages – exactly the task that all imperial rulers struggle with. Religions are potentially the great unifiers, as they can be the great legitimizers of rule.

Most of the gods in the world of the first century BC were attached to particular regions and would never rise above their local identity. Even when their worshippers carried them to a faraway city, these gods stayed within their own group. But, by the early first century AD, the Isis cult had transcended its local Egyptian roots and taken hold throughout the Roman Empire, especially in Italy, but even in Gaul and North Africa. Freeborn and slave, men and women, poor and to a lesser extent rich, were devotees. It was almost the only cult where women could become priestesses, and they celebrated Isis in hymns as the goddess 'who gave women the same power as men'.[16] By the time that the Romans destroyed the Temple in Jerusalem in AD 70 and the Gospel of Mark was being written, Isis had even become a patron deity of the imperial family.[17]

Isiacism was indeed the only pagan cult apart from Mithraism that would be a serious competitor to Christianity.* Isiacism almost made it as a world religion,** but not quite; it had many – though not all – of the ingredients that would eventually make Christianity fit so well into the Roman world.

---

* The cult of the Persian god Mithras was, along with the cult of Isis, one of the most serious competitors of Christianity. But since its development really began in the second century AD, I have excluded Mithraism from this book.

** The world religions are traditionally considered to be Christianity, Islam, Hinduism, Buddhism and Judaism. The term 'world religion' is a slightly awkward one since it is historically based on a classification of religions according to what was considered theologically and historically important from a Western Christian-centred perspective; modern classifications are based much more on numbers of adherents, although Judaism is still considered to be a world religion, despite having only about fourteen million adherents and ranking therefore below Sikhism with its nineteen million followers.

Isis seemed to be offering her worshippers what they demanded from a religion and doing so more effectively than most pagan cults under the new, disturbing conditions of the trading city. Like other pagan gods, she granted favours and offered protection against disaster, but because she was loving she was less unpredictable. Her love and association with the afterlife gave comfort. Her initiation ceremonies gave the devotee a hugely powerful sense of belonging to a community, far greater than that provided by most pagan cults, and in addition gave the devotee a sense of his or her own significance, a heightened sense of meaning and an ecstatic, exalted experience. The 'mystery religions', in particular the Isis cult, transformed the religious experience from a mundane to a supra-mundane one. Isis enabled each worshipper to escape the terrors, or merely boredoms, of the everyday and be overwhelmed by a passionate ecstasy. But once the sacrifice had been made, and the feast eaten, Isis could be shut away behind the curtain and impinged no further on most worshippers until the next time she was needed or the next festival.

If power can be measured along the twin axes of both the number of people an institution, person or belief attracts and how much they actually change people's behaviour, then Isiacism scored highly on the first axis, but less well on the second. Isis demanded that her priests were chaste and ascetic; but as far as most scholars can tell she did not demand a lot from the rest of her followers, though she did seem to require some sort of purity from them, moral as well as physical (see chapter 6). The Jewish God, on the other hand, laid down rules that covered every aspect of living, from eating, to taxation, to having sex. He was deeply embedded in a Jew's life. The pagan gods, and even the gods of the mystery religions like Isis, exerted that much less power over their worshippers and consequently had that much less significance for them.

As Rodney Stark, the contemporary sociologist of religion, has pointed out, the more demanding a religion, the more value it has for the devotee because of the sacrifices they have had to make and think worth making for it. And the more value they place on their religion, the more committed they will be to it. Paradoxically, it was the fact that the pagan gods demanded so little that helped, in part, to kill them off.

But, of course, the religion that makes too many demands will deter potential converts. Augustus' imperial cult was intended to reach out to all of his eighty million subjects, but to affect their behaviour only to the extent that they should feel themselves to be Roman and therefore would be loyal tax-paying subjects. Judaism and that even more demanding religion of the East, Jainism, exercised an enormous influence over their worshippers, but did not have mass appeal and would therefore not be integrated into the political process, while Christianity would arguably not alter behaviour so profoundly but would appeal to millions.

There is a trade-off between how many followers a religion has and how deeply it can alter its followers' behaviour. Religions settled at different points between those two axes of power – breadth and depth – just as they did on how far they addressed themselves to the individual or the group. Why religions took up their different positions along these axes is one of the central questions of this book. But no position intrinsically guaranteed more success than another. Confucianism was pre-eminently a religion, or more accurately a philosophy, of the group, concerned, just as Hinduism was, with how the individual helped create a flourishing social whole; while Buddhism, like Christianity, was concerned with the perfection of the individual. All four have survived to this day.

But the traditional *place-bound* pagan gods have vanished. Cities – certainly the racially diverse, disruptive trading cities – were no place for the old gods. The traditional, more homogeneous societies, where they had found a home, were changing.

Just south of Egypt, the kingdom of Meroe was in the process of developing from a simple society into a more complex trading empire, under the direction of the most powerful woman in Africa. She represented an older generation of god, the type of god that Augustus never could be – however much he might have wished it.

4

THE AFRICAN GODDESS-QUEEN

As the stag pants after the waterbrooks,
So pants my mind after you, Elohim!
My mind thirsts for gods! for living gods!

Psalm 42, ascribed to King David, *c*.1010–970 BC

Now the Ethiopians [Meroites], as historians relate, were the first of all men... And they say that they were the first to be taught to honour the gods and to hold sacrifices and processions and festivals and the other rites by which men honour the deity... And they state that, by reason of their piety towards the deity, they manifestly enjoy the favour of the gods, inasmuch as they have never experienced the rule of an invader from abroad; for from all time they have enjoyed a state of freedom and of peace one with another, and although many and powerful rulers have made war upon them, not one of these has succeeded in his undertaking.

Diodorus Siculus, *Historical Library*, *c*.60–30 BC

In general they [the Meroites] consider as gods benefactors and royal persons, some of whom are their kings, the common saviours and guardians of all.'

Strabo, *Geographia*, XVII.2.3, *c*.20 BC–AD 23

In about 21 BC, Candace Amanirenas led 30,000 men armed with rawhide shields and hatchets along the mudflats of the Nile into Roman-controlled Egypt. Candace (meaning Queen or Queen Mother) Amanirenas ruled the semi-desert kingdom of Meroe, or Nubia as it was later called, today's southern Egypt and northern Sudan. Towering above her troops on an elephant, sporting three scars on her cheeks, as some Sudanese women still do today, 'of masculine build and blind in one eye' (she had lost the other one in an earlier clash with the Romans, according to Strabo),[1] and gleaming with gold, she was arrogant warrior-queen, high priestess of Isis, fabulously wealthy, monumentally fat – and divine.

In the ancient world, there was nothing unusual about god-rulers. Augustus had consciously set out to construct an imperial cult amongst many peoples who had worshipped divine kings for centuries – with the notable, and for Rome problematic, exception of the Jews. The idea of a divine ruler was as necessary for rulers as it was natural for their subjects. Nothing could be more in the rulers' interests than to convince their people that they were the agents of god on earth and that their power was bestowed by the gods.

But what a living god-ruler actually meant to the ruler and to the people who worshipped that ruler differed between the Hellenized, civilized (city-filled) East and the non-Hellenized, non-civilized (city-less) West. And the wealthy – whether in the East or West of the empire, but especially the erstwhile Republican Roman elite – were likely to be far more sceptical than the poor. The divine ruler could mean anything from an impostor pretending to be a god in order to gull his people into obedience, to an intermediary between the gods and humans, to being no more than *like* a god in power, to being quite literally a god.

Meroe probably provides our best glimpse of the most traditional form of ruler worship – the ruler as literally divine – even though we know tantalizingly little: scholars still cannot understand Meroitic hieroglyphics. What follows is therefore no more than an interpretation based on archaeological finds and the few surviving accounts by classical authors such as Strabo (writing in about 7 BC) and the Sicilian Greek historian Diodorus Siculus (*Siculus* simply means Sicilian), writing several decades earlier.

The Candace, I believe, was accepted as a god in a way that Augustus never could be. She was the natural inheritor of a tradition, while he had to consciously manipulate the tradition to make it acceptable to at least some of his subjects.

When Diodorus visited north-east Africa in 59 BC, Meroe's ruler-gods still commanded such obedience that when they died and were buried under the slender pyramids in the royal cemeteries, all their palace servants committed suicide. Less than forty years later, Candace Amanirenas was in the eyes of most of her people not just their magnificent warrior-queen but their living god, though she was probably ranked amongst the lesser gods, like her pharaonic predecessors. The Meroites had ruled Egypt as Pharaohs of the twenty-fifth dynasty from the mid-eighth to the mid-seventh century BC, and had been ruled directly by Egypt for nearly 600 years. Meroe was the inheritor of a fifteen-centuries-old tradition of the pharaonic god-ruler.

Everything about the Candace emphasized her separation and complete difference from ordinary mortals. To her subjects, she was the most powerful person in the world, the owner of their fate, who lived in inconceivable splendour behind impenetrable palace walls. If the Meroites ever caught a glimpse of their Candace beyond her palace, or in the chaos of the battlefield, she was probably surrounded by chanting priests in tall pointed felt hats, wielding great sceptres with asps carved in coils around the ends that signified, according to Diodorus, 'that it will be the lot of those who shall dare to attack the ruler to encounter death-carrying stings'.

Surrounded by her bodyguard priests, her plump ankles, arms, fingers and neck encased in gold and bright glass jewels, a fringed and tasselled robe revealing one pendulous breast, the Candace was the divine incarnate. Reliefs etched into every mudbrick temple wall show the Candace towering over her midget enemies whom she grasps by the hair with one hand, while holding the weapon with which she is about to kill them in the other. The Candace was superhuman; but with the gods she was on an equal footing.

In the desert, near the modern town of Shendi in northern Sudan, squat the gold-brown ruins of the Naqa Temple. On the back wall a relief shows Amanirenas' successor, Candace Amanitare. Her face in Egyptian-style profile, her visible eye heavily underlined with kohl, she stands stolidly shoulder to shoulder with Meroe's most important deity, the three-headed lion god Apedemak, god of war and fertility. On the god's other side stand the Candace's husband (or perhaps son), King Natakami, and the crown prince Arikhankharer. And in a gesture that is exclusive to Meroitic art, the three-headed and four-armed lion god touches the Candace familiarly on the elbow. It is a symbol of recognition. The god's touch means she is the rightful ruler of the kingdom.

At the end of the first century BC, Meroe was a society in transition between a primitive/nomadic and a civilized, that is, city- and trade-based, society. It was a land of extreme contrasts – of endless desert, interspersed with fertile strips beside the River Nile; a land rich in natural resources where trade with Rome was beginning to boom, yet which relied on barter; of nomad herders and a tiny, fabulously wealthy elite. It was becoming one of the two richest kingdoms in sub-Saharan Africa, rivalled only by the kingdom of Axum to the south-east, in the highlands of modern Ethiopia.

Romans had money to spend and they wanted slaves, gold, ostrich feathers, tortoiseshell, ivory, leopard skins, pet monkeys and exotic animals like rhinos, which they could watch killing or being killed by gladiators. (Strabo saw his first rhinoceros in Axum and was not impressed – he thought it looked like a wild boar.)

In the extreme lights and shadows of the desert near modern Khartoum, in what classical writers described as an island between the east bank of the Nile and the Atbara River, lay the walled capital city of Meroe (the kingdom took its name from the city). About 24,000 people lived there in mudbrick flat-roofed houses that lined the meandering alleyways of the city, the houses of the rich standing out several storeys higher than the rest. There the Candace ruled from one of her labyrinthine palaces, its massive brick-vaulted rooms lined with gold leaf, pale ivory, glowing wood and ostrich plumes. The palace gardens were filled with fruit trees, screeching parakeets and monkeys; colonnades and statues sculpted by Greek artisans surrounded an artificial lake filled by a system of aqueducts from the

Nile; there were temples dedicated to Heracles, Pan, Isis (one of Meroe's most popular deities) and, in Strabo's words, 'some other barbaric god'. And, beyond the gardens, slag heaps from the city's ironworks made mini-mountains in the flat desert. They were mined by men in fetters who were naked except for the lamps fastened to their foreheads, and were worked continuously day and night, according to Diodorus Siculus.

Meroe was becoming a substantial city, but not yet one requiring layers of administration. The Candace, and probably a tiny group around her, controlled all trade. Her palace was a warehouse stocked with great blocks of ebony and ivory tusks in vast jars, baskets, sacks and wooden chests. She imported a little wine and olive oil from Italy, cheap cloth and corn from Egypt to supplement the Meroites' scanty crops, but mainly – just like the Romans – luxury goods, such as elegant vessels of bronze bowls and glassware made in Alexandria and possibly as far away as Gaul. But unlike the Romans she was trading by direct barter rather than with coins – a simple form of trade that did not require a middleman.

Meroe was not a Roman trading city like Alexandria, with its moneylenders, money exchangers, large- and small-scale merchants, and its many layers of power that intervened between the ruler at the top and the slave at the bottom. Nor was it home to all the diverse peoples with their different gods and customs that the Roman Empire had acquired.

When the Candace invaded Roman-controlled Egypt in 21 BC, she was confronting a vastly more efficient and complex regime. It was a clash of different worlds. Her ragged army of ill-trained, if frenziedly fervent, troops were up against the military discipline of Rome. The Candace had been fighting periodically with the Roman legions stationed on her northern borders ever since Augustus (as Octavian) had conquered Egypt in 31 BC. But the Roman troops were now on the other side of the Red Sea, struggling vainly to push the borders of the empire into Arabia (a story for the next chapter). Their garrison towns were half empty. Under the command of Candace Amanirenas, the Meroites poured into the southern Egyptian cities of Syene (now Aswan), Elephantine, and Philae, home to the great temple of Isis. They enslaved the fleeing inhabitants, looted what they could and, as a final insult, lopped off the head of a statue of the Emperor Augustus. The Candace had the bronze head with its neatly disarrayed hair, protuberant ears and startlingly open eyes of coloured glass buried under the threshold of a temple built to commemorate her victory, so that she could trample the head of her enemy underfoot.*

In 20 BC, a year after the Candace's symbolic beheading of Augustus, the new prefect of Egypt, Publius Petronius, retaliated. Phalanxes of unwavering Roman soldiers, on foot, horseback and camels, ploughed through a far larger – but undisciplined and ill-assorted – force of 30,000 nomads from different tribes, who were, according to Strabo, 'badly marshalled' by the Candace's son, and 'badly armed'. They had 'large oblong shields, and those too made of raw ox-hide, and as weapons some had only axes, others pikes, and others swords'. Petronius and his men struck across the desert and marched all the way to the Second Cataract,** where, said Pliny, 'the river Nile, as it thunders down the precipices, has quite deprived the inhabitants of the power of hearing'. Several thousand men, women and children were dragged from Meroe to be sold as slaves in Rome's marketplaces.

But though she had been worsted by Rome's military machine, the Candace behaved as a god-ruler should: she was unbowed. She sent her envoys to the Greek island of Samos to meet her enemy Augustus, who was just about to set off from there for Syria. Did the Candace send her envoys to parley with a fellow god? If so, she must have felt herself to be the stronger. The envoys brought with them a bundle of golden arrows, and, according to legend, this aggressive message: 'The Candace sends you these arrows. If you want peace they are a token of her friendship and warmth. If you want war, you are going to need them.'

---

* It is now in the British Museum.
** It is now submerged under Lake Nasser.

Augustus yielded. 'The ambassadors', said Strabo, 'obtained all that they desired, and Caesar even remitted the tribute which he had imposed.' Augustus may have decided that Meroe was too poor to be worth invading, but the Candace had certainly been an effective deterrent. She had made it clear that any attempt at encroaching on her territory would be extremely expensive. The peace treaty endured for three centuries and for all that time Meroe remained the southernmost frontier of the Roman Empire. Meroe never attempted another invasion of Egypt, and the border area prospered under the influence of Rome and trade.

In this clash between the old and the new worlds, the Candace's survived: arguably, it prevailed. Augustus was dealing with a new world where the person – the combative, wilful, troublesome individual who has to be cajoled and persuaded – was emerging. By the end of the first century BC the religions, the art, the writings of the peoples of the Roman Empire showed a passionate concern with the individual. Roman historians like Tacitus, Suetonius and Cassius Dio laced their histories with juicy gossip about the emperors and their wives, even inventing elaborate bedtime conversations between Augustus and Livia. In every bust, fresco and coin of Livia and Augustus their subjects could pore over their rulers' faces to read their individuality, however idealized: Augustus' intelligence and vanity; Livia's daunting coolness.

The Candace, on the other hand, ruled an older world of the collective group where the individual was not salient. It is clear from every image of her on temple walls that she was never considered as a person; her subjects could get no hint of her character; nor would they have wanted to. And they probably did not see themselves as – certainly did not prize themselves as – individuals.

In this traditional homogeneous society, the god-ruler prevailed more easily. According to the Princeton psychologist Julian Jaynes, members of small-scale ancient societies actually 'heard' commands issuing from the statues of the gods, and built temples to store their voices. The authority of the Candace-ruler would have come from the fact that she was a mouthpiece for the gods' commandments. Although eccentric, this theory could be taken as a metaphor for the collective responsiveness and behaviour that was brought to an end by society's increasing complexity (thanks to trade, population movements and military conquest). The hallucinatory voices of the gods were no longer heard because the cohesive group had been shattered. The marked diversity of Roman cities, in part the result of trade, in part a reason to trade, propelled the rise of the individual, which in turn made space for the philosophies of the self, like Stoicism, and for religions of the self, like the mystery religions and Christianity. Complex society, kept together by written law and the individual's understanding of his or her allotted position, replaced those simpler traditions.*

In AD 50, less than seventy years after Candace Amanirenas had made her peace with Augustus, an important Meroite was on his way home from a trip to Jerusalem, where he had been to worship. He was 'a man of Ethiopia, a eunuch of great authority under Candace Queen of the Ethiopians [possibly one of Amanirenas' successors, Gersamot Hendeke VII], who was in charge of all her treasure', according to the Acts of the Apostles, an account of Paul and the first missionaries of Christianity. The treasurer may have been a Jewish convert, or a 'God-fearer' as Gentiles interested in Judaism were called. Sitting in his chariot, reading the Book of Isaiah, he was spotted by Philip the Evangelist, a Greek Jew and one of Paul's missionaries. Philip ran alongside the chariot and kept on talking until he was invited to climb up and sit beside the treasurer. As the chariot jolted past dusty olive groves and low stone walls enclosing small fields of grapes, figs and chickpeas, Philip preached the message of Jesus. He was so successful that before long the treasurer asked him what he had to do to be baptized. Nothing, was the answer, except believe with all your heart. (In chapter 19 I will explain why

---

* In their different ways, Marx and Hegel would celebrate this development from collective group consciousness to the distinctively Western social order that is based on the self.

this was such a radical, successful, but also accommodating answer for a man on the border between the traditional and the modern worlds, as so many were at this time.)

The chariot stopped beside some water. The eunuch proclaimed, 'I believe that Jesus Christ is the Son of God.' He was duly baptized and the two men parted company, Philip to preach in the villages and towns of Galilee and the eunuch to return to Meroe, where, according to the Early Church Fathers Irenæus and Eusebius, he became the first Christian evangelist and may have converted the Candace herself.

According to a tradition within the Ethiopian Orthodox Church, the treasurer brought Christianity to Meroe's neighbour Axum.[2] In AD 335, 300 years later, Axum's Emperor Ezana converted to Christianity, around the same time as Constantine, and made Christianity the official state religion. Only twenty years later, Axum swallowed up Meroe, thanks, proclaimed Ezana, to the power of the Lord of Heaven, though the conquest was also thanks to the power of trade: Axum had taken over from Meroe as the chief supplier of luxury goods – and slaves – to the Romans.

The eunuch treasurer was Christianity's first Gentile convert to hold an important office of state. It may be that Christianity offered him the reassurance of a loving God and loving community as trade propelled Meroe from a homogeneous traditional world order into a more complex disruptive one.

Hegel may have tried to explain history by his mysterious 'march of the spirit of freedom'; Marx in terms of material and economic forces. I follow Weber's view that beliefs also have their causative part to play; it is the specific beliefs people acquire which interact with their interests and motives to shape human history.[3] Shaping, even manipulating, beliefs is therefore one crucial way by which states exercise control over their subjects.

Augustus' own attempt to co-opt religion as a way of consolidating his empire became ever more necessary after the failure of one of his last attempts at military expansion. Early in his reign, Augustus had his eyes on the gum from a scrubby little tree that grew across the Red Sea from Meroe in South Arabia (today's Yemen and Oman). It was probably the most essential luxury of the ancient world, and it had made the kingdoms of South Arabia fabulously wealthy. It was the reason why Roman soldiers, under the command of Strabo's friend Aelius Gallus, would die in their thousands.

5

THE MIRAGE OF ARABIA: ROME'S FIASCO

No power on earth can stand against Roman arms.

Livy, *The Early History of Rome*, c.29–27 BC

... these chaps [the Romans] were not much account, really. They were no colonists; their administration was merely a squeeze, and nothing more, I suspect. They were conquerors, and for that you want only brute force – nothing to boast of, when you have it, since your strength is just an accident arising from the weakness of others. They grabbed what they could get for the sake of what was to be got. It was just robbery with violence, aggravated murder on a great scale.

Joseph Conrad, *Heart of Darkness*, 1902

All of Arabia exhumes a most delicate fragrance; even the seamen passing by Arabia can smell the strong fragrance that gives health and vigour.

Diodorus Siculus, *Historical Library*, c.56–30 BC

The Roman invasion of Southern Arabia was a disaster from the outset, not just because the man who led it was 'a bungler of the first order',[1] but because the Romans had overestimated the prize they coveted. This failure, coming at the same time as the inglorious outcome of Augustus' confrontation with the Candace of Meroe, marked a turning point for Rome: the moment when religion took on a new significance in the Roman state and became an important political tool for its rulers.

In 26 BC, the incense kingdoms of Southern Arabia seemed

intensely desirable and easily obtainable. The Romans believed *Arabia Felix*, as they called Southern Arabia, was fantastically wealthy. Pliny – author of the thirty-seven-volume *Natural History*, whose subject, he said, with all the imperial confidence of Strabo, was 'Nature, that is to say Life' – thought these kingdoms were the 'richest nations in the world'. They produced and distributed two of the most sought-after commodities of the ancient world. As a result, the Romans believed the kingdoms themselves must be inconceivably rich. And the Southern Arabians were willing accomplices in creating the myth of their incomparable wealth.

Under the scorching sun on the red-clay mountain slopes of southern Oman, slaves and labourers camped every spring to harvest a gum 'brilliant white and gathered at dawn in drops or tears in the shape of pearls' that dripped from a squat and prickly tree, filling the air with a cloying sweetness. Having tapped the trees, the harvesters collected these 'pearls of the desert', as Pliny called them, and stored them in mountain caves to dry during the summer, while outside the monsoon rains wrapped the coastline and mountains in thick clouds and fog. By September, the rains had stopped and the ground was firm enough for herds of camels to set off, loaded with the resin – now dried in flat round cakes – on a journey of 1,600 miles to Gaza, where the goods could be transported around the Mediterranean and beyond.

The resin was frankincense. At the time of Jesus it was as expensive as gold. Frankincense was the ancient world's equivalent of crude oil. It was an indispensable element of public and private life, of all religious and state ceremonies in the Roman Empire as in the rest of Strabo's known world. Its sweet, woody-smelling white smoke wafted heavenwards in temples to the Greek sun-god Apollo, the Roman god of war Mars and the Babylonian sun-god Bel, in the Temple of Jerusalem, in Buddhist temples in India and at the small field shrine of a peasant farmer in Italy praying for a good crop. At his wife's funeral in AD 65, the allegedly heartbroken Nero burnt 3,000 tons of frankincense, though this may have been a guilt offering: his enemies were convinced that Nero had murdered her. Frankincense was used to fend off the stench of ordinary living if you could afford it, in oils for massages at the baths, in face packs for pampered women and in the kohl with which they made up their eyes. It was used to perfume the sails of Cleopatra's barge when she sailed up the River Cydnus to St Paul's birthplace of Tarsus for her first encounter with Mark Antony. It was rubbed into the fur of spoiled dogs and mixed into the mortar of houses. Frankincense was the aspirin of its time, used as a cure for anything from depression to dysentery.

For 900 years, ever since – according to biblical legend – the Queen of Sheba (the richest of the kingdoms of Southern Arabia) had travelled to Jerusalem to negotiate a deal with King Solomon, Southern Arabia had been growing rich on its virtual monopoly of the production and transport of frankincense and myrrh.* Myrrh, a thorny bush, which like frankincense grew in southern Oman and what is now Yemen, was the essential ingredient for embalming bodies. More expensive than frankincense, it was less in demand and used less frequently in religious ceremonies. But like frankincense it was mixed in cosmetics and perfumes and was used as a cure-all: to prevent poisoning and induce menstruation. It was also used to relieve pain, which may have been why Jesus was offered a mixture of myrrh and wine before the crucifixion; his mother, Mary, may well have been given myrrh to relieve the pains of childbirth.

Frankincense and myrrh were also produced across the Red Sea in Meroe and Axum, with whom the Arabians had been trading for centuries. But Southern Arabia produced the finest quality. Frankincense and myrrh were the reason so many Southern Arabian tribesmen had given up their nomadic life to found cities from

---

* The Queen of Sheba's negotiations with King Solomon (the son of King David) were presumably successful. They apparently resulted in a son, Menilek, who inherited from her the kingdom of Axum, the lands of Ethiopia and Eritrea, across the Red Sea. His dynasty, it is said, only ended in 1974 with the overthrow of Haile Selassie, Ethiopia's last emperor, who still carried Menilek's title of 'King of Kings, Lord of Lords, conquering Lion of Judah, and God Incarnate', and who is now worshipped as a god by modern-day Rastafarians. The god-ruler survived in Axum after all.

which the incense kingdoms like Sheba had developed. In the comparative peace brought by Augustus at the end of the first century BC, demand was soaring. Thousands of pounds of incense were making their way by land and sea to Alexandria, Rome and Gaza, to the former Persian Empire now controlled by the Parthians, to India and even to China.

Like some great city on the move,[2] thousands of camels, smelling of bad breath and coughing like angry old men, set off from the Southern Arabian peninsula and trudged across mountains and desert. The caravans with their merchants stretched for miles, the precious cargo protected by tribesmen archers sitting tensed on their camels or horses, on the lookout for bandits who might be lurking in every cave they passed, ready to swoop on them in narrow mountain passes or by wells of precious water. As Pliny said of the 'Arabs', 'one half of these almost innumerable tribes live by the pursuits of commerce, the other half by rapine'. At night, when the desert winds picked up, the travellers, if they were lucky, would stay in one of a network of caravanserais stretched every twenty-five miles along the route.* Some caravanserais offered no more than basic protection, a dormitory to sleep in and food; some provided stabling, fresh camels, lavish suites, coffee rooms, shops and, of course, 'dancing girls', their long hair braided in plaits. Other caravanserais had expanded into full-blown cities.

First stop along the overland incense route, according to Pliny, was the oasis city of Sabota (modern Shabwa in Yemen), capital of one of the four main frankincense kingdoms of Southern Arabia. Set on the edge of the desert among grey pebbled hills, salt mines and fields which were watered, like all the major cities, by an elaborate network of canals and dams, Sabota was the most feared city on the frankincense route. It was so determined to maintain its grip on the incense traffic that caravaneers caught trying to avoid the city and its tolls were executed. Priests stood outside their temple to the moon god Sin, with its colossal bronze statue flanked by statues of animals,

---

* Twenty-five miles was the average distance a caravan travelled in a day.

exacting a tithe from every caravan that passed through the massive gateway into the walled city.

All along the incense routes the merchants had to pay their way. They paid the local guides, the priests lining the entranceways to the cities and the customs collectors in the cities and on the mountain passes; they paid bribes and protection money; they paid for food and wine, camels and entertainment. And they paid with their lives. Turrets and tombs still mark where the caravans buried their dead along the route.

At the frontier crossings into Roman territory, merchants were charged a further 25 per cent tax by customs agents. The Romans required their cut just as the bandits did. The difference between a protection racket and an ordered state is sometimes just one of organization and monopoly. Indeed, the basic logic of a trading empire can perhaps be seen as replacing a series of bandits with a single bandit.

Rome's customs agents methodically searched each traveller, confiscating anything which had not been declared, and exacting taxes on everything from a corpse being transported for burial to eunuchs, handsome youths or slaves – any attempt by an owner to smuggle a slave across a border would result in the slave being freed on the spot.

By the time one camel-load of frankincense (about 350 pounds in weight) had reached Alexandria in Egypt – one of the main sorting and processing centres for frankincense, where it was usually impounded in a public warehouse until the tax had been paid – it had become so valuable that the workmen were strip-searched to make sure they did not take any of the precious grains away with them. Roman citizens paid 6 denarii a pound for top-quality frankincense – more than the average man could earn in a fortnight or an ordinary soldier in a week, though a night with a good prostitute could cost one denarius according to graffiti scratched on a wall by a lonely man in Pompeii (whether he was boasting or complaining is not clear). At such prices, frankincense was inevitably adulterated by dealers, but there were ways to detect the fraud: Pliny recommended biting it to make sure it crumbled easily. And demand was so great that Rome was paying about £7.5 billion in today's terms a year, while, as Pliny sourly noted, the Arabian kingdoms 'purchased nothing in return'.

Sadly, we have no Arabian Tacitus or Suetonius, no indigenous written sources except the countless inscriptions on votive offerings left by caravaneers at wells and temples, like the tribesman who 'dedicated to his lord Dhu Samawi... a bronze statuette of a she-camel that Dhu Samawi may grant him the well-being of himself and his children as well as the well-being and safety of his camel'. It is the foreigners Strabo and Pliny who have left us almost the only written descriptions of pre-Islamic Arabia at around the time of Christ, although neither of them ever actually went there. Pliny's account relied heavily on the great scholar and African King Juba's *Peri tes Arabias* (*On Arabia*), written in about AD 2, which is now lost (see chapter 16 for King Juba). Strabo's relied, like King Juba's, on earlier Greek sources, but also on the account by his 'friend and companion' Gallus, of his wretched 'expedition'.[3]

Both Strabo and Pliny faithfully recorded the earlier Greek descriptions of the untold splendours of the incense kingdoms and contributed to the legend of *Arabia Felix*. In Sheba, the wealthiest incense kingdom of them all, the inhabitants 'lived in effeminate luxury', according to Strabo, lying on gold couches, eating and drinking from gold and silver vessels in rooms whose walls, doors and ceilings were inlaid with ivory, gold, silver and precious stones.

It was not surprising, therefore, that Augustus had cast covetous eyes on *Arabia Felix*. 'He was... influenced by the report which had prevailed from all time, that this people were very wealthy,' said Strabo. Augustus was determined 'either to compel the Arabs to be Rome's allies or to conquer their territory outright'.

The Southern Arabian kingdoms had themselves carefully nurtured the legend of their own wealth in order to protect their secret knowledge of the monsoon winds, which gave them and the

Indians a monopoly of the sea trade between East and West. For centuries, the Arabian traders had convinced the Greeks and Romans that the pepper, cassia, cinnamon, nard, pearls and diamonds they imported by sea in their galleon-shaped dhows from India, Sri Lanka and further East, and even the teak, and ebony from Meroe and Axum, actually came from *Arabia Felix*.[4] Unfortunately for the Arabians, a shipwrecked Indian sailor had finally revealed to the Romans how to take advantage of the monsoon winds so as to radically reduce the sailing time between Arabia and India and thereby cut the cost of transport by sea.

The Red Sea was still only navigable in the winter months and even then the ships had to contend with pirates (though these had become scarcer since the Roman imperial fleet had started patrolling the Red Sea), storms, strong currents and treacherous coral reefs. According to the Sicilian historian Diodorus, who had just completed his history of the world from mythological times to 60 BC, the ships most at risk were those transporting elephants. Because of their heavy loads, the ships were driven on to the rocks or ran aground; as provisions on board slowly ran out, the weak and dying were thrown overboard. Long after the mariners had died a lingering death, the wreckage of the ships survived 'as so many solitary sepulchres and at length, being buried in heaps of sand, their lofty masts and mainyards remain only spectacles to move compassion in those that see them afar off'.[5]

Despite such hazards, more and more Roman trade was taking to the sea. Ships could now leave Egypt in early June and be blown by the monsoon winds to India by September. After doing trade and business for two months, the ships could be back in Alexandria by February. By the mid-first century AD the overland traffic through Arabia would dry up as increasing amounts of goods were transported more rapidly and cheaply by sea.

Strabo, luckily for him, did not join the Arabian invasion, although he did all he could to whitewash its leader, his friend Aelius Gallus, the prefect of Egypt. Overtrusting, overconfident and poorly informed,

Gallus had put his faith in the last man he should ever have trusted – the young, handsome but 'unscrupulously ambitious and cruel' Syllaeus, chief minister of the kingdom of Nabataea.

Nabataea, in what was then called Northern Arabia (the southern part of modern Jordan), controlled the trade at the northern end of the incense route. It charged a 25 per cent tax on all merchandise passing through – myrrh, spices and frankincense from South Arabia, rich silk fabrics from Damascus and Gaza, glassware and purple from Sidon and Tyre, pearls from India and the Persian Gulf, and raw silk from China.

Much of the caravan traffic from Southern Arabia headed north through the desert for Nabataea's great city of Petra. After plodding through bleak mudflats and endless waves of desert with their trains of camels, donkeys and horses, the caravaneers would see a great circle of cliffs rising up before them in dazzling colours of red, lilac, grey, brown, black and yellow. The travellers filed through a narrow canyon, passed crenellated towers and hundreds of tombs carved in the multicoloured rock, until suddenly they turned a corner, the walls of the narrow canyon opened up and there in front of them, shining in the sun, was a massive pinkish-orange temple (though it is called the treasury, the 'Khazneh' was more likely to have been a temple, possibly to Isis), its classical columns, arches and pediments soaring up 40 metres out of the sandstone rock face.

Petra was another boom town, profiting from its command of the trading routes to South Arabia, west to the port of Gaza on the Mediterranean, north to Damascus and east across the desert to the Persian Gulf. Around this time all the great monuments were being built that would make Petra the famed 'rose-red city' beloved by tourists, though John William Burgon, the Victorian cleric who coined this phrase, admitted later that he hadn't actually visited the ruins and 'peach' might have been more accurate. A city of 25,000 inhabitants, Petra was filled with Romans (who were, according to Strabo, extremely litigious) and other foreigners; even neighbouring Judaea's King Herod the Great, a longtime foe of Nabataea, had spent much of his formative years in Petra.

Nabataea did not want to see Rome controlling any of its profitable trade, all the more so as its trade by sea was beginning to be threatened by Roman merchants who were bypassing Nabataea altogether and transporting their goods via Egypt's Red Sea ports. Syllaeus, the Nabataean chief minister, therefore conducted what was in effect a covert war against the invading Roman troops while ostensibly acting as their guide. His first victory was in convincing Gallus that there was no overland route for an army from Egypt to Northern Arabia, when in fact, as Strabo ruefully pointed out, vast trading caravans regularly took the overland routes there 'with ease and in safety... with so large a body of men and camels as to differ in no respect from an army'. Instead Gallus decided to risk the notoriously difficult Red Sea crossing and compounded his error by 'building long vessels of war at a time when there was no war, nor any likely to occur at sea'. When he discovered that these would be totally unsuitable for the crossing, Gallus ordered the shipbuilders to construct another fleet, this time of 130 light troop-carrying boats.

Finally, in 26 BC, more than 10,000 Roman soldiers embarked from Arsinoe, near modern Suez in Egypt. Hundreds of them drowned on the fifteen-day journey; their boats, driven by winds that made the journey almost impossible, were wrecked on reefs, and ran aground on shifting shoals. By the time the surviving soldiers arrived at the Nabataean port city of Leuce Come (probably at the mouth of the Gulf of Aqaba, about 300 kilometres south of Petra), they were so debilitated by scurvy and what Strabo called 'skeloturbe' – a paralysis of the legs – that they were forced to spend the summer and winter there.

The following spring the Romans headed south with Syllaeus as their guide. With them went 1,000 Nabataean soldiers – Syllaeus presumably felt they were a sacrifice worth paying for the greater cause of leading Gallus's army to ruin. Nabataea's neighbour, Judaea, also sent a contingent of 500 men, including mercenaries from Thrace, Galatia and – probably – Germany, from where Herod the Great had just begun hiring troops.

The soldiers' march to Southern Arabia took them through one of the most inhospitable places on earth, though it was a trek that the incense caravans took regularly. On one side of them was a wall of high mountains, which drop into the Red Sea, and on the other was one of the world's largest deserts – 'the Empty Quarter' (in today's southern Saudi Arabia) as travellers called it. Roman soldiers were trained to march fast – an average of 4 to 5 miles an hour – carrying a heavy load of rations, waterskin, saw, rope, shovel and pickaxe. But Gallus' soldiers were marched 'through places that had no roads and by circuitous routes and through regions destitute of everything, or along rocky shores that had no harbours or through waters that were shallow or full of submarine rocks'. From Strabo's description, it sounds as though Syllaeus deliberately took them off the well-worn incense route, although once past Yathrib (Medina) even that route was punishingly hard. The villages were far apart, there were few wells, the standing stones that regularly marked the route and told travellers how far they were from the nearest water source were absent, and the nights were freezing cold. They marched about 25 miles a day. Barren, dried mudflats and sand stretched out into the distance, punctuated by craggy peaks of sandstone.

In this burning landscape – inhabited only by Bedouin Arabs, their sheep and goats and a few palm trees – the precious water carried by the camels turned bitter and had to be sweetened with grains of sand.[6] Not even Gallus' skills as a doctor could help the soldiers. He was able to cure snakebites, but could do nothing to alleviate the effects of thirst, heat and exhaustion.

Once they had passed Mecca, however, it looked as if the troops' fortunes might pick up. After six months, the Roman army finally reached the first of the Southern Arabian kingdoms and captured its major city. Nejrani (modern Najran, close to Saudi Arabia's border with Yemen) was an important staging post on the frankincense route where the caravans branched west or east. According to Strabo, the inhabitants of Nejrani did not even try to repel Gallus' army. Their king had fled and they gave up without a struggle.

Six days later, the army scored another easy victory. According to Strabo, 'the barbarians attacked the Romans and lost about ten thousand men; the Romans lost only two men. For the barbarians were entirely inexperienced in war, and used their weapons unskilfully, which were bows, spears, swords, and slings; but the greater part of them wielded a double-edged axe.' Even allowing for some hyperbole on Strabo's part, the soldiers clearly met little resistance. And no doubt they stripped the city bare and terrorized those inhabitants who had not managed to flee, for that was considered the soldiers' right. Rome was exceptional even at the time for the savagery with which it treated its defeated enemies. Victorious soldiers entering a conquered city were free to – indeed were expected to – rape and massacre its inhabitants and, most importantly of all, to sack it for anything of value.[7] But for the Roman soldiers and their commanders who had believed the fabled reports of *Arabia Felix*'s wealth, who were waiting for the loot which would make their year-long campaign worthwhile, Nejrani, and the few other cities they conquered, probably seemed deeply disappointing. They were built as bulwarks to repel invaders, not as showcases of the inhabitants' wealth and culture.

Like many Southern Arabian cities and villages, Nejrani was protected by an unbroken ring of houses several storeys high, which made a formidable wall to keep out nomadic raiders. Even the greatest houses, sometimes as much as eight storeys high, were built mainly of mudbricks. Resembling towers or forts, they lacked the decorative magnificence of Roman villas. In contrast with the Roman villa's light and airy atrium, its courtyards adorned with fountains, and adjacent rooms decorated with mosaics, the entrances to the houses of the Southern Arabian wealthy were built a few metres above ground level to prevent easy access; the dark rooms on the ground floor were used to stable goats and store grain; and were lit by windows which were only large enough for arrows to be shot from.

Southern Arabian cities were built for defence, not for display.

Unlike the deliberately imposing public buildings of the Roman Empire, which shouted the majesty and might of the state, the buildings of these incense cities made no distinction in style between public buildings and private homes. There were irregular paths rather than streets. And by Roman standards these cities were small – with populations of considerably less than 10,000, compared to a prosperous city in Italy like Pompeii which had a population of about 20,000, or Ephesus in Rome's province of Asia with its 50,000 people.

Nevertheless, the cities of Southern Arabia were wealthy, as evidenced by their huge temples stuffed with silver and bronze images. And they were probably more organizationally sophisticated than the African cities of Meroe and Axum with whom the incense kingdoms traded across the Red Sea. The Arabian cities maintained an effective control over the profits from the incense trade, regulating taxes and penalizing dishonest merchants.* The city elites of merchants and landowners – who lived in the cities while collecting rent and taxes on the vast lands they developed and owned on the fringes of the desert – ran sophisticated irrigation systems which demanded a high degree of cooperative work from the townspeople and peasants. The elites were too powerful for any Arabian king ever to attain the divine status of Meroe's Candace Amanirenas. In Tumna, capital of the incense kingdom of Qataban, the merchants even banned their sovereign from conducting business within the city. Such a measure would have been unthinkable in Meroe.

But, despite their level of economic and social organization, Southern Arabian cities must have seemed disappointingly primitive to Gallus and his soldiers. The Romans had assumed that because frankincense and myrrh were so expensive by the time it reached them, the place where these aromatics had originated must be extraordinarily rich. They had expected to find one single source of wealth, not realizing that the aromatics were increasing in price as they journeyed along the incense route, as every city, every dancing

---

* Dishonest merchants in the city of Tumna were fined fifty pieces of gold; see Highet, 2006.

girl, priest, tax collector and bandit made their profits from the traffic.

Frustrated and exhausted, the Roman army reached the city walls of Marib, capital of Sheba, the most famous incense kingdom of them all. Marib (today's Yemeni town of Ma'rib) is now just a rubbish-strewn truck stop between Oman and Saudi Arabia, but at the time of the Roman invasion it was the greatest oasis city in South Arabia, surrounded by groves of date palms. In a final supreme piece of military incompetence, Gallus had decided to besiege a city that was famous even then for its dam and irrigation works. The dam was one of the greatest feats of engineering of the ancient world. It watered 24,000 acres (100 sq. km) of rectangular fields. Criss-crossed by an elaborate system of canals, the fields fed about 50,000 people with wheat, barley, sorghum, pulses, dates and grapes. The dam was so big that 300 camel-loads of wine had to be provided for the workmen when they repaired it.[8] Gallus was faced with the most expert masters of water in the ancient world, yet unless he could gain control of their water supply, he would not be able to force Marib to surrender.

Nevertheless, Gallus should have been the victor. The Romans were the more experienced soldiers, and excelled in siege warfare, using not just catapults and battering rams but the far more menacing *testudo*. The 'tortoise shell' was in effect a human tank made up of a compact body of men with shields over their heads who were tightly surrounded by a wall of troops facing outwards with their shields drawn up; it was so strong that 'whenever they come to a narrow ravine even horses and vehicles can be driven over it', according to Cassius Dio. To the besieged, this glittering machine of shields which relentlessly advanced, almost impervious to the missiles hurled at it, must have seemed invincible.

But at Marib, time was not on the Romans' side: Gallus' troops ran out of water. After besieging the city for six days Gallus finally gave up and decided to make the humiliating journey home. It had taken him more than a year to reach Marib. The return journey took him about two and a half months. Of his original army of 10,000 men, most had died from the burning heat of the desert sun, from bad water and from disease. Only seven men had died in battle, according to Strabo, because the Arab kings had put up hardly any resistance. The Romans never got further south than Marib and they never again tried to conquer South Arabia.*

Gallus' Arabian expedition had been a humiliation for Rome, although one would not think so from the way Augustus recorded it in the *Res Gestae*, Augustus' own summary of his reign: 'At my command and under my auspices two armies were led almost at the same time into Ethiopia [Meroe] and *Arabia Felix*; vast enemy forces of both peoples were cut down in battle and many towns captured.' Augustus may not have wanted to consider this setback as a defeat, but it signalled the end of an era. Rome was finally coming up against its natural borders. Its standard formula of conquering new territory, milking it for a speedy and large injection of booty, and then farming it for taxes and recruiting its men to enlarge the Roman army, had failed. It was a formula that had worked successfully for 500 years.

Originally Latin tribesmen from a collection of small villages which coalesced into the city of Rome, the Romans had conquered the whole of Italy, defeated the Mediterranean superpower Carthage, extended west over Gaul and Spain, north over the Balkans and east into the territories of what had been the empire of Alexander the Great. By the time Augustus defeated Mark Antony and Cleopatra in 31 BC, Rome controlled virtually the whole Mediterranean area, a feat which no other power had ever managed or ever would again.

The Roman state had been almost permanently at war for 500 years. 'They seem to have been born with weapons in their hands,' wrote the Jewish historian Josephus. Plunder from conquest was the fuel that kept the state going; it was the bribe it offered to its people and its elite. Conquest was the quickest way to wealth for members of the competitive aristocracy, who were military warriors as well as

---

* More than 100 years later, the Roman Emperor Trajan annexed the North Arabian kingdom of Nabataea; the Nabataeans put up almost no resistance.

senators. Each new piece of conquered territory meant a new injection of wealth.

Loot from temples, towns and ransacked houses was grabbed by the generals, the treasury (the generals had to give some portion of their plunder to the state) and the ordinary soldiers, who were also given land to colonize. The amount of booty from a successful campaign was such that in 29 BC, three years before the Southern Arabian debacle, Augustus could afford to give 120,000 soldier-colonists 1,000 sesterces each (more than an ordinary soldier's yearly wage). All citizens, including the plebeians (the non-aristocrats), were treated to lavish handouts, the waiving of their rents, and spectacular gladiatorial contests from an elite eager to display their military success and buy popularity at the same time. The men, women and children captured in battle provided a fresh supply of slaves. In due course, men from the conquered territories became auxiliaries in the Roman army, which thereby grew with each new conquest, though, of course, auxiliaries might have divided loyalties and were therefore never completely trustworthy, as the auxiliary who led the slaughter of Roman legions in Germany would prove (see chapter 16). And, after the initial bonanza, the newly conquered peoples shouldered the tax burden. Roman citizens paid no direct taxes at all, though to their fury this changed under Augustus.

Augustus did not, of course, call a halt to imperial expansion. Rome's armies advanced into north-west Spain and along the Rhine and Danube and decisively subdued the Alps. But he concentrated on consolidating, not expanding, his territory. According to Cassius Dio, Augustus advised his successor Tiberius and the Roman elite 'to be satisfied with their present possessions and under no conditions to wish to increase the empire to any greater dimensions. It would be hard to guard, he said, and this would lead to the danger of their losing what was already theirs.'[9] Rome was involved in no major conquests from about AD 6 until Claudius' invasion of Britain in AD 43.

Augustus established an era of relative peace that would continue until the death of Marcus Aurelius in AD 180. The break with Rome's martial past was certainly not greeted with enthusiasm by Roman traditionalists. Looking back nostalgically on the golden age of the great wars, the besieging of cities and the overthrow and capture of kings, which had been the subject matter for more fortunate Roman historians, Tacitus complained of his 'narrow and inglorious' theme. 'Peace was scarcely broken – if at all. Rome was plunged in gloom, the ruler uninterested in expanding the empire.'

If Tacitus was too much of a Republican to appreciate the benefits brought by the *pax Augusta*, he was right to downplay its blessings. Peace threw up new problems for ruler and ruled. Augustus could no longer rely on conquest to finance the state and soothe or seduce a discontented Roman elite with promises of military adventure. He could no longer rely on military glory to bolster his position and justify his move from co-ruler of a republic to sole head of an empire. He had to seek alternative sources of legitimacy, something other than military prowess to mark him out as worthy of loyalty – hence the importance of the cult of the divinity of the emperor. Divinity could be as effective as military prowess, and would certainly be cheaper.

The ruler of a Rome at war could bribe his own people with loot and his conquered people, or certainly the conquered elite, with the promise of some share in its wealth and power. A Rome at peace could still offer wealth to its people. But the wealth that was generated by peace was no longer in the gift of the ruler but the result of the trade that flourished in peacetime, created by multiple transactions between thousands of people. Divinity maintained the emperor's position as the source of blessings. But trade provided an alternative source of good fortune and would eventually kill off emperor worship by creating the conditions for a new all-conquering religion. And when the Christian God became more popular than the pagan gods, demand for incense would fall, along with the Arabian kingdoms that had grown fat on it, and the once great cities along the overland trade routes would crumble as more and more traffic took to the seas.

Trade, the carrier and moulder of religions, builds empires and kingdoms – and destroys them. It was because Augustus ended the civil wars that had torn Rome apart that trade flourished and created new wealth for empires like Meroe and Axum. It was trade that created a climate for the growth of religious cults – either newly formed or born of the fusion of existing ones; they offered spiritual solace to the many thousands of people, of different backgrounds and cultures, who were settling in the cities along the trade routes. And it was trade which had brought Gallus' wretched soldiers to their deaths in the Arabian desert.

Although Strabo loyally maintained that 'if Syllaeus had not betrayed him [Gallus], he would have conquered the whole of *Arabia Felix*', Gallus was recalled to Rome in disgrace and replaced in Egypt by a far more competent prefect. As for the handsome Syllaeus, he managed to slip away from the Romans and returned to Petra a hero. Over the following twenty years, Syllaeus continued his picaresque career. He assassinated his enemies and plotted – unsuccessfully – to become king. Syllaeus gained the love of Herod the Great's sister, tried but failed to get Herod killed, and for a short while managed to persuade Augustus to favour him at the expense of Herod. But Herod was an even greater schemer than Syllaeus and finally outmanoeuvred him. He accused Syllaeus of offences ranging from treachery to murder, bribery, corruption and adultery with Roman (as well as Nabataean) women. Tried in Rome in 6 BC, Syllaeus was found guilty and pitched headlong from the Tarpeian Rock above the Forum – the standard punishment for murderers and traitors. Only two years later, Herod was faced with yet another protest from the people who would be the most resistant to Roman rule and to Augustus' bid to win his subjects through divinity.

6

HOW HEROD
AND THE PHARISEES
RADICALIZED
THE JEWS

… you chose the descendants of Abraham above all the nations, and
you put your name upon us, Lord.

Psalms of Solomon, 9:8–9, first century BC

They sit apart at meals, they sleep apart, and though, as a nation,
they are singularly prone to lust, they abstain from intercourse with
foreign women; among themselves nothing is unlawful.

Tacitus, *The Histories*, Book V, c.AD 100–110

For the Jews have long been in revolt… against humanity; and a race
that has made its own a life apart and irreconcilable, that cannot
share with the rest of mankind in the pleasures of the table nor join
in their libations or prayers or sacrifices, are separated from ourselves
by a greater gulf than divides us from Susa or Bactra or the more
distant Indies.

Philostratus, *The Life of Apollonius of Tyana*, v. 33, c.AD 217–238

One midday in Jerusalem, in the year 4 BC, a group of
students gathered at the Temple, newly rebuilt by Herod in
what had been the greatest building project of the times.
From miles away, pilgrims and sightseers could see its dazzling gold
gates and roofs, its white marble walls and pillars glittering like a
mountain covered in snow. The Temple was the embodiment of God's

contract with the Jews of Palestine,* and with all Jews scattered throughout the Roman Empire and beyond. And it was here that the students, inspired by their Pharisee teachers, climbed up the 65-foot-high inner walls and let themselves down by thick ropes to the great golden statue of an eagle perched over one of the Temple's massive gates, so big it took 200 men to close them.[1] The students toppled the eagle to the ground where a crowd smashed it to pieces with axes.

For religious Jews, the statue of the eagle was profoundly shocking. It was a flagrant violation of their God's second commandment forbidding any representational images (less strict Jews argued that the commandment only forbade *worshipping* such images, not representational art in general). But the eagle was also a symbol of Rome's domination – it was carried on soldiers' standards, etched on to coins and flew from temples and public buildings. Ironically, the new statue was part of the rebuilding of the Temple that Herod had undertaken in order to convince his subjects of his religious devotion. But for many Jews it was seen as the ultimate outrage committed by their king in a long list of violations against their religion. And the Pharisee teachers, along with their students, were prepared to die rather than permit such a transgression of their God's law.

The Pharisees, an increasingly popular politico-religious movement, had helped put Herod on the throne, but it was also the Pharisees who led the resistance against him for being too Romanized. They, or at least their extremist offshoots, eventually made any compromise with Roman rule impossible for the Jews of Palestine. Herod's loyalty to Rome and the Pharisees' religious objections to it radicalized many Jews who felt forced to make a choice between Rome and their religion. Together, Herod and the Pharisees paved the way for the Jewish terrorists who would murder their fellow Jews and help ignite the 'revolts' or 'wars', depending on which side you supported, against Rome of AD 66, when the Temple and Jerusalem

---

* By 'Palestine' I mean the physical territory comprising the districts of Galilee, Samaria, Peraea, Judaea and Idumaea; by 'Israel' I mean the land Yaweh promised to his chosen people. The Jews lived in a small area around Jerusalem called Ioudaia in Greek, hence Ioudaioi.

itself were razed to the ground and of AD 132, when the Jews were barred from Jerusalem.

Herod had been playing a difficult and, it would turn out, an impossible game. He was trying to be a good enough Jew to satisfy his Jewish subjects, while preserving the confidence of his Roman masters. The smashed eagle symbolized his failure. Alone of all the multifarious religions of the empire, the religion of the Jews was uniquely resistant to, and to some extent incompatible with, Roman rule. Rome had come up against the physical limits of empire in Arabia; it came up against the mental limits of empire in Palestine.

Machiavelli, that superbly pragmatic political theorist, writing with all the enthusiasm of a Renaissance admirer of Rome, thought there were three ways by which an empire could exercise hegemony over its peoples: occupying them by force, living amongst them (that is, colonization), or co-opting the elites (that is, bribing them by making it in their interests to be loyal). Rome, like China, used all three methods. Force was always Rome's ultimate resort, though it was not always successful. Rome also planted colonies of retired soldiers throughout the empire, which were sometimes Roman islands in a sea of 'barbarian' otherness, but whose Romanness would, it was hoped, overawe and convert the natives if they had not already been civilized by Graeco-Roman culture. Rome's client kings were part of Machiavelli's third method of imperial control, co-option. It was a method that worked particularly well in the Eastern, more urbanized, part of the empire, where the local elites were the products of centuries of imperial rule by Assyrians, Babylonians, Persians and Greeks. In the less urbanized Western part of the empire, in Spain, Gaul, and later Britain, Hellenized/Romanized elites were fewer in number, and tribal loyalties and customs persisted. In these territories, Augustus created veteran colonies but also imposed much more direct control.[2]

The relationship between client king and emperor was no different from any of the other client–patron relations that permeated Roman life: it was a mutually self-supporting system of benefits conferred and services rendered. The good client king had to pay tribute – tax – to Rome, provide soldiers for Rome's wars when required and keep order within his own territory. In return he was given considerable freedom to rule his kingdom (though he could never go to war unless authorized to do so, and never bequeath his kingdom to an heir without Rome's say-so); his country could prosper under the protection offered by Rome, and he and his elite individually gained from all the status and wealth that connection with one of the two most powerful empires on earth gave them. And Rome was spared the expense of administrators and avoided having to commit its scarce legionary forces. It was adept at turning a conquered elite into one that was willingly loyal to Rome. Juba, King of the North African kingdom of Mauretania, had walked in chains through the streets of Rome when his father's kingdom had been conquered; but he was then brought up within the imperial household and became the most faithful, as well as most learned, of all Augustus' client kings with the single exception of Herod (see chapter 16 for more on King Juba).

The Romans' usual pattern of military conquest followed by co-option extended even to the gods. The third-century lawyer and Christian apologist Minucius Felix noted that 'after they have captured a town, when brutality in victory might be expected, the Romans pay honour to the deities of the conquered people. They invite to Rome gods from all over the world and they make them their own.'[3]

Rome's religious 'tolerance' was, of course, still conquest, though in subtle guise, as the fourth-century Roman Christian poet Prudentius pointed out:

As her [Rome's] valour conquered cities and won her famous triumphs, Rome got herself countless gods; amid the smoking ruins of temples the victor's armed right hand took her enemies' images and carried them home in captivity, worshipping them as divinities. One figure she seized from the ruins of Corinth by the two seas, another she took for booty from burning Athens; the defeat of Cleopatra gave her some dog-headed figures, and when she conquered the sands of Ammon there were horned heads among her trophies from the African desert.[4]

The local gods in the conquered territories became Romanized, as we will see in chapter 8, while the Graeco-Roman gods established themselves, though with local colouring. It was a deliberate policy of inculcating Roman mores and Roman patriotism.

But the Roman model of conquest followed by co-option never worked for the Jews. Every conquered people is haunted by the problem of assimilation – how much to allow themselves to become absorbed within the dominant culture and how much to assert and preserve their own separate identity. But only for the Jews was the problem fundamentally a religious one which forced them to choose where they stood in relation to their God and to Rome.

In 4 BC, the Pharisee teachers Judas and Matthias chose God and incited their students to smash the golden eagle in the Temple. Half a century later, the historian Josephus, Jewish aristocrat and priest, plumped for Rome. Josephus' two major works *The Jewish War* and *Jewish Antiquities*, both written towards the end of the first century AD, are the main sources for Palestine at this period and provide some of the few near-contemporary references to Jesus outside the New Testament, although some historians believe these references were additions made by a later Christian editor to provide a first-century proof of Jesus' existence.[5] In the revolt of AD 66, Josephus began by commanding his fellow Jews in Galilee, believing, as he confessed, that 'the people will unite against the Romans'; after being captured by the Romans he switched sides, and provided the legions with intelligence on the revolt, convinced, he claimed, that the Jews' only hope of survival was surrender.[6] He would be with the Emperor Vespasian's son Titus and his troops when they razed Jerusalem and its Temple to the ground in AD 70. Josephus became a prosperous citizen of Rome and was granted a pension and land in conquered Judaea by the emperor. But he still tried to play a double role: in his history of the Jewish people, which was written for Titus and his Jewish mistress Berenice, he tried to exonerate the majority of Palestinian Jews from the revolts against Rome, and to blame instead a handful of rebel-bandits.

It would be Saul of Tarsus, ardent Pharisee yet loyal Roman citizen, who, about forty years after Herod's death, would find a way round the problem of assimilation by creating a new person, Paul, who was 'neither Jew nor Gentile'. For many Jews, Paul's route was the only way out of an increasingly impossible tension between Jewishness and Romanness. According to some modern scholars, Jewish converts would become the backbone of Christianity for several centuries.[7] By the fourth century, Rome was certainly able to benefit from Paul's universalist cult which was deliberately non-nationalist, but it could not accommodate, integrate or crush a religion based on exclusive nationalism.

The Jews had survived centuries of conquest, exile and Diaspora by insisting on their difference. Forced by famine to leave Palestine for Egypt, taken into captivity by the Assyrians and the Babylonians, the Jews survived without a land because they had turned exclusiveness into a religion. Ever since the sixth century BC, when the Babylonians destroyed Jerusalem and its Temple and took thousands of Jews into captivity, a majority of Jews had lived outside Palestine. By then Yaweh had become not just the supreme God but the only God.

It was their God Yaweh who kept them together and protected them against the huge dissolving pressures of assimilation. He had singled out the Jews as his chosen people. He promised them that he would one day deliver them safely home. In return they must worship only him and – crucially – obey his law, that is, the commandments and prohibitions God had revealed to Moses on Mount Sinai, which were set down in the Torah, the first five books of the Bible. For Yaweh ensured their survival (and his own) by extending his dominion over every aspect of their lives. The ethnic god had become the only God. As the historian Paul Veyne points out, jealousy was

Yaweh's first big religious invention: it was the seed of exclusive monotheism.[8] The religious Jews who stayed faithful to Yaweh in a foreign land were following his command to ignore the temptation of worshipping local gods. And Yaweh made great demands of his followers, for, unlike any other god, he made the whole of living a religious matter.

The pagan gods were also omnipresent in everyday life, but when it came to how life should be lived, they had nothing to say. Spirits lived in every wood and stream; farmers offered daisy chains to the gods of the fields; in every home families worshipped the protectors of the household, the spirits of departed ancestors; in the city streets passers-by would hang garlands on the statue of a god or touch their fingers to their lips and hold them out towards the image; potters at their kilns invoked the name of Vulcan; sailors prayed to Neptune for a safe voyage.

But these gods had almost no control over their worshippers' behaviour, and if they did it was restricted to how they should recite prayers and perform sacrifices. Jupiter's chief priest was subject to an eclectic range of behavioural rules, from not being allowed to ride a horse, touch or even name a female goat, raw meat, ivy or beans, to the injunction that his nail trimmings and hair had to be buried under a healthy tree, and being forbidden to remove his underwear 'except in covered places, lest he appear nude under the open sky, which is the same as under the eye of Jove', according to Cicero. But such detailed rules only applied to the priests. The mystery cults demanded even more of their priests, to the extent of requiring they castrate themselves and lead ascetic lives (see chapter 8), and they seem to have required some moral as well as ritual purity from their 'lay' worshippers, but from what little we know they did not exert much influence over people's day-to-day lives. Stoicism laid down the broad principle that individuals should live in such a way that they became autonomous beings, but did not concern itself with rules laying down the practical details, for that would be to detract from the individual's autonomy. 'A cucumber is bitter. Throw it away.

There are briars in the road. Turn aside from them. This is enough.'[9] The Jews' jealous and solicitous God, on the other hand, was concerned with the preservation of his tribe, with keeping it distinct; he had developed a far more explicit – and reciprocal – relationship with his people than any pagan god, even Isis, had with their devotees.

Jewish law made no distinction between the religious and the secular. Everything came under its remit, from how to treat Yaweh himself, to what you ate, how you farmed and did business. Deceiving one's neighbour was as serious as accidentally eating food that should have gone to the priests. All pagans had their taboos about food, but only for the Jews were these rules divine commandments; only the Jews' God commanded that they should not possess inaccurate weights and measures or delay paying a hired man his wages.

Yaweh did not say 'Obey me', but 'Obey my law', and that law was written down. Other gods spoke directly to their people – if they bothered at all – but that meant they had to be physically present in some way to their worshippers, even if, like Isis, they had their sacred books in which the prescribed rituals were inscribed. But once the law was written down, Yaweh could disappear. Indeed when in 63 BC Pompey and his Roman soldiers committed the ultimate violation by entering the Temple's inmost sanctuary, the Holy of Holies, into which only the high priest was allowed to enter once a year, they were amazed to find nothing to loot; the gleaming gold sanctum was empty. There were no statues to him; nor did there need to be. No other pagan god had reached Yahweh's level of abstraction, though some gods had not yet been anthropomorphized (see chapter 8). Worship of Yaweh was, according to the Roman historian Tacitus, 'a novel form of worship, opposed to all that is practised by other men. The Egyptians worship many animals and images of monstrous form; the Jews have purely mental conceptions of Deity.' Yaweh was the most portable of all the gods, because he was the Word.

The Jews' religion, portable and exclusive, was extraordinarily successful as a recipe for survival in the Diaspora. 'It is hard to find a place in the habitable earth that hath not admitted this tribe of men, and is not possessed by them,' noted the geographer Strabo. Five to six million Jews lived in the cities of the Roman Empire – like Paul, an ardent Pharisee, who was born in the port city of Tarsus (in today's southern Turkey). There were in fact more Jews living outside Palestine than in it. They constituted about 5 to 10 per cent of the empire's entire population and were a sizeable minority in most of the important cities of the empire, from the Persian Gulf to Spain.[10]

Because of their extraterritorial cohesiveness, Rome had to treat the Jews in Palestine and in all the cities of the empire as a single group, and had to make special concessions to them. Julius Caesar's gratitude to the Jews of Palestine for supporting him against Pompey in the civil wars was translated into privileges, not just for Palestinian Jews but for all Jews throughout the empire. Augustus confirmed these privileges. He waived Rome's general ban on associations, which were considered to be a potential breeding ground for subversion, and allowed the Jews to assemble for worship. (In gratitude, the Jews in Rome named two of their thirteen synagogues 'synagogues of the Augustans'.) Jews did not have to appear in court on the Sabbath. Rome even permitted the Diaspora Jews to levy their own tax and protected them in doing so. This was an extraordinary concession from a tax-farming empire, and one that was deeply resented by the Greeks who still ran so many of the cities in the Eastern part of the empire. Every male Jew in the ancient world contributed to the daily sacrifices made at the Temple in Jerusalem, and to its upkeep, by paying a Temple tax. Every year gleaming convoys of gold and silver coins left the cities of the empire for Jerusalem. As far as the Greeks were concerned, money was visibly leaking out of their cities, and the convoys were regularly hijacked. But Augustus extended his protection to this rival tax extractor by issuing edicts that the thieves must be delivered up to the Jews and the money returned to them.

Rome recognized that its usual policy of religious co-option, and of absorbing foreign gods into its own pantheon, could not work with the Jews. The jealous Jewish God could not tolerate other gods. Tolerant, inclusive polytheism was up against intolerant, exclusive monotheism.

Monotheist Jews forcibly converted the Palestinian regions of Galilee and Idumaea in the second century BC. Monotheist Christians would later knock the heads off pagan statues, spit as they passed temples, ruthlessly suppress other cults and heavily penalize the Jews. Augustus, on the other hand, was happy to acknowledge the Jews' God and 'ordered that for all time continuous sacrifices of whole burnt offerings should be carried out every day at his own expense as a tribute to the most high God', according to the Jewish Alexandrian philosopher, Philo. Pagan Rome was, by virtue of its polytheism, much more tolerant of other gods, though the Roman religion – its gods and festivals – predominated. But failure to participate in or contribute to the Roman cults was considered suspicious, a sign of potential disloyalty, since it was through the cults, and above all through the countless festivals associated with them, that Rome tried to make its subjects Romans, to give them a pride in Rome and a sense of solidarity.

In 16 BC, however, Augustus excused all Jews from participating in the new imperial cult, even though the cult was such a crucial part of Augustus' strategy to unify a vast empire in loyalty to him and legitimize him as Rome's emperor. Sacrifices to the emperor were required of every province and city; they symbolized allegiance to Rome. Only the Jews were exempted, though they did have to make sacrifices for the emperor's welfare. As a good client king, Herod the Great ordered that the priests of the Temple should make daily sacrifices (two lambs and a bull) 'on behalf of' Augustus and 'the people of Rome'.[11] These sacrifices would become a running sore for a growing number of Jews, until in AD 66 the Temple priests finally refused to perform them. Their refusal marked for Josephus 'the true beginning of our war with the Romans'.

Of all the myriad peoples scattered around its empire only the

Greeks outdid the Jews as a racially identifiable group with special privileges, which was why the Greeks resented the Jews and were occasionally perpetrators of appalling pogroms against them. Ever since the Macedonian Greek Alexander the Great had conquered the Persian Empire in the fourth century BC, Greeks had colonized and ruled countless cities from the Mediterranean to Afghanistan, and were a dominating presence even in the Judaean capital of Caesarea. But in Alexandria, Antioch and other major Greek cities of the empire, the Jews lived in what was virtually a city within a city. They were 'citizens' of the *politeuma*, which administered its own internal affairs through its own officials.

The *politeuma*'s powers relative to that of the city-wide Greek-run council, the *demos*, was always a source of friction. To be a citizen of the *politeuma* did not entail, as being a citizen of the *demos* did, Roman citizenship with all its privilege: exemption from taxation, the right to stand for office in the wider city outside the *politeuma*, and protection under the law.

After his stay in Jerusalem in 15 BC, Agrippa, accompanied by Herod, had visited numerous Greek-run cities in the Eastern provinces and listened to the complaints of delegates from the Jewish communities. The Jews complained that the Greeks were clawing back the religious privileges and exemptions that had been granted them by Rome. Herod's minister and biographer, the lean red-faced Nicolaus of Damascus, a Greek or Hellenized Syrian, put the case for the Jews at a tribunal presided over by Agrippa: the Greeks were forcing Jews to appear in court on the Sabbath and other holy days and interfering with the transmission of the sacred Temple money to Jerusalem. The Greeks did not deny this, but argued that the Jews were not fulfilling their side of the bargain; in order to be citizens with the rights that that entailed, they must integrate themselves into pagan civil life and worship the local gods, but they refused to do that. Agrippa sided with the Jews and confirmed their privileges. The Jews expressed their gratitude by naming one of their synagogues in Rome 'synagogue of the Agrippans'.

The extraordinary concessions that the Jews had won from Rome came at a cost: the Jews were resented for their privileges and for the exclusiveness by which they had won those privileges. Furthermore, that exclusiveness made it impossible for religious Jews to live easily under their imperial rulers or with all the diverse peoples who found themselves violently jammed up against each other in the Graeco-Roman cities. 'The lawgiver fenced us about with impregnable palisades and walls of iron, so that we should in no way have dealings with any of the other nations,' wrote Aristeas, the pilgrim from Alexandria who visited Jerusalem in the first century BC.[12] The Jewish creed was precisely one of anti-assimilation: assimilation was in a sense forbidden by God.

Jews took different approaches to the problem of accommodating Roman rule and the Gentile world, and were more or less strict followers of the law. They often chose to live together, as did other ethnic groups in the empire's packed cities – any one of the strangers who streamed into the cities every day could find the street or quarter where his fellow countrymen lived and had established cults of their native gods. But while some Jews tried to maintain as little contact as possible, others visited pagan shrines and temples, performed pagan rituals, attended the public games and called their children after the pagan gods – Isidora (Isis), Serapion (Isis' consort Serapis), Herakleides (Hercules).[13] Synagogues welcomed 'God-fearers' – Gentiles who were attracted to Judaism by its very exclusiveness, its monotheistic rigour and high moral standards – and all Gentiles were allowed to bring offerings for sacrifice at the Temple.

But such inclusiveness only went so far. Gentiles caught trespassing beyond the Court of the Gentiles in the Temple could be, and indeed were, killed. On the stone wall separating the Court of the Gentiles from the inner courts were tablets inscribed with a warning notice in Greek and Latin: 'No foreigner is to enter within the forecourt and the balustrade around the sanctuary. Whoever is caught will have himself to blame for his subsequent death.'[14] It was no light threat. In AD 57 Paul, the former ardent Pharisee and persecutor of Jesus' followers, was arrested in the Temple on suspicion of having taken a Gentile beyond the Court of the Gentiles. The ultimate penalty for such a blasphemy was to be stoned to death; Paul successfully pleaded his rights as a Roman citizen to be tried under Roman law. Leviticus may have told Jews to 'love thy neighbour as thyself', but the neighbour was 'a child of thy people',[15] and Deuteronomy told them 'Not to intermarry with Gentiles'.[16] Tacitus noted sourly: 'among themselves they are inflexibly honest and ever ready to shew compassion, though they regard the rest of mankind with all the hatred of enemies'.

Judaism attracted God-fearers, but it deterred converts – proselytes. Not only did proselytes have to obey the strict law, and the men have to be circumcised, but they were told that 'the world was created only for the sake of Israel, and only Israel were called children of God, and only Israel are dear before God'.* Jews in antiquity were divided about how 'Jewish' these proselytes could ever really become. On the whole, Gentile converts were treated as a separate and sometimes less privileged group.[17] They prayed to 'your God' not 'our God'; they were denied a seat on the Sanhedrin, the legislative and judicial body that governed Palestinian and to some extent Diaspora Jews; and women converts were barred from marrying into priestly families.

Herod's alienation from his subjects was compounded by the fact that he was considered not just as a usurper by the aristocratic supporters of the Hasmonean regime he had ousted, and not just as an irreligious, sometimes blasphemous, Jew by the religious, but also as being only 'a half Jew', and not a proper Jew at that.[18] Herod's mother was probably a Gentile from the neighbouring Arabian kingdom of Nabataea, home of Rome's nemesis in Arabia, Syllaeus; Herod's father's family came from Idumaea, the district south of Jerusalem. Like Galilee, Idumaea had been forcibly converted to

---

* *Babylonian Talmud, Gerim* 1.1. See also *Exodus* 19:5–6. This is admittedly part of a Palestinian conversion formula written after the Jewish revolts, when Jewish identity became even more of an issue.

Judaism only 100 years earlier by the Hasmoneans when they ruled over an independent and expansionist Palestine. As a result, Idumaeans were often despised by the religious Jews, who considered themselves to be inheritors of the real Judaism while the Idumaeans were only converts.

But Herod's major fault in the eyes of the religious Jews was that he was too much of a Roman and not enough of a Jew. The Jewish religion, certainly as conceived by the Pharisees, was particularly unsuitable for an empire: the jealous and demanding nature of their God meant that the Jews had constantly to decide if and when God's law and Rome's law were at odds, and if so whose law they should then follow. Rome never experienced such a catastrophic breakdown of relations with any other of its conquered peoples as it did with the Jews of Palestine in AD 66. Other regions of the empire revolted against Roman rule and the Romanization of their rulers, but in most of these cases local patriotism died remarkably quickly.[19] But, for the Jews, religion and nationalism were inextricably bound together in a way that was unique in the empire. Yaweh's promise of the promised land was in a sense a call to revolt against Roman rule: the massive glittering Temple, where the Pharisees had staged their protest against the eagle, was the embodiment of that promise whose fulfilment was frustrated by Rome.

It was the Pharisees who began the radicalization of a growing number of Jews. They were in a sense the fundamentalist populists of their time. Although the Gospel writers portray the Pharisees as over-scrupulous hypocrites – and indeed the Pharisees delighted in referring to themselves as 'the righteous' and all their opponents as 'the wicked'* – they were deliberately trying to create a more sympathetic, more egalitarian religion than the other two major movements within the Jewish religion, the Essenes and the Sadducees.

The Essenes believed in a religion for a religious elite. Judging

---

* 'Pharisee' probably derives from the Hebrew word *parush*, meaning 'separate'.

from the content of the Dead Sea Scrolls,* which most scholars now believe were written by the Essenes, they demanded a rigorously monastic life of chastity and poverty, which few were able or willing to lead. Pliny the Elder, in a rare moment of enthusiasm, described the Essenes as 'marvellous beyond all others throughout the whole earth, for they have no women among them; to sexual desire they are strangers; money they have none; the palm-trees are their only companions.'[20]

Josephus, who sampled all three groups and eventually plumped for the Pharisees at the age of nineteen, disliked the 'boorish', arrogant behaviour of the Sadducees, the lay and priestly aristocracy. Living in their spacious Roman villas in Jerusalem's upper city on the hills, cut off from the densely populated alleyways of the poorer part of Jerusalem below, the Sadducees had dominated the religious and political life of Jews by controlling the priesthood and the Temple, the spiritual and political heart of Jewry. The priesthood was hereditary and only priests could perform the essential sacrifices and rituals to God in the Temple. The Sadducees also formed the majority on the Sanhedrin which met in the Hall of Hewn Stones built into the north wall of the Temple.

But, probably during the first century BC, the Pharisees started taking the Jewish religion out of the Temple and out of the hands of the Sadducee priests. The Pharisees were part of the new wave of the urban 'middle classes' who were prospering under the *pax Romana* and beginning to assert themselves against the old aristocratic hold over religion and government. They were mostly merchants or traders, as were their sympathizers. Excluded from the aristocratic priesthood, the Pharisees were lay scholar-theologians, who remoulded the Jewish religion into one that was both more populist but also more demanding – the paradoxical combination common to so many religious fundamentalist movements. Like all

---

* The scrolls, a collection of documents found in caves near Qumran by the Dead Sea, contain the Essenes' rules of initiation and for living in their religious community nearby, as well as their biblical interpretations.

fundamentalists, the Pharisees were a mix of modernizer, traditionalist and egalitarian. 'God gave all the people the heritage, the kingdom, the priesthood, and the holiness', the Pharisees maintained.[21]

In particular, the Pharisees were anxious to redefine the Sadducaic conception of the law that Yaweh had given his people. The Sadducee priests had claimed the law for themselves. In their view, the ritual purification rules, including those that related to unclean meat, were intended for them alone: it was they and the meals they celebrated at the Temple that were sanctified, not the ordinary people and their everyday meals.

Not only had the Sadducees taken possession of the law, but they had further excluded ordinary Jews by making it extremely difficult to follow. According to the Sadducees, the law consisted only of the commandments which God gave to Moses on Mount Sinai and which were written down in the first five books of the scriptures, the Torah. This meant in effect that ordinary Jews struggled to follow rules that were prescribed centuries earlier under vastly different social and economic conditions; it meant that only a specialized priestly caste could really obey God's law. The Torah was equally sacred to the Pharisees, who would bless themselves by tracing the shape of the sacred letter tau from forehead to breast and from shoulder to shoulder (a gesture only given up when it was adopted by the Christians).[22] The Pharisees' brilliant innovation was to claim that God had imparted to his people not only the commandments and prohibitions that Moses had written down, but also a body of laws and traditions that had been passed down orally from generation to generation, what Josephus called the 'tradition of the fathers'.

By including oral tradition within Jewish law, the Pharisees could interpret the law more flexibly and so transform an austere religion tailored by and for the elite into a warmer, more all-embracing one. The Sadducees saw the Sabbath and holy days as Temple festivals, restricted to the religious elite. According to their strict interpretation of Moses' command, on these days ordinary people should 'bide

1. Apollonius, the miracle worker and wandering holy man, was a near contemporary of Jesus, and at the time, much more famous.

2. Livia, a 'Ulysses in petticoats' and alleged murderess, engineered the deification of her husband, Augustus, and headed his cult.

3. A house in Marib in the incense-rich kingdom of Sheba (today's Yemen). The wealthy built their houses for defence not display, much to the disappoint- ment of looting Roman soldiers.

4. Maecenas, aristocratic aesthete, 'soft comforter of adulteresses' and brilliant spin doctor. In the battle for Augustus' favour, he lost to the morally upstanding populist, Agrippa.

5. Agrippa, the 'man of the people', played a major role in constructing an imperial regime under the guise of restoring the republic.

6. Tiberius, the charmless and politically inept successor to his stepfather, Augustus. Tiberius appointed Pontius Pilate and was emperor at the time of Jesus' death.

7. Josephus commanded his fellow Jews in the revolt against the Romans of AD 66, but then switched sides. Apart from the Apostles and Tacitus, he is the only near-contemporary writer to mention Jesus.

8. The Kiosk, a small temple at Naqa in the kingdom of Meroe (today's Sudan), ruled by the fat, one-eyed goddess Candace Amanirenas – one of the last traditional ruler gods. The temple mixes an Egyptian-style entrance with Roman columns and arched windows.

9. Bronze statue believed to be the chief of the Suren clan who led the Parthians to victory over the Romans. He was later beheaded for his success by his insecure king.

10. Banqueters from a second century AD tomb in Palmyra. Reflecting the city's position in the Syrian desert between the Roman and Parthian empires, the elite were Hellenized yet retained their Near Eastern identity, this carving also combining Near Eastern stiffness with Hellenistic forms and dress.

11. Merchants from Babylon (in modern Iraq) imported their supreme god Bel to Palmyra and built a temple to him at the eastern end of the main street. The temple combines Corinthian columns with Babylonian-style, triangular-wedged battlements.

every man in his place', and were not allowed to carry anything in or out of their homes. The Sadducees had considered 'place' to mean a single dwelling. But according to the Pharisees' far more accommodating definition, which was frowned on by the Sadducees, 'place' meant something much larger; they defined 'place' as that which was included within the *eruv*, a ritual enclosure which created a single unit, a place beyond the actual physical boundaries of the home. A neighbourhood could therefore become a 'place' if it was enclosed, and a number of houses could count as a single house if they were surrounded by a wall or 'fused' together by doorposts and lintels. So neighbours and friends could visit each other in their walled courtyards, and along their narrow alleyways, carrying their babies with them; they could bring each other food, and share meals. The Pharisees turned an austere, rather joyless day into a festal one.

The Sadducees, with the naturally conservative tendency of all aristocracies that want to maintain their own hold on power, clung to an interpretation of the Jewish religion that was colder, more difficult and less welcoming than the version that was being fashioned by the eventual victors in this battle for the soul of the Jewish religion, the more flexible Pharisees. Sadducaic Judaism was a religion for the powerful. It emphasized that man alone was responsible for his good and bad actions. As Josephus pointed out, the Sadducees shared with the Epicureans this bleak but splendidly self-reliant view of man in relation to God. The Epicureans believed that the gods existed but did not believe that they influenced human life (they also denied the idea of an afterlife); the Sadducees similarly rejected the comforts of an interfering God – their God was an all-powerful but disappearing God who left man to his own devices. The Sadducean view was a sort of 'practical atheism'.[23] The Pharisaic view, on the other hand, was more comforting. Josephus thought it had similarities with Stoicism, which was overtaking Epicureanism in popularity amongst the Roman elite (see chapter 2).

The Pharisaic liberation of the law from total dependence on the Torah, meant that the Pharisees could offer one of the most comforting prospects that religion can provide – life after death, and the promise of eternal happiness for the righteous (with the downside, naturally, of eternal punishment for the wicked). The Pharisees were happy to embrace such an obviously appealing idea, even though it was only hinted at in the Book of Daniel, and may have been imported from Zoroastrianism by the Jews returning from Babylonian exile in the sixth century BC. The Sadducees denied any form of afterlife; it was not explicitly mentioned in the Torah.

Not surprisingly, the Pharisaic scholars' more accessible interpretation of the law gained in popularity, especially amongst the socially aspiring who had previously been excluded from the privileges of the religious hierarchy. Josephus reckoned that, during the reign of Herod the Great, there were 6,000 men who explicitly identified themselves as Pharisees. Given that they also had a number of supporters and sympathizers, this made the Pharisees a significant force in Herod's Judaea, which had a total population of about 800,000.[24]

The Pharisees, Josephus said, had 'the support of the masses and are extremely influential among the townsfolk', while the Sadducees 'have none but the rich on their side'.[25] The Pharisees preached in the synagogues they were building in the cities and villages of Palestine and throughout the empire. They formed groups devoted to mutual support, where Pharisees could together observe the strict ritual purity laws they believed were essential for a religious Jew. They preached to hundreds of students – Paul would later be one of them – some of whom would be radicalized by the Pharisees' fundamentalism, their religious fervour and their religious egalitarianism.

By insisting that obedience to the law was possible for everyone, not just the priests, the Pharisees were saying that everyone must obey the law; by including within the law the oral interpretations and customs that had grown up around it, the Pharisees extended the law's remit beyond the ritualized activities of the priest to all aspects of everyday life. The Gospel writers caricatured the Pharisees as being obsessed with minor points of religious law and show Jesus attacking the burdens of legal observance that the Pharisees put on ordinary people.[26] But for the Pharisees the whole of life, including its smallest detail, was invested with religious significance. And that had political consequences. For the more the Jews observed their own religious law, the more difficult it became for them to live as good Romans under pagan rule in what the scriptures told them was their promised land.

Yet the Pharisees had initially backed Herod, the 'half-Jew', the candidate of Rome, in his battle for the throne against the ruling Hasmonean dynasty of Palestine. In 37 BC, supported by thousands of Roman troops, Herod, the son of one of Palestine's chief ministers, camped in the olive groves outside the walls of Jerusalem where the Hasmonean King Aristobulus and his Sadducee supporters were making their last stand. After the siege had dragged on for five months, two of the Pharisees' most influential scholars, Hillel and Shammai, urged the starving inhabitants to open their gates to Herod. Herod, they said, 'was an infliction from Heaven, God's scourge and instrument of judgement', but he had to be endured.

The Pharisees were not concerned about who ruled them. They were engaged in a battle for the soul of Judaism – their efforts to open up the religion to ordinary Jews versus the Sadducees' desire to keep it under the tight control of a few aristocratic families. For the Pharisees, rule by Rome or by a king who was loyal to Rome was not in itself a problem. As long as their law was not violated and they could impose their version of it, quietism was the price they were prepared to pay. And Herod was happy to have the support of the Pharisees. They shared a mutual enemy in the Sadducees who had supported the Hasmonean king against Herod. On taking the throne of Judaea, Herod executed about forty Sadducean members of the Sanhedrin and replaced many of them with Pharisees.

But it was clear even at the celebrations for his coronation in 37 BC, when he sacrificed at the temple of Jupiter on the Capitoline Hill in Rome, that Herod was on a different mission from the Pharisees.

The Pharisees were ambitious for their religion, Herod for his kingdom. He believed that success for him and for Palestine meant acknowledging Rome's dominance. The Romans were, he said, 'the rulers of the whole world'. Herod became one of Rome's most loyal client kings and in many ways his loyalty paid off. Augustus rewarded him with a large territory east of Galilee, including the modern Golan Heights, and Palestine grew more prosperous as trade expanded.

Because of the Jewish ban on images, we know almost nothing of Herod's appearance except that he probably dyed his hair, and wore magnificently decorated greatcoats imported from Parthia. But, thanks to Josephus and the Gospel writers, Herod still lives vividly for us as the archetypal tyrant: cruel, mad, sexually rampant and a murderer. According to Josephus, Herod 'was brutish and a stranger to all humanity', though Josephus was not an entirely impartial judge: he claimed to be related to the Hasmonean dynasty that Herod had ousted and was writing his history not just for the Emperor Titus but for Titus' Jewish mistress Berenice who was also a Hasmonean.

Herod was, in fact, probably only marginally more appalling than the imperial family of Rome or his fellow Near Eastern rulers in the savagery with which he kept the lid on opposition and ruthlessly exterminated his suspected enemies – including large numbers of his own family whom he accused of conspiring with the remnants of the Hasmonean royal family. He had three of his sons executed and the most beloved of his ten wives, Mariamne, killed, along with her mother and her seventeen-year-old brother Aristobulus, the last of the male Hasmoneans. During a royal feast Aristobulus was drowned in Herod's swimming pool by a group of Herod's guards, who held him under the water while pretending to play a boisterous game in the deep end.

Herod's potential enemies were not just the former ruling party of Hasmoneans and their Sadducean aristocratic supporters, but an increasing number of Pharisees who found Herod more and more suspect as a Jew the better he became as a loyal Roman client king. He 'left no suitable spot within his realm destitute of some mark of homage to Caesar,' according to Josephus. Herod's massive building works created mini Romes in Jerusalem, Jericho, Stratonospyrgos (which he renamed Caesarea), and his favourite city Samaria, which he renamed Sebaste, the Greek form of Augustus.

The Temple itself, one of the biggest building projects in the entire empire, which was Herod's attempt to prove his religious piety to his Jewish subjects, was Hellenistic in style. The giant Corinthian pillars, topped with bronze capitals in the Court of the Gentiles, testified to Graeco-Roman domination at the very heart of the Jewish nation.

Jews were also shocked by his introduction of barbaric Roman entertainments. Every five years Herod laid on spectacular games in honour of Augustus at the amphitheatres in Jerusalem and Caesarea. Naked athletes, wrestlers, charioteers and musicians from around the empire competed for the great prizes Herod offered. But what was anathema to many Jews were the contests between lions or other wild beasts and condemned criminals; they thought it was 'barefaced impiety', said Josephus, 'to throw men to wild beasts, for the affording delight to the spectators and it seemed a further impiety to change their established ways for foreign practices'.

According to Josephus, Herod apologized to his Jewish subjects for being obliged 'to transgress the customs of his nation, and to set aside many of their laws' by saying 'that all was done, not out of his own inclinations, but by the commands and injunctions of others, in order to please Caesar and the Romans'.

But for Herod it was easy to please Rome at the cost of what seemed to him merely minor infractions of Jewish law. He had become part of the global Hellenized aristocracy created by the Roman Empire, connected by ties of marriage, friendship and diplomacy: his daughter-in-law, the Anatolian Princess Glaphyra, married the brilliant polymath King Juba of Mauretania, while Herod himself travelled to Ionia in modern-day Turkey with his great friend Agrippa, the second most powerful man in the empire (see chapter 2). It was an aristocracy whose members sent their sons and daughters to be educated in Rome, who were steeped in Graeco-

Roman culture and who had probably more in common with each other than with their lowlier fellow countrymen.

The client king's relationship with his subjects was always a potentially uneasy one. For a people who felt their own traditions and customs to be under threat, the embrace of Rome by the king and his elite could all too easily be seen as collaboration with the conqueror. King Juba of Mauretania, as loyal a client king as King Herod himself, was considered to have become too Romanized by many of his tribesmen, who would eventually rise in revolt (see chapter 16). But in Judaea, thanks in part to the Pharisees' insistence on wider obedience to the law, Herod's Romanization had become not just an offence against their customs and identity, but an intolerable offence against God.

When the rumour spread that Herod had decorated his new theatre in Jerusalem with armoured statues, religious Jews were outraged. Herod had in fact been sensitive to the issue of idolatry and had ensured that the 'statues' at the theatre were actually just pieces of wood with armour and weapons attached. Unaware of this, ten men plotted to enter the theatre with daggers hidden under their cloaks and kill Herod. An informant alerted Herod's guards. The conspirators were dragged to the palace where they willingly confessed and proclaimed that their plot was 'a holy and pious action' to preserve 'those common customs of their country which all Jews were obliged to observe, or die for'. The men were led away to execution and, in the words of Josephus, 'patiently underwent all the torments inflicted on them until they died'.

In 6 BC Herod ordered his people to swear a joint oath of loyalty to him and to Augustus, as was common practice among many client kings. When some Pharisees refused because they feared it might involve worship of the emperor's statues, he executed them.

Two years later, Pharisee students smashed the golden eagle Herod had placed in the Temple, spurred on by their teachers Judas and Matthias. Armed with their new doctrine of resurrection, they proclaimed – or at least Josephus proclaimed for them in the sort of set speech that all ancient historians delighted in putting in their subjects' mouths – that it was 'a glorious thing to die for the laws of their country; because that the soul was immortal, and that an eternal enjoyment of happiness did await such as died on that account'.

As the Pharisees and their sympathizers began hacking the golden eagle to pieces with axes, Herod's soldiers came running through the underground passageways that linked the Temple to the Antonia Fortress where they were stationed. Most of the crowd fled but forty held their ground along with Judas and Matthias. They were taken in chains to Jericho. In order to preside over their trial, Herod – now terminally ill, probably with bowel cancer – endured the agonies of the 17-mile journey (about a day's horseback riding) along the dry riverbed hemmed in by steep cliffs that threaded its way through the barren hills and valleys of the Judaean Desert.

Jericho, below the cliffs of the desert in the Great Rift Valley west of the Jordan River (in today's West Bank; the state of Israel continues to use the names 'Judaea and Samaria'), was Rome transplanted to an oasis of date palms and balsam. It was here that Herod had his winter palace with its red and black colonnaded courtyards, and its gardens where storks paced amongst the fountains and pools of clear water, and where Herod's entourage cooled themselves in the palace's Roman baths.

From the palace Herod was carried to the amphitheatre where the rebels were tried. Their fate was probably a foregone conclusion, and would inevitably be inflammatory, because of the Pharisees' growing influence and popularity. So that the anger the trial was bound to provoke was not focused solely on him, Herod had ordered that the rebels should be tried publicly by the most important Jews of the country. Too weak to sit up, Herod lay on a couch and delivered a violent tirade against the ingratitude of his Jewish subjects. In Josephus' account of the trial, 'He enumerated the many labours that he had long endured on their account, and his building of the Temple, and what a vast charge that was to him; while the Hasmoneans, during the 125 years of their government, had not been able to perform any so great a work for the honour of God.'

If Herod had done no more than publicly display his devotion to God, then he would have been exactly the sort of ruler that the Pharisees had hoped for when they supported his struggle to seize the throne – a client king who kept Rome happy by paying taxes and keeping order, but otherwise remained a good religious Jew who allowed the Pharisees space to impose their version of the Jewish religion on the Jewish people. But politically, culturally and by accident of birth, Herod could not do this. He saw Palestine's future as dependent on Rome's goodwill, and therefore wanted overtly to prove his country's loyalty; he was attracted by Graeco-Roman culture and by the glamour of the Hellenized global aristocracy; and as an outsider, an Idumaean Jew with a non-Jewish mother, he perhaps never quite understood the visceral importance of the law.

The Pharisee rebels' defiant answer to Herod summed up why he and Rome could never win in Palestine. 'We will undergo death', they said, 'and all sorts of punishments which you can inflict upon us, with pleasure, since we are conscious to ourselves that we shall die, not for any unrighteous actions, but for our love to religion.'

On 13 March 4 BC, the two Pharisee leaders and their forty students were burned alive. That evening there was a total eclipse of the moon. And probably around this time Yeshua or Joshua (Hebrew for 'saviour'; Jesus is the Greek rendering) was born.

7

GALILEE: JESUS AND THE MESSIAH-BANDITS

Can anything good come from Nazareth?

Gospel of John,1:46, *c.*AD 90–100

Surely the Messiah is not to come from Galilee?

Gospel of John, 7:41

And now Judaea was full of robberies; and as the several companies of the rebellious lighted upon anyone to head them, he was created a king immediately, in order to do mischief to the public.

Josephus, *Jewish Antiquities*, XVII.285, AD 93–94

The Jews have a passion for liberty that is almost unconquerable, since they are convinced that God alone is their leader and master

Josephus, *Jewish Antiquities*, XVIII.1.6

In Galilee, the most beautiful and fertile of all the districts of Palestine, a young Galilean became famous for his holiness, his loving kindness and his miraculous powers. He preached to huge crowds of peasants amongst walnut, fig and palm tree groves, or to the fishermen on the shores of the heart-shaped Sea – or rather freshwater lake – of Galilee. With his followers, he wandered through Galilee's dense network of fortified villages, where families shared a courtyard for cooking, where the whitewashed houses were filled with the sweetish smell of rancid olive oil and on hot summer nights families slept on the roofs under tents of branches. He exorcized demons, healed sick children from a distance, created bread out of nothing and transformed vinegar into oil. This holy man addressed his prayers to his father in Heaven, and was called 'son of God' (in Hebrew or Aramaic this was meant in the metaphorical sense of being a child of God rather than the more literal Graeco-Roman sense of being of the same nature as a god[1]). He lived a life of total poverty – much to his wife's annoyance. His name was Hanina ben Dosa and he was probably the most famous of all the holy men in Galilee.

Galilee probably had more holy men, or Hasidim, living a life of poverty and performing miracles and healings than any other district of Palestine. During the days when Josephus was sampling all the major religious movements within Judaism, he went to live in the desert for three years with Bannus, a man who 'used no other clothing than grew upon trees and had no other food than what grew of its own accord, and bathed himself in cold water frequently, both by day and by night, in order to preserve his chastity'.[2] As for miracles, people in the ancient world found nothing surprising in the idea of exceptional people performing exceptional deeds: Tactitus, a supremely level-headed historian, reports without mockery that the Emperor Vespasian (the former Roman general who would capture and then befriend Josephus during the Jewish revolt of AD 66 to 73/4) healed a blind man and a man with a diseased hand, adding in corroboration: 'Persons actually present attest both facts, even now when nothing is to be gained by falsehood.'[3] Many Jews relied on the healing powers of an exorcist since they believed that demons were responsible for spiritual as well as bodily evils; an exorcist was anyway probably as efficacious, certainly cheaper, than a medical doctor, and desperately needed. Life expectancy at birth was around 30 per cent, women suffered chronic infections from childbirth and abortion, and disease was visible everywhere, in stunted limbs and deformities and the skin rashes and leprosy which barred Jews from entering the Temple because they were impure.[4]

The Judaeans despised the Galileans for being country bumpkins living in a rural backwater; they mocked their guttural accents and their mispronunciation of Hebrew. But they especially criticized

Galileans for their ignorance of, or pragmatic approach to, the law – which they put down in part to the fact that Galilee had only been converted to Judaism in *c.*104 BC (see chapter 6), but which was also due to Galilee's distance from Jerusalem.

Partly because they were geographically so far from Jerusalem to the south, the Galileans were relatively free of the control of the Sadducee priests in the Temple. Galileans still made their pilgrimages to Jerusalem, passing through the hostile district of the Samaritans to do so. But the Temple priests could not dominate political and religious life in Galilee as they still did, despite the growing popularity of the Pharisees, in Jerusalem and the surrounding district of Judaea. The Galileans developed their own distinctive form of Judaism, under the control of the holy men, not the Sadducee priests in the Temple. Hanina, and his fellow holy men, posed a threat to established religious authority and orthodoxy. The Hasidim were as lax about strict observance of the law as Jesus would be.

Hanina was called the 'man of deeds', meaning that he was a miracle worker, though some scholars now say that a 'man of deeds' meant simply a Hasid. He was probably younger than Jesus, whose miracles were also described as 'deeds' by Luke and by Josephus. But Hanina never claimed to be the Messiah, whereas Jesus, or at least his disciples speaking for him, did. This was an extraordinarily dangerous claim to make, since it represented a direct challenge to Roman rule. At the time of Jesus' birth around 4 BC, would-be Messiahs were 'sprouting as quickly as mushrooms in damp soil', according to the historian of religion Martin Hengel.[5]

Originally 'Messiah' meant simply the king or high priest anointed with holy oil.* But in what are thought to be the later parts of the

---

* Until the time that Christians took over the symbol of the cross, the high priest was anointed with the shape of the Hebrew letter *tau*, the last letter of the alphabet, which could be written as an upright or diagonal cross. For Jews, as for the earliest Christians, the symbolic meaning of *tau* was attached to a letter, not a shape: it was the Word of God, not the cross. It was only later that the shape itself, the cross, took on a defining religious significance and the Hebrew *tau* came to be connected with the Greek letter that perhaps looked most like it, the letter *chi*, the first letter of the word *Christos*, Greek for Messiah, the anointed one.

Book of Isaiah, written during and after the Babylonian exile in the sixth century BC, the Messiah king as prophesied by Isaiah took on a far more elevated role. He became the focus for the Jews' longing for their homeland. With the coming of the Messiah, God and the Jewish people would have fulfilled their promises to each other. The Jews scattered around the world would be returned to their homeland and the Messiah would rule over a righteous nation. 'The Jewish people will experience eternal joy and gladness', proclaims the Book of Isaiah; 'Nations will recognize the wrongs they did Israel'[6] (a prophecy which must have been balm to exiled, conquered, scattered Jews) and the Jews' God would be recognized by the whole world: 'For My House [the Temple] shall be called a house of prayer for all nations,'[7] a triumphal but inclusive proclamation which is written on the front of synagogues to this day. The Messiah combined the spiritual and the nationalistic.

According to the prophecies of Isaiah, Jeremiah and Mikah, the Messiah would be descended from David, who ruled over the first united Jewish kingdom based in Jerusalem in the eleventh century BC, and had over the centuries become idealized as priest-king. The two Gospels that mention Jesus' birth are keen, therefore, to establish Jesus' connection with King David, in order to 'prove' that Jesus was the Messiah. Matthew's Gospel indeed begins with a laborious family tree tracing Jesus' adopted father Joseph's descent back to David (and beyond that to Abraham), while in Luke's account, the angel Gabriel refers to Jesus' 'father David'.

In order to emphasize the fact that Jesus was indeed the Messiah, it was important that Jesus and his messianic precursor King David should share the same birthplace, the large hilltop village of Bethlehem, in Judaea, that was famous even at the end of the first century BC as the home of the young David. He had watched his father's sheep in the surrounding terraced hills, with their low stone walls, vineyards and olive orchards, the purple-tinted Mountains of Moab above and the valleys below stretching away eastwards to the Wilderness of Judaea and the Dead Sea. Matthew implies that Jesus' family was already living in Bethlehem (just 6 miles from Jerusalem) at the time of Jesus' birth. Although Luke describes the family as living in the tiny white limestone village of Nazareth in Galilee, far to the north of Jerusalem, he also has Jesus born in Bethlehem. Unfortunately, the reason he provides for the family's journey there from Nazareth undermines his credibility as a historian. According to Luke, the family was obeying an order from Rome to take part in a census so that Judaea could be properly assessed for tax. There was indeed a census, but it was not until AD 6, the year when Rome took over direct control of Judaea. However, Luke, like Matthew, explicitly states that Jesus was born during the reign of King Herod. Herod died shortly after a lunar eclipse, which has been dated by astrologers as March 13 4 BC. He was, therefore, most definitely dead by the time of the census in AD 6. Furthermore, there was no reason for Joseph to take part in the census at all. Luke's explanation was that Joseph's ancestor, King David, was born there. The Romans, however, were not interested in ancestry but in the people they could tax there and then; and since Joseph was living in Nazareth in Galilee, which was still nominally independent of Roman rule, its inhabitants were not subject to the census.

The census would polarize the Jews and turn some into terrorists. Some would refuse to comply with the census; others – Jesus' family among them, according to Luke – would obey. By that time the figure of the Messiah, descended from David of Bethlehem, had acquired a more militant edge,[8] which would cost Jesus his life (see chapter 18). This new, more aggressive Messiah was defined most clearly in the Psalms of Solomon, probably written by the Pharisees some time either during the reign of Herod the Great or a little earlier, around 63 BC during the civil war between Pompey and Julius Caesar, when Pompey's troops had battered down the walls of Jerusalem, and desecrated the Temple.

The Psalms were an attempt to explain how God allowed the Romans to violate the Temple, bring an end to Palestine's independence and take thousands of Jewish prisoners of war to

Rome as slaves (when they were freed, they formed the backbone of the sizeable Jewish community in Rome). The Pharisees may also have been trying to absolve themselves from their initial support of the Romans, and subsequently Herod: Roman rule, according to the Psalms, was God's way of punishing the nation for the irreligious and blasphemous behaviour of the Hasmonean rulers and perhaps by implication their Sadducee supporters. The Hasmoneans 'laid waste the throne of David in tumultuous arrogance. But Thou, O God, didst cast them down and remove their seed from the earth, In that there rose up against them a man that was alien to our race'.[9] Whether this 'alien' was Pompey or Herod is not clear, but crucially the Psalms now envisage a Messiah who is not just appointed by God to *rule* over a righteous nation but must *vanquish* the Jews' oppressors in order to do so. 'Gird him with strength that he may shatter unrighteous rulers', the Psalmists beseech God, 'And that he may purge Jerusalem from nations that trample (her) down to destruction... He shall destroy the godless nations with the word of his mouth; At his rebuke nations shall flee before him.'

For some Pharisees and their supporters this was, in fact, a hymn to insurrection. The new Messiah could not be anything but a rebel and a violent one who would 'smash the arrogance of sinners like a potter's jar'. He had to overthrow the irreligious, alien ruler before he could preside over an eternal kingdom of righteousness ruled according to the law. And his coming was now expected imminently. Such a message could not but be inflammatory and destabilizing. And the more Roman Herod made the country, the more salient the new militant Messiah became.

When 'wise men from the East' arrived at Herod's court in Jerusalem, enquiring after the new King of the Jews – as described by the Gospel of Matthew – it was hardly surprising that Herod 'was troubled'. In a land rife with Messiahs, here was yet another apparent threat to his rule. But this one was invested with the dual authority of the wise men themselves and a star traditionally associated with the birth of all great men: Augustus' own birth was, according to Suetonius, heralded by a star.

The writer of the Gospel of Matthew is entirely vague as to who the wise men were or where they came from, and certainly never mentions how many there were. The earliest Christians assumed they were Zoroastrian priests, or magi, from Parthia, probably from the Parthian city of Babylon (in modern Iraq).* It was not until the end of the second century AD that the North African Church Father Tertullian gave the wise men the grander status of kings, so that they would fulfil the Old Testament prophecies that the Messiah was worshipped by kings.[10] And it was not until the sixth century that the kings acquired what have become their traditional names of Balthasar, Melchior and Caspar.

For Matthew, it was important that the first worshippers of Jesus should be non-Jews.** His Gospel was written, like the other Gospels, after Paul had remoulded Jesus from a holy man for the Jews into the saviour of all mankind. Moreover, it was probably written only ten or twenty years after the Romans had defeated the rebel Jews and razed Jerusalem and the Temple to the ground in AD 70. Jesus, the Jew and the Messiah, had to be distanced from the Jews who had become so fatally tainted by revolt.

It was a testament to Jesus' appeal to Gentiles that the wise men, members of an esteemed and learned elite, should make the 500-mile journey from Parthia, bringing with them gifts of gold, frankincense and myrrh, the most expensive commodities in the ancient world. To some early Christian writers these gifts showed that the wise men were not magi at all, but merchants from Southern Arabia, though a tradition had also grown up that one of them was

---

* Jews from the Parthian city of Babylon were often mistaken for magi. These Jews, descendants of the Jews who remained in Babylon after their release from exile in the sixth century BC, still travelled regularly to Jerusalem for the important religious festivals, dressed in the same long black robes as the magi.

** Matthew's Gospel is, however, inherently contradictory in both emphasizing the universal nature of Jesus' mission while simultaneously proclaiming that his mission was only to the Jews; see chapter 19.

the Parthian Gondophares (or 'Gudapharasa', which evolved into Gaspard, Caspar), king of a vast territory in today's northern Pakistan and eastern Afghanistan (see chapter 11).

The Gospel ascribed to Luke, who may have been one of Paul's missionary companions, was also keen to emphasize that Jesus' message would embrace all mankind. But for Luke it was not so much the Gentile as well as the Jew, but the lowly as well as the exalted. Luke lays stress on Jesus' humble beginnings. He describes how Mary, presumably heavily pregnant, and Joseph, having travelled south from their undistinguished little Galilean village, tried but failed to find room in an inn (inns were often rough places with women for hire). Although Luke never actually states that Jesus was born in a stable, it has always been taken as implied by his reference to Jesus being laid in a 'manger', a trough. The stable is in fact only explicitly mentioned in the 'infancy Gospels' of the second century AD, the texts that tried to fill out the meagre Gospel descriptions of Jesus' early life. In Luke's account of the Nativity it was the local shepherds, ranked about as low down the social scale as fishermen,[11] who were the first to recognize Jesus as the Saviour; Matthew's wise men do not appear at all. Matthew also gives Jesus a setting more fitting for his elite visitors from the East – a house in a prosperous and renowned Judaean village-town, where the family had probably been living for some time.

Only in Matthew's account does the political significance of Jesus' role as the future Messiah play a major part. According to Matthew, it was because King Herod felt so threatened by the idea of a rival king that he ordered the killing of every baby boy in Bethlehem and forced Jesus and his family to flee into Egypt. Such a response was not, however, uniquely savage. As the biblical historian Geza Vermes has pointed out, the Republican Senate reacted to a similar threat in just the same way as Herod. When, around the time of Augustus' birth, a star was sighted which was said to herald the coming of a great king, the Senate decreed that all male babies should be killed, so that Republican Rome would be spared an autocratic ruler. The decree was in fact never enacted – it was stopped by senators whose wives were pregnant – and in due course Augustus became de facto emperor. According to Suetonius, in AD 64, after two comets had appeared in the skies, Nero was so fearful that he ordered the execution of all the leading men of Rome. Their surviving children were driven from the city and died from hunger or poison.

There is no evidence as to whether the infant boys of Bethlehem were in fact massacred (given that the population of Bethlehem was probably no more than a thousand, scholars reckon that seven to twenty babies would have been killed, had the massacre taken place), but we know from Josephus that Herod's mood became ever more murderously insecure as he succumbed to the agonizing disease that was destroying his body and his mind.

In 4 BC, the same year as the Pharisee students and their teachers had smashed the eagle in the Temple, Herod lay dying in excruciating pain, half mad, his breath stinking, his body bloated with dropsy and rotting with gangrene, his genitals gnawed at by worms – at least according to Josephus' gloating description. Herod was well aware of how much he was hated. He had ordered one member of every distinguished family in Palestine to be rounded up and imprisoned in his new hippodrome in Jericho. On his deathbed, he called his sister and brother-in-law to him and begged them to kill all of the prisoners – presumably many hundreds – so that when he died, 'the whole nation should be put into mourning'. But the eminent men of Palestine were fortunate. After Herod's death his sister and brother-in-law reneged on their promise.

The body of the dead king, dressed in a purple robe, wearing his diadem and gold crown, and holding a sceptre in his right hand, was placed on a bier of solid gold, studded with jewels. The bier was borne in a glittering procession led by the whole of his mercenary army, followed by the surviving members of his family, his bodyguard of burly menacing Germans, Thracians and Gauls and 500 of his courtiers, servants, eunuchs and slaves, swinging censers. They climbed the steep cliff road out of Jericho, crossed the barren rolling downs of the Wilderness of Judaea until they came to Herodium, Herod's massive fortress palace soaring up out of the desert 3 miles south-east of Bethlehem. The procession wound through the pleasure gardens, up 200 steps of pure white marble, and into the palace where Herod was buried in his royal tomb. But the hatred felt by many Jews for Herod the Great lived on. Seventy years later, Jewish rebels would hold Herodium against the Romans, and smash Herod's tomb to pieces.

At the news of his death, revolts broke out all over Palestine. They were the first revolts to have an overtly political as well as religious tone, and they were led by self-proclaimed Messiahs. Josephus was totally disparaging of these Messianic leaders, describing them as thuggish bandits.[12] Of course, it suited Josephus to characterize them as criminals: his histories were precisely intended to exonerate the Jews as a nation from blame for the revolt of AD 66 by putting the responsibility on a few rebel bandits. In Roman eyes, the Messiah – whoever he was – could not be anything but a rebel and it is true that the self-proclaimed Messiahs who led the revolts of 4 BC were probably more bandits and rebels than Messiahs. No doubt bandits, like emperors, found the divine sanction a useful one. Indeed, Judas, the leader of a major revolt in Galilee (not the disciple who betrayed Jesus), was the son of a notorious bandit whom Herod had hunted down and killed. Judas and his followers captured the royal arsenal in the hilltop city of Sepphoris, and created chaos in the surrounding countryside, including the nearby village of Nazareth, and all 'out of an ambitious desire of the royal dignity', according to Josephus. Certainly, the rebel leaders drew people who were poor enough to be attracted by the rewards of pillage. A mob led by one of Herod's former slaves, the tall and 'comely' Simon, from the district of Peraea to the south of Galilee across the Jordan River, burned down and looted Herod's palace in Jericho, along with other royal buildings. Perhaps in gratitude as much as belief, his followers declared him to be king and 'put a diadem on his head'.

Josephus, with his usual flexible attitude to numbers, says there were 10,000 other disorders in Judaea, though by this he probably just meant 'a lot'. Messiah-bandits and their peasant followers no doubt felt they could profit from the interregnum between the autocratic rule of Herod and that of his successor, yet to be announced by Rome. In his will, Herod had divided the kingdom between his three surviving sons, but though he had been a loyal king Herod was still a *client* king – and Rome had the final say as to who should rule Palestine. Unfortunately for the Jews of Palestine, Herod had wanted Archelaus, probably the least politically competent of his sons, to inherit the most politically and religiously charged part of the kingdom, the district of Judaea, with Jerusalem the jewel at its centre.

While Archelaus prepared to go to Rome to further his claim to Judaea, Jews from the whole of the Roman Empire and beyond were gathering in Jerusalem to celebrate Passover. Josephus claimed that some two million pilgrims descended on the city. Jerusalem had been preparing for their arrival for weeks. Roads and wells had been repaired, city squares cleaned, and special ovens had been built in Jerusalem so that the pilgrims could roast their paschal lambs for the Passover feast. Great caravans of pilgrims had travelled – overland or by sea – from every part of the Near Eastern world: Jews from Palestine in their tunics and white and brown striped cloaks, with rings on their fingers and toes; Jews from Phoenicia (modern Lebanon) in tunics and striped trousers; Jews from Anatolia (modern Turkey), dressed in goats' hair cloaks; Jews from Syria and North Africa; and Jews from Parthia, gleaming in silk brocaded with gold and silver or trailing black robes. The men had unplaited their long hair or unrolled it from under their turbans; under their cloaks, the ritual deep blue tassels hung from the ends of their tunics as a constant reminder to walk according to God's law. The more religious women were veiled; the others had covered their hair with a net or cloth. They were wearing their brightest and most richly embroidered cloaks of deep purple and maroon. Hundreds of beggars held out their stunted limbs for alms, road sweepers tried vainly to clear the streets of animal dung, as the pilgrims passed through the Temple gates (which were in effect tunnels leading from the lower, poorer part of the city to the Temple precinct), or climbed the Temple's monumental stairways, three storeys in height, which led to the upper, wealthy part of Jerusalem.

Beyond the Court of the Gentiles, the Court of Women and the Court of the Israelites, where only Jewish men were allowed, thousands of priests in billowing trousers and white turbans prepared for the sacrifices of the paschal lambs. A Levite assistant priest blew one long unwavering blast of his shofar (ram's horn), followed by nine rapid notes and another long blast, and the hundreds upon thousands of pilgrims and priests burst into their song of thanksgiving and deliverance to the sound of harps, lyres and cymbals:

All nations surrounded me:
In the name of the Lord I cut them off!
They surrounded me, surrounded me on every side,
In the name of the Lord I cut them off.[13]

Passover was a celebration of national liberation commemorating God's freeing of his chosen people from slavery in Egypt. It was the time when Jews expected the Messiah to reveal himself, and when Roman control would seem most intolerable; it was the time when, according to Matthew, Joseph felt safe enough, now that Herod was dead, to bring his family back from Egypt.

The barefooted pilgrims brought their lambs to be slaughtered. Row upon row of priests caught the blood in silver and gold basins and flung it against the base of the altar where it ran into a channel and was flushed out of the Temple area and into the River Kidron, a river so rich in blood that its water was sold as fertilizer.[14] Amidst clouds of smoke and burning incense, the priests waded barefoot in water and blood, their ankle-length white linen tunics hitched up by crimson, purple and blue sashes. They worked silently in a flowing routine, flaying the animals, cleaning their entrails and cutting them up on a series of marble tables. The best fatty pieces of the animals were burned on the altar. The rest of the meat was divided between the priests, their families and the pilgrims.

As the Passover rituals continued, a new and different sound was heard above the singing and the terrified bleating of the lambs – that of pilgrims protesting in the Court of the Gentiles. Their protest was, inevitably, a mixture of the religious and the political. They wanted to avenge the Pharisee martyrs who had smashed the golden eagle by punishing those responsible for their deaths and dismissing the high priest Joazar. But they also wanted their taxes reduced.

Archelaus, the aspirant ruler of Judaea, had been expecting trouble. As insensitive to Jewish sensibilities as his father Herod had been, he had stationed about 1,000 soldiers on the rooftops of the huge porticoes in the Courtyard of the Gentiles. When the clamour from the crowd became louder and more unruly, Archelaus ordered his troops in to put down the disorder. The crowd pelted them with stones, killing some of the soldiers and forcing them to retreat. Archelaus responded by sending in reinforcements mounted on horseback. The cavalrymen, probably foreign mercenaries, came clattering across the paved stone courtyards, trampling and butchering the stampeding crowd. Thousands of terrified pilgrims tried to escape but were hunted down by the mounted soldiers. In all, some 3,000 Jews were killed, according to Josephus. After the bloodbath was over, Archelaus ordered the remaining pilgrims in Jerusalem to return to their homes, while he set out on his three-month journey to Rome to ask for Rome's blessing to govern Judaea.

In Archelaus' absence, Rome took Judaea under its direct control. A legion of 5,000 soldiers – mostly Gauls and Spaniards – was brought in from Rome's neighbouring province of Syria and stationed in the Antonia palace-fortress (named in honour of Herod's first Roman patron Mark Antony), which loomed over the Temple. Herod had controlled his kingdom without the need of Roman troops. Now these soldiers were a visible presence in Jerusalem. Their shining bronze helmets, short tunics, 7-foot-long javelins and short swords, and the waving plumes on the centurions' helmets, symbolized Roman control with all the thoughtless arrogance that imperial power entails. Later, when Roman rule was established more overtly, the soldiers were ordered to cover their standards so that religious Jews would not be offended by the sight of the emperor's portrait. But in 4 BC such tact was unlikely.

Only fifty days after the Passover massacre, revolt broke out in Jerusalem as Jews gathered for the feast of Pentecost (from the ancient Greek meaning 'fiftieth day', that is, the fiftieth day after Passover). Jews from all over Palestine besieged the Antonia Fortress, the headquarters of the military in Jerusalem. In response the soldiers set fire to the Temple cloisters. The Jewish rebels were burned or mown down as they fled; some threw themselves on their swords, while the Roman legionaries looted the Temple treasure. It was the second time in fifty days that the Temple had been desecrated. The response was more revolts. In the town of Emmaus, another would-be Messiah, the shepherd Athronges, accompanied by his four strong brothers, 'superior to others in the strength of their hands', began attacking Roman troops. They ambushed a convoy of soldiers who were bringing grain and weapons to the troops who occupied Jerusalem.

Roman retaliation was predictably savage. Varus, the governor of Rome's province of Syria, who would see his legions slaughtered by the Germans in AD 9, brought in two extra legions (leaving just one behind in Syria) and, with the help of Herod's old enemies the Nabataeans, burned and looted his way to Jerusalem. Emmaus and Sepphoris were completely destroyed: Sepphoris' inhabitants were sold into slavery and 2,000 rebels were crucified – their bodies strung up along the roadways as a dreadful warning to the inhabitants of Nazareth and other local villages whose stonemasons, carpenters and craftsmen were employed in rebuilding the ruined city.

In Rome, outside the temple of Apollo that Augustus had built next to his 'modest' house – at least by later imperial standards – on the Palatine Hill, Augustus listened to the rival claims put forward by the Jews as to who should be the next ruler of Judaea. Nicolaus of Damascus, the brilliant, red-faced lawyer who had been Herod's confidant and would become his biographer, pleaded Archelaus' case for ruling the district of Judaea as stipulated in his father's will. But Archelaus was opposed by his brother Antipas, and by a delegation of fifty Jews from Judaea. They were probably part of the Romanized Sadducee elite, and they preferred to be incorporated into the province of Syria and be ruled directly by Rome rather than by Archelaus, who was responsible for the deaths of thousands of Jews at the Temple. Herod had been, they said, 'the most barbarous of all tyrants'; but Archelaus had already proved that he would be even worse. As far as the delegation was concerned, a client king was a far riskier bet than direct rule from Rome. The large community of Jews in Rome, most of whom were freedmen living on the north bank of the Tiber in what is now Trastevere, confirmed this view. About 8,000 of them, according to Josephus, clearly felt well enough treated by Rome to back the Judaean delegation's request for direct Roman rule.

But after the competing parties had argued their cases for two days, Augustus made his ruling and divided Palestine as Herod had wished. Philip, the gentlest, least tyrannical and least ambitious of the brothers, was made tetrarch (literally 'ruler of a quarter') of the territories to the north and east of the Sea of Galilee – including the modern Golan Heights – where Syrian and Greek Gentiles predominated. He remained a loyal client ruler and until his death ruled over a peaceful territory. Antipas, the ablest of the three, was given Galilee and Peraea, though again, not as king but as tetrarch, a subordinate ruler. 'That fox', as Jesus called him, would sidestep the Roman governor Pontius Pilate's attempt to involve him in the trial of Jesus, and survived as ruler for forty-three years until he was exiled to Gaul in AD 39 for allegedly conspiring against his erstwhile friend Caligula.

Surprisingly, for such an astute politician, Augustus confirmed Archelaus as ruler of Judaea, Samaria and Idumaea. And it was because of this, according to Matthew's Gospel, that after their self-imposed exile in Egypt Joseph decided to take his family to Galilee rather than return to Bethlehem in Judaea. Joseph would have feared Archelaus as much as Archelaus' father Herod, and preferred the safety of rule under Antipas in the tiny Galilean village of Nazareth, with its population of about 450 people,[15] to the potential dangers of life under Archelaus in the substantial Judaean hilltop village of Bethlehem.

In the early first century AD the safest way to travel from Egypt to Nazareth was along what the Romans called the Via Maris, an ancient trade route even then, that connected Egypt with the Mediterranean port cities to the north and with Damascus to the north-east. Camel trains set off from the mouth of the River Nile. They entered the sand-dune desert where the sunrises blazed in oranges and blues, skirted a shallow lake, tantalizingly undrinkable because it was too salty, passed small villages and gleaming cities on the Mediterranean coast of the Sinai Peninsula and entered what is now the Gaza Strip, the land which had once been controlled by the Jews' enemies, the Philistines, until King David defeated them in the eleventh century BC. The sand dunes grew larger, the going more difficult, but then the dunes gave way to forest and there, set on a hill, was Gaza, where the Jewish Samson had brought the temple to the god Dagon crashing down on him and his Philistine enemies. The city had declined since the era of the Philistines but was now reviving under the impetus of trade. Herod had built bathhouses, fountains, colonnades, an aqueduct and a palace. From its port, which had been silted up with sand, ships could now set sail for Greece and Rome. It was the meeting point of the Via Maris and the incense route. Caravans lumbered south to the city of Petra and the incense kingdoms of Arabia, or headed north along the sandy coast past the port city of Ascalon, newly rebuilt by Herod, and Azotus, a city forever threatened with being buried in sand, where the Philistine woman Delilah had once shorn Samson's hair. At Jaffa (now part of Tel Aviv), the Via Maris split in two, one branch turning inland towards Damascus, the other continuing up the coast through the rolling wooded hills of the plain of Sharon, past prosperous villages and Herod's new city of Antipatris.

At the Romanized and renamed city of Caesarea travellers on the Via Maris could carry on north up the Phoenician coast or travel inland through the Plain of Esdraelon (Jezreel Valley) passing below the village of Nazareth, before going round the west of the Sea of Galilee to Capernaum and on towards the Golan Heights and Damascus.

Today, Nazareth is a predominantly Muslim city of about 65,000 people. In the early first century AD it was a tiny village of rough stone houses built round open courtyards set in a hollow surrounded by terraced limestone hills, where the villagers tended their vines and olives and stored their goods in the caves that pockmarked the steep slopes. From the hilltops 500 feet above, Mount Hermon's snowcapped peak was visible to the north, and to the south the uplands of Samaria, home to the potentially hostile Samaritans. Galilean and Judaean Jews regarded the Samaritans as racially impure heretics because they had assimilated with their Assyrian conquerors in the eighth century BC. Jews were forbidden to marry them; Herod the Great had married a Samaritan, but then he was insensitive to Jewish sensibilities and was anyway only half Jewish.

In AD 6, however, Herod's son Archelaus – newly installed ruler of Judaea, Samaria and Idumaea, who had already shown his political heavy-handedness with the Temple massacre – had managed to unite the Samaritans and Jews in opposition to his rule. It was an extraordinary piece of incompetence given that the relationship between the two neighbouring districts was so charged with hatred. A joint delegation of Judaeans and Samaritans complained to Augustus about Archelaus' 'barbarous and tyrannical usage of them'. Augustus exiled Archelaus to Gaul and placed Judaea under direct Roman rule with a Roman governor. That same year, a radical freedom movement, based on the Pharisees' increasingly popular form of Judaism, was born (see chapter 18).

147

The clash between Herod and the Pharisees had laid the ground for the emergence of an ultra-militant Jewish religious nationalism and for the later far bloodier Jewish revolts. Other peoples in the Roman Empire rose in occasional revolt but no revolts ended so catastrophically as the Jews' did. At root was the particular nature of their religion. What made it so successful for a stateless people also made it particularly tortuous for a people living in a colonized country that should have been their promised land.

It would take the trial and execution of the proclaimed Messiah Jesus for a new type of religion to be created that would accommodate itself more easily to the Roman Empire. In Paul's hands, the crucified Jesus was refashioned into a totally new sort of Messiah. As created by Paul, Christ (*Christos* is the Greek translation of 'Messiah') was shorn of his militant, liberationist role; he became the slain not the slaying Messiah, a cosmic not an earthly saviour.

8

CASTRATING PRIESTS AND TRADING GODS IN PALMYRA

The Greek, the Roman, and the Barbarian, as they met before their respective altars, easily persuaded themselves, that under various names, and with various ceremonies, they adored the same deities.

Gibbon, *Decline and Fall of the Roman Empire*, vol. 1, ch. 2, 1776

She [the goddess Atargatis] is undoubtedly Hera, but she has something of the attributes of Athene and of Aphrodite, and of Selene and of Rhea and of Artemis and of Nemesis and of the Fates.

Lucian, *De Dea Syria, c.*AD 150

The ridiculous actions and passions of superstition, the phrases and gestures, the running around and drumming, the impure purifications, and filthy sanctifications, the barbarous and shocking penances and mortifications before shrines; these are the things that allow some people to say that belief in no gods at all is better than belief in gods who accept and take delight in this sort of thing, gods who are so arrogant, so captious, so petty.

Plutarch, 'On Superstition', *Moralia*, late first century AD

From Jerusalem, the embodiment of resistance to assimilation, it is 300 miles to Palmyra, the quintessential city of fusion. Palmyra was a frontier city, set in the Syrian desert between the two empires of Rome and Parthia, trading goods, cultures and religions between the East and the West. Everything about the city – from the way people dressed, to the languages they spoke, the frescoes that decorated their houses and their tombs, the temples that they built and the gods they worshipped – reflected the mix. Palmyra represented the model of an assimilated city, its gods fusion personified; the antithesis of Jerusalem. When Rome took control of Palmyra in about AD 30, the Palmyrenes and their religions could accommodate themselves to Roman rule in a way that the Jews of Palestine could not.

Travellers and merchants from Jerusalem would travel north on their sturdy white donkeys, climb eastwards over the Golan Heights and drop down into a fertile valley where they stopped at Damascus, which was home to at least 10,000 Jews. Leaving Damascus, travellers would plod through a black and desolate region, over and around deep fissures, through narrow passes and confused masses of fallen rocks. If they could afford it, a bodyguard of archers rode with them, ready to fend off the Bedouin robbers who might be lurking in every cave they passed.

After nights crossing the freezing lunar landscape of the Syrian desert in order to avoid the intolerable heat of the day, the travellers would see with relief a walled city in the distance, lit up in the pink glow of morning. Around it, thick groves of palm, olive and pomegranate trees kept the surrounding desert at bay. Nearing the city walls, the travellers passed stone towers several storeys high, the 'houses of eternity' where the mummified bodies of the city's rich were buried. At the south gate, they struggled amongst thousands of sulky, growling camels, flocks of sheep, high-strung horses from Persia, and nomads and fellow merchants from every part of the known world to enter the golden limestone city of Palmyra.

Amongst the traders could sometimes be seen a frenzied, shrieking procession of shaven-headed eunuch 'servants' of the mystery goddess Atargatis, hurling themselves backwards and forwards. Their faces were daubed with white clay, their eyes outlined with eyeshadow, their hands and necks tattooed; they wore earrings, saffron-coloured robes, billowing red and white striped tunics belted tightly at the waist and yellow slippers; they brandished great swords and mightie axes... Now and then they bite their own flesh before finally cutting their arms with a double-edged blade... you could see the soil soaking up the foul blood of these effeminates, under the slashes of the swords and blows of the whips... When at last... this butchery came to an end, the people vied with one another to offer bronze, even silver, coins which they gathered in the ample folds of their robes.[1]

The priests, or 'street-corner scum' as the sceptical Syrian observer Lucian called them, even brought along sacks to collect the pitchers of wine, milk, cheeses, flour and wheat which were donated by thrilled onlookers of these devotees of Atargatis. It is not clear how far Lucian, writing in the second century AD, was caricaturing the cult's sheer wildness and barbarity as he witnessed it in Hierapolis (in the south-west of modern Turkey), the centre of Atargatis worship. Many scholars, however, think Lucian provides a pretty accurate eyewitness account of the Atargatis cult in the first and second centuries AD. If we can believe Lucian, the Atargatis cult even continued to make human sacrifices, though Romans found the practice totally abhorrent and usually banned it, as they did with the Druids. Atargatis worshippers, according to Lucian, tied ribbons on their victims, even sewed their own children into sacks, and threw them headlong to their deaths from the top of the temple steps.

Atargatis was probably the most famous deity in Syria. She was simply called 'the Syrian goddess' by most Greek and Roman writers, including Lucian (hence the title of his observations on the Atargatis cult, *De Dea Syria*).[2] Statues depicted her as half woman, half fish (according to legend, Atargatis had fallen into a lake and been changed into a fish), with small red painted lips and wavy hair falling in two thick braids.

Twice a year worshippers held a phallic vigil at her temple. An acolyte climbed up one of the giant phalli standing at the entrance to the temple by securing himself with a small chain and attaching wooden pegs on the phallus to give him footholds. When he reached

151

the top, he let down a longer chain to haul up wood and clothing and perched 'as it were on a nest' for seven days, a less self-punishing ordeal than that of the Christian ascetic St Simeon Stylites who sat on *his* pillar in Syria for thirty-seven years. Visitors would bring the Atargatis ascetic offerings of gold, silver and brass. They shouted their names up to him so that he would utter a prayer for each of them, in between prayers shaking what Lucian called a 'brazen instrument… which gives forth a loud and grating noise'. The man never slept or if he did, we are told, a scorpion would creep up and sting him awake, though as Lucian points out – whether mockingly or in earnest – 'his wakefulness is in no small degree due to his fear of falling'.

Like so many of Palmyra's peoples and gods, Atargatis was a foreigner. She and her consort Hadad had been brought to Palmyra by merchants from Damascus in southern Syria, just as the Phoenician (Lebanese) settlers in Palmyra had brought Ba'alshamin and Astarte, the Egyptians had brought Isis, and Arab tribesmen – the original settlers – their goddess Allat who had set up home beside other Arab deities in the western quarter of the city. At the eastern end of the great main street, thousands of craftsmen and labourers were building a massive temple to the great god Bel, imported by merchants from Babylon (in modern-day Iraq); the temple's soaring bronze Corinthian columns carried Babylonian-style triangular wedged battlements. Yaweh had also been brought to the city by the Jews who formed a sizeable community (probably at least 2,000) as they did in every city in Syria.

Palmyra was home to hundreds of deities. They formed part of the great jumbling mass of gods that were merging, amoeba-like, in the cosmopolitan cities of the empire. Throughout the empire, from Gaul to the Sahara, local gods were fusing with each other and with the Graeco-Roman gods. Fusion – syncretism – was almost inevitable in a city: close proximity meant that the gods could not help affecting each other. The Roman gods themselves had been assimilating with the Greek gods since at least the fifth century BC, when Romans first came into contact with Greek culture. And since the age of Alexander the Great, in the second half of the fourth century BC, the Greek gods themselves had owed a great debt to the gods of the Near East (today's Turkey and the Middle East). Even the Jews' God had not been immune to the syncretic process and had borrowed features from the Persian gods. Judaism was profoundly influenced by Zoroastrianism during the Jews' exile in Babylon in the sixth century BC.

Supremacy was, for some of the gods, part of the process of syncretism. Indeed, some sociologists of religion, from Émile Durkheim to Raymond Stark and Robert Bellah today, have seen the development of the supreme God as almost inevitable: when societies become larger and more complex, gods meet new gods and extend their sphere of influence over a larger, more diverse group. By the beginning of the first century AD, Atargatis had grown from being the goddess of the sea to being the great universal mother goddess. She had fused with the Babylonian god Bel's Arabian consort Allat, with the Syrian and Phoenician goddess of love Astarte, as well as with the ferocious Canaanite goddess of war Anath, and with Asherah, the Canaanite goddess of fecundity. Atargatis was goddess of fertility and virginity, of love and of war. For most worshippers such contradictions were not a problem, since their religious practices did not require any very fixed set of beliefs; they performed rites but had little creed. There was no such thing as 'heresy' or religious law that could be contravened.

It was the ease with which most of the gods of the Roman Empire could accommodate each other that enabled Rome to use religion so effectively as a tool of imperial control. Although Rome failed to co-opt Yaweh, it usually exported its deities and deliberately identified them with the local deities of its conquered territories. The local gods thus became Romanized in partnership with their worshippers.

How Romanized the local gods became varied. Some gave way entirely to the Graeco-Roman ones; others took on some of their features while maintaining their own identity, and some refused to submit at all. Their degree of Romanization depended on whether they were worshipped by the elite or by ordinary people, by townspeople or people in the country. And that depended to a large extent on whether they were in the Eastern part of the empire (the Greek-speaking part which had been conquered by Alexander the Great and stretched from Greece and North Africa to Syria) or the Western and Northern parts of the empire (from modern Portugal and Spain to the River Rhine in modern Germany and to modern Croatia), which had never been conquered by Greece or any other empire until they were absorbed by Rome.

If religions are, as Feuerbach, Marx, Durkheim and most succeeding social scientists would argue, a reflection of the political and social order, then the Near Eastern gods had become as well adapted as the cities' inhabitants to surviving the pressures of assimilation. Unlike their counterparts in the Western and Northern parts of the empire, the inhabitants and gods of the Near East had lived for centuries under foreign rule and amongst foreigners. For 900 years they had seen empires come and go. The Assyrians (934–609 BC) and then the Babylonians (626–539 BC) had founded their empires between the Tigris and Euphrates (in modern-day Syria and Iraq). They had been succeeded by the Persians in 540 BC, then the Greeks in the late fourth century BC, and in 63 BC by the newcomers, the Romans. The peoples of the Near East were the inhabitants of the most ancient cities in the Roman Empire. Augustus' *pax Romana*, in stimulating trade and the concomitant growth of cities, had only encouraged the further development of an environment that the gods and their worshippers had lived in for centuries. But the Western and Northern parts of the empire had few cities; their gods, like their peoples, had no experience of surviving the impact of the foreigner as had the Near East. The Jews and their God had survived by refusing to assimilate; other Near Eastern gods and their peoples chose a middle route between refusal and total submission.

The members of the Palmyrene elite were Hellenized, but they, like some of their gods, never lost their own Near Eastern identity. At first glance, the men and women staring out from the frescoes which decorated their tombs and palaces seem to be portraits of a thoroughly Hellenized elite painted in a Greek style. They lie stretched out on couches strewn with Near Eastern rugs, but members of the same family are dressed in culturally contrasting styles: some in the Greek fashion of sleeveless tunics covered with a long cloak and some in the fantastically embroidered and bejewelled Persian/Parthian dress – the men in baggy trousers, soft boots and conical caps, their veiled wives in long belted tunics, dripping with necklaces, rings and strings of pearls. And their stiffness, their lack of all personality, the artist's concentration on the gold and silver embroideries, the rows of pearls and square jewels on the men's flowing trousers, depict what is still essentially a Near Eastern culture.

Atargatis, too, had become Graeco-Romanized without losing her Near Eastern identity. She acquired a Graeco-Roman name – Lucian called her 'the Assyrian [that is, North Syrian] Hera' – and also a Graeco-Roman form. The Jews, the Phoenicians, Herod's unfriendly neighbours the Nabataeans and many of the desert Arabs had all thought of their gods in the abstract and refused to worship anthropomorphic images of them. The mother goddess Cybele was worshipped as a black stone. The Nabataeans' sun god Dushara was worshipped as a large conical stone; in a superb syncretic sleight of hand he would be renamed in Christian times St Zeus Doushares, the Greek form of Dushara.* But, unlike the Jewish God, these other Semitic gods were falling under the influence of the Greeks and Romans and adopting human shape.

Only the most senior priests were allowed inside the sanctuary of Atargatis. But the sanctuary had no doors, and awestruck worshippers could see the great gilt statue of Atargatis seated between two lions, flashing white, sea-green and wine-dark jewels, the gifts of adoring pilgrims from Arabia, Egypt, India, Ethiopia (that is, black Africa),

---

* Dushara went from being chief of the Nabataean pantheon, to becoming associated with Zeus as high god, to taking on human form, before being incorporated into the Christian pantheon of saints.

Babylon, the country of the Medes, Armenia and Sardinia. 'Golden Hera' was even more mysterious and terrifying to her worshippers because she had clearly taken on the lifelike characteristics of Graeco-Roman art. Unlike the stilted, lifeless Palmyrenes staring out from their funerary frescoes, the image of Atargatis-Hera gave the unnerving sense of watching her worshippers: 'it looks you in the face', wrote Lucian, 'and as you pass it the gaze still follows you, and if another approaching from a different quarter looks at it, he is similarly affected.' Beside her, seated on two bulls, was her consort Hadad, or, as Lucian called him, Zeus – since Hera was the wife of Zeus.

Atargatis had taken on Graeco-Roman form, but she did not, like the gods of the Western and Northern parts of the empire, succumb to the Graeco-Roman gods and melt away. In order to survive centuries of foreign gods and foreign rulers, Atargatis had needed to secure the commitment of her worshippers.

Every cult sought to build a body of loyal members by creating some sort of community. Communal dining was at the heart of pagan religion, as it would soon be of Christianity. Guests at religious banquets in Palmyra received a little clay tablet inscribed with the picture of their god on one side, and on the other the name of the person or group issuing the invitation. The clay tablets of Atargatis showed her dressed in a Greek tunic, sitting on a lion, with a large figure of a fish standing on its tail in front of her. The priest offered a sacrifice, musicians played, servants brought round bowls of wine and served roasted meat on spits and vegetables to the cult members as they lay on couches – observing, one hopes, the rules carved on the temple's walls: you were not allowed to vomit up your wine, sing or create a disturbance, or carve your initials on the walls of the temple's banqueting rooms; you were to be suitably clothed, uncontaminated by recent childbirth, by sexual intercourse with a woman or dog, by sight or touch of a corpse, or by having consumed pork or garlic or milk.[3]

Devotees of Atargatis and other mystery cults, however, were required to do much more than attend the occasional riotous banquet. While most pagans only went to their temples for festivals, mystery devotees were expected to go daily, or to meet in each other's private houses, as the early Christians would do. And the mystery cults demanded from their priests a level of commitment which not even Christian monks, in a later era, were expected to attain. According to Lucian, the would-be Galli, or eunuch-priest, of Atargatis would take part in an increasingly frenzied procession in order to commit 'the great act'.

> Any young man who has resolved on this action, strips off his clothes, and with a loud shout bursts into the midst of the crowd, and picks up a sword from a number of swords which I suppose have been kept ready for many years for this purpose. He takes it and castrates himself and then runs wild through the city, bearing in his hands what he has cut off. He casts it into any house at will, and from this house he receives women's raiment and ornaments.[4]

What greater sign of loyalty to your goddess was there than to become a cross-dressing eunuch – someone who had literally cut himself off from the pleasures of the physical world so that he could be faithful only to Atargatis?

In vaunting the punishment of the flesh, Atargatis, like Isis and Cybele, was signalling a disdain for this life compared to the immortal life in a better world. These gods were moving into the moral world and in doing so were extending their control over their worshippers and therefore the level of commitment they could demand of them. Priests and ordinary worshippers had to atone for wrongdoing by self-punishing behaviour: sinful Galli whipped themselves; in Apuleius' *The Golden Ass*, a worshipper who had offended Atargatis by eating her sacred fish did penance by dressing himself in 'sordid rags', covering himself with a sack and sitting in the public highway proclaiming his sins. The asceticism of these cults became the butt of jokes among sceptics. Juvenal mocked the self-mortifying Isis devotee who 'three times, in the depths of winter... will dive into the chilly waters of the Tiber, and shivering with cold, will drag herself around the temple upon her bleeding knees'.[5]

The move from an array of gods with limited powers to a supreme or only God, to a single, *moral* God controlling the behaviour of his worshippers, was not an inevitable one, although it was probably more likely in the increasingly complex and diverse society that the city created. As the sociologist Guy Swanson has pointed out, people need a moral ruler to lay down the rules when they are no longer controlled by the conventions of tribe and village, when they start acting as individuals and not as part of a group. The moral god created a new group of individuals bound together by morals rather than by tribe.

The Isis cult and other mystery cults were transforming themselves into 'religions' by creating an internal spiritual world which could be inhabited by everyone because it was based on each individual's relationship with their god (see chapter 3). The gods of the mystery religions were building up a stable body of committed worshippers. They were providing the essential requirements of a religion more effectively than their rivals. They gave their worshippers transcendence and meaning, protection and insurance against the vicissitudes of life, and the security and sense of specialness of belonging to a chosen community. Mystery devotees were united in a loyalty to their religion by their initiation rites, the behaviour expected of them and the passionate intensity with which they were encouraged to worship their gods. As a result, the gods of the mystery religions were both resistant to the disintegrating pressures of assimilation suffered by so many gods, and were also hugely popular beyond the confines of their own *ethne* and place.

The mystery cults were particularly well served by the merchants who became adherents. Because the Eastern part of the empire was so much more commercially successful than the less urbanized, more primitive West, Eastern traders travelled and settled throughout the empire. They were enthusiastic carriers of their cults, as they would later be of Christianity. Merchants took Atargatis west from Palmyra to Nabataea, to the port city of Ascalon (north of Gaza, in modern Israel) where they built a temple to Aphrodite/Atargatis overlooking the Mediterranean Sea; in the city of Smyrna, on the Aegean coast of what is now Turkey, a religious law threatened anyone who ate her sacred fish with being devoured by them. Syrian merchants settled along the Mediterranean coast of Egypt, in Sicily, and in the Italian ports of Naples and Ostia. They made their homes and built their temples along the trade-bearing rivers of the Danube and by the Rhone in Lugdunum (Lyons) in Gaul, and near army camps where they set up stalls and shops. Atargatis also travelled with the Syrian soldiers who worshipped her. They took her to upper Germany with a cohort of archers from Damascus; auxiliaries from Palmyra took her to Mauretania in North Africa. She was taken to Britain where one inscription in the first century AD called her 'the Syrian goddess', Ceres, Cybele (her fellow mother goddess from what is now Turkey), and even 'the Virgin'.[6] A Roman officer carved an inscription to her on Hadrian's Wall and another soldier offered an altar to her in north Yorkshire; she had followers on the north-eastern fringes of the Roman world at Romula (in modern Romania) and in Pannonia (along the fertile plains of the upper Danube).

Many gods in the Roman Empire were rooted to the spot, in the natural features of the landscape. There were few people in the empire who did not believe that all nature was inhabited by gods. Wherever travellers went, according to Apuleius, who had described his hero's adventures with the Isis cult in *The Golden Ass*, they would come across sacred features of the landscape which local people had decorated with offerings: 'an altar wreathed with flowers, a cave shaded by leafy boughs, an oak weighed down with horns, a beech crowned with pelts, a little hill sanctified by an enclosure, a tree-trunk hewn into an effigy, a turf altar moistened with libations, a stone smeared with unguent', and there the traveller would 'make a vow, offer fruit, and sit for a while'.[7]

But most gods, even if they were portable and travelled with the merchant, soldier or slave, were never really worshipped beyond their own peoples. They were what the historian of Roman religion James Rives calls 'diaspora cults' – none more so than Yaweh. The Celtic goddess Epona, the goddess of horses, was taken from Gaul to Spain, northern Britain and the Balkans by Gallic soldiers who made up a large part of Rome's auxiliary army (the soldiers who, unlike the legionaries, were not Roman citizens). The soldiers were faithful to her and never even Romanized her name. But she was only ever worshipped by the Gauls, never by foreigners.[8] Epona was too tied to her own people; she had nothing special to offer the foreigner.

What distinguished the mystery gods was that they appealed beyond the boundaries of their own ethnic community. However, the very features that enabled Atargatis and Isis to spread around the empire, and find their home in its trading cities, also made them a potential political threat. They created communities which had an alternative focus of loyalty beyond Rome and its rulers.

Atargatis, in fact, inspired the first major slave revolt in Italy, the so-called First Servile War of 135–132 BC, which eventually involved 200,000 slaves and spread throughout Sicily. Syrians enslaved by the Romans during their Eastern conquests had taken Atargatis to the great landed estates of Sicily. Just as the exiled Jews, bound together into a tight community by Yaweh, had their Messiahs, so the exiled Syrians, bound together by Atargatis, found one for themselves actually present among them.

According to the Roman historian Florus, who was writing in the early second century AD, Eunus, the leader of the slaves' revolt, proclaimed that Atargatis had come to him in a dream and foretold that he would become king.[9] In order to prove to his followers that he was acting under divine inspiration, Eunus 'secreted in his mouth a nut which he had filled with sulfur and fire, and, by breathing gently, sent forth a flame as he spoke'. When he was crowned by his rebel slave followers, 'King Antiochus' declared that he was Atargatis' consort. King Antiochus was both holy man – his followers called him a 'wonder-worker' – and king who had delivered his people from his enemies. After just one month, he was so firmly established that he issued his own coinage and had a royal bodyguard of 1,000 men. A delegation of ten Roman senators, who were responsible for religious affairs, even travelled to Sicily during the revolt to placate 'Ceres of Enna' (Atargatis) by offering sacrifices.

It took Rome three years to suppress the revolt. Some 20,000 slaves were crucified and hung in chains, but Eunus was left to rot in prison, perhaps because the authorities were reluctant to create a legendary hero – a sensible precaution that the Romans would fail to take in the case of the rebel Jesus in Judaea a century and a half later.

Despite crushing the Atargatis-inspired slave revolt, Rome could not suppress the religion itself, which was adopted in the very heart of the empire. There was a temple to Atargatis in Rome's Trastevere quarter, where many Palmyrenes and Jews lived.[10] Rome was equally powerless against the other mystery religions. In 205 BC, possibly as a result of popular pressure, the Roman Senate had made the great mother goddess Cybele (or, as they called her, Magna Mater) an official cult in Rome, which meant her temple and ceremonies were funded by the state. But the Senate was clearly fearful of its subversive potential for they hedged the cult round with restrictions. Romans were not permitted to become Galli. Cybele's priests and priestesses were allowed to hold only one procession a year and Roman citizens were forbidden to take part. Nonetheless, the Senate did not – probably could not – ban the cult: it had too many devotees. The cult's practices were, 'unseemly for men of respectability', said the Spanish Stoic Seneca, 'so unlike the doings of sane men, that no one would doubt that they are mad, had they been mad with the minority; but now the multitude of the insane is the defense of their sanity.'[11]

By the first century BC, the popular Isis cult (see chapter 3) had taken root in Rome, though the Republican Senate tried five times to tear down its altars and statues, as did the Emperor Augustus and his successor Tiberius. The Isis cult's independent priesthood, and its special fellowship knit together by secret initiation rites, created a powerful organization which was not controlled by Rome and could compete with it. Temples would be shut down, processions banned, but they soon resurfaced. Rome was always forced to give in to the protests of Isis' followers. They were too numerous and too devoted; the cult flourished, as did the mystery cult of Cybele.

By the middle of the first century AD, the Emperor Claudius looked with enough favour on Cybele (or was forced by popular pressure into doing so) to lift the ban on Roman citizens becoming Galli and taking part in her processions. His successor Nero, who 'despised all forms of religion, for a while had eyes only for *Dea Syria* [Atargatis]', though according to the gossip-loving second-century biographer Suetonius, Nero was then distracted by another deity and 'afterwards showed her [Atargatis] such disdain that he soiled her with his urine'. The future emperors Vespasian and his son Titus celebrated their suppression of the Jewish Revolt in AD 73/4 by spending the night in the sanctuary of Isis on the Campus Martius in Rome. Not surprisingly, the mystery deities found even more favour 150 years later with the Syrian emperors of the Severan dynasty.

The adoption of the mystery religions by the Roman elite and the emperors should have signalled their victory. Yet, of all the Near Eastern gods, it was Yaweh, the most demanding, the most ineluctably tied to tribe and most opposed to imperial rule, who survived. Even Isis, whose cult was one of the most popular and widespread in the empire, bowed out after 1,000 years when the Byzantine Emperor Justinian closed her most important temple at Philae in Egypt in the sixth century AD. Christianity, which had followed in Isis' footsteps around the world, overtook her.[12] Isis could withstand the assault of the Roman gods but she could not withstand the Christian God.

Elements of Isaicism, however, and of the other mystery cults, lived on in the religion that killed them off, perhaps the most syncretistic of them all. Christianity would be more welcoming than Judaism, but the Christian God would be more demanding and exclusive than the mystery deities. Yaweh and his Christian reinvention could not tolerate other gods, while the mystery deities were henotheists – supreme gods but gods who recognized and tolerated the existence of other, lesser gods. That made them well adapted for an empire but also less able to keep their worshippers in the face of the jealous monotheistic God. Christianity might even be seen as the 'mystery cult of Yaweh': it would have the mystery cults' universalism, that is, openness of membership, their concentration on the individual, the relationship between the deity and her devotee, and the high drama, but would attach them to the unique, jealous and morally demanding God of the Jewish religion, who brooked no rivals.

The exclusive Jewish religion survived, but of course by its very nature could not have a large membership. Paul's Christianity would take over from the imperial cult and the other Roman cults as the state religion of the empire. But it could only do so because the Roman state was still stable enough to be able to take advantage of religion as a means of controlling its subjects, and strong enough to promote or impose a state religion.

Across the desert to the east, the rulers of the Parthian Empire were never secure enough either to need or be able to impose a religion, though the original supreme, quasi-monotheist god was born there. The Iranian deity Ahura Mazda was regularly encountered by the merchants of Palmyra when they left their city and set off for the Euphrates and beyond.

The journey was risky and expensive, though the profits could be huge, and most merchants could only afford it by enlisting the backing of a wealthy Palmyrene patron, or 'synodiarch'. At Palmyra's bars, cafes and in the marketplace, groups of merchants wanting to import pearls and cinammon from India, or pomegranates and rugs from the Parthian Empire, met to make a deal with a synodiarch. In return for a share of the profits, the synodiarch provided the finance, a bodyguard of archers, the necessary pack animals from his landed estates outside the city walls and probably led the vast cavalcades as they headed at dusk out of the gates of Palmyra.

The 'sons of the caravan', the merchants, wearing leather

breastplates, holding a dagger in one hand and a heavy spear in the other, with richly embroidered and fringed saddle bags hanging from their camels' saddles, made their sacrifices to the caravan god Azizu. Leaving the city walls and the groves of palm trees, they set out in the hazy mauve light of evening to cross the desert, relying on the skills of their synodiarch to guide them safely through the flatlands. He had to negotiate his way past every tribe grazing their great flocks of sheep, goats and camels along the way, and through every flourishing oasis settlement. According to Strabo, some of these tribes were friendly, some rather less so. And they demanded money, in varying amounts, for safe passage and for use of their precious wells; the 'chiefs of the tent dwellers', living farthest from the Euphrates, were apparently the most moderate and accommodating. Some tribesmen, however, refused to negotiate and simply wanted plunder. And then the caravan, under the command of the synodiarch, had to fight its way through. Palmyra is full of inscriptions from grateful merchants to synodiarchs who had saved their caravans. The Romans would soon erect a chain of watchtowers across the desert, manned by troops who could signal to each other with flags or by flashing their shields to warn of bandits approaching.

In the freezing night winds the caravan ploughed across the flatlands, hearing only the screams of foxes and jackals. But after six days the monotonous landscape changed to fields and villages. The caravan had reached the fertile fringes of the Euphrates. At the city of Hit (in what is now central Iraq), on the banks of the river, the merchants left the pack animals to graze and recover while they boarded boats. Garrisons of Palmyrene archers, stationed on islands in the river or on the banks, guarded them from attacks as they sailed downriver towards the Persian Gulf. Across the muddy-brown, fast-flowing river was Parthia, the birthplace of monotheism and the most unstable empire in the world, where a former slave girl turned empress had just murdered her emperor-husband.

9

POLITICAL AND RELIGIOUS CHAOS IN PARTHIA

Religion and kingship are two brothers, and neither can dispense with the other. Religion is the foundation of kingship and kingship protects religion.

Attributed to Ardashir, the vassal king who defeated the Parthians in
AD 224; cited in *The Cambridge History of Iran*, p. 877

Jesus was born during the reign of Augustus, the one who reduced to uniformity, so to speak, the many kingdoms on earth so that he had a single empire. It would have hindered Jesus' teaching from being spread through the whole world if there had been many kingdoms.

Origen, *Contra Celsum*, II.30, AD 248

In AD 2, Parthians and Romans feasted each other on the banks of the Euphrates, the unacknowledged boundary between their two empires. After two months of negotiations they had settled their differences by diplomacy rather than warfare. On the western – Roman – side of the Euphrates the Roman delegation, led by Augustus' eighteen-year-old heir Gaius, feasted the Parthians. Then it was the turn of the twenty-five-year-old Parthian King Phraataces to host a banquet on his side of the river.

Minstrels played, endless carcases of kid, lamb and wild boar were served, as the Roman delegation watched with appalled fascination the drunken behaviour of the Parthian king and his court. The

Romans thought the Parthians were 'arrogant, treacherous, and violent'. They feared the Parthians' military prowess, and admired their cuisine; they despised their barbarism and were appalled by their effeminacy.[1] The king and his court flung bones at their bodyguards and friends, drank vast quantities of palm wine from drinking horns made in the shape of horses, stags and female deities. They twirled their swashbuckling moustaches and combed their pointed beards (hairiness meant barbarism to the clean-shaven Romans). Their long hair was curled in neat rows, they had make-up on their faces, pearls on their soft boots, and richly embroidered belts for the swords that never left their side.

Phraataces, their king, was the most magnificent of them all, in purple cloak and dazzlingly coloured tunic. Above his royal headband, with its long ribbons trailing down his neck, his hair was ringleted; below, it was carefully waved, his fine moustache curled up at the ends, a small beard jutting forward from his chin. A wart on his forehead, the result of a genetically inherited disorder of the nervous system, was proof that he belonged to the Arsacid clan. The Arsacids were the most important of the clans that made up the tribe of Iranian Parni nomads who had conquered the small kingdom of Parthia in today's north-eastern Iran in the mid-third century BC. From there, they had slowly wrested the Persian* Empire from the Seleucids (the dynasty descended from Alexander the Great's general Seleucus). Parthia's kings had always been selected from the Arsacid clan. It was one of the few stable elements in what was the most unruly empire in the world.

Clean-shaven Gaius and his soberly dressed entourage looked on in scorn as Parthia's 'effeminate' nobles and vassal kings grovelled at Phraataces' feet and kissed the hem of his richly embroidered garment. To the Romans, it was no more than they expected. Ever

---

* I use the term 'Iranian' to refer to the peoples of the Iranian plateau – an area larger than modern Iran which stretches from the Hindu Kush to central Anatolia and from Central Asia to the Persian Gulf – and 'Persian' to refer to the Persian Empire that was ruled by Iranians, starting with Cyrus, and resuming after Alexander the Great and the Seleucids with the Parthians.

since the historian Herodotus had written his triumphalist explanation of what it was about the Greeks that made them uniquely capable of defeating the mighty Persian Empire, the Romans – the Greeks' successors – had conceived of themselves as virile, freedom-loving, independent citizens. Of course they would triumph over the decadent, luxury-loving, slavish peoples of the East who bowed down before their autocratic kings; 'orientalism', thanks to Herodotus, was alive and well in the ancient world. Young, handsome slaves from the East were de rigueur for wealthy Romans. The tables in their villas were supported by marble figures of Oriental cupbearers, often in Parthian dress.² The Romans were inordinately proud of their Republican heritage, though it was being seriously eroded by Augustus, who had more power over his senators, cities and even his far-flung territories, as well as more wealth and more control over his vast well-disciplined armies, than King Phraataces could ever dream of. His nobles might prostrate themselves before him, but Phraataces had good reason to fear them. In two years' time, some of them would send him into exile and probably assassinate him and his Queen Musa.

Musa was Phraataces' mother, wife and – probably with his connivance – the murderer of his father and her husband, King Phraates. A slave girl from Italy, she had been a gift to the king from Augustus. A marble bust of Musa, found in the Mesopotamian city of Susa, shows a young woman whose large wide nose and sober stare elevate her above mere prettiness. The sculptor has even depicted the first wrinkle that has appeared on her neck. She looks determined to win, though not a likely murderess. According to Trogus, a historian writing at the time of Augustus, Musa's murdered first husband, King Phraates, had murdered his father and his twenty-nine brothers to get to the throne, though how much this is a caricature of Parthian barbarity it is hard to tell. We only know the Parthians through the prism of Roman superiority and hostility to the only empire on its doorstep. The Parthians themselves left virtually no record of themselves.

167

Parthia, which stretched from modern Iraq, through Iran, Turkmenistan and Afghanistan to Pakistan, in a sense started with the same ingredients as Rome. It too had its formidable fighting force; Parthia was, in fact, Rome's most feared opponent. Parthia's wealth, like Rome's, was based on trade: in Parthia's case on controlling, or trying to, the overland trade routes linking East and West. Yet both empires evolved in very different ways. Rome was an empire held together and ruled by a strong central authority. After 200 years, however, no Parthian King had imposed central authority across the empire. The kings tolerated what was essentially a fissiparous federation made up of huge semi-independent kingdoms (Pliny counted eighteen), of territories – especially in the Eastern part of the empire – owned by mighty Parthian nobles, and of estates owned by the old nobility of Persia. The great trading cities of Mesopotamia (in what is now Iraq), home of the former Assyrian and Babylonian Empires, were almost autonomous city-states.

Parthia's kings ruled by war, diplomacy and intrigue – not the style of rule that allowed them to enlist the aid of religion to give them authority and loyalty. They supported 'Zoroastrianism', but neither religion nor ruler used the other in the mutually reinforcing way that Rome did.

There were different ways for an empire to survive, ranging from the imposition of strong central authority over the empire's constituent parts to an acceptance of a virtual federation of independent kingdoms. At the beginning of the first century AD, China was settling on the authoritarian end of this spectrum; Rome was somewhere in the middle, giving some measure of independence to its conquered territories, but ready to clamp down at any hint of trouble; while Parthia, at the opposite end of the spectrum from China, was more a collection of semi-independent parts loosely bound together under a weak central authority. The Parthian model in this – inevitably oversimplified – picture was perhaps the most unstable. Nevertheless, it endured – however turbulently and uncomfortably for its rulers and subjects – for 500 years, roughly the same lifespan as the Han dynasty in China (206 BC–AD 220). The Roman Empire also lasted for about 500 years (from 27 BC to the sack of Rome in AD 410), although it could be said to have lasted for 1,500 years, if one takes the fall of the Eastern half of the empire in 1453 as the end point.

Phraataces and Gaius had spent two months negotiating on an island in the middle of the Euphrates, watched by their armies on either side of the river. In the delegation of expert field staff that Augustus had assembled to support the young and inexperienced Gaius on his first major mission was Juba, the Berber king of Mauretania (now part of modern Algeria and Morocco), a client king who rivalled Herod in his loyalty to Rome.* Juba's father had been Rome's enemy. His kingdom had been conquered by Julius Caesar in 46 BC. But Rome had turned Juba from enemy to faithful servant in a single generation, as it did with so many members of its conquered royal families and elites (see chapter 16).

Rome was able to rule through its semi-autonomous kingdoms and cities, because it had both the power to turn their elites into willing agents of the empire, and the ever-present threat of force if that failed. Parthia's rulers, on the other hand, did not have a sufficient monopoly on power and wealth to be able to bribe or force their elites into becoming loyal subjects. In Parthia, the heads of clans, the 'vassal' kings and the Greek elites who ran the cities did much better by shifting their allegiances from king to pretender to the throne in Parthia's unending civil wars, while behind them lurked the Roman Empire, ever happy to help Parthia disintegrate by playing one faction against the other. 'Disloyalty was their [the Parthians'] national habit,' wrote Tacitus, who recorded two chieftains switching sides three times in probably as many weeks.

While Augustus rewarded his loyal Juba with the kingdom of Mauretania, albeit with significant constraints on his power, Parthia's king rewarded the general who inflicted one of the most serious

---

* It was probably on this expedition that Juba, as a member of the transnational elite, met and fell in love with his future wife Glaphyra, who would later divorce him to marry Herod's son Archelaus.

defeats Rome ever suffered by beheading him.

Despite 'his painted face and parted hair', even Plutarch, the only source for the battle, recognized the brilliance of the thirty-year-old commander of the royal armies, a chief of the mighty house of Suren, especially in contrast to his Roman counterpart.[3] Vainglorious Marcus Licinius Crassus was twice the Suren's age and looked even older, according to Plutarch. The richest man in Rome and, in the last decades of the Republic, its unofficial ruler along with Julius Caesar and Pompey, Crassus was determined to prove himself a better general than his fellow triumvirs. In 53 BC, against all advice, he invaded Parthia, the only major power the Romans had to encounter at any point along their borders.

Crassus was probably as incompetent as Aelius Gallus would be in Arabia twenty-seven years later (see chapter 5) and, like Gallus, he was duped by a 'crafty and treacherous' Arab chieftain who led the Romans straight into an ambush on the desert plains of Carrhae (in modern south-eastern Turkey). Crassus' troops outnumbered the Suren's by four to one. But the legionaries, in this case mainly Gauls, were trained to fight as a solid mass, advancing slowly but relentlessly towards the enemy. They were unused to the nomads' flexible guerrilla-style tactics, which relied on speed and brilliant horsemanship. The legionaries formed into tight squares. Shield locked with shield to protect themselves, they wheeled this way and that as they were penned in tighter and tighter by the circling Parthian horsemen on their black mail-clad horses. Stumbling over the bodies of the dead and wounded, choking in the dust raised by the galloping horses, the soldiers were sitting targets for the Parthians' light cavalry who did not even bother to aim but lined up loosely to shoot black-feathered arrows from their huge bows, while the mail-clad horsemen in front plunged their long spears and pikes into the far less well-protected Gauls. 'The sword slipped into the armour like water;... the arrow slid into the eyes like sleep... the spearpoint glided into the heart like love,' wrote the magnificent poet of the eleventh-century Iranian epic *Vis and Ramin*, which is based on the heroic stories sung by the Parthian minstrels.*

A legion led by Crassus' son Publius tried to rescue them, but fell victim to the 'Parthian shot'. The Parthians seemed to be fleeing. Publius and his cavalry pursued them, but the Parthian horsemen – probably the best in the whole of Asia – turned in their saddles and, gripping only with their legs as they galloped full speed, loosed their arrows at the Romans. When he saw his men being massacred around him, Publius took the easy way out and committed suicide. His severed head was brought to his father Crassus who lay paralysed by despair. It fell to Cassius, his deputy – who less than ten years later would be the 'lean and hungry' co-assassin of Julius Caesar – to lead the panic-stricken, disordered remnants of the army in a retreat through the night, abandoning the dead and the dying whose despairing shouts alerted the Parthians that their enemy was escaping. Two thousand men were cut off on a hillside by the Parthians and were cut to pieces – all except twenty. In one of those extraordinary moments in warfare when the enemy soldier suddenly becomes a fellow human, 'the Parthians, admiring these men, who tried to push their way through them with drawn swords, made way for them and suffered them to pass through'. Only 10,000 soldiers made it back to Syria with Cassius out of an original force of more than 40,000. Crassus himself was tricked by the Suren into a meeting to negotiate peace and was killed by the Parthian general's bodyguard. His severed head was brought to the Parthian King Orodes II and used as a stage prop before cheering courtiers as they watched Euripides' *Bacchae*.

A year later, King Orodes had the magnificent Suren beheaded. The Suren's success had made him too dangerous. The Suren family was one of the most powerful clans in Parthia, ruling over the fertile region of Sistan and even minting their own coins. Victory at Carrhae had been won by the Suren's own private army of vassals and slaves.

---

* Even though *Vis and Ramin*'s author Gurgani was writing centuries after Parthian rule had collapsed, scholars consider that he faithfully conveyed the atmosphere of the Parthian Empire, and I have therefore used his superbly evocative epic to provide some of the descriptive details of this chapter.

The 'Parthian army' consisted of the king's small standing army supplemented by large private armies, like the Suren's, who owed their allegiance to their local clan chief, and not to the king. In the Republican period, Rome's soldiers too had had their loyalty to their own generals, enhanced by the fact that it was their general who enriched them with booty after a victory. But in the post-civil war era, Augustus had power and wealth enough to assert his control empire-wide over the army and to buy their loyalty. The Roman army remained an organization under central control even if succeeding emperors often failed to retain their soldiers' loyalty as successfully as Augustus had done.

By the beginning of the first century AD, China had already exchanged a warrior elite for an elite of civil servants; Rome was embarking on a similar process, painful though that was for its senators. But the Parthian elite were still nomadic warriors; they were superb soldiers but bad subjects. Their loyalty was to their clan, not their king. They were descended from nomads, most of their territory was only suited to nomadic life, and they were still at heart the nomads that their ancestors had been.

The Parthian elite, owners of vast herds of horses and cattle, preferred hunting with cheetah and hounds to almost any other activity except perhaps drinking. Strabo noted that Parthians carried on their most important deliberations when they were drinking date wine and 'considered that the decisions they made when drunk were more lasting than those made when they were sober'.[4] The Parthians still lauded the nomad lifestyle and nomad skills. From the age of five, highborn boys were still taught the nomad's arts. Strabo says they were woken at dawn for competitive races; in the late afternoons they were shown how to plant trees and gather roots, make weapons, clothes and hunters' nets; after dark, they were taught how to 'tend flocks and live outdoors all night and eat wild fruits, such as pistachio nuts, acorns, and wild pears'.

Nomadic warrior culture, with its diffuse centres of power based on clan leaders, is inimical to the static hierarchical organization that centralization requires. And the Parthian king did not have the power to offer the Hobbesian contract – wealth and security in return for obedience – that Rome could offer its elites.

Trade and the wealth created in cities funded most empires. But the Parthian kings never really conquered their cities, especially the big trading cities of Mesopotamia. These were still run by the Macedonian Greeks who had originally settled there with Alexander the Great's conquering army in the fourth century BC. The huge Jewish population of Mesopotamia (descended from the captives dragged to Babylon after the destruction of Jerusalem by the Babylonian King Nebuchadnezzar II in the early sixth century BC) had their own hereditary ruler. In the towns and villages which had a large Jewish community, or were sometimes exclusively Jewish, the exilarch fixed market prices, collected duties from trade, presided over a supreme court and appointed local judges. In return the exilarchs paid tribute for their lands to the Parthian kings.

Rome too had its semi-autonomous cities, which in the Eastern part of its empire were also run by Greeks. Roman cities, like Parthian ones, often had their own separately administered Jewish communities. But Rome could rely on its cities and virtually ran its empire through them because it had the power both to make loyalty attractive and disloyalty utterly ruinous: that power was based on the wealth that Rome could extract from its cities. Parthia's kings never did the same, even though Parthia's position as geographical 'middleman' in the increasing traffic of goods between East and West was making its cities extremely rich.

Big trading cities like Seleucia (18 miles south of modern Baghdad) and Dura Europos (further to the north-west on the right bank of the Euphrates in what is now Syria) made their separate contracts with the king. They could mint their own coins, which effectively allowed them to control the value of money – a huge concession since these cities were becoming centres of enormous wealth.[5] They taxed all the goods passing through, and in theory handed some of the revenue, as well as land taxes from the surrounding territory they administered, to Parthia's kings. But the flow of revenue to the centre was dependent on the cities staying loyal and the Parthian kings could never rely on that, despite ingratiatingly calling themselves 'Philhellene' on their coins. The Greek-run cities remained, according to Plutarch, 'invariably hostile' to Parthia's rulers, ready at any moment to switch allegiances in the endless civil wars that bedevilled the empire. Rome's rulers had the wealth to bribe its cities because it controlled taxation, and if bribery failed it could always fall back on the threat of overwhelming military force – itself paid for in large part by taxation. Parthia's rulers could neither bribe nor threaten so successfully; they were dependent on local chiefs for most of their army, and they, like the cities, could never be relied upon.

Seleucia, which lay at the confluence of the Tigris River and a major canal from the Euphrates, was the richest and most successful commercial city in Parthia. It rivalled Alexandria in its wealth and size. Like the great Roman trading cities, it had a large and mixed population (Pliny put it at 600,000, though he probably overestimated) of Iranians, Arab nomads, Babylonians, Assyrians, Phoenicians, Palmyrenes and Jews (5,000 Jews, if Josephus' figures are to be believed, were massacred there in 41 BC). Boats bringing frankincense from Arabia sailed up the Tigris from the Persian Gulf, or arrived from the other direction carrying goods from the Mediterranean. They docked at Seleucia's harbour and were charged for the right to do so. Caravans using the overland routes to Samarkand and beyond to China stopped to do business, or take on new merchants for the next stage of the journey. Apricots, cast iron and above all silk, the most sought-after material of the ancient world, came from China, while Parthian pomegranates and rugs made the reverse journey to the kingdoms of India, to the newly developing empire of the Kushans, to Samarkand and China, or went west to the oasis city of Palmyra and on to the Mediterranean. But the city was almost always opposed to the Parthian king. In AD 36 it would back a pretender to the throne and rebel against the king for seven years.

Across the Tigris from Seleucia was the new city of Ctesiphon. It was the Parthians' attempt to create a rival to Seleucia, which would be, like Rome, the centralizing force and focus of the empire. The two cities confronted each other across the great trading river: Seleucia, ancient, and ineluctably Greek, was built on the rectangular Greek grid system with streets at right angles to each other, though, as Strabo noted, it also had its own local flavour: the single-storey houses had brightly painted pillars, made of palmwood (the only tree that grew in the area) with ropes of twisted reeds wound round them, and the rooms were vaulted with sun-dried mudbricks, because wood was so scarce and expensive. But the city still sounded and looked Greek. It still had its gymnasia and theatre. Its Greek elite still jealously guarded their control of the city, excluding most non-Greeks from citizenship – and therefore from the right to hold office and vote on the affairs of the city.

The modern city of Ctesiphon, on the opposite bank, was Parthian rather than Hellenistic in style; it was built to a circular plan, which made it much easier to defend and required considerably less walling than the Greek-style rectangular city. According to Marcellinus, the fourth-century Roman historian, King Pacorus I enlarged the city 'by an immigration of many citizens' in 39 BC, though how big Ctesiphon was is unclear: Strabo describes it as both 'a large village' and a city 'that lodges a great number of people... provided by the Parthians with wares for sale and with the arts that are pleasing to the Parthians; for the Parthian kings are accustomed to spend the winter there because of the salubrity of the air'.[6]

But Ctesiphon never became the focus of an empire, a true capital city like Rome. The variation of official titles used throughout the empire was a clear sign that each city-state, kingdom and small territory was going its own administrative way and that Parthia's rulers had failed to impose any simple uniformity in administration over the whole empire.

Even the court never remained at Ctesiphon that long. Phraataces and Musa were constantly moving around the empire – evidence perhaps that there was no one sufficiently trustworthy to whom they could delegate power. They stayed in the palace at Ctesiphon, where every surface was covered in designs of dogs, winged dragons, battles and hunting scenes, picked out in brilliant yellow, red, green and brown stucco. But they were only there during the winter and even then they probably divided their time between Ctesiphon, Babylon and possibly the palace at Seleucia. In the summer, they travelled north-east to their palaces at Ecbatana in the Zagros Mountains and to the oasis city of Merv on the edge of the Turkmenistan desert. In general, the Parthians preferred to avoid city life.

Unable to rule the city, unwilling to live in it, the Parthian rulers lacked the base from which they could impose themselves on their subjects. For the 500 years they ruled they were indeed considered outsiders by the peoples that made up their empire. Augustus, Rome's first de facto emperor, made himself visible in every city of his empire through the great public monuments, statues and temples he erected. Seleucia, Parthia's richest city, still kept the name and used the calendar of the Seleucids, the Greek rulers of the former Achaemenid Persian Empire. Even more significant, the city still worshipped the Seleucid dynasty the founders of the city.[7] The Parthians had ousted the Seleucid rulers physically, but had not managed to dislodge them mentally. Augustus, on the other hand, stamped himself on the minds of every city-dweller in his empire through the imperial cult he inaugurated (see chapter 2). The Parthian rulers may have tried to do the same. Certainly Musa, the former slave and gift of Augustus, was called 'Goddess Musa' when she was married to King Phraates. On their coins, the kings inscribed themselves as gods. What that actually meant is unclear. They may have thought of themselves as god rulers or as earthly incarnations of the Zoroastrian supreme god Ahura Mazda ('Lord Wisdom'), or, less arrogantly, as having the divine blessing of an impersonal force, a sort of divine right of kings which the Iranians believed was conferred on every legitimate ruler (see chapter 14 for China's version of the divine right of rulers).[8]

The Parthians may not have been credible as god-rulers – their grasp on the throne was too tenuous – but they did try to wrap themselves in the aura of Zoroastrianism to give them the authority they lacked. The great Persian Emperors Cyrus and Darius, who had been Zoroastrians or at least had placed Ahura Mazda at the head of the pantheon before Alexander the Great, 'the accursed' as Zoroastrians called him, had conquered their empire and all but destroyed their religion. His soldiers had killed their priests – preservers of the prayers and rituals, which were handed down orally – and looted their temples. According to later Zoroastrian texts, when the Greek Seleucid rulers were defeated, the new Parthian conquerors proclaimed their allegiance to Zoroastrianism. They claimed that their Arsacid clan was linked with the legendary kings of the *Avesta* – the sacred poems and hymns of Zoroastrianism. They appeared on coins standing with their nobles beside the fire altar. Fire, the great purifier, was the sacred symbol of Ahura Mazda, the Zoroastrian supreme god. They built fire temples in their palaces, and were crowned by Zoroastrian Magi priests.

The Iranian epic *Vis and Ramin* describes a royal coronation when the king rode through the city of Ctesiphon, which was decked out with flowers and royal arches, while the kettledrums rolled and the trumpets blared. 'Every hand cast jewels in his path. Every tongue called down blessings upon him... Above hung a cloud of smoke from musk and ambergris.'⁹ Surrounded by his nobles and vassal kings, he entered the palace. A member of the mighty Suren clan exercised the clan's traditional right of crowning the new king. He placed a jewel-encrusted tiara on the king's ringleted head, while the surrounding nobles and vassal kings hailed their new 'king of kings'. One after another, they came forward and flung cupfuls of pearls at his feet.

Then the king and his retinue processed through the palace's vast vaulted halls hung with rich tapestries, and carpeted with the finest rugs, and through the courtyards to the fire temple where Magi priests waited, holding bundles of myrtle branches and wearing round their heads high felt turbans which covered their cheeks as far as their lips. Great mounds of ash covered the floor of the domed sanctuary. The king processed to the mudbrick altar, where the priests

177

had prepared a fire. He poured oil on the dry wood, and lit the sacred fire, feeding the flames with sandalwood, aloe, camphor and musk, but being careful not to blow on it, for, according to Strabo, 'those who blow the fire with their breath or put anything dead or filthy upon it are put to death'. The sacred fire blazed up, a fire that the Magi priests had to keep permanently alight, and the king's reign was dated from that moment.

Zoroastrianism,* that is, the body of beliefs and rituals which had been slowly evolving since the prophet-poet Zoroaster started preaching his message to the Iranian nomads, at some time between the eighteenth century BC and 1000 BC, had all the potential of becoming a world religion. Indeed, it had in itself the seeds of three of the five world religions – the monotheist religions of Judaism, Christianity and Islam. It had a supreme god who was also a moral god in constant battle with the self-created force of chaos and evil. Ahura Mazda required moral behaviour from his worshippers who had to prepare for his imminent arrival and last judgement by their prayers, good thoughts and good deeds. Zoroastrianism had messiahs who would defeat the enemy on the battlefield and resurrect the dead; the righteous would be sent to Heaven and the wicked cast into hell, though they only remained in hell for three days, after which a life of bliss was guaranteed for all creation. Only the evil divinity Angra Mainyu and the forces of evil are assigned to eternal darkness.

Zoroastrianism gave its worshippers not just ritual but a way of living. It offered them the promise of a blissful afterlife and the assurance of a supreme god; it bound its worshippers together in festivals which were both holy days and holidays of feasting and dancing when the king rode in procession mounted on an elephant, with galloping horses in front and 'moonlike beauties' carried in litters behind, while the people picnicked and danced in the fields.

Parthia's large trading cities in the west, with their mixed

---

* 'Zoroastrianism' – like 'Buddhism', 'Confucianism' and most religions of the ancient world – had not yet coalesced into a concrete set of practices or beliefs. But though it is misleading to call any of them 'isms', I will do so for the sake of brevity.

populations, provided just the sort of context that in the Roman Empire would create the perfect conditions for the mystery cults and Christianity, as the trading cities in the kingdoms of India would for Buddhism. Zoroastrianism had its followers throughout the Parthian Empire. Yet it never established itself, so far as it is possible to tell, as the overarching religion that linked together the peoples of Parthia. Zoroastrianism, reflecting the society from which it was emerging, was not a uniforming, centralizing religion, just as the Parthians were not centralizing rulers. Like Parthia's rulers, Zoroastrianism did not generate enough commitment amongst its worshippers to become strong enough to impose itself.

Zoroastrianism, at that time, never demanded sole allegiance from its followers. Like the mystery deities, Ahura Mazda allowed other gods their existence. Nothing prevented a good Zoroastrian from paying his reverence to all the many gods that thronged together in the Parthian Empire as they did in the Roman Empire. Ahura Mazda was recognized as supreme, but he was worshipped along with Anahita and Mithra (the progenitor of the Mithras cult which would become so popular with Roman soldiers in the second century AD). Zoroastrianism would have no martyrs as the Christians did; indeed it specifically told its worshippers that they were free to reject their own religion under torture. Nor did it require from its worshippers the sort of self-punishing behaviour that the 'world-rejecting' religions of Buddhism, Judaism and Christianity did. The hardships that these religions demanded meant that their worshippers had to be hugely committed and prepared to forfeit worldly delights, but the more the worshippers put into their religion the more valuable it became to them. Zoroastrianism, on the contrary, enjoined on its followers the duty of being happy; it rejected all forms of monasticism, of separation from the world in order to be devoted to the spiritual; there were no fast days, because hunger, along with sorrow, belonged to the evil spirit; Zoroastrian festivals were, like Roman ones, a time of lavish banquets, with unstinting wine and music, often played by women who were permanently attached to the temple.

For religion and kingship to be mutually advantageous, the religion had to be powerful enough to make itself worth enlisting by the king, and the king had to be strong enough to be able to impose a religion on his people. The great Emperor Ashoka imposed Buddhism on his Indian Empire in the third century BC; Christianity had its Constantine in the fourth century AD, but Parthian kings struggled just to keep their grip on the throne. The 'king of kings' had to recognize the gods of the constituent parts of his empire. Although the Parthian rulers embraced Zoroastrianism, they were in a sense no use to Zoroastrianism, just as Zoroastrianism was of no use to them in shoring up their kingship.

By AD 4, only six years after Phraataces had been crowned king, the nobles had sickened of him as they had of his mother-wife Musa, who by now was depicted on coins looking like a rather frumpy matron, with a developing double chin, hawkish nose and protruding eyes. The nobles plumped instead for Orodes, one of Phraataces' half-brothers, who was living in Rome as a 'hostage' – part prisoner, part guest of the Romans, but either way an extremely useful pawn in Rome's diplomatic battle with Parthia.

Orodes was escorted by his Parthian supporters – and, probably, a contingent of Roman soldiers – across the Mediterranean, through the Syrian Desert and the oasis city of Palmyra to the Euphrates and the edge of the Roman Empire. There, on the right bank of the river where wild boar grazed, the pretender paused before crossing the river to fight for the Parthian throne. He offered a sacrifice of a finely harnessed horse; in their turn, the Romans offered a boar ram and bull to Mars. Then both Parthians and Romans crossed the river on a bridge made of boats.

On the Parthian side of the river, they were joined by the supporters of the coup, nobles on horseback, daggers in their belts, protected by fur caps and capes. Court officials who had turned against their former king brought treasure from the court as proof of their loyalty – purses of gold and silver, golden goblets, jewels, coins and royal regalia.[10] The commander of the Roman troops had discharged his duty – he had delivered up the pretender – now it was up to Orodes and his supporters to fight it out with the incumbent king. Leaving them with a patronizing speech, the Romans marched back to Syria. The contender and his entourage rode off through the fruit groves and marshlands of Mesopotamia, which was littered with visible reminders of the precariousness of empires. They rode past ruined and looted temples, half-deserted villages and crumbling cities, past bustling new mercantile centres with their half-built new temples and building sites. Each civilization in turn – Assyrian, Babylonian, Persian and Greek – had built their colossal monuments in the certainty that they would last forever and each in turn had crumbled away.

Orodes successfully claimed his kingdom, becoming Orodes III. Phraataces and Musa fled across the Euphrates to Syria where they were probably murdered. They were never heard of again. But, only three years later, Orodes himself was assassinated by his nobles. Another Parthian delegation set off for Rome to ask the emperor to give them another 'hostage' from the Parthian royal family on the grounds, according to Josephus, that the previous king had become 'too cruel and of a violent disposition'. It was a pattern that repeated itself time and time again in Parthian history.

Perhaps because the Parthian nobles knew the new king's reign would not be a long one, they were never very particular about their candidate. Tacitus recorded one delegation as saying when they appeared before the Emperor Tiberius in about AD 35: 'All that was needed... was a name and an authorization: the name of a Parthian royalty and the authorization of Tiberius.'*

In AD 38, the newly installed Parthian King Vardanes I found his fragile grip on power threatened, like so many of his predecessors.

---

* In case a note of Roman triumphalism should creep in here, it is worth pointing out that while Rome's emperors may have had more authority than their Parthian counterparts, they too were not immune from disloyalty. Post-Augustus, they were always in danger of losing control to the army. The mad Caligula was assassinated by officers of the Praetorian Guard in AD 41; Nero was abandoned by his bodyguard and forced to commit suicide in AD 68; and in the one-year civil war of AD 68–69 two short-lived emperors – Galba and Vitellius – were both killed by troops loyal to their imperial successors.

Vardanes lost control of Seleucia, his most valuable city. That same year one of the most renowned holy men of the time, a 'son of god' who after his death appeared to one of his doubting followers, visited Vardanes in Babylon.

10

A 'PAGAN CHRIST' IN BABYLON

But the people of the country say that just at the moment of the birth, a thunderbolt seemed about to fall to earth and then rose up into the air and disappeared aloft; and the gods thereby indicated, I think, the great distinction to which the sage was to attain, and hinted in advance how he should transcend all things upon earth and approach the gods, and signified all the things that he would achieve.

Philostratus, *The Life of Apollonius of Tyana*, I.5, *c*.AD 217–238

A girl had died just in the hour of her marriage, and the bridegroom was following her bier lamenting as was natural his marriage left unfulfilled, and the whole of Rome was mourning with him, for the maiden belonged to a consular family. Apollonius then witnessing their grief, said: 'Put down the bier, for I will stay the tears that you are shedding for this maiden.'

And withal he asked what was her name... but merely touching her and whispering in secret some spell over her, at once woke up the maiden from her seeming death; and the girl spoke out loud, and returned to her father's house,

Now whether he detected some spark of life in her, which those who were nursing her had not noticed – for it is said that although it was raining at the time, a vapor went up from her face – or whether her life was really extinct, and he restored it by the warmth of his touch, is a mysterious problem which neither I myself nor those who were present could decide.

The Life of Apollonius of Tyana, III.45

A pollonius was the contemporary of Jesus but more famous at the time. Like many Hellenistic charismatic men, he was called the 'son of god' or 'son of Zeus'. By the third century AD his followers thought of him as the pagan Christ, but far holier; the Stoic Hierocles, one of the fiercest persecutors of the Christians, argued that Apollonius was a much greater miracle worker. In the fourth century pagans and Christians were still arguing amongst themselves as to whether Christ or Apollonius was the holier man. The debate continued into the eighteenth century, though a sceptical Edward Gibbon was 'at a loss to discover whether he [Apollonius] was a sage, an imposter, or a fanatic'.[1] Apollonius' hagiographic biographer, the third-century Sophist Philostratus, records the love he inspired for his universal goodness, his exorcisms and his miracles.[2] After his physical disappearance from the world in AD 100 – Philostratus is hesitant to say that he actually died – Apollonius appeared to a doubting disciple. Maybe Apollonius did not have the right message. Certainly Philostratus did not have the genius of Paul to be able to turn one amongst many holy men into the saviour of mankind who would be beloved by billions.

According to his biographer, Apollonius' birth had been foretold by the Egyptian god Proteus who appeared to Apollonius' mother in a vision. At an early age he was renowned for his learning. By the age of eighteen he had become an ardent follower of the teachings and rigorous disciplines of Pythagoras, the sixth-century BC Greek philosopher, mathematician and mystic. Apollonius abstained from women and wine and wore nothing made from the skin of animals. Dressed in white linen, his hair and beard uncut, he wandered barefoot through the cities and villages of the Roman Empire preaching his message of the supreme god, the immortality of the soul, and reincarnation – a somewhat similar message to that of the mystery cults and Pauline Christianity, except that Apollonius was far more interested in the need to purify the many cults of the empire, than in creating a community.

> He would call the priests [of the cults] together and talk wisely about the gods, and would correct them, supposing they had departed from the traditional forms... and then he would go in quest of his followers [there were only seven of them] and bid them ask any questions they liked... And having answered all the questions which his companions addressed to him, and when he had enough of their society, he would rise and give himself up for the rest of the day to haranguing the general public.[3]

For five years, however, Apollonius left the public in peace and kept a vow of silence before deciding he wanted to learn the wisdom of the Magi in Parthia and of the Brahmins in India. In about AD 38, approximately seven years after Jesus had been crucified, Apollonius set off with a disciple, Damis, for the Parthian province of Mesopotamia where the Parthian King Vardanes I was embroiled in yet another civil war.

The great city of Seleucia was in open revolt, refusing to recognize Vardanes and supporting his brother Gotarzes instead. From the nearby city of Nehardea two Jewish outlaw brothers were ruling their own independent territory. King Vardanes was staying at his palace in the crumbling city of Babylon, about 35 miles from the rebellious Seleucia. Babylon, which straddled both banks of the Euphrates, was, according to Strabo, half deserted. Great chunks of the city walls, once wide enough for four chariots, had collapsed; patches of wasteland and rubble lay between the surviving houses. Yet Babylon still survived even if Seleucia and the Parthians' own city of Ctesiphon had superseded it in importance. A community of

Greeks still attended its gymnasium and theatre. The Babylonians still worshipped their supreme god Marduk, or Bel ('Lord') as he was more often called, at their temple south of the tower of Babel. And the king himself spent some of the winter at his palace there – as long as the city was not hostile to him.

When Apollonius and Damis arrived at the city gates, the 'Satrap', the governor in command of the city, held out a golden statue of the king.[4] Everyone, except ambassadors from the Roman emperor, had to prostrate themselves before it or be arrested and barred entry to the city. Apollonius, however, refused. The Satrap ran to the palace to inform the 'Ears of the King' – the royal spies. Apollonius was questioned. Had he brought presents for the king? Courage and justice, answered the twenty-five-year-old Apollonius. His brave and wise answers to their questions so impressed the officials that they took him to meet the king. They escorted him through endless pavilions and halls with blue or red lacquered pillars embedded with jewels, the ceilings coffered with painted panels, dripping festoons of pearls. Apollonius passed rooms set aside for playing chess, galleries of royal statuary glittering with silver and solid gold, hung with rich tapestries and lined with the finest rugs, and through the throne room where the king gave judgement below a domed sky-blue ceiling of lapis lazuli decorated with images of the gods, 'looking like golden figures shining out of the ether'. The gods had been placed there by the Magi, the 'tongues of the gods', as Philostratus said they were called.

Refusing to be impressed, Apollonius looked neither to right nor left until he came to the palace temple, where the king with his Magi 'was on the point of sacrificing a horse... adorned with trappings as if for a triumphal procession'. Vardanes, unlike his officials, recognized Apollonius as the renowned Pythagorean holy man from the Roman Empire and begged him to stay. Apollonius, however, preferred to stay with a Babylonian 'of good character' rather than be 'housed above my rank'. 'I cannot', he said, 'become either for you or for anybody else a companion in drinking or an associate in idleness and luxury' – not a happy message to a Parthian – 'but if you have problems of conduct that are difficult and hard to settle, I will furnish you with solutions, for I not only know matters of practice and duty, but I even know them beforehand.'

For over a year, Apollonius and the king talked regularly. Apollonius was a friend of kings – unlike Jesus, who addressed himself to the non-elite. In the cool of the evening, Vardanes and Apollonius wandered in the gardens lit by flaming torches and lamps or sat on the glittering bronze roof of the palace. At midday and midnight, Apollonius talked with the Magi priests attached to the palace, learning from them but also instructing them: 'They are wise men, but not in all respects,' he told his disciple Damis.

Perhaps thinking that he had learned all he was going to learn from the Magi after his year in Babylon, Apollonius became anxious to continue his journey and visit the holy men of India. King Vardanes provided him with four camels and a camel driver, as well as water and provisions for the journey. The king embraced Apollonius and he and Damis headed north.

They rode past groves of dates and apple trees, past fields of wild barley and chickpeas and through towns where families ate and slept on the flat roofs of their mudbrick houses, their courtyards lit by oil lamps. Villagers greeted them respectfully, for the leading camel of the caravan 'bore upon his forehead a chain of gold, to intimate to all who met them that the king was sending on their way some of his own friends'. They left the low-lying Mesopotamian plain and climbed uphill through the Zagros Mountains, where wild asses grazed and in the springtime mountain sheep and goats lay hidden amongst the tulips and violets.

Near the Parthians' summer palace in Ecbatana was the rubble of a once breathtaking gold and silver temple to Anahita, the goddess of water and fertility, who along with the supreme god Ahura Mazda, and Mithra, the god of light, was worshipped by Zoroastrians. Alexander's soldiers had looted Anahita's temple, leaving only a few gold bricks and silver roof tiles scattered among the stumps of gilded wooden columns. By the western gateway to the city pilgrims reverently touched, as they still do today, a massive stone lion, in the hope that it would make them fertile. The lion was all that remained of a sepulchral monument to Alexander the Great's friend and lover, the Macedonian nobleman Hephaestion.

Past Ecbatana, the travellers rode east towards Rhagae (near modern Tehran) by fields of wheat and herds of horses for which the area was famed. The land shelved gently down to the Iranian plateau and became increasingly arid. They crossed inlets of the Great Salt Desert of Iran. Mountains rose up to their north as they reached the fertile corridor that led to the Caspian Gates, the most important mountain pass in the ancient world. Today it is just part of the motorway between Tehran and Meshad. But when Apollonius and Damis rode through, it was the only overland way for travellers and goods to get from the West to the East. Once through the pass, the travellers turned south for Kabul (in modern Afghanistan) and left the Parthian Empire behind them.

About five years later, in AD 45, by which time Paul had begun spreading the cult of Jesus beyond the Jews to the Gentiles, King Vardanes, who had listened so eagerly to Apollonius, was assassinated while out hunting, and was succeeded by his ever-troublesome brother Gotarzes. Over the next century, the power of the Parthian kings progressively weakened as that of the nobles increased. They refused to pay levies and failed to answer the king's call to arms. The empire broke up into 240 independent states and the Arsacid royal family continued to murder each other in their constant succession struggles. Parthian rule finally collapsed in AD 224 when Sasan, a vassal king, killed the last of the Parthian kings in battle. The succeeding Sasanian dynasty also suffered from a rapid turnover of kings and overmighty nobles, but it was more successful at imposing its authority over the empire, and indeed adopted Zoroastrianism as the state religion. Its Magi priests became increasingly powerful and as ministers of state would persecute rival religions, including Judaism, Christianity and Buddhism. Zoroastrianism became the popular religion in Iran and Central Asia, practised from the Middle East to the western border of China.

But when Arab tribesmen conquered the Sasanian Empire in the seventh century AD, Zoroastrianism crumbled in the face of a more powerful religion. The empire's elite converted to Islam or fled to India.* Zoroastrianism did not aim to conquer the world; it was not a proselytizing religion. Buddhism, however, which had its home to the east of Parthia, had from the beginning its missionary monks. Even the organizationally brilliant Paul was never so explicit about proselytizing. By the time Apollonius the pagan Christ was making his journey to India, Buddhism had already arrived in the eastern parts of the Parthian Empire. Buddhism would prove immensely popular and would spread from India throughout the East. It also found its Constantine, the great Indian Emperor Ashoka, yet he never managed to establish Buddhism permanently in India. Buddhism became the only one of the world religions to wither in its birthplace.

---

* In 2002, there were only about 125,000 Zoroastrians left in the world, of whom the majority were Parsis whose ancestors had fled from Iran to India to escape the Muslim invaders. Christianity, the largest religion in the world, claimed over two billion adherents, while the second largest, Islam, which took over the former Parthian Empire, claimed over one billion.

11

INDIA: BRAHMINS VERSUS MONKS

A bureaucracy is usually characterized by the thorough contempt of all irrational religion, combined, however, with the recognition of its usefulness as a means of the domestication of the governed.

Max Weber, *The Sociology of Religion*, 1922

It is the king in whom the duties of both Indra (the rewarder) and Yama (the punisher) are blended, and he is a visible dispenser of punishments and rewards; whoever disregards kings will be visited with divine punishments, too. Hence kings shall never be despised.

Kautilya, *Arthashastra*, late fourth century BC

No Brahman is such by birth. No outcaste is such by birth. An outcaste is such by his deeds. A Brahman is such by his deeds.

Vasala Sutta (Discourse on Outcasts), v.136, *Sutta Nipata*, the earliest Buffhist scriptures, written down in 29 BC

When Apollonius and his disciple Damis had crossed the Hindu Kush Mountains – where Damis saw the chains that had pinned Prometheus to the rocks, 'though you could not easily guess at the material of which they were made'[1] – the monsoon rains were over.

Muddy water sparkled in the channels dug around the small fields of wheat and barley, protected by scarecrows made out of buffalo skeletons. Mongoose and porcupines rustled in the hedges. Great wooden bullock carts lumbered by, loaded with fruit, long pepper, spikenard, muslins and cottons, lion, leopard and tiger skins. They were on their way through what is now the northern part of Punjab province (in present-day Pakistan) to the great port cities from where the goods would be shipped eastwards to China and west to Parthia, Arabia, the Roman Empire and the African kingdoms of Meroe and Axum. Even the Temple in Jerusalem was hung with fabrics from India.

Like the rest of Strabo's known world, trade was booming and the kingdoms of India (by which I mean the whole of the Indian subcontinent) were catering to an ever increasing demand for Indian goods from the Roman and Chinese Empires. Great trade routes criss-crossed the continent. Though Strabo never visited India, he reported in his *Geographia* that the Indians 'make roads, and at every ten stadia place pillars showing the by-roads and the distances'.

The travellers discussed elephants as they rode, quoting the great expert King Juba, of Mauretania, who had been part of the Roman peace delegation to Parthia (see chapter 9). The fields gave way to orchards and gardens growing vegetables and flowers as Apollonius and Damis neared walled villages, their entrances marked by two thin wooden poles stuck in the ground and joined at the top by festoons of greenery. Women washed their laundry in pools outside the walls.

Smoke from offerings rose in the sweet clear air; men and women hung garlands from deep-spreading banyan trees. They sprinkled the trunk with sugared water, smeared it with red-coloured powders and oils, or spurted water at the trunk with their mouths; between the dripping roots they placed little cakes and left incense sticks to smoulder. Villagers venerated their trees as home of the Yaksas, the spirits who might grant them fertility, prosperity and long life in exchange for the right offerings.

Buddhist monks in saffron-coloured robes walked by with downcast eyes, for fear of meeting a woman's glance, and rattled the iron rings that dangled from the top of their pilgrim staffs. The travellers passed a half-naked Brahmin, a member of the highest caste according to Brahmanism, which was developing into the religion we know as Hinduism.* The Brahmin had left his wife and family to devote the end of his life to being a wandering holy man (a *sannyâsin* or *sâdhu*). His body was smeared with ash. In one hand he held a bamboo cane to ward off evil spirits; a spare loincloth, a begging bowl and a water pot hung from a yoke balanced on his shoulders. Like all Brahmins, his hair was gathered up in a knot on top of his head, and a sacred thread was looped across his bare chest.

The travellers saw Buddhist stupas (shrines), Jain temples, and timbered Brahmanic temples, their doors garnished with garlands of flowers, their walls marked by the imprint of hands dipped in sandalwood, their courtyards crowded with pilgrims, beggars, the sick and the dying. They passed groves of wild olive, and entered a valley which was, in the words of the seventh-century Chinese scholar Xuanzang, 'a land of rich harvests, flowing streams and fountains, abundant flowers and fruits',[2] though today the surrounding hills are brown and barren most of the year.

Towards morning, Apollonius and Damis passed the Ionic columns of a Zoroastrian fire temple and approached the massive 19-foot-thick mudbrick ramparts topped by serrated parapets, which guarded the city of Taxila (near Islamabad in today's Pakistan). As they got nearer they heard 'trumpeting elephants... the neighing of horses in their stalls... the sound of drums being beaten and conches blown in time in Shiva's great temple and in the sanctuaries of all the other gods... the Vedas [the Brahmanic collections of sacred hymns and rites] being chanted by the learned Brahmins and the prayers being recited by the monks, filling the morning air with their holy murmur'.[3] A great city was waking up to the sounds of the three great religions of India, captured for us in the *Shilappadikaram* (*The Ankle Bracelet*), the sensuous poem written by a Jain prince who may also have become a monk. Though Prince Adigal was writing about the Tamil

---

* Many scholars would argue that 'Hinduism' is in fact a colonial, specifically British, invention of the nineteenth century, corralling together under one umbrella what were in fact a variety of different beliefs and practices. I follow the opposing scholarly line that though there are many varieties of Hindu thought, they have enough in common to justify the term.

kingdoms in the south of the Indian subcontinent, and he could have been writing at any time between the first and third century AD (ancient Indians were far more interested in theorizing than in chronicling and dates are therefore notoriously elusive), he provides a rare glimpse, and scholars think a reasonably accurate one, of life in ancient India.*

Buddhism and its more austere sister Jainism were enjoying their heyday in India. They had developed in the sixth and fifth centuries BC in reaction to the caste dominance of Brahmanism. The caste system on which Brahmanism was based ineluctably separated man from man into a series of groups, ranked in order of superiority, which determined both spiritual and temporal life. Each caste had its own different social and moral duties and capacity to attain salvation.

Brahmanism defined people according to their group identity, their caste. In this collectivist hierarchical view of mankind all men were not alike or equal – perhaps a more accurate description of their world than the Buddhist and Jainist one which offered the prospect of liberating men and women from their group identity. For Buddhists and Jains, men and women were no longer defined – and separated – by what group/caste they belonged to; they were defined by the abstract individuality that everyone shared. Paradoxically, by individualizing mankind, the 'heretical sects' of Buddhism and Jainism universalized and therefore equalized it: all men and – in a somewhat grudging concession by Siddhārtha Gautama, the Buddha – women, too, could share the same spiritual goals, the same moral duties and the same route to salvation.

The group religions tend to exclude, while a universalist religion can unite peoples from a multiplicity of cultures, and languages – the task that all rulers of empires struggle with. There are many different ways for a religion to be successful, however, and universalism is not the only route; nor does it guarantee popularity. Though the

---

* Because of the paucity of material, I have relied, for this and the following chapter, on sources ranging from the more historically reliable to the literary and legendary. The interested reader should consult E. Lamotte, *History of Indian Buddhism* (Peeters, 1988) for a thorough treatment of sources.

universalist message might in theory be a useful tool for the empire-builder trying to weld his peoples together, it does not always work.

The move from the group-oriented religion to the individually oriented and therefore universalist religion was the same move that Christianity would make from Judaism. Christianity, however, was a hymn to the unique preciousness of every self: it is no longer the tribe that is elect, but every soul. For Buddhists, on the other hand, the attainment of nirvana depended on realizing that the 'I' was a pernicious illusion, that it was simply a transient bundle of desires that chained one to the world. Nevertheless, both religions used universalism to dissolve old hierarchies, a move that made them particularly attractive to new and rising elites. Just as Christianity would do, so Buddhism and Jainism found their greatest support amongst the wealthy merchants of the city and amongst aspiring empire-builders.

Taxila, like all India's trading cities, was a relatively tolerant host of diverse religions and gods. 'The greatest city in India', according to Apollonius, as quoted by his biographer Philostratus, was renowned as much for its commerce as for its religious teachers who attracted students of all persuasions. But when Apollonius and Damis visited Taxila it was predominantly Buddhist. With its numerous merchants, mixed population and newly installed foreign king, Taxila was the perfect home for Buddhism.

The travellers entered the city over a bridge that crossed a series of moats, and went under one of the pillared porticoes high enough for elephants to get through with their swaying palanquins. Officials at the gatehouse collected tolls. Apollonius and Damis were told to wait at the Brahmanic temple of the Sun, while the king was informed of their presence.

Records of the period are minimal and muddled, but it is likely that the king in question was the Parthian Gondophares, who may well have been a member of the powerful Suren family – like the chief who had been beheaded following his victory over the Romans at Carrhae in 53 BC (see chapter 9).

Whether Gondophares ruled his vast kingdom in the Gandhara region (in today's northern Pakistan and eastern Afghanistan) as a reasonably loyal client king of Parthia's, or had broken away from the Parthian Empire, is not clear. Nor do we know for certain whether 'Gondophares' was his actual name or simply a title for members of the ruling dynasty he founded; he may even be two separate Gondophares who have through time been rolled into one. What we do know is that he was part of the invasion into the region, which had started around the middle of the first century BC, of Parthians from the west and tribes from the vast grasslands of Central Asia to the north who had pushed out the former Greek rulers. The Indo-Greeks were still, however, a dominant presence when Apollonius and Damis were escorted through the streets of Taxila to Gondophares' palace.

The city was, according to Apollonius' Greek biographer Philostratus:

> divided up into narrow streets in the same irregular manner as in Athens, and the houses were built in such a way that if you look at them from outside they had only one storey, while if you went into one of them, you at once found subterranean chambers extending as far below the level of the earth as did the chambers above.[4]

Each neighbourhood had its shrine, temple or Buddhist stupa, with their Corinthian or Ionic columns, their pilasters and pediments.

Artisans and small tradesmen sat cross-legged on the ground in their small stalls. Bankers made silent deals by touching fingers. Powdered and perfumed merchants strolled under bamboo umbrellas, their eyes rimmed with kohl, and their lips reddened with lac.* Near the heart of the city the royal escort passed great houses with battlemented parapets, their smooth stucco walls relieved only by slit-like windows. Inside, the tiled and carpeted rooms were filled

---

* A scarlet resin secreted by lac insects, which was used in cosmetics and as a dye.

with Graeco-Roman bronze statuettes, furniture inlaid with a riot of figures in gleaming white ivory, Chinese lacquer boxes and glassware from Rome. Parrots and parakeets squawked in gilded cages hanging from the verandahs. As many as fifty people lived in these big houses – a large extended family, servants, slaves, workmen and craftsmen, and perhaps some resident young students who were studying under a Buddhist, Jain or Brahmanic teacher in this university city. These were the homes of the merchants and bankers who were accumulating great fortunes. It was to them above all that Buddhism and Jainism appealed.

Under the Brahmanic caste system, the merchants, however wealthy they became, would always be inferior to the two castes above them. Priests could only come from the Brahmin caste. Only Brahmins could perform the Vedic rituals and teach the Vedas (the sacred writings on which Brahmanism was based). According to some interpretations of the sacred writings – and of course these interpretations were made by the Brahmins as the scholarly and priestly caste – only Brahmins could attain *moksha*, release from the endless cycle of rebirth; everyone else had to ascend the caste ladder in successive reincarnations. Below them in the hierarchy of caste, at least theoretically, was the Kshatriya warrior caste – the protectors of the community – from which India's kings were usually drawn. Between them the Brahmins and Kshatriyas controlled spiritual and temporal power in an alliance which held firm, though there was always a struggle as to which predominated – 'church' or 'state'.

In theory, the Vaisyas, the caste of traders and farmers to which the merchants belonged, should have been treated as equal in status to the Kshatriyas. The Vaisyas, like the two castes above them, were also 'twice-born', that is, they were born both physically and spiritually, since after their initiation ceremony in childhood they were entitled to read the sacred scriptures and thus gain access to the knowledge that might enable them to achieve *moksha*. But the Vaisyas found themselves on the whole excluded from the tight alliance between the Brahmins and the Kshatriyas. In the *Laws of Manu*, compiled some time between the third century BC and AD 200, in which Brahmin scholars set out the divine laws of right conduct (the duties of each caste), the Vaisyas were firmly classed with women and Sudras, the lowest caste, whose duty it was to serve the three higher castes.

The Vaisyas, like the Sudras, were materially as well as spiritually disadvantaged. Brahmins and Kshatriyas, the spiritual and temporal protectors of the community, did not pay taxes; Vaisyas, the wealth creators of the community, had to pay heavier taxes and duties and higher interest rates. Brahmins were exempt from capital punishment, such as being trampled to death by an elephant; Kshatriyas were punished more lightly for crimes such as sexual intercourse with a Brahmin woman: 'a Vaisya shall forfeit all his property after imprisonment for a year; a Kshatriya shall be fined one thousand panas and be shaved with the urine of an ass.'[5]

It was true that caste boundaries could be more or less restrictive, depending on the dominance of Brahmins in the region, the caste of the local ruler, his political strength and the size and economic fortunes of the various castes; and inter-caste marriages were frequent enough to provoke laws banning them. But it was only by accepting one's caste status and faithfully performing the duties required that an individual acquired the necessary merit to enter a higher caste in the following life. Brahmanism was a powerful recipe for social stability. But it was hardly likely to suit the beneficiaries of India's booming trade, whose new wealth did not match their caste status.

In the port cities of Barbaricum (the nearest port to Taxila, near the modern-day city of Karachi, in Pakistan) and further south at Barygaza (near modern Mumbai) ships from the Roman Empire docked alongside ships from Meroe, from its neighbour Axum, from Arabia and from the Indian subcontinent itself. Great bales of merchandise marked with the quantity, weight and name of the owner were loaded and unloaded in a city that never slept. 'All night lamps were burning, the lamps of foreigners who talk strange tongues, and the lamps of the guards who watch over precious cargoes near the docks', wrote the author of the *Shilappadikaram*. Arab ships brought slaves, many of them women, who entered the Indian kings' harems or were enrolled into the female militia who guarded them.[6] Roman ships brought 'very costly vessels of silver, singing boys, beautiful maidens for the harem, fine wines, and gold'.[7] On their homeward journey, Roman ships loaded up with pearls, exotic animals for the games, peacocks and parrots to have as household pets and, above all, pepper to fill their silver pepper pots and spice their food.

A papyrus, recording a shipment of goods from Muziris on the Malabar coast of south-west India to Alexandria, listed a consignment containing over 4,700 pounds of ivory, nearly 790 pounds of textiles – muslins and cottons – and between 700 and 1,700 pounds of nard. Nard or spikenard was a plant found only in the region of the Himalayas from which an extremely expensive ointment was extracted.* The total value of the consignment recorded on the papyrus was about 131 talents, a huge sum, which could have purchased about 2,400 acres of Egypt's best farmland. And this was only one consignment, owned by a single individual or partnership. If the vessel had been a 500-tonner (no great size by Roman standards), there would have been as many as 150 such consignments in the hold.[8]

The risks were great, especially for the mariners. If they survived coral reefs, pirates and gale-force winds, they might not survive being becalmed when one of them was chosen by ballot and abandoned in the middle of the ocean on a raft as inducement to the gods to bring wind to fill the sails again. But if the ships reached their destination, the Indian merchant or banker involved could become very wealthy indeed, so wealthy that he needed a handbook, the *Kama Sutra*, written some time between the first and third centuries AD, to tell him how to spend his days and nights most pleasurably.

---

* Judas had good reason to be appalled at Mary's extravagant gesture of pouring this ointment on Jesus' feet when he visited her and her siblings Lazarus and Martha – the amount she bought was equivalent to a year's wages for a farm labourer.

In the morning, he should rise from his canopied bed, wash his teeth, perfume his body, colour his eyelids and lips, smoothe down his hair with beeswax and admire himself in the mirror. After breakfast he should teach his parrots how to speak, and watch a cock or ram fight. Then it was time for a siesta, followed by a change of clothes. In an outer room looking on to his pleasure gardens, he should lie chatting with his friends on couches covered with crimson cushions, spittoon at hand. At night he should entertain his courtesan with 'loving and agreeable conversation', watching her dance for him on carpets inlaid with gold and silver. And 'thus,' says the *Kama Sutra*, 'end the duties of the day.'[9]

The merchant with his long painted fingernails could afford to shower his courtesan with jewels and she in return would spend the day preparing herself for him, as the *Shilappadikaram* records with lingering delight. She 'bathed her fragrant black hair, soft as flower petals, in oil mixed with ten kinds of astringents, five spices and a blend of thirty-two pungent herbs. She dried it in the smoke of incense and anointed each tress with heavy musk paste.' She lined her eyes with kohl, plaited her hair with garlands, and painted her breasts and arms with filigree patterns of sandal paste.

> She then adorned her tiny feet, their soles dyed red, with well-chosen rings on her slender toes. She loaded her ankles with jewelry made of small bells, rings, chains, and hollow anklets. She elaborately ornamented her shapely thighs, fastened round her hips a girdle of thirty rows of pearls set on blue silk and embroidered with figures and flowers. Armlets studded with pearls, and bangles made of carved precious stones, embraced her arms... her rosy fingers disappeared under rings of dark rubies and flawless diamonds. Her frail throat was adorned with a chain of gold.[10]

By the evening, after the dancing and conversation on the pillared veranda, 'the breeze gently caressed many a lotus-eyed woman lying voluptuously against the strong chest of her lord'.[11]

Yet, according to the Brahmanic system, the merchant was inferior to the Brahmin and Kshatriya castes. He was lumped along with 'prostitutes, and musicians, and those who trade in cooked rice, liquor, and flesh'. He was told that the Brahmins are 'gods among humans' or 'human gods', that a Brahmin 'is born as the highest on earth, the lord of all created beings'[12] who should receive donations so that the donor could attain merit.

It is hardly surprising that merchants should find Buddhism and Jainism so attractive. These religions preached against the idea that only Brahmins could become priests; that they alone were the indispensable intermediaries with the gods, the sole holders of sacred knowledge. The ultimate goal for both Jainism and Buddhism was still, as in Brahmanism, to be free from the cycle of rebirths. But the spiritual and temporal path of their adherents was not determined by where they were born in the caste hierarchy. 'I do not call him a Brahmin merely because he is born of a Brahmin womb or sprung from a Brahmin mother. He is merely a "Bhovadi" [one addressed as "Sir"] if he is with impediments. He who is free from impediments, free from clinging, him I call a Brahmin,' proclaimed Siddhārtha Gautama, the Buddha.[13] Siddhārtha himself was the son of a king or chief of what is now part of Nepal; he may have been a Kshatriya, though it is possible that the area where he was born had not yet been conquered by the Aryans,* and was therefore outside the caste system altogether.

Buddhism taught that everyone, irrespective of caste and sex, could reach enlightenment. Mahavira, the sixth-century BC teacher who moulded a loose body of Jaina ideas into a coherent sect, and who may, like Siddhārtha, have been a Kshatriya, also stressed spiritual equality, though not for women: they had to be reborn as men before they could gain salvation. Every single living thing – the king as well as the slave or the tiniest insect – was an individual and

---

* The Aryans or Indo-Iranians were nomads from Central Asia who settled in the north-western part of the Indian subcontinent in about 1500 BC.

eternal soul, which was why *ahimsa* (non-violence) was such an essential part of Jainism.

The doctrine of equality naturally appealed to all those who were struggling to find a place in the new social order created by trade and empire. The city was Buddhism's home. The Buddha's first two converts had been merchants. Guilds of corn traders, bamboo workers, ironmongers, jewellers and perfumers, caravan traders, merchants, bankers and scribes all contributed land, money, cisterns or ivory doors to the great Buddhist and Jain cave monasteries that were being hewn out of the rock, and to the dazzling white temples being built throughout the subcontinent.

By cutting free from the group – from being born into a particular caste, or a particular race – Jainism and Buddhism potentially expanded their appeal from the local to the horizons of their known world, as Christianity would do when it freed itself from its ethnically exclusive, Jewish, roots. Brahmanism, on the other hand, was not well suited to the trading cities; it excluded rather than embraced the foreigner. It found its main support outside the city in the more traditional rural areas.[14] It was a mode of living for people who were welded together socially and religiously through the hierarchical ranking of caste. If you were not born into the caste system with the ritual rights and duties that implied, you could not be part of the Brahmanic community. Trading cities like Taxila were attracting increasing numbers of foreigners. Taxila was home to communities of Greeks, Bactrians from today's northern Afghanistan, Sakas (or Scythians, as the Greeks called the tribesmen who came originally from Central Asia) and Parthians, especially merchants from Mesopotamia. Even Taxila's new ruler, the Parthian Gondophares, was a foreigner. Slotting foreigners into the caste system was a problem. Brahmanism did not seem well adapted for an empire.

Everyone in the Roman Empire – except strictly religious Jews – participated in some way in the Roman religion, that is the rituals and festivals attached to its gods, and as a result became to some degree Romanized. As priests of the state cults, the elites gained access to Roman offices of state with all the wealth and status that implied. But the elites of the conquered tribal territories of the Indian subcontinent could not in theory become Brahmanized, if they were not already part of the caste system. They were equivalent to, though not subject to, the same indignities as the 'untouchables', the sweepers, tanners and disposers of dead bodies who, because they were so polluted, had to drink from a separate well, attend separate temple services, live beyond the burial grounds of the city and use only the dark, winding lanes leading off the main avenues so that the higher castes could avoid coming into any defiling contact with them.

In practice, Brahmanism tried to get round the problem by stipulating that a territory could be considered 'suitable for sacrifice', that is, Brahmanic, when the conquered or conquering king had established the four castes. He and the ruling strata could create the fiction that they were 'fallen Kshatriyas', that they were in fact descended from Kshatriyas who had immigrated from an ancient Brahmanic region, and had subsequently ceased to practise the sacred rites and to consult the Brahmins.[15] But many high-caste Brahmins would not accept this. And just as the 'half-Jew' Herod and Gentile converts to Judaism were considered of inferior status to the full Jew, so anyone who was not born into the caste system remained to some extent an outsider. In the territories that were Brahmanized, ordinary people who were not born into the caste system were still considered to be outcastes, and the castes could only be filled by genuine members of those castes immigrating into the area.

Brahmanism was not the easiest way of welding peoples together into an empire, although it was espoused by the founder of India's first and greatest ever empire, Chandragupta Maurya, who is thought to have conquered Taxila and the Gandhara region from the Greeks in the late fourth century BC. But he was fortunate in having a brilliant Brahmin chief minister who wrote for him a manual of statecraft that is one of the greatest political treatises of the ancient world.

A mixture of the prescriptive and the descriptive, the *Arthashastra* (*Treatise on Worldly Gain*) is an astute and wonderfully cynical examination of how to run an empire and how to exploit religion in the interests of the state. 'Compared to it Machiavelli's *The Prince* is harmless,' wrote Weber in his major work on the sociology of Indian religions.[16] The author, Kautilya (he is also known as Vishnugupta and Chanakya), probably wrote his treatise in the city of Taxila at the end of the fourth century BC; it was subsequently added to and amended in the second century AD.

Kautilya was a Brahmin, but though he insisted that it was the ruler's duty to ensure that everyone within the caste system followed the duties of their caste, or else 'the world will come to an end owing to confusion of castes and duties', he was too much of a political realist not to believe that when it came to a conflict of interests, state not church must prevail.

The Brahmanic caste system had in theory made a clear distinction between spiritual and temporal power, as Christianity would also do. The Brahmins held the spiritual power; the Kshatriyas, the warrior caste from which the kings usually came, held the temporal power. But in ancient India, as in medieval Europe, the theoretical distinction between church and state did not stop them struggling between themselves for dominance. Over time and throughout the varied kingdoms of India, the pendulum of power swung between the two castes, determining whether the kingdom was more centralized (when the temporal power wielded by the king and Kshatriyas was more dominant) or more feudal (when the power of the Brahmins backed by their vast landed endowments predominated).

At the time that Kautilya was writing, the balance of power was tipped in favour of the state, which was extremely centralized. It was paternalistic and autocratic, underpinned by a vast network of spies. In the *Arthashastra*, Kautilya recommends enlisting spies in the elaborate stings that he devises to test the loyalty of ministers and ordinary people. One test specifically involved getting the emperor's ministers to choose between their Brahmanic religion or their ruler.

For this test, Kautilya recommended that the emperor dismiss a Brahmin on the grounds that he had refused the emperor's order to teach Vedic scriptures to an outcaste, since to do so was forbidden by Brahmanism; the emperor's spies, posing as the injured priest's supporters, were then meant to encourage a rebellion against the unrighteous ruler. If the ministers refused to rebel, they were to be considered 'pure' and therefore fit for employment.

Kautilya had the cynic's – or perhaps just a member of the elite's – understanding of the vital political uses to which religion could be put. 'Winning over the enemy's people' was as important as 'intrigue, spies... siege, and assault' for successful conquest.[17] Kautilya was well aware that religion was the mental glue required to weld together the disparate parts of an empire, and that Brahmanism was incapable of fulfilling that function. The religious strategy he recommended was in fact that adopted, though in more inchoate fashion, by most emperors, from Parthia to Rome. Kautilya concentrated his attentions on a threefold policy of creating loyalty to the emperor by a quasi-deification of the ruler himself, suborning the conquered elites by using their religions, and moulding the people into good subjects by using theirs.

Weber has made the useful distinction between popular and elite religions. Popular or 'folk' religions, the religions of 'the masses', are quasi-magical and emotionally satisfying; they are more a set of rituals than a set of beliefs. The religions of the elite, on the other hand, are austere and rational. Weber saw the elite religion's gradual incorporation of the popular as one of the most significant characteristics in the evolution of a religion – one that was particularly noticeable amongst the religions of India as they developed in competition with one another (see chapter 12).

Kautilya, like so many members of the elite, whether in Rome, China or Meroe, whether in the ancient or the modern world, despised the religion of ordinary people with its gods, charms and spells, which didn't even attempt to concern itself with the meaning of the universe and mankind's role in it. He thought of it as mere 'superstition'. But, while Kautilya may have despised popular religion, he shamelessly recommended manipulating the people's belief in it for political purposes with the assistance of the empire's spies. If the king urgently needed money, Kautilya suggested that 'by causing a false panic owing to the arrival of an evil spirit on a tree in the city, wherein a man is hidden making all sorts of devilish noises, the king's spies, under the guise of ascetics, may collect money (with a view to propitiate the evil spirit and send it back)'.[18]

Kautilya never went so far as the Romans would do, over 300 years later, in encouraging a cult of the divine emperor. But he did exploit the Brahmanic association of the ruler with divinity. (It is unclear whether, in this tradition, the ruler was actually considered to be divine or merely had divine qualities.) Kautilya recommended that the emperor surround himself with the trappings of divinity, and show himself to be on speaking terms with the gods, as a way of impressing and inspiring loyalty in both his existing subjects and his newly conquered peoples. And he suggested a series of tricks in order to convince the people of the emperor's divinity, or at least his association with it:

Proclamation of his omniscience is as follows:... pretensions to the knowledge of foreign affairs by means of his power to read omens and signs invisible to others when information about foreign affairs is just received through a domestic pigeon which has brought a sealed letter....

Proclamation of his association with gods is as follows: Holding conversation with, and worshipping, the spies who pretend to be the gods of fire or altar when through a tunnel they come to stand in the midst of fire, altar, or in the interior of a hollow image; holding conversation with, and worshipping, the spies who rise up from water and pretend to be the gods and goddesses of Nágas [snakes]; placing under water at night a mass of sea-foam mixed with burning oil, and exhibiting it as the spontaneous outbreak of fire.[19]

Kautilya describes how 'Astrologers, sooth-sayers, fortune tellers, story-tellers' and the ubiquitous spies were to spread wide the news of the king's power 'to associate with the gods and of his having received from Heaven weapons and treasure'. Spies were to hold arguments – Kautilya virtually script-wrote them – in public places, proving that the king had the right to exact taxes because of his divine status, and warning that anyone who disobeyed the king would be afflicted with divine punishment.

The divine or semi-divine emperor should also be religiously tolerant. The king, said Kautilya, should not only 'adopt the same mode of life, the same dress, language, and customs as those of the people'; he should also 'follow the people in the faith with which they celebrate their national, religious and congregational festivals or amusements'. Such tolerance would have been frowned on by Plato, who, 100 years before Kautilya, considered a state cult to be so important to maintaining the integrity and unity of the state that it justified religious persecution: those who violated the beliefs and practices of the state cult should be imprisoned or put to death.

The Emperor Chandragupta followed Kautilya's advice. He never imposed Brahmanism as the state cult and in fact turned away from Brahmanism and became a fervent Jainist. He is credited with having brought Jainism to southern India. Tradition has it that at the end of his life Chandragupta became a Jainist monk and starved himself to death in the manner of Jainism's 'founder' Mahavira.

Chandragupta's grandson, however, did try to impose a state cult, albeit one that preached tolerance of all religions. In the third century BC, Ashoka controlled virtually the whole of the Indian subcontinent, more territory than any individual ruler would ever have again until the British in the nineteenth century AD. The sheer size of the empire, its new communities of foreign traders forming in the cities, its multiplicity of cultures, languages and religions, cried out not just for an extremely well-run administration, which it had, but for some means of uniting the people to each other and to their ruler. Buddhism was Ashoka's means of 'mass domestication' as the historian of ancient India, Romila Thapar, puts it. But the policy never really worked, despite the stupas that Ashoka built in every important city of his empire, and the 50-feet-high columns, the pillars of Ashoka, each topped with a snarling lion, on which were inscribed his Buddhist edicts calling for social harmony based on respect for all life and tolerance of all people, whatever their background or religion.

Ashoka chose the wrong religion. Despite its democratic, universalist message that men and women were equally deserving of respect, and equally capable of attaining salvation, Ashoka's brand of Buddhism was designed for an elite, not for the people. It was an austere, atheistic religion, with no gods to pray to, which preached detachment from the world, not enjoyment of it; Ashoka's Buddhism was not interested in providing the reassurance and emotional satisfactions which made ordinary life more bearable and pleasurable, and which made the religion that offered such consolations an essential part of people's lives. Ashoka dismissed rites of passage and rituals as 'vulgar and worthless'. He banned festivals and dances because they were distractions from the pursuit of spiritual truth and salvation, and as a result deprived himself of one of the most effective means of community-building. Ashoka's grandfather's minister, Kautilya, had understood that it was by making religious festivals part of the ordinary person's experience of life in the empire – by weaving together state, ritual and the sheer pleasure of dancing and feasting – that subject peoples can be persuaded to become loyal subjects and to feel part of a larger political entity. Kautilya had in fact specifically urged the emperor to 'show his devotion' to the religious festivals of his conquered peoples.

When Ashoka died at Taxila, around 232 BC, the Maurya Empire that had been founded by his grandfather virtually died with him. The empire broke up into separate kingdoms, and most of its rulers reverted to Brahmanism.* But though austere Buddhism had not worked as an imperial religion for Ashoka, the north-western part of the Indian subcontinent – the Gandhara region which included Taxila – remained under 'Buddhist rule'. This may have been because it was ruled by a succession of foreigners: from the early second century BC by the Greek descendants of Alexander the Great's army; from the early first century BC by Saka (Scythian) tribesmen from Central Asia; and, at the beginning of the first century AD, by the Parthian Gondophares, whose kingdom was always threatened by, and would eventually submit to, the expansionary aims of nomads.

Gondophares' guests Apollonius and Damis were deeply impressed by the modesty of his living. When they had passed the almshouses, the stables, cowsheds, elephant stalls and coach houses of the outer palace, they had expected to see bejewelled pavilions and halls, and rooms lined with sheets of ivory, as they had at the palace of the Parthian King Vardanes. But, to their great pleasure, Apollonius and Damis

> saw no magnificent chambers, nor any bodyguards or sentinels, but, considering what is usual in the houses of magnates, a few servants, and three or four people who wished... to converse with the king. And... they admired this arrangement more than they did the pompous splendour of Babylon, and their esteem was enhanced when they went within. For the men's chambers and the porticoes and the whole of the vestibule were in a very chaste style.[20]

King Gondophares was twenty-seven years old. Coins show him as rather unbuddhistically fearsome, solidly built, verging perhaps on the stocky, with a thick beard, wearing a headband, with huge

---

* 'There was no lasting "Pax Indica" comparable to the "Pax Romana",' as the classicist Kurt Raaflaub has pointed out (Raaflaub, 2007, p. 60) , although, of course, India is now mainly reunified, while the Roman Empire still has not reunited and its successor states have continued warring amongst themselves.

earrings and a necklace. 'Our customs', he said, 'are dictated by moderation.' Gondophares took Apollonius off to bathe in the palace gardens in a pool fed by fountains of cold water. Beside the pool were javelins and quoits with which the king exercised 'after the manner of the Greeks'. A philhellene, like many Parthian rulers, the king also talked to Apollonius in Greek.

After their bath, Apollonius was crowned with wreaths and was led into the banqueting chamber. The king sat modestly on a cushion, with five of his closest relatives and his honoured guest Apollonius. They ate a meal of vegetables and fruits that Gondophares claimed he had grown himself in his 'well-watered garden'. The rest of the court – about thirty people, including the master of ceremonies, and probably ministers, ambassadors, the royal equerry, the treasurer and Taxila's most prominent bankers and merchants – sat on chairs and were served 'fish and birds... whole lions and gazelles and swine and the loins of tigers; for they decline to eat the other parts of this animal'. At the end of the meal, great silver and gold goblets were brought in and wine was served. In most palaces the cupbearers were dwarves who doubled as court jesters, and the wine pourers were women in Graeco-Iranian dress in honour of the origins of this extremely expensive import. Apollonius' biographer Philostratus does not tell us who the servants were, though he does note rather disapprovingly that the goblets were big enough 'for ten banqueters, and out of these they drink, stooping down like animals that are being watered'. Even the king drank wine – moderately, of course – but Apollonius, who called himself one of 'the Bacchantic revellers in sobriety', declined and refreshed himself with water instead.

As they drank, the entertainments began. A boy was tossed lightly in the air and performed tumbler's leaps in order to avoid the arrows shot at him by an archer – the archer, like all good magicians, having previously gone round all the banqueters asking them to test the sharpness of his arrows. After the illusionists and conjurors came the acrobats (the human pyramid was particularly popular), the snake charmers and mongoose handlers. Then the court musicians sang their hymn of goodnight to Gondophares, praying that he might have 'good dreams, and rise up propitious and affable towards his subjects'. As he did, rising at dawn to talk some more with Apollonius, before attending to the business of state and giving audience to embassies.

After three days, the king reluctantly let Apollonius and Damis go. He provided them with four white camels, a guide, provisions, white linen cloaks and a letter of introduction to his own spiritual teacher Iarchas – the leader of a community of holy men in the Tibetan mountains. Whether they were Brahmin *sadhus*, or Buddhist monks, it is hard to tell. Apollonius' biographer simply calls them 'holy sages'.

Apollonius and Damis rode out of Taxila, heading for the Himalayas. If Apollonius had tried to proselytize for his religion he had failed. Either his religious message was not attractive or distinctive enough, or he was never out to win converts anyway. Only a few years after he and Damis left Taxila, Gondophares and his brother Gad are said to have converted to Christianity. According to the third-century text, the 'Acts of St Thomas', they were converted by the Apostle known as 'doubting Thomas'. The 'Acts of St Thomas' is considered apocryphal within mainstream Christianity. But scholars have found evidence to corroborate its account of Thomas' presence and missionary activity in the south of India, where he was eventually murdered by Brahmins, so it is possible that he also visited Gondophares' court in the north-west. According to Christian apocrypha and Eastern Orthodox tradition, however, Gondophares had been converted much earlier, since he was said to have been one of the three kings, 'Gaspard [Caspar], King of India', who made the long journey to attend the birth of Jesus.

In a sense, the conversion of the Buddhist Gondophares and his brother was not surprising. The new Christian sect had much in common with, and may well have been influenced by, a new populist version of Buddhism which emerged around this time and which, scholars think, originated in Taxila. This new brand of Buddhism, known as Mahayana Buddhism, would spread far beyond the Indian subcontinent: it would be adopted by nomads from China's north-western border as they invaded Gondophares' kingdom.

12

THE BUDDHA IN A TOGA

It is better that I [the bodhisattva] alone suffer than that all beings sink to the world of misfortune. There I shall give myself into bondage, to redeem all the world from the forest of purgatory, from rebirth as beasts, from the realm of death. I shall bear all grief and pain in my own body for the good of all things living.

From *Siksasamuccaya* (*Compendium of Doctrine*), compiled in the seventh century AD from earlier Buddhist writings

Around 65 AD, about a year after Paul and a group of fellow Christians were probably put to death by Nero, the inhabitants of Taxila desperately tried to bury their gold jewellery and their precious silver and bronze vessels. They were trying to escape from the Central Asian nomads who came thundering into the city on horses and elephants. The nomads, from what is now Mongolia, wore felt caps, thick fur-lined knee-length coats and baggy trousers – silk in the summer, woollen in the winter – tucked into soft padded boots. The Chinese called them Yuezhi; the Indians called them Kushans. Their chief and first king, Kujula Kadphises, was building an empire and using Buddhism to do so.

It was a new version of Buddhism, one which was remoulding a severe, ascetic religion fit for a spiritual elite into a more comforting religion fit for ordinary people. Yet though Mahayana Buddhism spread to China and around Asia, it never displaced Brahmanism/Hinduism, the religion that confined people to their caste, in the affections of the people of India. Buddhism tried to break down divisions and differences, just as Pauline Christianity tried to do. But Buddhism failed to oust Brahmanism, while Pauline Christianity, universalist and populist like Mahayana Buddhism, managed to supplant the old Roman religions. Why one universalist religion established itself and the other did not, will, I hope, start to become clear in this chapter.

The Yuezhi/Kushan nomads were 'excellent soldiers', but better merchants. They were 'skilful at commerce and will haggle over a fraction of a cent. Women are held in great respect, and the men make decisions on the advice of their women,'[1] according to the Chinese diplomat Zhang Qian who visited them in 126 BC. The Yuezhi had been trading with the Chinese since the sixth century BC, exchanging jade and 'heavenly horses' for silk. But in the second century BC they had been squeezed out from the steppe pastureland on China's western borders as China expanded its empire. In a great ripple effect, the tribes forced to migrate from China's borders displaced other tribes, triggering a series of invasions west and south into the Indian subcontinent. The Kushans were already conquerors of the vast Greek kingdom of Bactria in Central Asia when their chief Kujula led them over the Hindu Kush Mountains and began encroaching on Gondophares' kingdom.

An illiterate tribe, the Kushans were becoming masters of highly literate kingdoms that had been ruled by the Greeks since the time of Alexander. Their self-styled 'Tyrant' Kujula had to convince the sedentary Indo-Greeks, suspicious of foreigners but even more of nomads, that they, the Kushans, were 'civilized' too, even if city life was relatively new to them. Coins – one of our few sources for the Kushans – show the initially awkward attempt to marry their Central Asian nomadic culture with the Indo-Greek culture of their conquered elites. Coins of Kujula show on one side his fierce and determined head, usually far too big for his body, with the fine features of the Mongolian tribesman, slanting eyes, moustache curled up at the ends, the raised artificial deformation of his skull probably a sign of his elite status; like the bound feet of Chinese women, the skulls of children of the Kushan elite were constricted from birth for about two years until they were distorted into the required shape. On the other side of the coins is an image of Hercules holding a club and lion skin or, in some cases, the head of a Roman emperor. The coins were inscribed in Greek and the local dialect, though, as Kushan rule progressed, the Greek became more and more debased and eventually disappeared from the coins altogether.

But throughout the Kushans' expanding empire a new image was being carved into the hillsides or sculpted in temples and monasteries. It was the figure of a man, standing or seated, his face square and rather plump. He had slightly protruding half-closed eyes, elongated ears, a Mona Lisa-like smile, and was dressed in a Graeco-Roman toga.

The man was Gautama Buddha, and these sculptures were the first ever depictions of him in human form. For 500 years, the Buddha, though he had been a real historical figure, had been represented by symbols – the stupa that housed his relics, the Bodhi tree under which he achieved enlightenment, and the wheel of rebirth. Under the patronage of the Kushans, the Buddha took on human form but also became a god. In their search for legitimation, the Kushans had adopted the religion of the Indo-Greek elites they were trying to suborn, but in its new, populist version.

Buddhism had always been a universalist religion; it accepted the foreigner, as it did the trader, in a way that Hinduism could not. But the original austere Theravada Buddhism had made no attempt to cater to the needs of ordinary people.

Mahayana Buddhism, or 'Great Vehicle' Buddhism, represented the mass marketing of Buddhism. Weber saw in the religions of India a trend that was symptomatic of the development of all religions – the adaptation of an austere, rational set of ideas and practices tailored for the elite to one that appealed to a far wider audience. In India, the three major religions were all, to varying degrees, trying to broaden their appeal, and in doing so they were both competing with and influencing each other. But the popularization took very different forms in each religion, and had very different outcomes. Of the three, Jainism made the least effort to be populist and would remain austerely elitist, although – like Buddhism – it was a universalist religion that emphasized what mankind shared in common.

Mahayana Buddhism really did try to adapt itself to people's needs, as Pauline Christianity would do. Yet it was Brahmanism/ Hinduism, which retained its particularist, hierarchically based view of man, that proved to be most enduring on the subcontinent. By the fifth century AD only a tiny community of Jains remained (a community that survives in India to this day). Buddhism began a slow decline and by the thirteenth century had virtually disappeared from India, though it has spread and flourished across the rest of Asia. Universalism does not automatically trump traditionalist particularism. Buddhism, which developed partly in reaction to Brahmanism, never managed to supplant it. Scholars differ as to the reasons for this, as they do about the origins of Mahayana Buddhism; my claim is that Brahmanism embedded itself more deeply into the lives of the Indian people than Buddhism.

Buddhism, Jainism and Brahmanism in their original forms had offered a view of the world where man determines the fate of his own soul at rebirth with no benevolent god to help him. Salvation for these religions meant release from the world, an absence from suffering; nirvana meant literally 'blowing out', as of a flame. It was a state of bliss in which the individual self with its desires and sufferings was annihilated, unlike the Christian paradise in which the purified self lived eternally. Perhaps only an elite, confident in their own power, could live with such a tough message, just as the elite Sadducees could afford to eschew the idea of life after death adopted by the more populist Pharisees, and the Stoics could seek the calm of reason rather than the comfort of love. Buddhism and Jainism had no gods to worship who might intervene to help the world and its people, who would be the object of worship and prayers. Salvation had to be attained without the aid of god or priest.

All three religions believed that a life of contemplation and asceticism was the only way to achieve complete understanding of the worthlessness of the world and therefore liberation from it.

Brahmanism made the understanding of this truth dependent on caste. Jainism and Buddhism proclaimed that everyone could reach salvation by the same ascetic route, whatever their caste. They were the first religions to found monastic orders; Jainism is indeed the only surviving religion to have begun as a purely monastic religion. But while in theory they had made the route to salvation open to all, in practice they had swapped an elitism based on birth for a meritocratic elitism based on religious commitment. The monastic life, which involved abandoning all attachment to family and possessions, was simply not possible for most people.

To be a Jainist monk in particular required an extraordinary level of self-sacrifice. Monks of the strict Digambara or 'sky-clad' sect had to go naked, as their name implies, because even clothes were a material possession, which chained people to the world. The only possessions they were allowed were a water gourd and a whisk of peacock feathers to sweep away any insects they might accidentally step on and thus break their vow of non-violence. They were not allowed to beg, but had to rely on the unprompted generosity of villagers, accepting whatever was offered with open cupped hands. A marginally less rigorous sect was, however, developing in the north of India. The Shvetambara or 'white-clad' sect of Jainism allowed its monks to wear simple white robes. It also allowed women to enter the monastic order, unlike the Digambara sect, which did not believe a soul could attain liberation from a female body; women had to be reborn as men to gain salvation.

The Jain layman was inevitably spiritually inferior to the ascetic, since only the ascetic could lead the life that would ultimately lead to liberation. And that life meant such disdain for the body that the Jain was allowed, if not encouraged, to take his own life. The most committed Jain monks starved themselves to death, following the example of their founder, Mahavira, as Chandragupta Maurya, India's first emperor, is said to have done.

It could only have been a Jain monk whose spectacular suicide caused a sensation in the Roman Empire at some time between AD 2 and 13. According to Cassius Dio and Strabo, who based his report on the eyewitness account of Herod the Great's secretary and biographer Nicolaus of Damascus, the monk was called Zarmanochegas (or S'ramanacharya, Sanskrit for 'spiritual teacher', though for Jains it also meant being the leader of a community of monks). Zarmanochegas was part of a delegation of ambassadors that set out from the kingdom of Pandya in southern India to visit the Emperor Augustus. Augustus was staying with his wife Livia in Athens where their 'court poet' Virgil had once lived for three years. A special ceremony was being held out of season to initiate the emperor and his wife into the Eleusinian mysteries. It may well have been this ceremony that Zarmanochegas attended. The ceremonial fire was blazing when, to the delighted horror of the onlookers, Zarmanochegas 'leaped upon the pyre with a laugh, his naked body anointed, wearing only a loin-cloth'.[1] Cassius Dio was unsure whether this self-immolation was 'because, being of the caste of sages, he was on this account moved by ambition, or… because he wished to make a display for the benefit of Augustus and the Athenians'.[2] Much more likely was that Zarmanochegas was seeking to accomplish the Jainist ideal: to be free of the body and attain moksha. The Athenians themselves simply inscribed on his tombstone: 'Here lies Zarmanochegas, an Indian from Bargosa, who immortalized himself in accordance with the ancestral customs of Indians.'[3]

For Augustus and his entourage, Zarmanochegas' suicide would not have been especially shocking. They were, after all, used to the sight of men dying for public amusement. And they were anyway mollified when 'eight naked servants, with girdles round their waists, and fragrant with perfumes' presented the gifts which the Indian delegation had brought. They included 'a partridge larger than a vulture'; a huge tortoise, an equally huge snake and a Hermes: 'a boy who had no shoulders or arms, like our statues of Hermes. And yet, defective as he was, he could use his feet for everything, as if they were hands: with them he would stretch a bow, shoot missiles, and put a trumpet to his lips.' Although, said Cassius Dio, 'How he did this I do not know; I merely state what is recorded.' Only three of the embassy survived the journey.

Buddhism was less demanding than Jainism, but its monks were meant to have few material possessions, and to live off alms – though, according to the monastic rules, they should be careful not to deter the potential donor by being too pushy. Entering the dusty compound of a village house, the monk was to stand a little distance away from its occupants, waiting – but not for too long – to see if they were going to give him anything.

If (the potential donor) puts down his/her work or rises from his/her seat or wipes a spoon, wipes a dish, or sets one out, he should remain (thinking), 'It looks like he/she wants to give.' Then, with averted eyes, he should offer his bowl. He should then observe, 'Do they want to give bean curry or not?' If the donor wipes a spoon, wipes a dish, or sets one out, he should remain, (thinking), 'It looks like he/she wants to give.'[4]

Once he had received his curry, the monk should then leave 'carefully and unhurriedly', with the steaming bowl concealed under his robe.

Buddhist monks and nuns were to have no home except during the rainy seasons when they lived in monasteries. They slept in small stone cells with their lamp and books in a niche on the wall, small cotton pillows, a stool, a spittoon and some matting on the floor. They prayed together in large halls or meditated and studied in the open courtyards where small bells tinkled in the wind. But when the rains had stopped, the monks and nuns shut the door of their cells, put their beds on four stones, laid the bedding on top, and set out to wander the villages and cities of India.

Buddhism, Jainism and Brahmanism were in their original forms religions for an intellectual and spiritual aristocracy that could afford to make an often quite extraordinary commitment to the pursuit of salvation. They were not religions for the ordinary householder who had a living to make. They had little to say to the 'field labourers, their arms blackened by exposure', to 'the lowborn women who cried obscene remarks to passers-by as they stuck the tender sprouts of the new rice into the water-soaked ground',[5] or the cities' coppersmiths, carpenters, goldsmiths, tailors and shoemakers who sat cross-legged in their small stalls, each in their own section of the city depending on the work to which their sub-caste confined them. For those already living a hard life, the monastic life was neither available nor appealing. Similarly, the ultimate goal of nirvana was a rational but not a consoling goal: most people did not just want nirvana: they wanted comfort in the here and now, along with the prospect of paradise to come.

Mahayana Buddhism's response was to create a god, a saviour and a Heaven. Siddhārtha Gautama the man became Buddha the trinitarian god. He was Truth, the embodiment of enlightenment. He was the embodiment of bliss and ruler of Heaven, the temporary home of enlightened beings before nirvana. He took on human form, and as a bodhisattva, 'enlightened being', became the redeemer of mankind.

The bodhisattva is a saint who has reached such a level of enlightenment that he could at his next rebirth be the Buddha. But out of love for mankind the bodhisattva is prepared to undergo the suffering of rebirths in order that he can share the merit of his own good deeds with all sentient beings so that they too may secure liberation. Like Christ, he suffers willingly in order to mitigate the suffering of others. Siddhārtha Gautama was, according to tradition, reborn 550 times as a bodhisattva. In the Mahayana tradition, anyone could become a bodhisattva. Buddhists do not consider Siddhārtha Gautama to have been the only Buddha. The world ran in epochs and each epoch had its corporeal Buddha.

The Mahayana tradition was humanizing Buddhism. It made compassion as important as understanding that the world is worthless or illusory. It gave worshippers a supreme god and a saviour to pray to. Mahayana Buddhism's growing number of devotees brought garlands of flowers, silk clothes, ointments, powders, pearls, gold and lapis lazuli as gifts to lay before the new images of the Buddha and the bodhisattvas in the hope of gaining merits from them.

It was this emerging populist version of Buddhism that the burly, bearded Kushan nomads from the western borders of China inherited from the Indo-Greeks when they invaded Gondophares' Gandhara region and began to build their empire. The Gandhara had been ruled by the Greeks for some 200 years. According to many scholars, it was the coming together of Indian and Greek culture in Gandhara that created the very conditions that would give birth to Mahayana Buddhism. It was here that Indian abstraction met Greek individualism to create a more personal, emotional religion that in its turn would profoundly influence the emergence of Christianity.[6] And this Indo-Greek syncretism was reflected in the great statues to Gautama Buddha that the Kushan rulers erected throughout their growing empire. In grey or blue slate stone or painted stucco, his right hand raised in the gesture of reassurance, *abhayamudra*, a halo behind his head, the human Buddha meditated before the gaze of his worshippers.

The anonymous sculptors gave him delicately carved fish-like eyes, the epitome of beauty, judging by the *Shilappadikaram*'s constant praise of the 'carp-shaped' or 'fish-curved' eyes of the voluptuous courtesans. The Buddha's eyes are underlined with kohl but the sculptors also gave him the features of a Greek god, though the Buddha is a squarer, plumper version. He has wavy hair bundled up in a pile on top of his head in the style of Greek statues of Apollo, though, according to tradition, Siddhārtha had shaved his head. Dressed in a toga, he sits cross-legged, Indian-style, or stands firmly planted on thick legs, swaying slightly to the right like a Greek god. He is surrounded by Greek as well as Indian gods, and by Kushan devotees still in their nomadic dress of felt cap, flared tunics and boots, with eyes slanting up and curling moustaches. Sometimes the Buddha himself is incongruously given a moustache and stands with his two feet pointing outwards in the typical posture of horse-riding people. The bodhisattvas were depicted as bare-chested, bejewelled, rather plump Indian or Kushan princes, though they might be carved into the acanthus capital of a Corinthian pillar.

The Kushans presided over a flowering of this Indo-Greek cultural fusion – adding their own Central Asian element to the mix – which found its expression in the artistic style now known as the Gandhara School from the region in which it originated. In a wonderful artistic syncretism, Indian sensuality and love of decoration merged with the impersonal naturalism of Greek sculpture; plump, languorous Indian bodies became leaner and tauter as they took on some of the characteristics of the Greek physical type.

Probably not long after Kujula had conquered Taxila – dates for this era are very uncertain because the Kushans left no written records – his successor Kanishka, the greatest of all the Kushan rulers, converted to Buddhism, just as Ashoka, the greatest ever Indian emperor, had done (see chapter 11). Kanishka controlled an empire stretching from modern Afghanistan all the way east to the Ganges Valley and far into Central Asia.

Unfortunately, we know almost nothing about him except that, despite his Buddhism, he was said to be 'cruel and temperamental'.[7] From coins we know that he had a luxurious beard. The fabulous sculpture in the Mathura Museum (in today's Uttar Pradesh, North India) of 'the mighty Kanesko' has lost its head; we are left with the rest of his body, which exudes kingliness and brute strength, dressed in a stiff tunic, one hand holding a broad sword, the other resting on a huge mace which is firmly planted between his oversize boots. The Taliban smashed the only other known statue of the king – also headless – in 2001, as they would also destroy the world's largest Buddha statues, the Buddhas of Bamyan, which were carved into the cliffs of central Afghanistan during the third and fourth centuries AD. Like English Puritan iconoclasts of the seventeenth century, the Taliban cannot tolerate representational art.

Kanishka undertook a huge building programme of Buddhist monasteries and stupas – thereby carving into the landscape his complete affiliation with the religion of so many of his subjects. At his capital in Purushapura, modern Peshawar in Pakistan, he built an enormous fourteen-storey stupa – allegedly 700 feet high – for Buddhist pilgrims and travellers crossing the empire. It was still famous hundreds of years later when the Chinese pilgrims Faxian and Xuanzang visited the site in the fifth and seventh centuries respectively. Nothing remains of it today but a small silver casket bearing Kanishka's name, and images of the Buddha and bodhisattvas representing the new Mahayana tradition.

Aside from Ashoka, Kanishka, is considered to be the most important Buddhist rulers the Indian subcontinent has ever had. Kanishka was indeed the first, and probably the only, ruler in the ancient world to mint coins with the image of the Buddha on them. But his gold coins also depicted images of the great Brahmanic god Shiva, or the Greek goddess Nanaia, or the Parthian god Mithra, or the Indo-Greek lunar goddess Mao, or the god of metals Athsho, or the flying Wind God Oado holding up his cloak to catch the wind like a sail, his hair streaming around him.

The Kushan rulers never restricted their allegiance to Mahayana Buddhism alone. They were magnificent in their tolerance, partly because as nomads they had tended to embrace the religions of the other peoples they encountered in their wanderings, but also because, like all empire builders, they had to support the diverse religions of their empire in order to enlist the support of their peoples. Kautilya, the Machiavelli of the ancient world, had counselled his Emperor Chandragupta Maurya to pursue a policy of religious tolerance when he was creating his empire. 'He should worship the local gods and favour the religious and intellectual leaders with gifts of land and money and remission of taxes.'[8] However, although multiculturalism might prevent disaffection, it could never turn heterogeneous peoples into imperial subjects united in loyalty to their empire. The best method of creating that loyalty was through the binding effects of a state religion – which is why cults of the divine emperor were so widely promulgated across the ancient world.

The Kushans ran a Parthian-style empire, exercising loose control over semi-independent rulers who could withdraw their fealty. In the absence of strong administration to keep the empire together, the Kushans tried to develop a powerful ideology which would do so. They certainly went further than any of the great rulers of the Indian subcontinent had ever done before in claiming divinity for themselves. The great Buddhist Emperor Ashoka had called himself *devanampriya*, 'beloved of the gods'; the Kushans, including the fervent Buddhist Kanishka, called themselves *devaputra*, a Sanskrit expression meaning 'son of god'. It could well have been modelled on the Chinese *tianzi*, 'son of Heaven', which was the title used by the Chinese emperor – a title that no doubt the Kushan tribesmen from China's western borders hoped would inspire loyalty and obedience as they built their own empire. Kanishka referred to himself as 'the great salvation, the righteous, just autocrat, worthy of divine worship, who has obtained the kingship from Nana ['the Lady', a Babylonian goddess] and from all the gods'.[9] He appears on many of his coins wearing a tall Kushan crown, the flames of divinity bursting from his shoulders, a nimbus of light around his head.

With an insouciant mixing of the grandest appellations from every neighbouring empire, Kanishka called himself 'the Great King [Indian], the King of Kings [Parthian], the son of god [Chinese], Caesar [Roman]' or sometimes 'King of Kings, Saviour, the Great'. It is impossible to tell how persuasive the Kushans' pretensions to divinity were, though they clearly did not convince Kanishka's soldiers. According to legend they smothered him to death. Despite being a convert to the religion of non-violence, Kanishka had remained addicted to warfare and his disgruntled soldiers had rebelled against the constant campaigning.

Thanks to Kanishka's support, Mahayana Buddhism went on its missionary journey along the trade routes to Central Asia and China. Within the Kushans' own empire, however, Brahmanism began to reassert itself. Kushan kings after Kanishka, rather like the kings who followed the Buddhist Ashoka, increasingly turned to Brahmanism.

Brahmanism had embedded itself into the social and political fabric of life on the Indian subcontinent in a way that Buddhism and Jainism had failed to do. The king (if he was not a Brahmin himself) acknowledged the Brahmins as his spiritual superiors who were essential to his rule, while they provided him with religious legitimation. His role was to preserve the caste, and therefore the social and religious order. Only the caste system prevented society from slipping into chaos. In order to preserve it, the spiritual authority of the Brahmins needed to be reinforced by the temporal power of the king. Without it

the stronger would roast the weaker, like fish on a spit; the crow would eat the sacrificial cake and the dog would lick the sacrificial viands, and ownership would not remain with any one, the lower ones would (usurp the place of) the higher ones... All castes would be corrupted (by intermixture), all barriers would be broken through, and all men would rage (against each other).[10]

So proclaimed *The Laws of Manu* – in effect the Brahmins' manifesto and assertion of their spiritual dominance.

The Brahmins' spiritual power would always trump the king's temporal power: 'Though dying (with want), a king must not levy a tax on *Srotriyas* (Brahmins learned in the Vedic scriptures).' Famine would strike the kingdom if the king allowed even one *Srotriya* to go hungry.[11] It was the duty of the king to appoint a Brahmin as chief minister with whom the king must consult before making any important decisions. It was the chief Brahmin priest who protected the people against natural and human calamities, not the king. The king might have divine qualities, but these were conferred on him at his coronation, and could be withdrawn or, as the *Ramayana* (the great epic probably written in the fourth or third centuries BC by the Hindu sage Valmiki) put it, he could be 'roasted in airless hell', if he failed to fulfil his duties.

Although the Brahmanic emphasis on caste, which tended to

exclude the foreigner, was not helpful to a new empire trying to create an entity out of different conquered peoples, Brahmins made themselves essential to the Indian ruler as Christianity would for Rome's emperor. But Buddhist and Jain monks could not, nor would they have wanted to. Salvation was through contemplation and contemplation did not go with the messy entanglements of political life. The primacy of monastic life within Buddhism and Jainism meant that they in effect relinquished their hold on everyday life.

Monks and nuns sought to detach themselves from the world. Performance of the daily rites and rituals that made life meaningful and safer, precisely what for most people made religion necessary, was considered by the monks to be a distraction. They left the performance of such rites to the Brahmins. So most people, whatever their religious preference, relied on the Brahmins to mark the fundamental transitions in their and their families' lives – birth, marriage and death. Brahmins lived with wealthy families as household priests, making offerings in front of the fire's altar before the midday and evening meals. They were consulted by householders of every sect about the auspicious times to perform sacrifices. They even performed some of the rituals in Jain and Buddhist temples that the nuns and monks did not want to be distracted by.

Ashoka, the Buddhist emperor of India's Maurya dynasty, had shared the Buddhist and Jain comparative lack of interest in rites of passage and festivals. The Brahmanic year, on the other hand, included festivals that were carnival high points of drinking, dancing and storytelling. The *Shilappadikaram* describes the twenty-eight-day spring festival to Indra, the god of war and weather, when 'nubile girls, splendidly dressed' brought offerings of rice, sesame cakes and brown sugar to the altar of the spirit or genie of the city. 'Hands on their generous hips, these virgins gyrated madly as if possessed by obscene devils, and then in a circle performed the dance of lust, the *Rasa-lila,* which the god Krishna had performed with the cowgirls'. Frenzied young men whipped themselves until their backs bled. The streets were garlanded with flowers. Lamps and golden vases filled with water stood outside every shop; brilliant-coloured streamers decorated with elephant tusks and dragons hung from the doorways. The rich watched from the balconies of their great mansions that were studded with emeralds, brilliants and strings of pearls. Singing and dancing crowds cheered as the king, his councillors, courtiers, princes and nobles rode by in chariots or perched on elephants that were crowned with gold tiaras, with great heavy clusters of jewels hanging from their pendulous ears, and bells and bangles jingling on their legs as they plodded by. In public squares Brahmin priests recounted stories. 'Through the city oboes and tambourines could be heard. The voices of the bards blended with the soft accents of the harps. Night and day the rhythm of drums filled every corner of the city with merriment.'[12]

Brahmanic festivals brought together king and peasant, state and religion, gods and local spirits, orgy and civic respectability. They were an essential, intensely pleasurable part of life. Buddhism and Jainism, in contrast, were far more concerned with detachment from life. And so the Brahmins became ever more bound into the social life of towns and villages, while the Buddhist monks, doggedly pursuing their ascetic life of meditation, became ever more isolated.

In theory, Buddhist monks kept in close touch with the people through living a life of wandering and begging. By the early first century AD, however, the Buddhist monasteries stretched out along the trade routes were growing rich. At Kanheri, near modern Mumbai, the monastery carved out of a massive outcrop of basaltic rock was expanding to become the biggest religious centre along the west coast. Wealthy bankers, money-changers, poor ploughmen, caravan traders, princes and royal officials came fortnightly from cities and villages with gifts of robes, food, medicine and oil for the lamps. Dazzling white monasteries were built far from the clamour of the city. Brightly painted and gilded frescoes, and stone bas-reliefs coated with fine gold leaf, covered the walls; pilasters and niches were crammed with a profusion of scenes from the life of the Buddha, of worshippers, attendants, and animals. Some of the monasteries were now so richly endowed and so vast that they had to employ slaves and hired labour, because the monks couldn't cope with the work. There could be up to 5,000 monks in a monastery.

But, as the monasteries became richer, so the monks no longer depended on begging for their one meal a day and for the rags from which to weave their clothes. They no longer lived off the alms they collected in the morning hours. Now they ate regular meals in vast monastic refectories. In giving up their begging bowls, they increasingly lost contact with lay people, the lifeblood of any religion.

The monks still slept in stone cells. And they certainly weren't living quite as well as their rich donors. Indeed, the monastic rules laid down in the *Cullavagga*, which was probably written at the end of the first century BC, explicitly forbade the type of beautification, adornments and luxuries recommended for courtiers and merchants in the *Kama Sutra*.[13]

The monks were only allowed a minimum of accessories when they bathed: no back scrubbers or sharing a bath with another monk who could perform this service for them. They weren't allowed to wear make-up and were obliged to have their hair cropped short. They couldn't wear necklaces, bangles, bracelets or rings. They couldn't have long fingernails because of their erotic connotations: they were visible reminders of lovemaking. The *Kama Sutra* in fact named eight different shapes the nails could make, including 'a tiger's nail or claw, a peacock's foot, the jump of a hare and the leaf of a blue lotus'. The monks were also forbidden to seduce other men's wives.

Instead, they retired within their monasteries and lost contact with the people. It was something that Jain monks, however austere, never did. Lay Jains were firmly connected to the monks of their local monastery. The monks supported the lay community pastorally, while it supported the monks materially. Jainism would never attract a vast following because of its austerity. But the very demands it made meant that Jain followers were highly committed, a commitment that was shored up by the strong organizational ties created between the lay community and their monks.

Ironically, the people of the Indian subcontinent preferred to live under the immutable hierarchical constraints of caste rather than seek the liberation from it offered by Buddhism or Jainism. The Brahmin priest who performed the domestic rites was needed much more and was a far more prominent figure in the lives of ordinary people than the Buddhist monks cut off from the world in their wealthy monasteries.

Brahmanism was anyway popularizing itself, as Buddhism was doing in the form of Mahayana Buddhism. Indeed, it may have been under the influence of Mahayana Buddhism that Brahmanism was developing its own consoling gods. In the early *Upanishads** salvation was gained through knowledge of Brahman – an Absolute who was not a god and who was without qualities. But the idea of a monotheistic personal god slowly began to emerge with the elevation and transformation of Vishnu and Shiva. And they, like the Mahayanan Buddha, became saviours.

Just as the Buddhists and Jains used folk tales to transmit their teachings, so the Brahmins adapted two of the most popular secular epics, the *Ramayana* and the *Mahabharata*, to preach their new theistic message. In the revised epics, Shiva was both ascetic creator, supreme practitioner of yoga, and the more human householder who lived in the Himalayan mountains with his wife, granting boons to those who propitiated him. He appeared on earth disguised as an untouchable, or as a naked yogi seducing the wives of the sages.

Vishnu, an old Vedic sun god, was transformed into Vishnu-Krishna, saviour of mankind. In the *Bhagavad-Gita* (the 'Song of God'), a section inserted into the *Mahabharata*, Vishnu takes on human form as Krishna to save humanity from evil. The Vishnu-Krishna of the *Bhagavad-Gita* presented a new conception of god and a new democratic route to salvation – *bhakti*, devotion to Krishna.

---

* The *Upanishads* are speculative treatises forming part of the *Vedas*, the hymns and texts that were composed between about 1000 BC and 500 BC. The *Vedas* are regarded by Hindus as embodying the essential truths of Hinduism (see Embree). For the *Upanishads* and the *Vedas*, see: <http://www.sacred-texts.com/hin/>.

Bhakti provided a route to salvation that was available to all castes and to women as well as men.

'And whoso loveth Me cometh to Me', proclaims Krishna.
'Though they be born from the very womb of Sin,
Woman or man; sprung of the Vaisya caste
Or lowly disregarded Sudra – all
Plant foot upon the highest path.'[14]

Even the merchant caste of the Vaisyas, lumped though they were yet again with the more despised elements of society, could find salvation through *bhakti*. And this salvation was not through knowledge of the impersonal Brahman, but through the intense devotion of the worshipper to a personal god and the grace that in turn the god bestowed on his worshipper. Salvation itself came to be seen as not just release from rebirth but a blissful union with Shiva or Vishnu. *Bhakti* became the moving force of Hinduism: Shivaism and Vishnuism its two main sects.[15]

Buddhist devotees in India turned back to Brahmanism. In the competition for hearts and minds, Buddhism, the universalist religion that proclaimed the spiritual equality of all mankind, lost out to the more exclusive hierarchical religion that was more deeply rooted in people's lives. Brahmanism had made itself indispensable to rulers and people alike. Ordinary people needed their Brahmin priests more than their Buddhist monks. And the rulers and ruling elites eventually found Brahmanism far more congenial than the more egalitarian messages of Buddhism or Jainism with their potentially disturbing social implications. The caste basis of Brahmanism legitimated the rulers' dominant position. The Brahmanic concept of caste provided a spiritual imperative for the non-elite to be obedient: their prospect of salvation was directly linked to accepting their place in the caste system and faithfully following the duties it imposed. All men were not alike; there was no perfect natural order towards which mankind should aim where all men were equal. Brahmanism was a recipe for social stability.

In about AD 450, yet another army of tribesmen from Central Asia, with what Gibbon described as 'broad shoulders, flat noses, and small black eyes deeply sunk in their heads, and little or no hair on their faces', tore through the Gandhara, their ferocious approach signalled by the dark cloud of vultures and crows which perpetually hovered above them in the certainty of having a feast of corpses to dine on. They were called the White Huns, and may well have been descended from those Kushans who stayed behind on the steppes of Central Asia when the rest of the tribe rode west to found an empire. Now the White Huns devastated the lands of what had been the Kushan Empire (the Kushans having long since been ousted by the Sasanian rulers of the former Parthian Empire), while another group of Huns from Central Asia ravaged the Roman Empire. The combined onslaught of both groups of Huns had a catastrophic effect on trade and therefore on the merchants who had formed the backbone of support for Jainism and Buddhism.

When the Chinese traveller Xuanzang visited India around AD 644, the great Buddhist city of Taxila was in ruins. It had never recovered from its destruction by the White Huns. The stupas were crumbling. A thousand monasteries in the Gandhara lay in ruins, overgrown with wild shrubs; the thousands of monks that had once chanted in the gleaming stupas and eaten in silence in the vast refectories had gone. The monasteries that still survived were virtually deserted. In the Kushans' former capital of Purushapura, where Kanishka had built his fourteen-storey stupa, only one monastery remained, housing just fifty Mahayana monks. In the city of Vesali (Vaiśālī) in eastern India, Xuanzang saw one of the great pillars crowned by a lion that the Emperor Ashoka had erected to proclaim his Buddhist message, but the magnificent monasteries were dilapidated and only a few monks still lived in them.

Beyond the Indian subcontinent, however, where it did not have to compete against an entrenched religious-social system with populist roots, Buddhism, especially the populist brand of Mahayana

Buddhism supported by the Kushans, found a vast audience in China and in Central and South-east Asia.

With the upsurge of trade from the beginning of the first century AD, Buddhist monks sailed eastwards from India's western and southern ports. The monks, periodically shouting or blowing trumpets with their fellow passengers to scare away the whales during the voyage,[16] took with them the harsher, older Theravada Buddhism, which is still today the predominant religion in Cambodia, Laos, Burma, Thailand and Sri Lanka. Meanwhile, from the Kushan Empire in the north-west, Mahayana Buddhism was travelling north and east to Samarkand and China, eventually reaching the original homeland of the empire's nomadic founders via the 'Silk Road'.

The first Kushan King Kujula Kadphises was probably the Kushan ruler who sent his ambassadors on a trade mission to Emperor Ai in China in about 2 BC. Amongst the ambassadors with their gifts for the emperor, and merchants with their cargoes of precious gems, spices, cosmetics and ivory, were Buddhist monks whose gift to the emperor was Buddhism: scholars believe that they recited Mahayana writings (unfortunately we do not know which ones).

Merchants, in groups of several dozen to several thousand, had been travelling the 'Silk Road' ever since the second century BC when, thanks to the Great Wall, China's rulers could offer travellers protection against the attacks of the Xiongnu nomads, the Kushans' old enemies. The 'Silk Road' was in fact many different routes stretching from the Mediterranean to China. Which route the caravans took depended on weather conditions, whether the local bandits were under control, and whether war was being waged in the area. Few if any merchants went the whole distance (over 7,000 miles), which would have taken them more than a year. Instead, they stopped somewhere along the route and in a kind of relay sold their goods on to the next group of merchants, who – with fresh horses, mules, donkeys or camels, fresh human porters and new caravan leaders – endured the next stage of the journey. Palmyrenes guided the caravans through the Syrian desert to the banks of the Euphrates where Parthian guides took over. They in their turn gave way to the Kushans, who then handed over to the Sogdians from Samarkand on the Central Asian steppes for the second and the most gruelling half of the silk route.

For the ambassadors and monks travelling from the Kushan kingdom to China, the shortest route would have been to cross the Hunza Valley between the Karakoram and Pamir Mountains over a terrifying network of hanging footpaths fastened to sheer cliff faces hundreds of feet above the river. The paths were too steep or zigzagged too sharply for pack animals, so they were left behind and their loads carried by humans for whom one false step could prove fatal. After negotiating the Pamir Mountains, where landslides and avalanches could force the travellers to take a longer, more difficult route, the snow freezing on their faces, they reached the endless steppes of Central Asia. They trudged through the deafeningly silent steppes, past staring nomads who came in their thousands to graze their flocks of camels and horses, and who might or might not be readying to attack the travellers' precious cargoes.

Beyond the steppe lands was the Taklamakan Desert (its name means the place where he who goes in does not come out), which they had to skirt around or cross. It was the driest, most relentless desert on earth, a billowing sea of soft yellow sand which occasionally rose to sand dunes 600 feet high.

Finally, they reached one of the great sandy-yellow watchtowers that punctuated the Great Wall as it swung its way beside the silk route, keeping the nomads out of China and protecting the merchants from them. About 1,200 miles ahead was Chang'an (meaning 'Endless Peace'), probably the largest walled city in the world. After days, weeks, months of hardship, this was their journey's end. Along with a stream of carts, mules, donkeys, camels and people anxious to get inside the towered gates before they closed for the night, the traveller entered Chang'an, where, in 2 BC, China's version of Richard III, the usurper Wang Mang, was plotting to take over the oldest, most sophisticated empire in the world.

13

CONFUCIUS' RELIGION FOR CIVIL SERVANTS

... kindness in the father, filial piety in the son, gentility in the older brother, humility and respect in the younger brother, good behaviour in the husband, obedience in the wife, benevolence in the elders, and obedience in the juniors, benevolence in the ruler, and loyalty in the ministers.

The ten basic human duties enumerated in
Liji (*Book of Rites*), 202 BC–AD 220

The course (of duty), virtue, benevolence, and righteousness cannot be fully carried out without the rules of propriety;... nor can (the duties between) ruler and minister, high and low, father and son, elder brother and younger, be determined; nor can students for office and (other) learners, in serving their masters, have an attachment for them; nor can majesty and dignity be shown in assigning the different places at court, in the government of the armies, and in discharging the duties of office so as to secure the operation of the laws.

Liji (*Book of Rites*)

What you do not want done to yourself, do not do to others
Confucius, *Analects,* XV.23, *c.*479–409 BC

In about 50 BC, a minor Chinese official proposed his daughter as a candidate for the imperial harem. Wang Zhengjun* was vetted for her looks, complexion and hair, and checked by a physiognomist to see whether she would bring luck to the imperial

---

* There are many different ways of transcribing Chinese characters phonetically into the Roman alphabet. I use the most popular, which is the Pinyin system.

family and – crucially – whether she would bear a son. After being presented to the emperor she entered the Lateral Courts or 'rear palace' as a Daughter of Good Family, the next to lowest rank of imperial concubines corresponding to that of a petty official in the state bureaucracy. For the sexual court of the concubines exactly mirrored China's civil service, the most meritocratic in the world.

Two years later, Wang Zhengjun was one of a select group of five girls forced by the empress upon the reluctant heir-apparent who 'had no desire for any of the five girls, but could not help himself, because of the Empress' order', according to the *Hanshu*, the official history of the Han dynasty from its foundation in 202 BC until AD 25. The *Hanshu* was begun *c*.AD 25 by Ban Biao, nephew of the great scholar, poet and emperor's concubine, Consort Ban. After Ban Biao's death, the *Hanshu* was completed by his son, Ban Gu, and his daughter, Ban Zhao, China's first woman historian. A hugely enjoyable mix of lurid gossip and the minutiae of government business, drawing on sources such as imperial messages, edicts, stenographical reports of imperial conversations, official annals, testimony at trials and the reports of informers, the *Hanshu* is our main source for the period.[1] Unfortunately, it cannot be regarded as completely trustworthy since its writers were commissioned by the Han rulers themselves.

As the *Hanshu* notes, Wang Zhengjun entered Prince Liu Shi's harem and began her spectacular rise through the ranks of the concubines. In a flowered, red silk short jacket (red was the colour of the Han dynasty, representing fire, the element by virtue of which the dynasty ruled) and long skirt, she was waited on by slave girls, some no more than eight years old, and guarded by eunuchs, ready to attend the prince whenever he commanded his 'handmaids'. She was promoted to Senior Maid and then to Beauty. When the prince was enthroned as Emperor Yuan in 48 BC, she moved into the Palace of the Blazing Sun, which the emperor had built for his concubines.

The palace is now little more than a sand dune. Then it was part of a vast complex of thirty-six palaces and offices for the emperor, his harem, his family and his officials, set on a hill in Chang'an (near modern Xi'an in north-west China). Slaves kept watch on the water clock and tolled the hours on a drum; 3,000 slaves worked in the kitchens.

In the autumn and winter Wang Zhengjun and the other concubines attended the great hunting parties in the imperial park outside the city walls, which was stocked with lions, camels, a giant panda, elephants from India, ostriches from Arabia (a species which is now extinct), grape vines and pomegranates newly imported from Parthia. After the mass slaughter of animals had ended in 'a wind of feathers and a rain of blood', according to Ban Gu, the historian and poet who took over from his father the work of writing the history of the Han dynasty, the concubines arrived in their carriages and were rowed in dragon-shaped barges on the ornamental lakes. The oarsmen would break into song as flaming torches were lit, while wild geese and cranes flew overhead. In the centre of the lakes, in the pavilions hung with kingfisher feathers, with vermilion and jet dragons and serpents carved on the rafters, the party watched strong men – usually 'barbarians' – grappling with lions, leopards, bears, elephants and rhinos. Unlike the Roman gladiators, who used weapons, these men used only their bare hands. 'Choirs dressed as fairies sang, and men in the skins of leopards and bears danced, and others as white tigers struck great lutes, whilst green dragons played flutes.'[2]

In 47 BC, one year after Emperor Yuan's enthronement, Wang Zhengjun bore him a son in the Painted Hall of the First Lodge, where the concubines gave birth and their babies were suckled by wet-nurses. She had beaten the rest of the harem (which could number as many as 3,000 concubines) in the battle to bear the emperor's heir. The following year she was made Favourite Beauty and could now ride in her own carriage instead of being carried on a litter by four men. Three days later, the twenty-two-year-old daughter of a minor official became empress. 'The mother of the Empire', as the empress was called, moved out of the harem into her own apartments from where she would fight her deadly battles with the emperor's 'inner court' of his favourites and their families.

Wang Zhengjun would eventually triumph, the losers commit suicide and her nephew Wang Mang briefly usurp the Han throne. In doing so, Wang Mang, with his bulging eyes, and platform shoes which he wore, according to the *Hanshu*, to enhance his height, like his Roman counterpart Augustus, would mould 'Confucianism' into the most successful state ideology the world has ever known.* Confucianism would provide the theoretical underpinnings of the empire until its demise in 1912. Even today, China's communist rulers still appeal to Confucianism to give themselves legitimacy. No other pairing of state and state ideology has had such a long partnership.

Yet, perhaps uniquely amongst state religions, Confucianism made almost no attempt to address itself to ordinary people. Most empires used religion to try to unite their followers in devotion to state and emperor. But Confucianism had no great public festive holidays where the people took to the streets to eat and drink too much, and watch spectacular processions in honour of their emperor and his gods. As far as we can tell from the admittedly court-centred focus of the sources, the Chinese people were mostly excluded from the extraordinarily elaborate state rituals. As the seasons rolled by, the inhabitants of Chang'an might see the emperor and his entourage riding through the walled districts of the city, the horses' hooves kicking up red dust as they rode down the broad, tree-lined tiled avenues, past evenly spaced raftered houses, but that was almost their only point of connection with the state rituals. These were performed in private by the emperor and his court. The state even forbade celebrations involving more than three people. Only in the 'second month of summer', when the great summer sacrifice for rain was performed by the emperor, were the people enjoined 'to sacrifice

---

* As with my use of 'Buddhism', 'Zoroastrianism', etc., I use the terms 'Confucianism' and 'Daoism' as shorthand for what are, at this time, very loose collections of ideas, values and traditions.

to the various princes, high ministers, and officers who benefited the people; praying that there may be a good harvest of grain'.[3] It was their sole involvement in the rituals of the state calendar.

Confucianism does not even qualify as a religion, certainly by Christian-based standards. It was a rational, conservative philosophy of government created by and for an elite. But, though it was in no sense a populist religion, it was a philosophy that impressed upon the elite its duty to create and maintain the good of everyone. Confucius, born in the sixth century BC, around the same time as the founders of Jainism and Buddhism, was not concerned with the individual's quest for fulfilment through self-perfection, but with the happiness of all. Only through the creation of a stable, harmonious and well-ordered society could the individual, an essentially social creature, find happiness.

Confucianism worked so effectively as a state ideology in part because it promised good government, though there were competing views as to what this actually meant. The 'modernists' believed in strengthening the power and authority of the state and throne; the 'reformists' put a primacy on the welfare of the people, and it was this ideal that was gaining the ascendancy. According to Confucius, the 'Grand Harmony' could not exist unless people were prosperous enough to be able to think of more than just the necessity of catering for their and their family's physical needs. The same ideal is described in the *Guanzi*, a collection of Chinese philosophical writings on statecraft, compiled in 26 BC : 'When granaries are full, the ordinary people will know propriety and moderation; when clothing and food are sufficient, the ordinary people will know honour and shame.'[4] Government must ensure its people had enough to eat. In elevating good government to be the essential prerequisite for the happiness of all, Confucius, a government official as well as scholar, gave his fellow officials a moral status that probably no other philosopher except Plato has ever done.

By the end of the first century BC, when the twenty-one-year-old Emperor Ai, thirteenth member of the Han dynasty, sat on the throne, government officials were the acknowledged leaders of society. Civil servants ran the empire. They governed the commanderies (the provinces into which most of China was divided that were directly under the control of central government); and they governed China's remaining kingdoms, although theoretically these were still ruled by the emperor's kinsmen. Officials collected the poll and land taxes – vital for an empire that was predominantly agricultural. They ensured the maintenance of stable prices for basic commodities, controlled trade between the provinces, ran the major state monopolies of iron and salt production, which employed about 100,000 convicts and conscripts fulfilling their annual labour duties to the emperor, and supervised the other elements of the corvée.*

There were officials responsible for religious ceremonial, the observation of the stars, and officials to inspect the work of other officials. And all of them were meticulously graded into twenty ranks, which determined the official's salary, the privileges and exemptions from the law to which he was entitled, the type of carriage he could ride in, the style of robes, aprons, mortarboard hats and ribbons – purple, yellow or black – that he could wear and the type of seal – gold, silver or bronze – that he could use to authenticate documents.

It was in the third century BC, when the Han dynasty founded their empire, that officials had replaced the landed aristocracy and the warriors in status. The great aristocratic families had been decimated in the fighting that brought the Han to the throne. And the Han rulers had capitalized on this destruction of feudal power by building up a centralized bureaucracy to do the work of running the state that the local aristocrats had once performed. As the new Han

---

* All able-bodied men aged between about twenty-three and fifty-six were required to provide one month's service to the state every year in their local county. Corvée labour ranged from working in the iron and salt mines, building and maintaining roads, city walls, government buildings and imperial monuments – Emperor Ai mobilized 50,000 men to build a tomb for his mother Empress Dowager (formerly Consort) Ding – or working on the vital task of trying to prevent the regular flooding of the Yellow River and other rivers and canals. On top of that, all males had to serve two years in the military; the first was spent training, the second in the armies garrisoned around the capital or on the frontier. High-ranking civil servants were exempt.

rulers consolidated their empire rather than expanding it, the glory days of the military warrior came to an end. Prestige and wealth no longer attached to heroism. Emperor Ai would not have dreamt of cloaking himself in military glory as Augustus did in Rome. Though the two empires were of roughly similar size (about 4 million square kilometres) and population (over sixty million),[5] the Han Empire was already 200 years old; it had moved beyond justification by might and found an alternative means of keeping the people loyal. The empire may have been 'won on horseback', but 'it could not be ruled on horseback', as the second-century BC Confucian scholar Lu Jia told Emperor Gao, the founder of the Han dynasty. Rome was only just beginning to grapple with this second phase of empire-building.

Confucianism legitimated the officials' status as it did the emperors'. *Hsiao*, filial piety, a concept at the heart of the Chinese people's ancient tradition of ancestor worship, was for Confucius the bedrock of social relations and ethical behaviour. A smooth-running harmonious society did not depend on the goodness or wickedness of mankind, but on everyone knowing their place and acting accordingly. Obedience, devotion and loyalty were due from the child to the father, and from the father to his superior, all the way up to the father of all the Chinese people, the emperor himself.

Liji, the *Book of Rites*, which laid out the correct way of behaving in every situation, stipulated the extraordinary devotion and obedience the son owed to his father: 'If the parent be angry and displeased, and beat him till the blood flows, he should not presume to be angry and resentful, but be [still] more reverential and more filial.' Both the son and his wife,

> while going out or coming in, while bowing or walking... should not presume to eructate, sneeze, or cough, to yawn or stretch themselves, to stand on one foot, or to lean against anything, or to look askance. They should not dare to spit or snivel, nor, if it be cold, to put on more clothes, nor, if they itch anywhere, to scratch themselves.[6]

The emperor himself was shrouded with even more protocol. A senior official, coming to present government business at the morning audience with the emperor, rode up to the palace in his two-wheeled carriage. Wearing a mortarboard hat with five jade strings dangling from it, dressed in a bright red silk coat with square-cut sleeves, the seals and ribbons of office hanging from a leather bag tied round his waist, and a mirror tied on his back to ward off evil spirits, the official dismounted and climbed three flights of steps which were flanked by gigantic bronze statues of soldiers. Then, as etiquette dictated, he half ran, half walked, trailing his heels 'like the wheels of a carriage', through the palace courtyards, down the long airy galleries with their latticed windows, past the Cool Pavilion, and the Hall of Proclamations, until he reached a vast vermilion audience hall the size of a football pitch. There sat the 'Son of Heaven' on his throne, under roof beams carved with dragons. The dragon motif was emblazoned on the emperor's robes and banners as a reminder of the emperor's 'dragon nature': he was majestic and terrible, but because of his power, virtue and correct behaviour he brought prosperity and happiness to his people.

Every official, with one exception, had to prostrate himself before the emperor; when told to rise, he had to look with downcast eyes, stand with his back 'curved in the manner of a sounding-stone', and hold his tablet before his mouth lest his breath should contaminate the emperor. The emperor's name could never be spoken or written; he could only be referred to as *shang* (meaning 'above' or 'the superior one'). Only the emperor could use the personal pronoun 'I'. The emperor never looked at anyone 'above his collar or below his girdle' and stood up for only one official – the imperial Chancellor.[7] In 4 BC, that man was Wang Jia, who would shortly die trying to defend his bureaucracy against the emperor.

Wang Jia presided over about 120,000 officials. He probably came from the educated gentry, but not necessarily. The Chinese civil service was extraordinarily meritocratic and had been ever since 135 BC, when Emperor Wu, the seventh emperor of the Han dynasty, decreed that anyone who wanted to enter government service had to be tested on their knowledge of the Confucian classics. His decree in effect made Confucianism the state ideology, binding the empire's entire body of educated men under one system of thought dedicated to good government and obedience. In theory, it also made entry into the elite a question of knowledge and ability as an administrator, not wealth, birth, or connections. A man who owned only one horse, and could barely support himself and his family, could rise through the ranks of the civil service and become rich. About half of China's annual tax revenue went on paying officials' salaries. The successful official invested his money in land, and lived behind high walls surrounded by his park. In his multi-storeyed house, its floors covered with embroidered cushions and rugs, every surface carved, plastered or painted, he was waited on by hundreds of slaves, and entertained by his five-piece orchestra, his house choir and the girls from his harem who danced for him.

The Chancellor Wang Jia had had an extraordinarily successful career. He had 'understood the Classics [the Confucian canon] and took the first place in the examinations'. He was appointed Gentleman and joined the pool of as many as 1,000 hopefuls waiting at court for an appointment, with a salary of about 100 piculs a year. Officials were paid in a mixture of cash and grain, but the salary was always defined in terms of the weight of grain; a picul was about 60 kilograms. As the most junior official, his salary was already almost as much as the average small farmer who struggled to get about 150 piculs from his parcel of land (on average about 5 acres).

Wang Jia's salary rose spectacularly over the following sixteen years as he sailed through the oral examinations, demonstrating his knowledge of Confucianism, his understanding of government and his good Confucian behaviour. His rise was temporarily stalled when, as an upper-class official responsible for security in the public parts of the palace compounds, he was dismissed for allowing someone to enter the doors of the palace hall without authorization. But 'Wang Jia was investigated, found incorruptible and made Assistant Prefect of Nanling'. He clearly did well and was promoted to Chief of Police at Changling. Every three years the provincial authorities submitted reports on the performance of their junior officials, including an assessment of their services as 'high', 'medium' or 'low', and a certificate of their ability to read, write and manage accounts and of their knowledge of the law. In the reports on his performance drawn up by his immediate superior and sent to the authorities at the capital, where promotions and demotions were decided, he was, according to the *Hanshu*, recommended as 'sincere and simple, able to speak frankly, and was summoned to an imperial audience in the Xuan Room, where he answered questions regarding the success and failures of the government'. From then on, Wang Jia rose rapidly. He became Grand Palace Grandee, was posted to rule a commandery, was brought back to the city and made Grand Herald, then Governor of the Capital until finally, on 12 May 4 BC, he reached the top of the ladder and was made Chancellor. The following day, he was ennobled, as most of the highest officials were. He became Marquis Zhong Xin and was granted a vast estate with 1,100 households attached, from which he was entitled to collect land and poll tax. His salary was now at least 10,000 piculs a year.

In principle the civil service was open to everyone, though in practice the majority of officials came from the wealthy educated gentry. Good family connections were an advantage for those looking to join the Chinese civil service – the officials themselves would often recommend their sons to fill vacancies. The prejudice against merchants, so widespread in ancient agricultural societies, meant that they were often banned from even applying for bureaucratic posts. But even Emperor Ai, whose abuse of power would eventually cause the downfall of the Former Han dynasty (so called to distinguish it from the 'Later Han' which resumed rule after Wang Mang's brief usurpation), paid lip service to the idea of a meritocratic civil service. He issued an edict, written on bamboo and wrapped in heavy green silk, declaring that the top officials should 'each recommend one person who is filially pious, fraternally respectful, true and honest, able to speak frankly, who understands government matters, and has arisen from a mean condition, so is able to love the common people'. Meritocracy was, in a sense, China's alternative to a populist state religion. Who needed heart-stirring public festivals when you had the promise of becoming part of the empire's elite?

The people looked elsewhere to satisfy their emotional needs and soothe their fears – to the cult of ancestor worship, and to their folk religions of gods, magic and rituals which were coalescing around what we now call Daoism. And the people would soon look to Buddhism, especially Mahayana Buddhism, which the Kushans were bringing to China along the silk routes. As long as the empire's rulers kept their side of the bargain and provided good government and at least the promise of open entry to the elite, the empire did not need a state religion that relied on the irrational, the magical, the divine and the ritualistic to create loyal and cohesive subjects. But of course the empire did not always deliver. Confucianism's offer of stability and good government depended on controlling the mighty and their destabilizing bids for power, including those of the emperor himself, and that was not always possible. Wang Jia, the Chancellor, was 'courageous, straightforward, strict, and bold, with a commanding presence', according to the *Hanshu*. And he needed to be. The emperor's 'inner court' of favourites was undermining Wang Jia's position and that of his 'outer court' of civil servants.

Although both shared the same vast compound in Chang'an, the outer court, with its thousands of officials serviced by red-kerchiefed male and female slaves, was a mental world away from the inner court, where the emperor's entourage fought its deadly battles behind pearl hanging screens and doors carved with jade. The outer court stood for hierarchy, rationality and order, the triumph of the group over the individual, where the officials, each in their rank, happily bent themselves to serving the interests of the empire and their emperor; the inner court, on the other hand, was a chaotic maelstrom of individuals battling for power. It is the world represented by the 'outer court' of Confucian scholar-officials that has dominated the

Western view of Chinese society ever since the early Jesuit missionaries of the seventeenth century worried that they had found a superior civilization that had no need of God. According to this view, 'outer court China' was diametrically opposed to the individualist world of ancient Rome.

Oversimplistic though it is, there is some truth to this picture. Rome was forced to accommodate itself to the individual because its empire was so diverse and fractured. It had too many different peoples, each with their own religions, languages and customs, to be able to create, let alone impose, a homogeneity where people could more easily take their place in a unified group. China's elites, on the other hand, had shared a common culture longer than any other group on Earth (apart, possibly, from the Egyptians). They were united by a common written language; even weights and measures were standardized across the empire. Rome was a trading empire; its cities crammed with a never-ending influx of foreigners. China, as I will describe presently, regarded commerce with deep suspicion, and its rulers accordingly subjected it to a high level of state control.

China, nonetheless, traded in one of the most sought-after materials of the ancient world. It had been producing silk since the thirtieth century BC; since the second century BC, asses, mules and camels had been carrying thousands of bolts of silk from Chang'an along the silk routes to feed the massive demand for this wondrous material, which was light enough to be cool on hot summer days but could serve as padding against the cold, and which, above all, could be dyed in brilliant colours. But silk required land not cities. It was often produced by rich landed families on their estates, who combined farming with running a silk factory which might employ up to 700 slaves or servants feeding the silkworms with mulberry leaves, unwinding their cocoons, spinning the threads, dyeing the silk and embroidering it.

China was predominantly an agricultural empire. In fact, its rulers, with the moral backing of Confucianism, viewed merchants – that group who throughout the ancient world found themselves battling the prejudices of the old agricultural and warrior order – as the enemies of the state. Merchants were motivated by self-interest, the desire for personal profit, rather than by the interests of society as a whole. They lured people with the promise of profits away from the essential task of farming, which put food on people's plates. Merchants were therefore to blame for China's food shortages – the perennial curse of the ancient world.

It was partly in order to curtail the wealth and power of the merchants, partly perhaps to control the disruptive effects of trade, that the government exercised such a tight grip over trade and manufacturing. It ran the iron and bronze foundries which manufactured everything needed for state and home use – farm tools and ploughs, swords, and bronze triggers fitted to crossbows, cooking stoves, mirrors, incense burners and bells, weights and measures. Each article was stamped with the names of the chief officials who had superintended production and passed it as fit for distribution. Imperial control reached down to the smallest shopkeeper and trader. Every market in the empire had its two-storey government building with a flag and drum on top, where officials fixed the standard price for the silks, lacquer, salted bean sauce, dried and salted fish, jujubes and dog cutlets, the fox and marten pelts, slaves, and all the other commodities sold by the small-time trader. Every trader was registered and paid a commercial tax.

Merchants had to wear white, as a sign of their lowly status; they paid the heaviest taxes. In 7 BC, Emperor Ai decreed that 'No merchants are to be allowed to own private cultivated land or become officials', a ban that had been periodically reinforced over the centuries. Penalized by the state, despised by the elite, and by its religion, it was not surprising that merchants should find Buddhism appealing. Confucianism had a vision of the world as conservative and authoritarian as Brahmanism in India.

The big, cosmopolitan Roman city would be the forcing ground for the new universalist religion of Christianity, which would try to neutralize the disruptive power of trade by stressing what all the differing peoples shared in common – their precious individuality. China, by contrast, did not have a trade-based empire. Its cities were more administrative centres run by imperial officials than the hub of commercial and industrial activities. (The latter were largely in the hands of imperial government and often conducted outside the city gates.[8]) As a result, the Chinese people never faced a strong need to find ways of coping with diversity nor their rulers to provide it. They needed a religion of the state to bind together the administrative elite more than the people, and that religion would naturally emphasize a morality of harmony, rather than of autonomy and individuality.

But, of course, there would always be an underlying tension between the well-ordered institution and the individual battle for power, the world of the outer and of the inner court. That tension was a fundamental characteristic of China at the end of the first century BC.

Ironically, it was because the outer court had provided such a smooth-running administrative machine that emperors had increasingly turned to their entourage in the 'inner court' as a counterweight. An official elite run on meritocratic lines may pose less of a threat than a hereditary elite or a military one, but nonetheless an efficient bureaucracy was potentially too independent; it could run very well without an emperor, and could certainly dominate him. Emperors turned instead to their own entourage, men who they thought would be totally dependent on them – wrongly, as it turned out.

By the time the young Emperor Ai came to the throne in 7 BC, the inner court was in the ascendance, thanks in part to the concubine-turned-empress, Wang Zhengjun. She had beaten off all the other concubines to bear Emperor Yuan's first son, but she had to fight to get him recognized as the heir. Emperor Yuan preferred the son of his new favourite concubine, the Brilliant Companion Consort Fu. But the empress prevailed, with the help of a brave official from the outer court. Shi Dan risked his life by stepping uninvited into the imperial bedchamber, where Emperor Yuan lay dying, to argue in favour of Wang Zhengjun's son.

With her son enthroned as Emperor Cheng in 33 BC, the demure Empress Dowager Wang ('Empress Dowager' was the title given to the mother of the emperor), who was 'uninterested in ruling', slowly circumvented the outer court and placed her own Wang family in the most influential positions. Members of the Wang clan became ministers, grandees, palace attendants or division chiefs. 'They divided the offices among themselves and filled the court,' says the *Hanshu*, which, as the official history of the Han dynasty, starts at this point to tread a difficult line between loyalty to the Empress Dowager Wang, since she was the wife and mother of Han emperors, and loathing for her clan, since it was her nephew Wang Mang who would briefly take the imperial throne away from the Han family.

Four of Empress Dowager Wang's five brothers were in turn appointed Commander-in-Chief, a position that had been restricted to heading the army, but which under the Wangs became the most powerful office in the empire. The Commander-in-Chief was regent in all but name and undisputed leader of the government. He cited officials for promotion or demotion, proposed governmental policies and acted as chief consultant to the ruler. The other ministers had become for the most part virtual executive officers to the Commander-in-Chief. As each of the brothers 'inherited' the position, they were ennobled as marquises and given the land and wealth that went with the title. These sons of a minor official 'vied with each other in extravagance, with several tens of concubines in their harem and slaves by the thousands or hundreds, musicians, singers, actors, dogs, horses, large residences with earthen mountains, cave gates, high verandas and pavilions'.[9]

By 8 BC, imperial power had been wielded for a quarter of a century by Empress Dowager Wang's brothers, but the last of her brothers to fill the post of Commander-in-Chief was seriously ill. According to the de facto hereditary succession that the Wang clan had established, the position should now have been filled by Shun

Zhang, chief assistant to the emperor. But the route to success in the inner court was never certain; because it was based on favouritism, it was always manipulable. Shun Zhang was outmanoeuvred by his thirty-seven-year-old cousin Wang Mang. Wang Mang had sensibly devoted himself to the care of his powerful uncle and now informed him that Shun Zhang was plotting against the emperor. Shun Zhang was executed for treason and Wang Mang was made Commander-in-Chief on 28 November 8 BC.

Only five months later, Emperor Cheng 'slept in the White Tiger Hall; in the evening he was quite well, but towards dawn, with his trousers and stockings on, he tried to arise but dropped his clothes and was unable to speak'.[10] His death was possibly the result of a stroke, though some suspected he had been given an overdose of aphrodisiacs by Consort Fu, the favoured concubine of the former emperor and Empress Dowager Wang's rival.

Now it was Consort Fu's turn to triumph. In 7 BC, her seventeen-year-old grandson, sickly and crippled with arthritis, was enthroned as Emperor Ai. From the start, he was the plaything of the inner court. His grandmother, Consort Fu, now Queen Dowager Fu, installed herself in the Yung-Hsin Palace (Northern Palace). The Fu clan and the Ding clan (the family of Emperor Ai's mother) were in; the Wang clan was out. In the Ding clan alone there were 'two marquises, one Commander-in-Chief, six generals, ministers, and officials ranking at 2,000 piculs, and more than ten Palace Attendants and Division Heads'. One by one, members of the Wang clan, once the most powerful in the empire, were singled out for criticism, removed from their posts, stripped of their marquisates and demoted to commoners.

Wang Mang had tried to oppose Consort Fu's demand to be called Grand Empress Dowager, a title for which she was not eligible since she had never been empress. This was not sheer pettiness on her part. The title would allow her to take part in the affairs of government and give her more status and power than that of her long-standing rival, Grand Empress Dowager Wang, which was why Wang Mang

12. A Kushan prince, AD 1. The Kushans, nomads from what is now Mongolia, enlisted Buddhism in their bid to create an empire in present-day Afghanistan, Pakistan and northern India.

13. Juba, the brilliant polymath ruler of the North African kingdom of Mauretania. He and Herod the Great were Rome's most loyal client kings.

14. St Paul, the greatest marketer a religion has ever known.

15. Coin of Varus, who led Roman legions to one of the worst defeats it ever suffered. The catastrophe in Teutoburg Forest effectively put an end to Roman expansion into Germany.

16. Coin of Gondophares, Parthian Buddhist King of the Gandhara (part of modern Afghanistan and Pakistan). Gondophares is said to have converted to Christianity and to have been one of the three kings who attended the birth of Jesus.

17. Model of the Antonia fortress in Jerusalem looming over the Temple. From the fortress, Herod the Great's soldiers stormed the Temple to quell a protest by Pharisee teachers and their students.

tried to oppose her. At a grand banquet in the Weiyang Palace, 'The Prefect of the Flunkies spread the canopy and seat for the Queen Dowager Fu at the side of the seat for the Grand Empress Dowager Wang.' Wang Mang furiously told the Prefect that the queen dowager was only a concubine. 'How could she be permitted to be honoured equally with the most honorable [lady in the palace]?' Queen Dowager Fu's place was moved. But it was only a minor victory for Wang Mang and his aunt, the Grand Empress Dowager. Wang Mang had incurred Queen Dowager Fu's loathing. He was forced to resign and to leave the city. Two of the top three officials of the outer court who dared oppose her elevation were demoted to commoners, while the most senior of them all, the Chancellor, was arrested for his opposition; he duly committed suicide as honour dictated. Wang Mang's protégés, the men he had recommended for office, were all dismissed. Empress Dowager Wang remained in her palace but as a minor figure, referred to contemptuously as the 'Old Dame' by her triumphant rival, now Grand Empress Dowager Fu.

But there was a far more serious competitor for control of the emperor and the emperor's favours, one of the Gentlemen of the Yellow Gate, who attended the emperor. Dong Xian 'was personally handsome and admired himself'. He was fifteen years old, just two years younger than Emperor Ai, and he was 'good at flattery'. In the course of ten months, 'he had accumulated 100,000,000 cash in grants and rewards and his greatness shook the court'.*

The emperor lavished gifts on Dong Xian's wife. Her father was made minister of palace supplies and created a marquis. She was given unprecedented permission to enter and leave the palace as she wished; she and her children moved into apartments in the Weiyang Palace, while Dong Xian himself shared the emperor's bed. In ancient China this was not necessarily the sign of a sexual relationship, although the emperor clearly loved Dong Xian tenderly. One

* A 'cash' was a type of coin. The annual tax revenue of the empire was about 4,000,000,000 cash coins; 100,000 cash was considered the value of the property of a reasonably prosperous family.

afternoon, the two men had taken a siesta together. When Emperor Ai woke, he found his sleeve was stuck under Dong Xian's head. Rather than wake him up, the emperor had cut off his sleeve. Dong Xian slept on undisturbed, and from then on *duanxiu zhi pi*, 'the fetish of the cut sleeve', was used as a slang term for homosexuality. The emperor made Dong Xian's sister Brilliant Companion, next in rank to the empress. Dong Xian's younger brother was appointed Director of Imperial Equine Operations; other members of the clan were made Palace Attendants and Deputy Ministers, 'receiving Emperor Ai's favour more than the Ding or Fu clan'.

Dong Xian and the Dong clan now overtook the Fu and Ding clans in power, wealth and position. A large and splendid residence was built for him just outside the main palace and a magnificent burial place was prepared beside the imperial tomb. Few officials dared criticize the jewels, the vast estates or the positions that the emperor heaped upon his favourite. But Wang Jia, the Imperial Chancellor, did. He sent a memorial (a memorandum) to the emperor, remonstrating against his intention of making Dong Xian a marquis. Emperor Ai ignored him. Several months later Wang Jia again presented a memorial, arguing against the extravagant favours that the emperor was granting his favourite. The only result was that 'Emperor Ai gradually became less and less pleased with him, and loved Dong Xian more and more.'

The increasing sway of the inner court meant that favouritism, not merit, was determining the most powerful offices in government. A lovely concubine, or, in Dong Xian's case, a beautiful young man who captivated the emperor could secure powerful positions for their kinsmen and themselves. Corruption at the local as well as the central level was rife. A system of promotion depending on intimacy rather than merit, where there was no transparent formal route to success, inevitably broke down into vicious fighting between members of the emperor's entourage, all of whom were struggling for his favour so that they could get the titles, the land, the gifts and the jobs for their own family. There was a general sense of political instability, of scandalous conditions at court and of administrative negligence. The high standard of ethics required, ostensibly at least, from Confucian officials who rose in the outer court did not have to apply to those who rose through personal favour in the inner court.

In 3 BC, the state's bargain with the people – their loyalty in return for meritocracy and good government – which had obviated the need to win their hearts through a populist state religion, finally broke down. One of the droughts that periodically blighted northern China was withering the fields. Peasants who had been precariously surviving on the margins of existence were going hungry; some were starving. For the average small farmer who had to till the land, as well as provide two months of labour service, three days' garrison duty annually and two years' military service, his small plot of land was never quite enough to support his household (on average about four to six people). A drought almost inevitably forced the farmer to sell his land, and often even his wife and children.

In an empire that was predominantly agricultural, the threat of peasant unrest had to be taken very seriously – the Han dynasty itself had been founded by the leader of a peasant uprising. Emperor Ai, or rather his officials, had tried to ease the problems of the subsistence farmers by proposing to restrict the amount of land owned by any one landlord. But by now the inner court, which had been so richly endowed with land by the emperor, was too powerful. In what must have been a rare moment of alliance, Dong Xian, the emperor's favourite, together with the emperor's grandmother, Empress Dowager Fu, and the Fu clan, found the proposal 'inconvenient', so it 'was temporarily postponed to a later [time]'.

The drought of 3 BC forced the peasants to leave their land in search of food. In increasing numbers, they took to the tracks and pathways. By February, thousands of people were marching through the kingdoms and commanderies of northern China towards the capital, Chang'an. They were part rebels, part religious pilgrims, 'processing with stalks of millet or yarrow', symbols of their goddess

Xi Wangmu, the Queen Mother of the West. According to the *Hanshu*, 'Some let down their hair and walked barefoot,' as pilgrims in China still do today, carrying the stalks 'and passing them to one another, saying, "I am transporting the wand of [the goddess]".' Some galloped on horseback, passing a written message to the pilgrims, which said: 'The Mother informs her people that those who wear this writing will not die.'[11] Desperate peasants looked to 'The Mother', who could bring rain and overcome the demon of drought.

The Queen Mother of the West may well have been the Chinese people's first personal deity.[12] She had evolved from a malevolent goddess of plague, drought and flood, with brilliant-white tangled hair, tiger's teeth – which were good for whistling – and a leopard's tail. Her companions were 'the stinkmeet', a scarlet pheasant that made a noise like wood being carved and caused floods wherever it appeared, and 'the trickster', a dog with the markings of a leopard and the horns of an ox, who was the harbinger of bumper harvests. By the end of the first century BC, she had become a goddess of immortality, who was kindly disposed to mankind and could make her favourites immortal. These lucky immortals, painted in the tombs of the less fortunate as skinny, scantily dressed men with long hair and wings, lived with the Queen Mother in the Paradise of the West, somewhere in the Northern Himalaya. There they 'feasted on phoenix eggs and sweet dew', by 'trees of deathlessness and rivers of immortality', accompanied by the nine-tailed fox, the dancing toad and the hare who ground a death-defying drug with his pestle and mortar.[13]

The Queen Mother offered hope, comfort, excitement and even deathlessness to her initiates. They prayed to her for life-giving rain, for help in times of trouble and for a long life, if not immortality. They sang, danced and offered sacrifices to her at the many local shrines scattered around the countryside. She was perhaps the nearest the Chinese got to the deities of the mystery cults.[14] Unlike Confucianism, which belonged to the ruling elite, she appealed to rich and poor alike, though especially to the poor. Her rituals involved everyone; while the state rituals excluded everyone but the emperor and his court.

By summertime, the 'common people' had reached the city of Chang'an and, though the *Hanshu* never states this explicitly, religious fervour had by then exploded into rebellion. 'Some at night broke door-bars and some climbed over walls, entering [houses].' The people were stealing or looting, commandeering carriages and horses. They were running wild in the wards, lanes and footpaths of the city, singing and dancing, climbing over the high walls that surrounded the gardens and courtyards of wealthy mansions to light flaming beacons on the rooftops.

Unfortunately, the *Hanshu* never tells us how the authorities dealt with this crisis. All we are told is that by the autumn, when what harvest there was had to be gathered, the cult had died down. But the Queen Mother herself lived on. (Until very recently, and maybe even today, offerings are still made to her in times of drought, and fifty-year-old women are presented with her image in order to lengthen their lives.[15]) By the second century AD, the Queen Mother had become the most important goddess in the Chinese pantheon of folk deities and her cult was one of the focal points around which Daoism was forming. She had followed the self-aggrandizing route of the pagan gods of the Roman Empire. From goddess of plague and calamity, to goddess of immortality, the Queen Mother of the West now held the cosmos in her keeping along with the King Father of the East.

The emperor and his inner court had learned little from the Queen Mother of the West 'rebellion'. Wang Jia, the Chancellor, the man who represented and ruled the outer court, tried one last time to make a stand against favouritism and the inner court. In February 2 BC, the emperor's domineering grandmother, Grand Empress Dowager Fu, died. Emperor Ai was determined to give some of her vast estate to his favourite, Dong Xian. The Chancellor again wrote a memorandum recommending that Dong Xian should not be treated with such great favour by Emperor Ai, ending in the traditional official style of humility: 'Your servants in their blindness have laid themselves open to capital punishment, by presenting this their request.' And indeed he had. Wang Jia was charged with having been unjust and with attempting to mislead the throne. His case was committed to the decision of the most senior courtiers. About fifty of them supported the emperor's charges; only ten recommended mercy. On 11 April, a messenger came to the Chancellor's office to arrest him. His weeping officials offered him poison – the honourable alternative to prison – but Wang Jia refused, because, he said, he had acted for the best interests of the state. 'So he put on his court robes and went out. When he saw the messenger, he bowed twice and received the imperial edict. Then he mounted a small carriage with the cover removed, to show that he had committed a capital crime. The Commandant of Justice took from him his seal and cord of marquis, bound him, and had him transported to the jail.' Once there, Wang Jia refused to eat. Twenty days later, he vomited blood and died. Not long after, Wang Jia's nemesis Dong Xian was appointed Commander-in-Chief. He was just twenty-two years old and now occupied the most powerful position in the state, the position that the Wang clan had made their own until they fell from grace.

Wang Mang, the last of the Wangs to have been Commander-in-Chief before he incurred the enmity of Grand Empress Dowager Fu, had not been inactive during his exile on his country estate. He had been slowly building up support amongst the Confucian scholar-officials and cultivating his reputation for Confucian piety and modesty. Confucians thought luxury was a sign of lack of virtue and was indirectly responsible for the peasants' poverty. Wang Mang made such a point of living abstemiously that his long-suffering wife had to eschew bright silks, red badger furs, tinkling jade jewellery and silk-lined slippers, and as a result was mistaken for a servant.

The failure of government under Emperor Ai and the inner court had created a growing number of critics, not just among the poor and powerless, but among officials and those who were the losers in the game of favouritism played in the inner court. They began to look to

Wang Mang who, according to the *Hanshu,* had a large mouth and receding chin and vainly tried to look like a leader, though his height was against him. 'He was 5 feet 7 inches tall, loved thick-[soled] shoes and tall bonnets, and used clothes padded with felt. He stuck out his chest and made himself look tall, [so that he could] look down on those who were around him.'[16] Wang Mang had once been the beneficiary of inner court politics when he and his family had virtually ruled the empire as regents, but he had also been the inner court's victim when he fell foul of Consort Fu. Now he was basing his support on the Confucian scholar-officials, the upholders of the outer court, and of meritocracy.

But how does the ruling elite criticize an emperor without fatally undermining the imperial institution itself and the very institutions of rule from which it benefits? How do you destroy an emperor but preserve emperorhood? Wang Mang would use the teachings and precepts of Confucianism, with all their emphasis on filial obedience to the supreme father of the empire, to justify the ultimate act of disobedience, usurpation.

14

WANG MANG THE PIOUS USURPER

> … it is unnecessary for a prince to have all the good qualities… but it is very necessary to appear to have them. And I shall dare to say this also, that to have them and always to observe them is injurious, and that to appear to have them is useful; to appear merciful, faithful, humane, religious, upright, and to be so, but with a mind so framed that should you require not to be so, you may be able and know how to change to the opposite.
>
> Machiavelli, *The Prince*, ch. 18, 1513

In the summer of 1 BC, as black gibbons and peacocks howled in the imperial gardens, Emperor Ai lay dying in his vermilion chambers, under a bedspread of seeded pearls, while his inner court engaged in their own life-and-death struggle for survival. Emperor Ai had failed to provide a son and to the dismay of officials and rival clans of the inner court alike had nominated Dong Xian as his successor, handing him the imperial seals and cords of office. On 15 August 1 BC, Emperor Ai died at the age of just twenty-one. The Wang clan moved fast.*

Wang Hung, Palace Attendant and Colonel of Cavalry, who was one of the few members of the Wang clan not to have been dismissed

---

* Readers should bear in mind that the *Hanshu*'s account of Wang Mang's usurpation, on which I draw heavily, is almost certainly biased against Wang Mang, given that it was commissioned by the Han dynasty following its restoration after Wang Mang's brief reign. For a defence of Wang Mang, even of his physical appearance, see Bielenstein, Hans, 'Wang Mang and the Restoration of the Han Dynasty and Later Han, vol. 4: The Government', *Bulletin of the Museum of Far Eastern Antiquities*, 51,1979: 1–300.

by Emperor Ai, put on his sword and rushed to Dong Xian, 'saying that Dong Xian had received great favours from the deceased emperor and should prostrate himself and weep instead of holding the imperial seals and cords and thereby bringing calamity upon himself'. Dong Xian 'did not dare resist him but kneeled down and gave him the imperial seals'. By surrendering the jade seals, the symbols of office, Dong Xian had in effect given up the emperorhood. Wang Hung galloped off and handed them over to the 'kindly old lady', Grand Empress Dowager Wang, now resurgent after the death of her rival, Grand Empress Dowager Fu.[1]

Although Dong Xian had relinquished his claim on the throne he was still Commander-in-Chief, the most powerful official in the empire. Grand Empress Dowager Wang summoned him to her palace to discuss Emperor Ai's funeral. She made him admit that he was not competent enough to manage the funeral arrangements alone and would need the help of her nephew, Wang Mang, who as a former Commander-in-Chief had conducted the funeral for her son, Emperor Cheng. It was a clear demotion and Dong Xian must have seen the writing on the wall. He 'bent his head to the ground and said he was deeply favoured'. Grand Empress Dowager Wang at once sent a messenger to summon Wang Mang.

On 17 August, the Grand Empress Dowager issued an imperial edict dismissing Dong Xian as Commander-in-Chief on account of his young age. Wang Mang, aged forty-five, was once again Commander-in-Chief, the position he had occupied all too briefly before Emperor Ai had sacked him and sent him into exile. That same day Dong Xian and his wife killed themselves. Their family furtively buried them that night. But a vengeful Wang Mang ordered that Dong Xian's corpse be stripped naked and reburied in a prison. The entire Dong clan was exiled and their assets forfeited to the imperial treasury; all the officials who owed their position to Dong Xian were dismissed.

As Grand Empress Dowager, Wang Mang's aunt was now entitled to choose the next emperor. No doubt with the help of Wang Mang, she selected her nine-year-old step-grandson. But his family were kept well away from court; the Wangs had seen how dangerous a powerful inner court could be and had suffered from it themselves. Little Emperor Ping was forbidden to see his mother who, according to the *Hanshu*, wept day and night, and the whole of his family were barred from Chang'an; they were too powerful and had too many connections in the city. Most of the clan were subsequently executed for their alleged involvement in a plot to restore them to favour. Wang Mang used the plot to implicate his enemies. He had hundreds executed; amongst them his eldest son.

Before the boy emperor had even been enthroned, Wang Mang took his revenge on the Ding and Fu clans who had caused the downfall of his family under Emperor Ai. He stripped them of their titles and positions and exiled them far from the capital. Bereft of support from her family, Emperor Ai's wife committed suicide. His stepmother, Empress Zhao Feiyan, whose 'gait was so light that her graceful carriage... was compared to the single stem of a flower dangling in the grasp of a human hand' (in fact she was no delicate flower but had lied, bribed, schemed and slept with as many men as she could in an attempt to have a baby she could pass off as the emperor's child), retired to her palace and also committed suicide. The bodies of Grand Empress Dowager Fu and Empress Dowager Ding were disinterred and reburied in simple wooden coffins, as befitted concubines rather than empress dowagers. Their original tombs were levelled and thorns were planted in their stead.

Members of the inner court rose spectacularly, but their fall was equally swift and often brutal. Few clans managed to maintain themselves as a permanent elite – perhaps only the Wang clan, until they rose too high and crashed. Just as the inner court rose and fell with their emperor, so did the senior officials of the outer court. The Fu and Ding families had sacked senior officials because they had been Wang Mang's appointees. Now Wang Mang reversed the process and reinstated them, while dismissing the senior officials whom he suspected would be hostile to him.

Not long after he had become Commander-in-Chief, Wang Mang 'hinted that the Governor of Yi Province should induce the barbarians outside the barrier [beyond China's south-western border] to present a white pheasant'. The head of the Yueshang tribe duly appeared at the imperial court with a tribute of one white pheasant and two black pheasants, though his speech had to be 'repeatedly interpreted'. The event exactly mirrored the tribute paid to the Duke of Zhou, the upholder and protector of the Zhou dynasty, which had ruled from the twelfth to the third century BC. For the Confucians, the Zhou kings were the exemplars of the good rulers who ran a well-ordered, moral society. The most revered of them all was the Duke of Zhou, who had acted as regent until his little brother came of age when he handed back the throne to its rightful heir. Wang Mang, regent in all but name, consciously modelled himself on the selfless duke who acted in the interests of his empire, not himself. Ironically, it was the Zhou rulers who provided Wang Mang with the Confucian justification for his usurpation. The sage-kings, as the Confucians called the Zhou rulers, had founded their own dynasty by usurpation. They needed moral legitimacy; the Mandate of Heaven gave it to them.

Vague though the concept was, certainly as it was incorporated later into Confucianism, Heaven, *Tian*, was a kind of impersonal force, which was concerned with the harmony and smooth running of the universe (Heaven was also a good official). Heaven conferred on the emperor the right to rule on earth, and thereby gave him a semi-divine status. Only the emperor, 'the Son of Heaven', could maintain the harmony between Heaven, earth and man. The emperor, indeed, followed a meticulous set of rituals to keep the natural world in order.

At the beginning of every month he would retire to the Ming Tang, the Hall of Distinction, in the southern suburbs of Chang'an. The room he slept in, the food he ate, the colour of his clothes, the horses – the dragon-steeds – that pulled his carriage, were all prescribed in the *Book of Rites*, the *Liji*. In spring the emperor 'rides in the carriage with the phoenix [bells], drawn by the azure-dragon and carrying the green flag; wears the green robes, and the [pieces of] green jade [on his cap and at his girdle pendant]. He eats wheat and mutton. The vessels which he uses are slightly carved, [to resemble] the shooting forth of plants.' In summer he dressed in red and rode in a vermilion carriage drawn by red horses with black tails; in autumn he wore white and his horses were white with black manes; in winter he wore black and rode 'iron black horses'.

But unlike the divine right to rule conferred by the Christian God, *Tian*'s Mandate was conditional. The emperor was responsible for maintaining harmony on earth; he must therefore run his empire well, that is, he must be concerned for the welfare of his people. Without *ren*, loosely meaning benevolence, acting humanely, understanding the hardship of people and doing something to help them, the ruler would lose the Mandate of Heaven. 'If the committing of evil and crimes by monarchs brings calamities to the people, Heaven will deprive the monarchs of the power to rule,' wrote Dong Zhongshu, the second-century BC scholar most responsible for incorporating the Mandate of Heaven within Confucianism. Once the ruler had lost Heaven's approval, the people no longer had the duty to obey him and Heaven would bestow its Mandate on a worthier ruler.

The emperor bought his supernatural legitimacy at the cost of conditionality and of handing over a huge amount of power to the interpreters of Heaven's will – the Confucian scholars, or rather scholar-officials, since all officials were to some extent scholars by virtue of the Confucian exam they had had to sit. Heaven warned of its displeasure through signs and portents, natural catastrophes and strange phenomena. But only the Confucian scholar could interpret these messages (at least that is what the texts would like us to believe) and only the scholar could suggest how the emperor could appease Heaven by altering his policies. If the emperor believed in the Mandate of Heaven, then the Confucian scholar-officials became virtually indispensable to him. The scholar-officials were the secular priests of the state. Unlike the Brahmins of India, they had ceded spiritual power to the emperor. But the emperor's sacred power and very right to rule were dependent on the officials, the defenders and interpreters of Confucianism. Not surprising, then, that emperors did not automatically greet the Mandate of Heaven as a legitimating principle with enthusiasm, and that they would seek to find alternatives.

Confucianism could also legitimize opposition to an emperor in another way – one that made him just as vulnerable, but absolved him of any blame. According to the 'doctrine of the five phases', emperors fell not because they had governed badly, but simply in accordance with the unvarying alternation between two forces, yin and yang. The yin and yang forces represented all dichotomies – male and female, Heaven and earth, day and night, active and passive, hard and soft. Yin and yang were neither good nor bad; Chinese religions were not that much concerned with good and evil. The dichotomies they believed in, like yin and yang, alternated with each other in an endless cycle to create harmony, rather than clashing to cause the triumph of one over the other. The eternal permutations of yin and yang operated through the five phases or elements of earth, wood, metal, fire and water, which succeeded each other in an unvarying sequence. Every system in the world in which humans and nature interacted – the seasons, the emotions, the months of the year, directions, colours, music, food, smells – partook of the properties of the five phases. Dynasties too rose and fell in accordance with which power was in the ascendance.

Even if he was not considered morally responsible, the doctrine of the five phases made the emperor as dependent on his Confucian officials as the Mandate of Heaven. Just as strange and disastrous phenomena were a sign of Heaven's disfavour, so they also heralded the decline of one element with its corresponding dynasty and the rise of the next. But although the changeover from one element to the next, and therefore from one dynasty to the next, was inevitable, it could be postponed, if the officials interpreted the signs correctly and suggested the appropriate policies.

Wang Mang used the Mandate of Heaven and the doctrine of the five phases with consummate skill. He and his Confucian supporters manufactured and manipulated portents and disasters to show that Heaven wanted him to rule. Once he was actually on the throne, Wang Mang became the slave and not the master-manipulator of the portents. But during the nine years that it took for him to manoeuvre his way on to the throne, the portents served him well.

When he received the gift of a white pheasant from the Yueshang tribesmen, the same tribute that had been paid to the great Duke of Zhou, protector of the dynasty that had created the doctrine of the Mandate of Heaven, the response was overwhelming. Confronted with such 'proof' of Wang Mang's virtuous government, 8,000 people as well as his Confucian officials immediately petitioned the Grand Empress Dowager Wang, who was officially regent, to reward him by increasing his escort when he left the palace compound: 'he should', they said, 'be followed by twenty Attendants at the Gates, thirty [members of] the Winged Forest, and that before and after him there should be ten great chariots'.

But Wang Mang was treading carefully. In what appeared to be the true Confucian spirit of humility, he submitted a letter decrying his ability: 'my nature is stupid and rustic,' he wrote; 'I myself know most sincerely that while my virtue is small and my position honorable, my strength is too little and my duties are too great. Day and night I am fearful and circumspect, continually being afraid that I will sully and disgrace your sage court.' The Grand Empress Dowager issued edict after edict urging honours on him; Wang Mang declined in letter after letter. After he had written to decline yet again, this time pleading illness, an increasingly exasperated Grand Empress tried to call his bluff. She issued an edict which said:

Every time that the Duke has an audience, he kowtows with tears falling, as he firmly refuses [his honours]. Now he has sent [Us] a communication [informing Us] that he is ill. Should [We] indeed accede to his yielding so that [We] may order him to attend to his business? Or should [We] indeed put into effect his recompenses and send him home to his residence, [that is, dismiss him from his position and from the court]?[2]

Finally, in AD 1, Wang Mang accepted far greater honours than had originally been pressed upon him. Like the Duke of Zhou, he was given the exceptional honour of being granted a title with the name of the ruling dynasty, and became – ironically given his intentions – the Duke Giving Tranquility to the Han Dynasty. In addition, he took over the office of Grand Tutor to the boy emperor, the most important position in the supreme cabinet of imperial advisers. He was awarded the distinctive insignia that went with 'the highest class of the highest ministers': special shoes, a scabbard tunic embroidered with dragons, a dragon banner, a chariot, a vermilion axe and a black axe (the axe symbolized the power to punish), as well as 300 Gentlemen-as-Rapid-as-Tigers to guard the gates to his new palace. Again, in the apparent spirit of Confucian modesty, Wang Mang refused to accept any increase in his wealth (not so difficult when he already owned 135,000 acres), but instead proposed that a huge number of officials who had supported him should be ennobled as marquises, and that members of the imperial Han dynasty should also be ennobled.

Wang Mang was becoming increasingly powerful, but 'as his noble rank and position became more and more honourable, his conduct became more and more humble', according to the *Hanshu*, which interpreted Wang Mang's display of Confucian humility as pure hypocrisy. 'When he wanted to have something done, he subtly indicated it in his bearing; his clique took up his intentions and manifested them in a memorial, [whereupon Wang] Mang bent his head to the earth with tears in his eyes, and firmly declined.' What Wang Mang wanted in AD 1 was to sideline his aunt, who was still nominally regent. His ministers duly presented a memorial suggesting that she should be spared the more trivial government matters and that Wang Mang should take on her duties. Grand Empress Dowager Wang agreed, citing her great age, which, given that she was seventy years old, seemed fair enough. Wang Mang was now the most powerful figure in the empire; Emperor Ping was his little puppet.

In AD 2, however, a great drought and plague of locusts descended on northern China. Poor peasants again wandered the countryside in search of food as they had done during the Queen Mother of the West 'rebellion'. Weakened by hunger, whole families were wiped out in an epidemic. Was Heaven showing its displeasure? Wang Mang immediately donated money and about 342 acres to the Minister of Finance, to be distributed to the poor.[3] His senior officials followed suit. The people who were suffering most severely were exempted from land and poll taxes, housed in empty imperial lodges and provided with physicians and medicines. Grants were provided so that the poor could bury their dead. A 'new town' with government offices and buildings, marketplaces and hamlets was built. Peasants were urged to move there, provided with food during their journey and, when they arrived, 'were granted fields, residences, productive instruments, and were made loans of oxen for ploughing, and of seed and food. Five hamlets were also built within the city of Chang'an with two hundred residences, for the poor people to dwell in.'[4]

It was a magnificent exercise of benevolent authoritarianism, although not unusual; Emperor Wu had done the same in 119 BC. An agricultural empire cannot afford to antagonize its peasants; they are too important and potentially too dangerous. The Han dynasty had been founded by one of the leaders of the peasant rebellion against the Qin dynasty; and the peasants would eventually help to bring down Wang Mang.

But, in AD 2, Wang Mang's concern for the welfare of 'his' people made him hugely popular. Not long after, a delegation from south-eastern Vietnam arrived, hauling a rhinoceros. Like the gift of the white pheasant, it seemed to be yet another tribute paid by the admiring and envious barbarians beyond China's borders to Wang Mang the benevolent ruler. In fact, it was again Wang Mang who was behind it. He had specifically asked the king of the area to send him the rhinoceros.

Just two years after Wang Mang had married his daughter to the twelve-year-old Emperor Ping, the emperor died. It was rumoured by Wang Mang's enemies that he had given the boy pepper wine spiked with poison. Wang Mang's daughter, widowed at seventeen, refused to remarry and withdrew from life at court. Seventeen years later, when rebels opposed to her father set fire to the Weiyang Palace, she threw herself into the flames and was burned to death.

Emperor Ping's death presented a problem. Five kings and forty-eight marquises were candidates for the throne, and they were all of age. Wang Mang was in danger of losing his position as effective ruler of the empire. But he 'discovered' that the adults were disqualified: it was 'unlawful' for the throne to pass to anyone of the same generation as the deceased emperor. Forced to select from amongst the minors, Wang Mang chose 'the most auspicious of all the candidates at the divination' – the youngest of all the available heirs, two-year-old Liu Ying.

By this time Wang Mang had built up a huge body of Confucian supporters. He had substantially increased the number of Confucian schools throughout the empire; even villages now had their schools teaching the Confucian Classics, in particular 'The Classic of Filial Piety'. In AD 4, he massively extended the Imperial Academy at Chang'an, the fount of Confucian learning, with a building programme to accommodate 10,000 extra students, and employed more scholars to teach them. That same year he summoned several thousand of the empire's scholars to the capital, where they were funded to write their interpretations of Confucian texts. Wang Mang was trying to co-opt practically the entire body of learned men in the empire.

For the next two years, reports of portents and omens came thick and fast. Wang Mang rewarded so many of the officials who reported them with a 'letter of appointment' ennobling them as marquises that it became a joke among the more cynical. They would, according to the *Hanshu*, say to each other: 'Were we alone without letters of appointment from the Lord of Heaven?'

In February, the same month that Emperor Ping had died, a white stone was found on which was written the command that the Duke Giving Tranquility to the Han Dynasty should become emperor. Now his loyal officials petitioned the Grand Empress Dowager to make him Imperial Regent. Wang Mang, they said, should be the acting emperor. That would place him on an equal footing with his exemplar, the Duke of Zhou, who while regent had been openly acknowledged as the de facto emperor, the 'Son of Heaven'. As acting emperor, Wang Mang, like the Duke of Zhou, should be allowed to refer to himself as 'I'; he should

mount the eastern steps, wear the apron and tasselled mortar-board hat of the Son of Heaven, turn his back to the axe-embroidered screen between the door and window, and face south as he holds court for the courtiers and attends to the business of government. When he goes in or out [of the Palace] in his chariot and robes, [the people] should be warned and [the streets] cleared. The common people and courtiers should call themselves his 'subjects' or 'female servants'.[5]

Grand Empress Dowager Wang had become increasingly suspicious of her nephew's intentions. She declared that the portent of the white stone was 'trumped up to deceive the empire. [Its message] cannot be put into practice.' But the officials had now become too strong for her. Wang Mang was appointed Imperial Regent in April AD 6. Under his influence, the worship of Heaven was officially made part of the emperor's religious duties. It remained so until the demise of the last Chinese imperial dynasty, the Qing, in the early years of the twentieth century.

And the portents kept coming, until the final clinching one on 8 January AD 9. Ai Zhang, a young student who 'had not distinguished himself except by bragging', delivered a bronze casket to an imperial temple in Chang'an. Inside the casket was a sealed message from Heaven which decreed that Wang Mang should become emperor. It also listed eleven people who were to fill the highest offices under the new emperor; among them, of course, was Ai Zhang himself. (The 'prophecy' came true. When Wang Mang became emperor and founder of the Xin (or New) dynasty, the untalented but supremely resourceful Ai Zhang was made State General, and Duke Beautifying the Xin.)

The next morning, the Elder of the Imperial House, the Marquis of Loyalty and Filial Piety, Liu Hong, reported the portent to Wang Mang, who summoned his ministers. But they obviously needed one more prompt from Heaven. 'When they had not yet reached a decision, the great supernatural stone man [a large stone statue] spoke, saying, "Hasten the Emperor of the Xin [Wang Mang] to the Temple… [where he is] to receive the Mandate. Do not delay."'

But Wang Mang did delay, for a little longer. 'He was', he said in an edict,

> startled and reverently awed, and worried and sad that the ending of the Han dynasty could not have been arrested… for three nights he did not go to his bed and for three days he did not touch food. He invited and questioned the highest ministers, marquises, high ministers, and grandees, and all said, 'It is proper that you should receive [the rule] according to the majestic Mandate of Heaven Above.'[6]

Wang Mang submitted. As he said in a memorial to his aunt: '[How can] your servant Mang presume not to obey [the Mandate of Heaven]?'

But the Grand Empress Dowager was, according to the *Hanshu*, bitterly opposed to Wang Mang's usurpation of the imperial throne. Indeed, it is quite possible that while the Grand Empress Dowager had been extraordinarily ambitious for her family, and was happy for them and herself to rule supreme in the inner court, she drew the line at usurpation, at what she felt would be the overthrow of authority, stability and tradition. When Wang Mang asked her to hand over the Han seal, as a formal symbol that the imperial authority had indeed passed to him, she called him 'a faithless subject; a pig or dog would not eat his leavings', and threw the seal on to the ground.

On 15 January AD 9, Wang Mang ascended the throne. Unlike the Duke of Zhou, he did not return the throne to his charge, the young Prince Liu Ying. Instead, 'He grasped the hand of the Young Prince, dropped tears, and sighed, saying, "Anciently, when the Duke of Zhou had the position of regent, he was finally able to 'return [the government] to his intelligent prince'. [But] now, only [because] I am pressed by the majestic Mandate of August Heaven, am I unable to follow my intention [to return the government to you].'" He pronounced one of his own surviving sons heir to the new Xin dynasty, and made the disinherited emperor Duke of Established Tranquility: 'forever to be a guest of the Xin House'. In effect, the baby prince was under virtual house arrest in a former government building, 'confined within the four walls, so that when he grew up, he could not name the six [kinds of] domestic animals'. Not even his nurses and wet-nurses were allowed to talk to him.

To the empire at large, Wang Mang proclaimed his right to the throne as conferred on him by the Mandate of Heaven and as the inevitable result of the rise of a new element. Twelve Generals of the Five Majestic Principles travelled around the empire, proclaiming that the Mandate of Heaven had been given through forty-two portents: 'There were five matters of "Happy Presages of Virtues", twenty-five of "Mandates Through Portents", and twelve of "Responses of Heavenly Favors".' In a further edict, Wang Mang announced: 'Since the calculated [number of years allotted] for the age of the Red [Lord] was exhausted I could not eventually have the power to save [that dynasty].' The element of fire, along with its associated dynasty, the Han, and its colour red, had now been succeeded by the element of earth and its colour yellow. The vermilion banners and the red silks of the officials and the concubines disappeared. Yellow was the new colour at court.

Confucian propaganda had done its work. Resistance to Wang

Mang's usurpation was minimal. There were scattered attempts at rebellion by members of the Han clan, but they had lost too much support; Wang Mang was too popular and the portents in his favour were too convincing.

Wang Mang had bought his emperorhood through the Mandate of Heaven. His determination to prove that the Mandate remained with him would, however, prove fatal.

15

THE DRAGON WHO
FLEW TOO HIGH

Among events which may occur, those which should be feared are
human portents. When careless ploughing causes crops to suffer
and those who weed leave weeds behind, when government is
reckless and loses the support of the people – the fields unkempt,
the crops meager, grain sold dear and people starving, corpses lying
in the road: these are what I mean by human portents.

Xun Qing, *Treatise on Heaven*, third century BC

'Fate' is not determined by Heaven but by chance.

Treatise on Heaven

All religion… is nothing but the fantastic reflection in men's minds
of those external forces which control their daily lives.

Engels, *Anti-Dühring*, III.5,1878

Wang Mang's reign was a disaster. So adept at getting to
the throne, he was totally inept once on it.[1] He began his
reign with the goodwill of almost the whole of the
empire; members of the ousted Han dynasty tried two ineffective
rebellions and then subsided into silence. But by the end of his reign,
Wang Mang had antagonized almost everyone. As his rule spiralled
down into chaos, he clung to the magical formulae of the twin
doctrines that had got him to the throne – the Mandate of Heaven,
and the doctrine of the five phases – and abandoned *ren*, the
underlying principle that bound them together, the concern of the
ruler for his subjects.

The Confucian scholar-officials had introduced the magical, the irrational and the supernatural into their rational, ethical 'religion'. But this was not a magic designed to capture the hearts and minds of the people. Confucian magic, like the rest of Confucianism, was for the ruler and the ruling elite. It enabled officials to criticize and even oust their emperor while absolving themselves and their own smooth-working bureaucratic machine from responsibility, and it gave the ruler, especially a usurping ruler, a supernatural legitimacy. Confucianism was on the whole supremely uninterested in the supernatural and the officials probably shared the scepticism of most ruling elites. Xun Qing, the great third-century BC Confucian master, was dismissive of the idea that Heaven sent omens or responded to sacrifices. To him, as to many Confucians, this was pure superstition: fine for the masses but misguided for the elite.

But though Wang Mang may have begun his journey to the throne as the ruthless, cynical manipulator of Confucianism portrayed in the *Hanshu,* he lost the throne primarily because he *was* a believer. In his desperation to prove that Heaven still favoured him, he concentrated on adjusting to Heaven's needs, not to the people's. Instead of trying to create the good society that would lead to favourable portents sent from Heaven, Wang Mang became obsessed with the portents themselves. If they could be manipulated into being favourable, then he could rest secure on the throne and the Mandate would not be taken away. For Wang Mang, the portents, rather than the well-being of his people, became the proof of his good government.

At the outset of his reign, however, Wang Mang was determined to prove his credentials as the benevolent Confucian ruler. In AD 9, he nationalized land. It was a populist move, which was no doubt also intended to weaken the landed aristocracy yet further. All the cultivated fields were renamed 'the sovereign's fields' and could not be bought or sold. Families containing fewer than eight males were restricted to about 12 acres of arable land per male; any surplus had to be divided up and given to their extended family or to people in the neighbourhood. Anyone who disobeyed the edict, or even criticized it, would be 'thrown out to the four frontiers [and be made] to resist the elves and goblins', that is, they would be executed. At the same time, Wang Mang announced a general ban on the buying and selling of slaves; only the government, the largest slave-owner, was exempted from this.

In any other empire, these measures would have been an extraordinarily radical move. In China, they were presented as part of a Confucian egalitarian tradition. For the 'reformists', the physical welfare of the people was, after all, necessary for the creation of a harmonious society – the goal of Confucianism.

Wang Mang claimed he was restoring the well-field system, *jĭngtián*, a system which had been advocated by the great fourth-century BC Confucian theorist Mencius and which had allegedly been universally used in the days of the great Zhou kings (who ruled from the twelfth to the third century BC), though this could have been a mythologizing invention. Wang Mang was so keen to show that he was following in the footsteps of the sage-kings that he cited them as precedents for every ill-judged reform he introduced. In particular, he relied on the *Zhouli*, the lost classic 'found' by Wang Mang's chief ideologue, the great Confucian scholar Liu Xin, which purported to be an account by the great Duke of Zhou himself of his policies and administration, though it may well have been a reconstruction of an idealized antiquity.

Liu Xin was probably behind the nationalization. He, like many Confucian scholar-officials, had long been concerned with how to prevent the agricultural unrest which was always in danger of erupting whenever droughts or floods afflicted China, as they regularly did. The scholar-officials blamed the unrest on the concentration of land in the hands of very rich families. The peasants had too little land to insure themselves against hard times and consequently were forced to roam the country and resort to banditry when natural disaster struck. In the edict announcing his reforms, Wang said:

Fathers and sons, husbands and wives plowed and weeded for a whole year, [but] what they got was insufficient to keep themselves alive. Hence the horses and dogs of the rich had surplus beans and grain and [the rich] were proud and did evil, while the poor could not satiate themselves with brewer's grains, became destitute, and acted wickedly.[2]

During the reign of Emperor Ai, Confucian officials had proposed restricting the amount of land owned by any one landlord, only to be thwarted by the opposition of the powerful inner court. But, at the beginning of his reign, Wang Mang was happy to follow the advice of his officials on whose support he had relied so heavily to get to the throne. The outer court was in the ascendance, though not for long.

Three years later, Wang Mang bowed to the fury of the landowners (the remnants of the old aristocracy and the senior officials who invested their wealth in land and were also granted huge estates when they were ennobled) and rescinded his nationalization of land. The ban on buying and selling slaves was also lifted, or, as Wang Mang's edict put it, people who violated the ban would 'be temporarily free from prosecution'. It would be more than 400 years before the government ever again tried to restrict great landholdings. However, the repeal not only failed to appease powerful landowners, who would later join in the revolt against Wang Mang; it also enraged the peasants, who saw the promise of land snatched away from them, and who had already swung from being fervent supporters to bitter opponents of Wang Mang.

Again claiming the Duke of Zhou as precedent, Wang Mang had imposed a tax on all the produce that the peasants gathered from 'no man's land' (common land) – birds, fish, turtles, wild honey, kindling and all those immensely valuable extras by which poor peasant families eked out their subsistence living. This 'tax on the mountains and marshes' was probably Wang Mang's most serious political blunder. Not surprisingly, it made him loathed by the peasants. But he desperately needed the money.

In accordance with the portents – but perhaps also as a diversionary tactic of the kind that unpopular rulers resort to in order to regain popularity – Wang Mang had embarked on a ruinously expensive military expedition against the mighty Xiongnu, or Huns (the same tribe that had pushed the Kushans out of Mongolia and into what is now northern India and Pakistan). The Chinese liked to think of the Xiongnu as their vassals and had been offering them magnificent 'gifts' as an inducement for them to stay outside the bounds of 'China Proper' on the other side of the Great Wall. But the Xiongnu had renewed their border raids. According to the *Hanshu*, Wang Mang had provoked them by demoting the title of their leader from king to marquis, as he had with the 'barbarian vassals' on the south-western borders. It was part of his obsession with the 'rectification of terms'.

According to Confucius, the 'rectification of terms' was fundamental to understanding one's true place in the hierarchy of relationships that made up society. Each person's social standing entailed responsibilities and duties; the person's title reflected that. If their title corresponded to their true position in the hierarchy – if they were correctly called marquis, rather than king – that person could then behave in the right manner towards his inferiors and superiors. For Confucius, the 'rectification of terms' promoted the creation of a harmonious society. But Wang Mang, like so many fundamentalists, mistook the rule for the principle. He thought that if he got the terminology right, that is, if he adopted the titles used by the Zhou sage-kings, social harmony would be restored and the problems of his government would evaporate. When his reforms proved unpopular, when he lost support amongst the poor, the landowners, and even his officials, Wang Mang turned increasingly to the rectification of terms as the solution to his difficulties. What was in essence a philosophical principle was transformed by Wang Mang into a magical formula.

Whether their leader's demotion in title from king to marquis was the trigger for the Xiongnu's border raids, the omens as interpreted by Wang Mang's increasingly sycophantic officials were certainly in favour of military retaliation. In AD 10, part of the western bank of one of the tributaries of the Yellow River collapsed, causing it to alter course and flow northwards. This was evidence of a very serious irrigation failure. Wang Mang, however, had begun to surround himself with officials who would provide him with the advice he wanted to hear. They 'offered congratulations' and said 'that earth pressing upon water is a happy auspice of the Huns [the Xiongnu] being destroyed'.

A huge army of 300,000 men, led by the General Making Barbarians Quake, the General Tranquillizing the Barbarians and the General Expelling Filth, was mobilized on the north-western border. Lacking adequate shelter and provisions, the soldiers battened on the local people who were already suffering from famine and now resorted to raiding neighbouring provinces in search of food. It took more than a year to restore order. The army meanwhile remained camped on the borders – a huge drain on the state's resources – but never saw action. They were still there, harassing the local peasantry, nine years later, while the Xiongnu continued their raids into Chinese territory. It was at this point that Wang Mang decided that 'repressing various military forces by incantation' was the solution. As the *Hanshu* commented: 'By nature, [Wang Mang] loved the numerology of lucky times and days. When moreover matters became urgent, he merely repressed them by incantations.' The Xiongnu remained an expensive menace for the rest of Wang Mang's reign.

Wang Mang was forced to raise taxes to pay for his costly garrison on the border – a single horse consumed as much grain as an ordinary family. Hence his deeply unpopular tax on the produce from the common land. Hence too the state's further encroachment into the merchants' realm of commerce and trade. Wang Mang deprived them of one of their most profitable livelihoods: the state took over the brewing and selling of alcohol, as it had taken over the mining and sale of salt and iron and the minting of coins 100 years earlier.

In AD 11, the Yellow River – 'China's sorrow' – broke its dykes, flooding vast areas of farmland in the flat muddy plains to the east of

Chang'an and making thousands of peasants homeless.

During the course of Wang Mang's reign (AD 9–23), China was racked by a series of natural disasters. Floods, droughts and plagues of locusts and caterpillars forced hundreds and thousands of peasants to leave their villages in search of food. Prices of grain rocketed. There were five famines between AD 11 and 22, when peasant lawlessness born of starvation transformed itself into political rebellion.

But the weather need not have destroyed Wang Mang. As the Nobel Laureate economist Amartya Sen has pointed out, droughts and floods do not cause famines: the fact that peasants are already struggling on the margins of existence, and the failure of the government to meet the strains put upon it, do.[3] China was hit by droughts every six to seven years. Between 119 BC and AD 188, there were fifty 'migrations' when starving peasants were forced to wander the empire.[4]

A famine year was a time when the competence of the government was tested. Wang Mang proved himself incompetent. He turned natural disaster into political catastrophe by diagnosing the weather magically and trying to treat it magically. During his fourteen-year reign there were seventeen peasant rebellions compared to eight during the whole of the first century BC.[5] As he antagonized a growing number of his erstwhile supporters and became increasingly isolated from his officials, so he turned more and more to magic as the solution to problems that he had in large part created himself.

Wang Mang had tried to solve the problem of food shortages but had in fact only exacerbated them. His temporary land nationalization disrupted food production. Increased taxation, including his 'tax on the mountains and marshes', on the fruits of the common land, pushed many peasants teetering on the edge of survival over the brink. Even a small rise in taxation meant that the peasant could not afford to eat. He and his family had to eat much of the grain supply they should have planted for the following year, and so they produced less grain in the next harvest, had less with which to pay their taxes, and faced ruin and starvation. Wang Mang had re-introduced price controls on grain which had been established by emporer Huan in 53 BC but then rescinded. Grain was sought when prices were low and stored in granaries to be sold when grain was scarce and therefore expensive. It was an attempt to protect the people against speculation by merchants when times were hard – one of the many charges levied against them by Confucian officials, although ironically it was rich merchants who were put in charge of administering the new policy. In principle, they were now buying and selling goods not for their own private profit but to prevent prices skyrocketing when there were shortages. In reality, the policy only exacerbated the food crises of Wang Mang's reign, since without the incentive of personal profit there was no reason for the merchant to go to the expense of transporting scarce goods. The government granaries were empty and the price of grain rose.[6]

Starving peasants thronged into areas where there was food, stealing what they could. In the years that followed, when famine struck again and again, the problem of banditry became more acute, and the empire less able to respond. The state was running out of money and the officials were unable or not competent enough to cope.

It was not just the wasted expense of the military expedition against the Xiongnu that was draining the state's finances. Usurpation is an expensive business. Even if the usurper has Heaven's Mandate, he needs earthly supporters too. In AD 12, the year after the Yellow River burst its banks and flooded, Wang Mang announced that he would increase the numbers of the nobility to several times what it had been under the former Han dynasty. As in the days of the Zhou dynasty, the nobility would have 1,800 members, and so would the inferior nobility. The aristocracy had been decimated during the wars to establish the Han dynasty in the third century BC. Wang Mang was now re-establishing it. It would be the only time in Chinese history when refeudalization occurred. The beneficiaries would increasingly carve out positions of power for themselves, and seize their opportunities as public order broke down.[7]

The granting of new titles, with the allowances, land and tax-paying households that went with them, was a huge cost to the state. Wang Mang was eventually reduced to promising titles that he could no longer afford to deliver. In addition to the cost of the new nobility, and the huge idle army on the north-western borders, state revenues were beginning to fall rapidly as increasing numbers of peasants were unable to pay their taxes. Each successive year of bad harvests reduced the tax revenues. And the fall in tax revenues had a further disastrous consequence: the government became less and less able to pay the salaries of local officials. Payment of the full salary had become so unusual that, in AD 16, Wang Mang announced that for the first time in his seven-year reign his officials would finally be paid their full salary, though adding that this would only apply in the years when there was a good harvest.[8] As a result, local officials increasingly resorted to corruption and theft from the state granaries to supplement their salaries. In a vicious circle, the famines became more severe as the officials stole more, and as the famines became worse so tax revenue fell still further, encouraging officials to pilfer yet more.

In AD 14, there was another famine on the north-western borders, where Wang Mang's soldiers had already been preying on the local people. Equally serious, for Wang Mang at least, was an eclipse of the sun that same year. Ill omens now came thick and fast:

in the fourth month, there was a fall of frost which killed the vegetation, especially at the sea-shore. In the sixth month, a yellow fog [filled up everything within] the four quarters. In the seventh month, a great wind uprooted trees and blew off the roof-tiles on [the buildings at] the Northern Portal [of the Palace] and at the Zhicheng gate [of Ch'ang-an] and hail fell, killing cattle and sheep.[9]

Wang Mang's response was to sack one of his most senior officials, the Grand Minister of Works, Wang Yi. In his letter of 'resignation',

Wang Yi wrote: 'I have overseen my affairs to the eighth year, and my efforts have not been successful. In my duties... I have [moreover] been more especially useless, so that recently there has even been the grievous vicissitude of an earthquake. I wish to beg to retire.' Although it was usually the officials who used portents to focus the blame for governmental failure on the emperor, it could also work the other way around – if the emperor was enough of an authoritarian.

As the portents kept coming, and as the opposition to Wang Mang gathered from all quarters and grew in intensity, Wang Mang became increasingly sensitive to criticism. He was suffering the usurper's affliction of suspicion. As the *Hanshu* noted: '[Wang] Mang had been set [on the throne] by fraud, so he suspected in his heart that his great officials would hate and malign him. He wanted to terrify them in order to make his inferiors fear him.' Minor officials were encouraged to inform on their superiors and promoted for doing so. Flattery and fear were replacing efficiency and obedience in the outer court.

Though he had relied on Confucian officials to get him to the throne and had built up the power of the outer court in order to do so, Wang Mang now built up the inner court just as the Han emperors had done. He placed more and more official power in the hands of eunuchs, who now became the gatekeepers of all government memorials submitted to the emperor and shielded him from any criticism of government policy. At the same time, Wang Mang was seriously undermining the outer court as an efficient bureaucracy by destroying its meritocratic nature and therefore its incentive to govern well. In AD 11, he had appointed his son Grand Master, one of the most important government posts, and decreed that from then on it would be inheritable. Three years later, in AD 14, the year of the solar eclipse, he made all the important provincial government posts hereditary. At a stroke, Wang Mang eliminated an officialdom whose basic principle, even if not practice, was that success should come through knowledge and ability rather than birth.

In AD 17 there was another famine. Tens of thousands of homeless peasants wandered the country and the old and vulnerable died by the roadside. Starving, desperate families crowded into areas less affected by famine. Men organized themselves into armed bands to raid villages in search of food.

Wang Mang could probably still have avoided outright rebellion had he listened to the few officials brave enough to tell him the obvious: these armed bands of peasants were not political rebels, as he insisted they were; their violence was the result of physical desperation. Solve that, and the unrest would disappear. The never-ending droughts, coupled with the 'tax on the mountains and marshes', had driven the peasants to lawlessness. They wanted food, not a new emperor. The tax on the mountains and marshes should be repealed.

Wang Mang sacked the officials. He was determined to see these peasant bandits as political rebels. To concede that the unrest was due to drought and flood, rather than wilful disobedience, was to acknowledge that Heaven had turned against him and was showing its disfavour through these natural disasters.

Of course, the dividing line between bandit and political rebel, or between political rebel and religious cult leader, was very muddied in the ancient world; the Messiah cults in Judaea were as potentially dangerous to the Roman emperor as the Queen Mother of the West cult was to the Chinese. Nonetheless, it is very likely that unrest would have died down if the peasants' physical needs had been addressed. After all, the Queen Mother of the West 'rebellion' had evaporated with the coming of the harvest season.

It was a wealthy widow from Shandong, the province worst hit by famine, who turned unrest into rebellion. Mother Lu was renowned for her generosity. When the peasants were starving, she provided rice at her own expense, and paid for the funeral of a local man whose family could not afford to pay for it. Her care and concern seem to have been shared by her son, the local county constable, but not by the senior officials of the province. In AD 14, he 'neglected' orders to punish those people who did not pay their taxes and was executed by the County Supervisor.

The death of her son made Mother Lu a rebel. She opened a tavern where, over the next four years, she secretly stockpiled crossbows, and recruited followers, often by giving local youths wine on credit or loaning food and clothing. She went from house to house, speaking out against the high taxation the government was imposing on ordinary people. In AD 18, 100 peasants, waving a great banner emblazoned with her name, marched on the county of Haiqu. They were under strict orders not to steal from the local peasants. Mother Lu clearly understood how important it was for a guerrilla army not to antagonize its source of recruitment and support – the local people. When her well-disciplined army took Haiqu and captured its Ruler (the official in charge of the county), the General, as Mother Lu now called herself, took revenge on the man responsible for her son's execution and refused to listen to pleas for mercy:

> The officials knocked their heads to the ground [they kowtowed] and begged for the Ruler's life, but Mother Lu said, 'My son committed a small crime for which he should not have died, but he was killed by the Ruler. He who kills a person should die. Why do you beg for the Ruler any more?' Thereupon she had him beheaded. She used his head as a sacrifice on the tomb mound of her son.[10]

Mother Lu died soon after these events, but the rebellion she had ignited gathered momentum. All over China, more and more peasants were turning to banditry. In Shantung, Mother Lu's rebels joined up with thousands of bandits to form one huge group that looted and pillaged its way through the province in search of food. This force would soon become the most formidable of the guerrilla armies attacking Wang Mang. Wang Mang ordered his provincial officers to levy troops. But by that time the bandit/rebel groups were too numerous and too strong, and the troops failed to put down the unrest. Wealthy landowners protected their estates with moats and fortified walls from which their retainers – or 'guests' as they were called – fended off the bandits with crossbows.

As the empire disintegrated around him, Wang Mang put even more faith in magic. He commanded his Grand Astrologer to draw up a calendar for the next 36,000 years of the Xin dynasty, the dynasty that he had founded, and ordered that the calendar should be published all over the empire. It was both a magical way to ensure the continuation of his dynasty and a desperate assertion of his confidence that the Mandate of Heaven was still with him.

And he again resorted to the rectification of terms. 'Because of my lack of penetration, my performance of [Heaven's] commands has not been intelligent,' he announced in an edict. He had wrongly changed the title of 'General of a New Beginning' to 'General of a Peaceful Beginning'.[11] Now, in order to accord with the Mandate of Heaven, he was reverting back to the original title; with the one-word change, harmony would be restored and lawlessness would disappear. According to the *Hanshu*, 'he wished, thereby to deceive and dazzle the people', but it was only the emperor who was taken in; 'the vulgar all laughed at him'.

Wang Mang's discussions with his officials about correct terminology were interminable. He obsessively changed the names of palaces, institutions and the currency, but above all the titles of his bewildered officials. He changed the title of the Superintendent of the Imperial Household to the Director of Palaces, the Grand Coachman to the Grand Charioteer, the Commandant of the Palace Guard to the Grand Guard, the Bearer of the Gilded Mace to the Inciter to Military Deeds. He changed names so many times, even changing the name of one commandery five times, 'that the officials and common people could not keep records of [these names], and whenever a written imperial edict was issued, the former names [of places mentioned therein] were each time attached'.

When a gale tore the roofs off houses in Chang'an and damaged the Weiyang Palace's Hall with the Royal Apartments, Wang Mang invoked both the doctrine of the five phases, which absolved him of any moral responsibility for the disasters afflicting the empire, and the Mandate which did not.

Verily, since I have ascended the throne, the *Yin* and *Yang* [principles] have not been harmonious, so that the wind and rain have not been timely, and [the country] has several times met withering drought, locusts and caterpillars, which became [calamitous] visitations. The harvests of grain have been sparse or lacking, so that the people have suffered from famine. The barbarians have troubled the Chinese and robbers and brigands have caused disorder outside and inside [the government, so that] the common people are fearful and disturbed and do not know how to move a hand or foot.[12]

As a result of the great wind, Wang Mang said, 'I was greatly excited. I was inspired with great fear. I was greatly terrified. I humbly reflected and after ten days the riddle was then solved... the blame for this [lies] in titles not being correct.' It was because he had opposed the will of Heaven by appointing his younger over his older son. Now Wang Mang would obey Heaven. His older son, Wang An, became the new heir-apparent; he was mentally disabled. A year later, Wang Lin, the younger son, tried to assassinate his father because they had shared the same concubine and Wang Lin was terrified his father would find out. Wang Mang had him executed, paying only this paternal tribute to his son: 'at an untimely age his life was destroyed. Alas! How sad!'

Although the empire desperately needed cash to support the starving, Wang Mang embarked on a massive building programme to erect nine temples to his ancestors outside the southern walls of Chang'an. Tens of thousands of conscripts and criminals worked and died building the temples, as Chang'an's inhabitants looked on in amazement. Their city was already a forest of towers and steeples, but the temples overtopped them all – the Temple to the Aboriginal Founder (Wang Mang's mythical ancestor the Yellow Emperor) was 170 feet high.

In AD 21, the year after work on the temples had begun, there was famine in eastern China. Grain was twenty-five times its normal price. Several hundred thousand refugees trudged westwards to Chang'an and the surrounding area; about 80 per cent of them starved to death. Wang Mang showed his solidarity with the starving peasantry by reducing the cuts of meat served at the imperial table. And he 'asked' officials to accept a voluntary annual reduction in their already vulnerable salaries, the amount to be determined each year according to the state of the harvest. This reduction, coupled with the fact that officials would not know until the end of the year what their salary would be, served only to encourage what was already endemic corruption amongst local officials.

Wang Mang had virtually silenced any official who would tell him the truth. When he summoned his officials to discuss what to do about the bandits, they obligingly said, 'These [people] are Heaven's criminals and walking corpses. Their lives will [last] only an instant.' Increasingly suspicious of his officials, except those who flattered him with the advice he wanted to hear, Wang Mang tried to take more and more control himself. He worked all night until daylight but he was, fatally, a tinkerer. 'He loved to change and alter the institutions and regulations, so that the government ordinances were numerous, and those which needed to be put into practice had each time to be asked about, before anything could be done.' His obsession with the minutiae of government meant he neglected the big issues. 'He did not have leisure to examine law-cases, decide complaints of injustices, or to settle the urgent business of the common people... [with the result that] the covetousness and injuriousness of all [his officials] alike daily became greater.'[13]

Floundering in worthless advice from toadying officials, squandering scarce resources on his massive temple-building project while hundreds of thousands of armed peasants roamed the country, Wang Mang became ever more isolated and ever more obsessed with the magical. Like a Shakespearean tragic hero haunted by the ghosts of men he had killed, Wang Mang became terrified of the spirits in the temple to Emperor Gao Zu, founder of the Han dynasty that he had toppled. In an appalling act of sacrilege, he 'sent [Gentlemen] As

Rapid as Tigers and Men of War to enter the Temple... draw their swords, throw and strike in all directions, destroy its doors and windows with axes, whip the walls of the building with ochre-red whips and sprinkle them with peach-water.'

Ever since he had taken the throne Wang Mang had feared assassination. A general search of the city was always made before he left the Weiyang Palace; one search had lasted twelve days. He had had a special ramp built in the palace parallel to the staircase, so that when the city was declared safe he could step into his imperial chariot in the palace audience hall and ride down the ramp to the front hall. From there, he would be escorted through the city by eighty-one carriages lined up in three columns. But now, if the emperor ventured out, his imperial chariot was preceded by a carriage bearing a feathered canopy 81 feet tall. The chariot was pulled by 300 men dressed in Xin dynasty yellow, chanting to the beat of a drum 'He will mount up to be an immortal'. Wang Mang's legendary first ancestor had used such a canopy to rise to Heaven. Wang Mang hoped he could do the same, though his more sceptical officials 'said secretly, "This is like a funeral cart, not a thing for an immortal."'

By AD 22, the people of Chang'an – the greatest walled city in the world – were starving. The river that fed the canal network providing water for the city and the surrounding rich farmland, which was the one region in northern China never hit by droughts or famines, had become completely blocked. Fields of millet, hemp, soybeans and wheat, and the groves of mulberry trees that fed the silkworms, were dying. The city had already had to absorb several hundred thousand destitute peasants from the east and south of the empire. And more and more were crowding in, hoping to escape the famine, which was now so bad that people were turning to cannibalism. Finally, Wang Mang recognized what his best officials had told him all along. Famine was at the root of the peasants' unrest. He opened state granaries throughout the empire but acknowledged this would not be enough, and rescinded the 'tax on the mountains and marshes'.

It was too late. Before the messengers had even ridden out across the empire to announce the news, the vast army of bandits in Shandong province, to which Mother Lu's group had attached itself after her death, clashed with government troops for the first time. They had no armour and no banners, and had only their painted red eyebrows to distinguish themselves from the imperial troops. The Red Eyebrows were led by the brilliant general Liu Bosheng, a member of the Liu clan from whom the Han emperors had been drawn. Peasant rebellion now became political rebellion, with the restoration of the Han dynasty as the rallying cry for the disparate rebel/bandit armies that formed around the empire. Other members of the Liu clan rose in revolt.

Local landowners, whom Wang Mang had so thoroughly antagonized with his attempt at nationalizing land, had been playing a waiting game. Now they joined the rebellion with their 'guests', in effect their personal armies. In the early spring, when provinces and cities were falling or surrendering to the triumphant Red Eyebrows and the other rebel armies as they marched towards the capital, Wang Mang dyed his hair and beard in order to appear more youthful, and remarried. The new empress came with 120 concubines, the number that the empress of Wang Mang's alleged ancestor, the mythical Yellow Emperor, had brought with her and which were said to have assured him immortality.

Not long after his marriage, the imperial troops suffered their worst defeat at the hands of the Red Eyebrows. Wang Mang called his officials and commanded the Baron of Brilliant Scholarship to expound on the power of earth that had brought him to the throne and on the Mandate of Heaven that had been bestowed on him through portents. The officials dutifully shouted, 'Long life,' but they knew the game was up and began disappearing from court. Even Liu Xin, Wang Mang's chief ideologue, now turned against his emperor and plotted to hand him over to the Red Eyebrows. The plot was discovered and Liu Xin committed suicide.

In the summer, a black cloud of locusts invaded Chang'an and crawled through the rooms of the emperor's Weiyang Palace, as the

Red Eyebrows advanced through villages that came out to welcome them. While the city starved and the alarm drum beat incessantly, Wang Mang organized great weeping ceremonies of 5,000 or more ordinary people who were bribed with food to cry morning and evening. If their grief was judged genuine, they were made Gentlemen. An official had told Wang Mang that in the days of the Zhou, a ruler was meant to weep in order to ward off evil.

Wang Mang knew now that he would be defeated, but he made one last appeal to Heaven; surrounded by his remaining courtiers, he laid out the record of all the portents which were proof that he had received the Mandate and, looking up to Heaven, said:

'Since thou, August Heaven, hast given thy mandate to thy subject, Mang, why doest thou not immediately order extirpated the bands [of troops] and the robbers? But if thy servant Mang has done wrong, I wish that thou wouldst send down thy thunderbolt to execute thy servant Mang.' Thereupon he struck his heart with his palm and wept loudly.[14]

It was the prayer of a true believer, but Heaven did not respond.

On 4 October AD 23, the rebel armies broke through one of the wooden gatehouses on the east wall and fought their way through the criss-crossing streets, the evenly spaced houses, and the walled markets of Chang'an. By the time the sun went down, they had reached the palace gates. Inside, sixty-eight-year-old Wang Mang sat on a rug dressed in purple, the colour corresponding to the North Star, the seat of Heaven. All through the night, he regularly shifted his position in line with the North Star as it slowly travelled across the sky. He was girded with his imperial seals and apron and held a dagger with a spoon on the end of its hilt, which was meant to have belonged to Lord Shun, another legendary ruler from whom Wang Mang claimed ancestry. Beside him sat an astrologer who hourly calculated the future with the aid of a divining board, exactly on the model of the Zhou sage-kings, while Wang Mang murmured to himself: 'Heaven begat the virtue that is in me. The Han troops – what can they do to me?' Occasionally he slept where he sat, resting his head on a stool.

The following day, young men from the city, eager to prove they were on the rebels' side, set fire to part of the palace and hacked open a side door of the Hall of Reverence for the Law, calling out: 'You rebellious caitiff, Wang Mang, Why do you not come out and surrender?' Wang Mang fled from room to room as the fire spread, while the women in the harem 'wailed, saying "What must we do?"'

On 6 October, exhausted from lack of food, Wang Mang was half carried from the Front Hall, down the palace stairs, and westwards out of the White Tiger Gate. A chariot took him through the vast imperial park, past the ornamental gardens, menageries and pavilions where emperors and their concubines had feasted, to the Tower Bathed by Water, set as its name suggested in the centre of a lake. Wang Mang planned to make his last stand there with the water as his magical defence. Water would vanquish fire, and hence the Han dynasty: the doctrine of the five phases held that every Chinese dynasty ruled under the power of one of the five elements, and the Han's was 'fire'. A thousand loyal courtiers and ministers followed him. They were joined by the remains of the imperial army who found a way past the rebels and galloped to the tower. They must have known they had no hope. The general's own son, in fact, took off his distinctive robes and bonnet in order to escape, but was called back by his father. Together father and son, soldiers and courtiers, faced the rebels when they finally surrounded the tower.

A Beauty in the harem had told the rebels where to find them. Holed up in the tower, they fended off the rebels with their crossbows. By the late afternoon most of the emperor's defenders had been killed, including the general and his son. Clutching the portents that proved he still had the Mandate of Heaven, Wang Mang and his surviving courtiers fled to the top of the tower where they were cornered and slaughtered. Rebel soldiers sliced up Wang Mang's body and killed each other in a feeding frenzy to grab a piece of his flesh or bones. His head was carried to one of the marketplaces and used as target practice by jeering crowds, while others cut out and ate his tongue.

'The dragon who flew too high', as the *Hanshu* described Wang Mang, had lost his empire in the space of just fourteen years. The Han dynasty was restored and would rule for another 200 years before collapsing, in part because of the resurgence of feudalism that Wang Mang had encouraged.

Wang Mang had let the magical rather than the rational element of Confucianism guide his policies. Yet, though the Mandate was a disaster for Wang Mang himself, it became the essential underpinning of the Chinese state. The notion that the emperor's right to rule depended on his delivering good government to the people was enshrined at the heart of the state's ideology. Such a pact with the people helped ensure the continuation of the Chinese Empire and bureaucracy for another 1,900 years, until the last emperor stepped down from the throne in 1912 after a rebellion – and after the Yangtze River had overflowed its banks, killing thousands of people. The emperor had failed in his duty of good government; the omens were against him. Though Confucianism addressed itself to the elite not the people, though it did not try to satisfy the individual's needs for comfort and satisfaction, no other pairing of empire and ideology would ever last so long – not even Christianity or its predecessor, the imperial cult.

Rome had to manoeuvre every subject in its disparate empire, an empire made more heterogeneous by its huge trading cities, into accepting imperial authority. China's ideological task was different. It didn't have to reach out to the individual because imperial diversity was less problematic. Unlike the chaotically diverse cities of imperial Rome, China's cities were small units of imperial officials, centres of administration for an agrarian hinterland. Wang Mang's subjects had rebelled against food shortages and bad government. Augustus' subjects did that too, but also revolted against being subjects at all.

16

RECALCITRANT SPIRITS:
THE GERMAN RESISTANCE

... this man [Augustus], having attained preeminent power and discretion, ruled over the greatest number of people within the memory of man, established the farthest boundaries for the Roman Empire, and settled securely not only the tribes of Greeks and barbarians, but also their dispositions; at first with arms but afterward even without arms, by attracting them of their own free will. By making himself known through kindness he persuaded them to obey him.

Nicolaus of Damascus, *Life of Augustus*, fragment 125, c.AD 14

You Romans are to blame for this; for you send as guardians of your flocks, not dogs or shepherds but wolves.

Bato, leader of the Pannonian and Dalmatian revolt against Rome, in Cassius Dio, *The Roman History: The Reign of Augustus*, LVI.16, c. 214–26

Moulding people into willing subjects is never easy. In AD 3, Augustus was faced with serious unrest from what appeared to be one of the most successfully Romanized of the empire's conquered kingdoms. Tribesmen in Mauretania (what is now Algeria and Morocco) rebelled against King Juba II, the most faithful of all Augustus' client kings bar Herod the Great.

Juba was the epitome of a member of the successfully co-opted elite. Julius Caesar had conquered his father's ancient kingdom of Numidia and incorporated it into the Roman province of Africa when Juba was a baby. His father had committed suicide, and Juba – he was probably no more than two years old – had been paraded through the streets of Rome in chains as part of Julius Caesar's triumph in 46 BC.

In a typical triumph described by Josephus the whole of the Senate – more than 1,000 men with their bodyguard – led the miles-long procession that slowly made its way through the cheering crowds who lined the streets or watched from scaffolding erected specially for spectators.[1] Behind the senators marched a phalanx of trumpeters. Hundreds of carts rattled by, displaying the riches that had been looted from the conquered – gold and silver, weapons, statues, vases and precious stones. Flute players were followed by a herd of white bulls with gilded horns, attended by the priests who would sacrifice them at the temple of Jupiter Capitolinus. Behind them padded a troupe of elephants and animals brought back from the conquered lands. Then came the defeated, clanking in chains. And riding in a chariot, his face and body painted red, wearing a gold-embroidered toga, a golden crown held over his head by a slave, sat the triumphant general himself. It was the nearest most generals got to being a god: to avoid hubris, a slave stood in his chariot whispering over and over in his ear: 'Look behind you! Remember you are but a man!' Adoring crowds showered him with flowers. Behind him marched the disciplined ranks of the infantry, their spears decorated with laurel. They held up placards praising their general and listing the cities and territories he had conquered. They shouted his name in praise but also made ribald jokes at his expense – a special licence granted to the soldiers for the triumph. As they ascended the Capitoline Hill, the procession stopped and the defeated leaders were led away to be strangled in the Tullanium, Rome's subterranean prison. Then the procession headed on to the temple of Jupiter Capitolinus, the largest and most beautiful of Rome's temples, where the white bulls were sacrificed.

Having inflicted its humiliation on Juba, the Augustan regime set out to Romanize him. Juba was brought up and educated by the imperial family. Under Augustus, this deliberate policy of Romanizing the children of barbarian royalty by 'incorporating' them into the imperial household became common practice and was extremely successful. Cymbeline, though he was king of a still independent Britain in AD 5, had been brought up at the court of Augustus and without demur paid tribute to Rome. According to Juba's modern-day biographer, the classicist Duane Roller, Juba became, as did so many of North Africa's elite, not just Romanized but Roman. In 31 BC, at Actium, he fought with Augustus against Mark Antony and Cleopatra, the parents of his future wife. Four years later, he accompanied Augustus and the young Tiberius on campaign to subdue the mountain tribes of Spain. Juba was such a trusted figure that in AD 2 he was part of the delegation that accompanied Augustus' grandson, the eighteen-year-old Gaius Caesar, on his peace mission to Parthia (see chapter 9).

In reward for such loyalty, Augustus gave Juba the kingdom of Mauretania, 'the Juban land, dry nurse of lions' as Horace called it, neighbouring the Numidian territory which had once been Juba's father's and now was Rome's. Juba was twenty-three. A bronze bust made of him at about that time shows him to have been astonishingly attractive, slightly plump, with curly hair and small full lips, but giving no hint of the great scholar that he was, an authority on India, writer of the best-selling guide to Arabia and of numerous historical works in Greek and Latin – he was considered to be a better historian of early Rome than his now more famous contemporary Livy.[2] Juba wrote on natural history, geography, grammar, painting and theatre; he was known as *rex literatissimus*, was friend and protégé of Strabo, and described by Plutarch as 'one of the most gifted rulers of his time'.

Before he left Rome to take over his new kingdom, Juba was married with Augustus' blessing to Cleopatra Selene, daughter of Mark Antony and Cleopatra. It was probably her influence that turned Juba into a keen follower of Isis whose symbols were engraved on his coins. Like Juba seventeen years earlier, Cleopatra Selene had been marched captive in a triumph – this one to celebrate Augustus' defeat of her parents at Actium – and again like Juba she was Roman in education and upbringing. Together, Juba and Cleopatra Selene created a Graeco-Roman capital city on the Mediterranean coast.

Iol (today's Cherchel in Algeria), which they renamed Caesarea – just as that other client King Herod had given the same name to the Judaean city that had formerly been known as Strato's Tower – was a small decaying city founded by Phoenicians from Carthage in the fourth century BC. Juba constructed a harbour, and on a small adjacent island added a lighthouse in the style of the wondrous Pharos of Alexandria. On the waterfront, he built a fine library which became a centre for Greek, Roman and indigenous African scholars; Juba's court became the most scholarly of all the royal courts of the time. By the second century AD, North Africa would be a major intellectual force in the empire. Set into the side of the hill, above the harbour and the royal palace, was the forum. Iol had a temple to Augustus, a sacred grove – the *Lucus Augusti* – and an amphitheatre that hosted games in his honour. Amongst the marble buildings, the busts and statues, was a colossal statue of Augustus wearing a breastplate that showed the battle of Actium where Augustus, with Juba's assistance, had defeated Cleopatra Selene's parents. Like all client kings keen to prove their Hellenistic credentials, Juba was a patron of Athens, judging by the statue the city erected to him; he was also made chief magistrate of two cities in Spain with whom Mauretania had close trading links.

As all client kings were meant to do, Juba had created a mini Rome in his kingdom. The ordinary people of Iol and the surrounding area, which was well watered by Juba's aqueduct system, were being acclimatized to Rome by the imperial festivals, the statues of Augustus and the increasing trade with Rome, encouraged by the Roman merchants who were settling in the city. But apart from Iol, there was only one other port city, and only one city further inland. Juba, his wife and the North African elite, like local elites throughout the empire, were happy to think of themselves as Roman, and indeed increasingly benefited from doing so. But this only distanced them from ordinary people who, though they may have become accustomed to Rome's presence, were not necessarily reconciled to it. The North African elite looked to Rome and the Mediterranean as their cultural home. Many of them had been educated in Rome; they Romanized their names and married into the Roman elite who were settling great swathes of land which were farmed by armies of slaves or let out to tenant farmers. Pliny the Elder, writing in the mid-first century AD, says that by his day 'six landlords owned half of Africa'.

Exaggeration though this might be, it was indicative of a trend. Rome's province of Africa and its adjacent client kingdom of Mauretania were beginning to displace Egypt as Rome's principal suppliers of wheat, providing more than half a million tons annually from the fertile coastal belt and even from the desert. North Africa had become, and would continue to be, one of the most prosperous regions of the Roman Empire. The Sahara Desert of the ancient world was wetter than it is now and in places agriculture was flourishing. In about 200 BC, over fifty years before the Romans began their colonization of North Africa with the conquest of Carthage (in modern Tunisia to the north), Garamantes desert tribesmen had constructed a network of miles of underground tunnels, and shafts which transported fossil water from under the desert sand to feed their wheat fields.[3] The Garamantes, with their ritual scars and tattoos, became not just brilliant engineers but also landholders, using slaves to farm their wheat fields, and, as their villages developed and expanded into towns, they became merchants trading slaves, wheat and salt in exchange for wine, oil and Roman tableware and pottery. The Garamantes' 'kingdom' in modern-day Libya survived until about AD 500 when, having extracted at least 30 billion gallons of water over some 600 years, they suffered the consequences of climate change: the desert became hotter and drier and the water ran out.

But though the Garamantes traded with Rome in the early first century AD, they struggled against its encroachment. The provinces of Africa and Mauretania were a potentially tense mix of Roman enclaves in a sea of indigenous peoples. There were a scattering of

Roman cities with their Romanized inhabitants and immigrant Roman merchants; the Roman and North African Romanized elite who owned the great landed estates; and there were colonies of veterans – Augustus planted twelve such settlements in Mauretania.

The tension between the Roman and the non-Roman was exacerbated by the conflict between the pastoralists and the agriculturalists, nomad and settler, the age-old conflict between Cain and Abel. The Gaetulian nomads, who ranged the desert from the Atlantic coast to the borders of Egypt, saw their traditional routes blocked by Roman frontier roads and Roman forts, and their common land being taken not just by big Roman landlords but by peasant farmers in the hundreds of villages of Mauretania. As Rome's presence became more visible, as land was increasingly appropriated, as population increased and the competition for land between agricultural settler and pastoral nomad became more intense, and as they were conscripted into the auxiliary forces or into Juba's Romanized army, the nomad tribes increasingly resented Rome and its puppet Juba.

Juba was confronted with the problem faced by Herod and all client kings – how to maintain the trust and favour of Rome while not being seen as a collaborator and losing the trust of his people. In AD 3, the 'rough and unkempt' Gaetulian tribesmen were, according to Cassius Dio, 'discontented with their king, Juba, and scorning the thought that they, too, should be ruled over by Romans, rose against him'.[4] It took Juba about four years of hard fighting and military assistance from Rome to put down the rebellion. But the Gaetulians were never completely subdued. Ten years later, following Juba's death, his son Ptolemy would face an even more serious rebellion.

The non-urbanized were always going to be the most difficult of Augustus' subjects to co-opt, and the nomads above all. They were not subject to a static central authority, refused to acknowledge boundaries, owed their loyalty to their tribal chief whose authority moved with him, and did not recognize the authority of a super-king.

Since they were not city-dwellers, they were usually immune to the influence of imperial cults and their manifestations in festivals and statues – though not always.

In about AD 4, Livia's nineteen-year-old son Tiberius was leading one of Rome's never-ending attempts to subdue the tribes of Germany. Both sides were camped on opposite banks of the River Elbe. Velleius Paterculus, who was then cavalry commander of a legion serving under Tiberius, described seeing 'one of the barbarians, advanced in years, tall of stature, of high rank, to judge by his dress, embarked in a canoe, made as is usual with them of a hollowed log, and guiding this strange craft he advanced alone to the middle of the stream'. There he requested permission to land on the Roman side of the river so that he could see Tiberius Caesar, the heir to Augustus. Permission was granted. The tribesman

> beached his canoe, and, after gazing upon Caesar for a long time in silence, exclaimed… 'I, by your kind permission, Caesar, have to-day seen the gods of whom I merely used to hear; and in my life have never hoped for or experienced a happier day.' After asking for and receiving permission to touch Caesar's hand, he again entered his canoe, and continued to gaze back upon him until he landed upon his own bank.[5]

The imperial cult had turned this tribesman into a Roman. But it failed catastrophically with his fellow tribesmen and with the mountain tribesmen of Pannonia (part of present-day Austria, Hungary and the Balkans) and Dalmatia (part of modern-day Croatia), who in AD 6 rose in revolt against Roman rule, Roman taxation and Roman maladministration.

The uprising in Pannonia and Dalmatia posed the most serious threat to the empire Augustus had yet faced. Tribesmen slaughtered Roman citizens, army veterans and traders. War engulfed the whole region, threatening even Italy itself. Augustus had to call out the largest number of forces since the civil war and even then they were not enough; he was forced to enlist freedmen who were normally banned from serving in the army.

The resulting diversion of food supplies to feed the army during its three-year-long campaign precipitated famine in Rome. Augustus, who was now in charge of distributing the corn dole, had limited the number of recipients to about 200,000. But there were about a million mouths to feed in Rome.

In true Roman fashion, free corn was distributed not on the basis of need, but to whoever had inherited or been sold a *tessera*, a piece of wood, terracotta or bronze which was a ticket of entitlement to the corn dole. Charity was an alien concept to the Romans for whom the idea of providing unearned help was laughable: it was both unjust and irrational. Roman giving was not for free and not to the poor. Better-off Romans despised the poor – the 'filth of the cities' as Cicero called not just the indigent, but craftsmen and petty shopkeepers. A piece of graffiti scribbled on a wall in Pompeii, random survival of popular opinion twenty centuries ago, still explodes with the scorn of its writer: 'I hate poor people. If anyone wants something for nothing, he's a fool. Let him pay up and he'll get it.' Rome's version of charity was patronage, which required an exchange of favours even if the favours were unequal. Augustus spent vast sums on his people, but it was to keep them sweet and celebrate his own magnificence rather than because they needed help.

So slaves and 'resident aliens', that is, the majority of immigrants who were not accorded the privilege of Roman citizenship, were excluded from the corn dole; gladiators, who were usually enslaved prisoners of war or criminals, were expelled from the city so that there would be fewer mouths to feed. Hungry mobs rioted and attacked the officials they believed were hoarding grain or profiteering.

Augustus' principal concern was, however, to keep the soldiers on his side and in AD 6 he was prepared to incur the wrath of the rich to do so. For the first time since 167 BC, Roman citizens were required to pay tax. Augustus imposed a 5 per cent death duty on all inheritances worth more than 100,000 sesterces (the cost of a pretty house slave) plus a 1 per cent general sales tax, so that there would always be enough funds to pay the soldiers' discharge bonuses (equivalent to thirteen years' pay). Such care for his soldiers strengthened Augustus' control over the army and loosened the soldiers' dependence on their former generals who had traditionally supported them.

But the empire was as vulnerable to its auxiliary troops as it was to its regular army of citizen soldiers. Just like the Chinese Empire, Rome relied on its conquered peoples to defend the territory it had taken from them. Each legion was composed of citizens only, but was supported by auxiliary forces of non-citizens drawn from outside Italy. It was a potentially risky strategy. The auxiliaries were usually conscripted, and would often be fighting for Rome in their own homeland – sometimes under the leadership of their own chieftain – against relatives, friends and neighbours who were resisting Roman rule. There was always the threat that the auxiliaries might desert and revolt. But they were cheaper to maintain than legionaries and, Augustus believed, posed less of a threat to his regime than a large army of citizen soldiers. China countered the threat of revolt with the threat of force. When it unilaterally incorporated a north-eastern tribe into its army, the wives and children of the conscripted men were kept as hostages who would be executed in case of treason. Rome was more blithely confident of the irresistible attraction of its own culture to foreign peoples, like America some two thousand years later.

Quintilius Varus, head of the Roman army in Germany, was so convinced of this 'that he came to look upon himself as a city praetor administering justice in the forum, and not a general in command of an army in the heart of Germany', according to Velleius Paterculus. Varus was perhaps not the most able of leaders; Velleius described him as 'somewhat slow in mind as he was in body'. He was clearly also tactlessly arrogant in his assumption of Roman superiority, 'issuing orders to them [the German tribesmen] as if they were actually slaves of the Romans'. He imposed taxes that were too heavy and was as rapacious in Germany as he had been when governor of

Syria, where 'he entered the rich province a poor man, but left it a rich man and the province poor'.[6] The Germans did not openly revolt, according to Velleius Paterculus, but 'duped' Varus into believing they were totally compliant. In AD 9, the Romanized Arminius, chief of the Cherusci, made himself a friend of Varus while engineering an uprising some distance from the Roman legate's headquarters.

Arminius – we do not know his real name, though in the sixteenth century Martin Luther would 'rebaptize' him as Hermann, the 'man of the army'[7] – was, according to Velleius Paterculus who had served in Germany only four years earlier, 'of noble birth, brave in action... possessing an intelligence quite beyond the ordinary barbarian'. He was twenty-seven years old, was a Roman citizen, had fought for Rome in its auxiliary forces and had 'even attained the dignity of equestrian rank'.[8]

Lulled into a false sense of security by his friend Arminius, Varus set off to quell the 'uprising', accompanied by three legions, auxiliary troops of Germans and Gauls, camp followers of women and children, servants, baggage trains and wagons hauling artillery and equipment for building bridges and roads. They marched unsuspectingly 'through what they thought was friendly country'. And just as the 'unscrupulously ambitious and cruel' Syllaeus had left Aelius Gallus and the Roman troops to their fate in Southern Arabia (see chapter 5), and that unnamed 'crafty and treacherous' Arab chieftain had left Crassus and his troops to be massacred at the battle of Carrhae in Parthia (see chapter 9), so the Germans escorted the Romans a little way and then, according to Cassius Dio, 'begged to be excused from further attendance, in order, as they claimed, to assemble their allied forces, after which they would quietly come to his [Varus's] aid.'[9] As Varus progressed further, the going became more difficult and more mountainous. The army had to traverse deep ravines and cut their way through the increasingly impenetrable Teutoburg Forest. The long trail of men, women and children slowly became more vulnerable as they split up into scattered groups. A huge storm hit them and they struggled to find a footing in the slippery ground and to avoid the trees that were crashing down in the gales. Soldiers were now mixed up with the unarmed, the wagons and the animals. When the 'barbarians' suddenly attacked, the legionaries and auxiliaries were unable to form into battle order 'and could offer no resistance at all'. The slaughter, which would last four days, had begun.

On the second and third days, the surviving remnants of the Roman army regrouped, having abandoned or burned everything that was not essential. Caught between swampland and thick forest, they tried to advance but were unable to manoeuvre; cavalry and infantry collided frequently and they suffered heavy losses. At dawn on the fourth day, fighting resumed with a blare of trumpets, horns and bugles. In a heavy downpour and violent wind, Roman foot soldiers and horses floundered in the sodden marshland. Their waterlogged chainmail, helmets and large iron shields weighted them down; their heavy equipment – slingers which hurled spears, turf-cutters and earth diggers – stuck in the mud; the ground was too wet and slippery for the infantry to throw their 9-feet-long heavy javelins or for the archers to handle their bows. The Roman army was too cumbersome to cope with the more flexible guerrilla tactics of the big German tribesmen who were used to the terrain and carried only lances or clubs and plaited wicker shields.

The Roman cavalry charged, but the horses were pierced by German lances and they slipped in their own blood, throwing their riders and trampling on those who had fallen. The remnants of the infantry retreated behind the last remaining bulwark built by their combat engineers – a bank of earth and trees – where they took out their short swords for hand-to-hand combat. Seeing that defeat was inevitable, their commander Varus and the most senior officers, distinguished by their cloaks of bright red, a colour that was also intended to conceal any demoralizing bloodstains, committed suicide. Whether this was the coward's or the noble Roman's way out, the officers' suicides spelt the end for their men.

None of the rest, even if he had any strength left, defended himself any longer. Some imitated their leader, and others, casting aside their arms, allowed anybody who pleased to slay them; for to flee was impossible, however much one might desire to do so. Every man, therefore, and every horse was cut down without fear of resistance.

When Roman soldiers visited the battlefield six years later, they found, says Tacitus, 'human heads, prominently nailed to trunks of trees', a pile of whitening bones, fragments of weapons, limbs of horses, the ashes of tribunes and centurions who had been burned on the Germans' 'barbarous altars', gibbets where the captives had been hung and pits where the living prisoners had been corralled. Over the course of the four-day battle, more than 15,000 Roman soldiers had been slaughtered. Rome had lost nearly the whole of its army of the Rhine. It was the worst defeat Rome had suffered since Crassus' defeat by the Parthians at Carrhae in 53 BC. Arminius' victory would ensure that millions of Germans remained outside the Roman world. The barrier between the Latin and German territories was now fixed.*

The defeat shook Augustus profoundly. Suetonius reported that he thought of suicide, left his hair and beard untrimmed for months – a shocking sign of neglect for the clean-shaven Romans – and would beat his head against a door, shouting 'Quintilius Varus, give me back my legions.'

The disastrous German campaign had diverted more food supplies away from Rome, exacerbating the shortages already caused by lack of rain and pestilence. There were riots in Rome. Faced with increasing criticism, Augustus began to clamp down. Once senators had been

---

* Over the following centuries, the victory of Arminius/Hermann at Teutoburg became a central symbol in the bid by Germans to create a sense of German identity and a German nation. Martin Luther enlisted Hermann in his struggle against the authority of the Roman papacy. In the nineteeenth century, following Napoleon's invasion of German territories, the battle of Teutoburg became ever more salient for German nationalists and, after Germany's defeat in 1918, was used in a far uglier way by the Nazis as a symbol of the triumph of the indomitable Germans over their decadent, overcivilized enemies.

allowed to shout out their complaints in the Senate; writers could profess their admiration for Republican heroes without endangering their career. Now critics were banished and their publications burned. There were rumours of conspiracies.

In China, Wang Mang's response to disaster was a magical one: he tried to influence the portents in order to convince his people that he was not losing the Mandate of Heaven. Augustus' response was far more pragmatic, although Cassius Dio acknowledged that 'by reason of the portents which occurred both before the defeat and afterwards, he [Augustus] was strongly inclined to suspect some superhuman agency'. Even the temple of Mars, which Augustus had built in his new Forum Augustum, had been struck by lightning.

> ... many locusts flew into the very city and were devoured by swallows; the peaks of the Alps seemed to collapse upon one another and to send up three columns of fire... numerous comets appeared at one and the same time; spears seemed to dart from the north and to fall in the direction of the Roman camps... a statue of Victory that was in the province of Germany and faced the enemy's territory turned about to face Italy.[10]

But if Augustus believed that a catastrophe as great as Teutoburg 'could have been due to nothing else than the wrath of some divinity', he did not simply try to appease the divinity as Wang Mang did, but took practical measures to protect the empire.

Arminius' triumph had revealed the empire's vulnerability. Augustus could never totally rely on Romanization to keep the empire loyal. He might have his faithful King Herod of Judaea and King Juba of Mauretania, but there was always the possibility that they could turn out to be an Arminius. Ultimately the empire relied on its military base; but Teutoburg had proved how fragile that was too. Augustus expected that, after their victory, the Germans would invade Italy and Rome itself. But with Roman manpower already stretched to the limits on other fronts, he was unable to call up enough volunteers. Augustus therefore enforced conscription; anyone who refused was executed; even freedmen were enrolled and veterans were recalled. All Germans and Gauls – including those in his personal bodyguard – were expelled from the city in case they were inspired by the example of Arminius. The loyalty of the conquered could never be guaranteed.

About eight years after their defeat in the Teutoburg Forest, the Roman army confronted Arminius and his fellow chieftains at the River Weser. With the Roman army was Flavus, Arminius' brother. According to Tacitus, Arminius asked to speak to his brother and permission was granted.[11] From opposite banks of the river, the two brothers, the 'very loyal' Roman soldier and 'the liberator of the Germans', argued passionately against each other, with their mother joining in on Arminius' side. Arminius asked Flavus how he had lost an eye and was told it had been while fighting with Tiberius, for which he had been compensated with higher pay, and a wreath of honour. '"The wages of slavery are low," sneered Arminius. Flavus spoke of Rome's greatness, the emperor's wealth, the terrible punishment attending defeat, the mercy earned by submission... His brother dwelt on patriotism, long-established freedom, the national gods of Germany.' Their mother implored Flavus 'not to be the deserter and betrayer, rather than the liberator, of his relatives and his country'. From across the river, Arminius shouted threats in Latin and challenged his brother to fight. Flavus called for his horse and weapons and had to be restrained by his senior officer. But Flavus would win the argument. The Romans defeated Arminius; a few years later he 'succumbed to the treachery of his own relations', according to Tacitus, and was assassinated.

The Augustan regime had reasserted physical control; mental control was always going to be the more difficult task. In AD 14, Augustus was dying. The *pater patriae* had embodied the empire. His immortality would ensure its survival.

17

ROME: THE EMPEROR
BECOMES GOD

God was preparing the nations for his teaching by submitting them
all to one single Roman emperor.

Origen, *Contra Celsum*, II.30, AD 248

My goodness, I think I am turning into a god!

Emperor Vespasian as he lay dying, AD 79, in Suetonius, *The Twelve
Caesars, Vespasian*, XXIII, early second century AD

No modern flattery is so gross as that of the Augustan age, where
the emperor was deified.

Samuel Johnson, *Life of Johnson*, 1791

On 19 August 14 AD, in his Italian villa in Nola, the seventy-five-year-old Augustus called for a mirror, had his hair combed and his lower jaw, which had fallen open from weakness, propped up. 'Have I played my part in the farce of life creditably enough?' he asked the friends who had gathered round his deathbed. Then, according to Suetonius, 'he kissed his wife with: "Goodbye, Livia: never forget our marriage!" and died almost at once'. Whether she had poisoned him with figs she had grown herself, as Cassius Dio believed, Livia now presided over the first imperial succession. With the future of the Roman Empire in her hands, she made sure that she had divinity on her side. The institution of emperorhood would receive the mantle of divine authority, thanks to Livia. Augustus would be officially recognized as a god, as he had been unofficially during his lifetime.

After the premature deaths of Augustus' heirs Lucius and Gaius in AD 2 and AD 4, given a helping hand by Livia, if the historian Tacitus is to be believed, Augustus had reluctantly picked her grim and charmless son Tiberius as his heir. But officially Tiberius was only the heir to Augustus' private wealth. In principle, any senator or group of senators could have succeeded Augustus as ruler, since he had only been *primus inter pares* with traditional powers granted him on a rolling basis by the Senate. There was, in the Republican fiction still maintained by the regime, neither emperor nor throne.

As soon as Augustus had died, Livia therefore moved fast to ensure the succession of her fifty-six-year-old son, just as Empress Dowager Wang in China had done to ensure the pre-eminence of her nephew, Wang Mang. According to Tacitus, Livia's guards sealed the house and neighbouring streets, while she continued to give the impression that Augustus was still alive by issuing regular bulletins about his health. That gave Tiberius – whom she had immediately alerted – time to get to Augustus' bedside, at which point Livia announced simultaneously Augustus' death and Tiberius' succession. Then either she or Tiberius (Tacitus, Cassius Dio and Suetonius differ as to who was to blame) ordered the murder of his one serious rival, Agrippa Postumus, Augustus' only surviving grandson, the child of Julia and Agrippa.

The whole city of Rome turned out for Augustus' funeral, which was described in detail by Cassius Dio.[1] Troops guarded the route. At the head of the cortege swayed a wax effigy of Augustus, dressed in triumphal purple on an ivory and gold couch, carried by senators in black togas; two more statues of Augustus followed, one of gold and one carried on a triumphal chariot. Behind them paced hundreds if not thousands of men wearing eerily lifelike death masks, their frozen features carefully painted to resemble exactly the ancestors of Augustus' family, and the greatest Romans of history. Rows of bronze statues representing all mighty Rome's subject nations followed. The whole of the 600-strong Senate and the equestrian order, also dressed in black togas, their wives in white along with the cavalry, infantry and Augustus' Praetorian Guard filed past. Flautists played a funeral dirge; the mourners beat their breasts and sobbed. The procession reached the Campus Martius, where the naval battle had been staged as part of Augustus' *pater patriae* celebrations, where Agrippa had built his pleasure park and baths for the people, and where Augustus had built his mausoleum in which Agrippa's ashes had been buried. In front of the great cylindrical building, which was surrounded by cypresses and topped with evergreen trees and a bronze statue of Augustus, Tiberius and his son Drusus delivered their funeral orations. The ivory and gold couch, with its wax effigy of Augustus and the body encased below in its coffin, were placed on the funeral pyre. The family filed past to kiss the effigy. The infantry of the Praetorian Guard ran round it, throwing on all the decorations that they had received from the emperor. Barefoot equestrians lit the pyre, and an eagle – the bird of Jupiter which took souls to Heaven – was released.

Numerius Atticus, a member of the Praetorian Guard, swore to the Senate that, as the eagle soared aloft, he had seen the form of Augustus on its way to Heaven. Romulus had ascended to Heaven in just the same way. It was proof that Augustus had achieved divine status. The Senate declared him a god. Atticus was paid a million sesterces (about $500,000 in today's money) by Livia, in gratitude for his keen eyesight. Thus did the Romans subsume even the making of a god into the realm of the political. Imperial deification was a legal process, requiring proof as, later, would the making of a Catholic saint.

The Augustan regime had so skilfully smoothed the transition from republic to empire that not only were the Senate prepared to deify Augustus, but they openly acknowledged the true nature of the regime. They offered Tiberius the title of Emperor, a title which now denoted supreme power. Though Suetonius says 'he went through the farce' of rejecting it to the exasperation of several senators who were heard shouting, '"Oh, let him either take it or leave it"' and '"Some people are slow to do what they promise; you are slow to promise what you have already done,"' Tiberius finally accepted the title, albeit 'with a great show of reluctance, and complaints that they were forcing him to become a miserable and overworked slave'.[2] Compared to the murderous succession struggles in Parthia, Tiberius' succession was remarkably bloodless. Rome had become an empire, reinforced by an imperial cult, which would remain in place for almost 400 years.

Livia became high priestess of the new cult of Augustus and took on the title of Augusta, bequeathed to her by Augustus. At the age of seventy, she became the most powerful woman in the world, with the clear endorsement of Augustus, who had never thought much of Tiberius' 'sour and stubborn character'. She gave formal audiences, signed agreements and received communications jointly with Tiberius. As super-patroness of the empire, she held, like Augustus, her own *salutatio*, the morning greetings which senators were expected to attend.

Tiberius was taller and physically more imposing than Augustus, but had none of his charisma and, more fatally, none of his political skills. Augustus had attempted, on the whole successfully, to appeal to both Agrippa's people and Maecenas' elite. Tiberius antagonized both and was eventually feared and loathed as a dictator. He neither bought his people's loyalty with public games and spectacles, great buildings and donations, nor inspired it by the imperial cult, which became in his hands a tool of tyranny. His mother, 'that feminine bully', as Tacitus called her, was a far more competent politician, using both her immense wealth and above all the imperial cult to build support for her imperial family and herself.

Unpopular and anxious to escape his mother, Tiberius increasingly turned to the head of his Praetorian Guard, the sinister, manipulative Sejanus. Like Maecenas, Sejanus was an Etruscan, and of equestrian rank. But whereas Augustus had chosen in Maecenas a brilliant, if dissolute, strategist who was willing to further the cause not just of himself but of the regime, Sejanus, in an unlovely 'blend of arrogance and servility', according to Tacitus, 'concealed behind a carefully modest exterior an unbounded lust for power'.

By succumbing so entirely to the influence of Sejanus, Tiberius earned the loathing of the elite. But as he lost popularity, so he increasingly feared opposition. Although, according to Suetonius, he 'lacked any deep regard for the gods or other religious feelings', Tiberius had promoted the cult of the divine Augustus. Now it became a deadly test of loyalty. People were executed 'for carrying a ring or coin bearing Augustus' head into a lavatory or a brothel; or for criticizing anything Augustus had ever said or done', wrote Suetonius.[3] Tiberius' desire that due reverence be paid Augustus was so well known that men wishing to ruin their enemies would claim they had sworn falsely by Augustus or had dishonoured his statue.

Tiberius was as sensitive to the role of the imperial cult in creating loyalty to the empire as he was to the potential of religions to subvert it. In Gaul he suppressed the Druid priesthood. Unlike Roman priests who were civic officials knitted into the state, Druid priests were a separate caste that represented a rival source of authority; they could too easily become a focus of opposition to Roman rule. Augustus had already forbidden Roman citizens to take part in Druid rituals. Tiberius went further. 'In Gaul, the heads of enemies of high repute they used to embalm in cedar oil and exhibit to strangers... But the Romans put a stop to these customs, as well as to all those connected with the sacrifices and divinations that are opposed to our usages,' wrote Strabo. In particular, the Romans banned human sacrifice.

> They used to strike a human being, whom they had devoted to death, in the back with a sword, and then divine from his death-struggle... they would shoot victims to death with arrows, or impale them in the temples, or having devised a colossus of straw and wood, throw into the colossus cattle and wild animals of all sorts and human beings, and make a burnt-offering of the whole thing.[4]

For the Romans, ritual human sacrifice by Druids was barbaric, while gladiatorial combats to the 'cut-off', and entertaining ways of executing criminals in the arena, were not.

Julius Caesar, during his campaign to conquer Gaul (from 58 to 51 BC), had noted one interesting fact about the Druids, that the most 'vital element of their doctrine is that souls do not die'. But though Druidism offered the allure of immortality, just as the mystery cults did, it never had their durability. Druidism succumbed to the Roman clampdown; the mystery cults did not, although Tiberius tried to drive them out of Rome, as Augustus and Agrippa had tried to do.

The mystery cults' strength lay both in the loyalty they inspired and the numbers they attracted, since they were tied to neither place nor tribe, but crossed geographical as well as social boundaries (see chapters 3 and 8). That strength made them potentially dangerous to the empire, more especially because by creating an internal religious world which emphasized the personal relationship between god and worshipper, they were not creating good Roman subjects but making individuals, with all their destabilizing potential for autonomy.

In AD 19, the year that Livia/the Augusta died, Tiberius – who failed to turn up at her funeral, 'pleading important business' – ordered all Roman citizens who had embraced either the Isis cult or the 'superstitious faiths' of Judaism to burn their religious vestments and accoutrements. The followers of Isis were banished from Rome. The Jewish privilege of exemption from military service was withdrawn; 4,000 Roman Jews and proselytes (converts) of military age were conscripted into the army to deal with brigands on the island of Sardinia. The rest of the Jews, including those 'who were unwilling to become soldiers, on account of keeping the laws of their forefathers', were expelled from the city along with proselytes. They were threatened with enslavement if they returned, unless they repudiated what Tacitus called their 'unholy rites'. Thirty years later, the Jews had in fact returned to Rome and in such numbers that Tiberius' nephew Claudius would once more banish them from the city (see chapter 19).

The Jews' loyalty to Rome was always suspect, but particularly so for Tiberius who felt himself to be so insecure. They refused to offer sacrifice to the gods of the Roman state; they would not recognize the emperor as divine; their allegiance was to another, infinitely more powerful God. Tiberius was concerned that 'the Jews flocked to Rome in great numbers and were converting many of the natives to their ways'. His suspicions, encouraged by Sejanus, were increased by news that two Jewish outlaw brothers had set up a breakaway state within the Parthian Empire (see chapter 10). Sejanus feared such irredentism might spread to Judaea.

And, indeed, Judaea was rumbling with political as well as religious unrest, which was only exacerbated by the appointment of the desperately maladroit Pontius Pilate as procurator of Judaea in AD 24.

THE DEATH OF JESUS

... when Pilate, at the suggestion of the principal men among us, had condemned him to the cross, those that loved him at the first did not forsake him; for he appeared to them alive again the third day as the divine prophets had foretold.

Josephus, *Jewish Antiquities*, XVIII.3.3, AD 93/94

Christus... suffered the extreme penalty during the reign of Tiberius at the hands of one of our procurators, Pontius Pilate, and a most mischievous superstition, thus checked for the moment, again broke out not only in Judaea, the first source of the evil, but even in Rome, where all things hideous and shameful from every part of the world find their centre and become popular.

Tacitus, *The Annals of Imperial Rome*, AD 109

Pontius Pilate was 'a man of inflexible, stubborn and cruel disposition' who ruled Judaea with a mixture of 'venality, violence, robbery, assault, abusive behaviour, frequent executions without trial and endless savage ferocity', according to Philo, philosopher and eminent member of the Jewish community in Alexandria.[1] Pilate may well have been a protégé of Sejanus. During his first year as procurator, he installed a new unit of Roman soldiers at the Antonia Fortress, built by Herod the Great next to the Temple in Jerusalem, and named in honour of Herod's first Roman patron, Mark Antony.

The presence of Roman soldiers was a perpetual irritant in Jerusalem. Between six and twelve hundred troops were stationed there. At night, the cries of the sentinels could be heard answering one another from the 100-feet-high towers that punctured the fortress. But whereas previous Roman governors had been sensitive to the Jews' religious prohibition of representational images and had been careful to remove any emblems from the soldiers' banners and standards, Pilate's new soldiers bore a bust of the emperor mounted on a pole at the top of their standards. This violation of the second commandment was perhaps not as appalling to religious Jews as Herod the Great's erection of a golden eagle in the very Temple itself had been, but nonetheless many were determined to sacrifice their lives for the sake of their religion, just as the Pharisee students had been when they tore down the eagle in 4 BC (see chapter 6). At Caesarea, on the Mediterranean coast, the seat of Roman rule in Judaea, Jews lay down in front of Pilate's residence for five days and nights in protest; 'when Roman soldiers surrounded them and drew their swords, the Jews fell to the ground, extended their necks and said they were ready rather to die than to transgress the law,' wrote Josephus.[2]

Pilate bowed to the pressure and ordered the standards removed, but further outraged the Jews by appropriating money from the Temple treasury to finance a new aqueduct. Thousands of Jews protested. Pilate ordered his soldiers to take off their uniforms, hide their daggers under their garments and mingle with the protesters. When the crowd failed to disperse, he gave the signal for the soldiers to attack. According to Josephus, the soldiers 'laid upon them much greater blows than Pilate had commanded... and since the people were unarmed, and were caught by men prepared for what they were about, there were a great number of them killed by this means, and others of them ran away wounded'.[3]

When Pilate then hung golden shields inscribed with his own name and that of Tiberius on the walls of the Herodian palace, his residence in Jerusalem, the Jews petitioned to have them removed. Pilate refused. The Jews asked permission to send an embassy to Tiberius. Pilate again refused. In desperation, the Jews wrote Tiberius a letter. Tiberius was sensitive enough to the particularly delicate relations of the Jews with Rome to order Pontius Pilate to remove his shields. Judaea was already restless enough for Rome not to risk provoking the Jews unnecessarily.

By this time, Tiberius, on the prompting of Sejanus, had isolated himself on the island of Capri off the coast of Italy. There, according to the salaciously gossipy Suetonius, Tiberius trained 'his minnows', his little boys, 'to get between his legs to lick and nibble him' as he swam; he brought young girls and men from around the empire to conduct orgies in front of him, and watched with delight as his victims – usually astrologers who had got their predictions wrong – were hurled from a cliff on to the beach below where they were 'whacked at with oars and boat-hooks to make sure they were completely dead'. According to Suetonius, Sejanus made access to Tiberius almost impossible: 'huddled indiscriminately on land and shore, men endured, night and day, the patronage and self importance of his door keepers. Finally they were denied even that, and returned to Rome', where Sejanus, Rome's most feared citizen, ruled as de facto emperor.[4]

Tiberius had moved to Capri in AD 26; he would never set foot in Rome again. A few years later, according to the Gospel accounts, Jesus was baptized by his cousin John in the grey-blue Jordan River, as it wound its way from the Sea of Galilee to the Dead Sea through thickets of reeds, willow trees and feathery tamarisk bushes, the locusts humming in the heat. Although John's father was a Sadducee who had probably made his peace with Roman rule, John inveighed against the evils of the world. Only God, he said, could eradicate its wickedness. With just a pelt of camel's hair around his loins, living off locusts and honey in 'the wilderness', the arid mountainous area that stretches from the Mount of Olives overlooking Jerusalem down to the Jordan Valley, John proclaimed the imminent arrival of the Kingdom of God and God's judgement on the visible world – as his cousin Jesus would do a few years later. The Jews, John said, must give up their sinful ways in order to prepare themselves. John's criticism of the world was by implication a criticism of Roman rule. And his fervent belief in the coming of the Messiah made him a potential troublemaker for Herod Antipas who, in the division of Palestine at his father Herod the Great's death in 4 BC, Antipas had been given the districts of Galilee and Perea, to the south of Galilee, across the Jordan River, where John the Baptist preached.

For the Jews of Palestine, the Messiah had taken on a far greater significance ever since Rome had made Herod the Great its client king of Judaea, the most politically important and sensitive district of Palestine (see chapters 6 and 7). Herod's struggle to reconcile the inevitable conflict experienced by all client kings within the empire – of remaining faithful to his local people while being faithful to Rome – was made that much more fraught because of the nationalistic elements in the Jews' religion. That he seemed to put his loyalty to Rome before his loyalty to his Jewish God had polarized and radicalized many Jews. It became clear to some that the creation of a Heaven on earth in Israel was not possible under the unrighteous rule of Rome; the Messiah had to expel the Romans in order to bring about the righteous nation that he would rule with God's help. The Messiah had to be not just the religious saviour, but the national saviour as well. As hope in the coming of the Messiah intensified, so the burgeoning messianic cults took on ever more seditious connotations in the eyes of the Romans. Every religious protest could be seen as a protest against Roman rule, just as any protest against Roman rule could be dressed in the magnificent colours of Messiahdom.

In AD 6, the same year that Augustus was confronted with the tribesmen's revolts in Pannonia and Dalmatia, he deposed Herod the Great's least competent son, Archelaus, the King of Judaea and Samaria. Rome took over direct control and, so as to assess tax revenue, ordered the census that in Luke's account of the Nativity forced Jesus' family to travel to Bethlehem (see chapter 7). Taxation from the provinces financed the empire. It took the form of a property tax on land, houses, slaves and ships and a head tax, which was levied on all adults between the ages of twelve or fourteen and sixty-five, regardless of income, hence the census. Although it was deeply unpopular as a symbol of Roman rule, the census had in fact been introduced by Augustus in order to reduce the burden of taxation on the provinces. It allowed the treasury to make a much more accurate calculation of how much they could expect from each province, thus saving the provinces from the extortions of the tax farmers and governors (see chapter 1).

Taxation was, nonetheless, always a cause for resentment around the empire, and provinces like Gaul would sporadically erupt in protest at the economic burden. As far as Rome was concerned, such protests were short-lived and could be put down with relative ease. But when Judas the Galilean and Zadok (or Saddok) the Pharisee called for a mass boycott of the census in Judaea in AD 6, it was far more serious. Unlike the leaders of revolts elsewhere in the empire, Judas and Zadok were not just fighting to preserve their political and social order but their religious one as well. Taxation hit not just their pockets but their souls. To Judas and Zadok, Roman taxation was both an additional economic burden for them and their fellow Jews, and a religious insult – it flouted the Torah's admonition that the earth and everything in it belonged to God. God alone was the Jews' king and ruler and His laws were supreme. And because their monotheist God was supremely powerful, Jews were prepared to risk death rather than disobey His commandments. Their commitment to protest was potentially therefore that much more steadfast and unbreakable.

Judas and Zadok's call for a boycott of the census marked the birth of the Zealots, the radical wing of Pharisaism. As Josephus remarked, both Judas and his fellow 'rebel' Zadok 'agreed in all other things with Pharisaic notions'. But neither man believed that the Pharisaic experiment in co-operating with Gentile rule while living a strictly religious life was possible. The Pharisaic belief that God's laws as laid out in the Torah not only could be but had to be followed by every Jew – not just the Sadducees – and that those laws applied to every aspect of life, made the potential areas of friction between the Jews and their Roman rulers too great. A choice had to be made between

God and Caesar and the choice was obvious: God must be 'their only Ruler and Lord'. Judas the Galilean may well have been the same Judas who at the death of Herod the Great had aspired to kingship and/or Messiahdom, and had led a major revolt in Galilee.[5] Political freedom, resistance to Roman rule, had become for him a religious duty. The Jews, he said, 'were cowards if they would endure to pay a tax to the Romans and would after God submit to mortal men as their lords'.

On the burning question of the relationship between Jew and Roman, the Jews had now become split between those who believed it was still possible to live under Roman rule and those who did not. Most Jews, including Jesus' family, thought they could juggle the demands of being both Jewish and Roman; Paul, who was born around the time of the census, came from a family who were Roman citizens while also trying to be good religious Jews. Some of Jesus' brothers had Greek names; some Jewish. The family had, according to the Gospel of Luke, followed the advice of the Sadducee high priest Joazar and had presented themselves to be counted in the Roman census.

Whether or not Joseph and Mary did travel to Bethlehem – and it was important for Luke that they did so in order to underline Jesus' role as the Messiah descended from King David – many Judaean Jews clearly did comply with the Roman census, as the high priest had bidden them. Joazar's loyalty to Rome, however, proved his undoing. There were protests against him. Appointed by Rome as high priest, he was sacked by Rome for becoming too unpopular with the people. As for the leaders of the boycott, Judas 'was killed, and all his followers were scattered', according to the author of Acts. Zadok's fate is unknown. But the Zealot party that he and Judas had founded proved to be the first organized movement opposed to Roman rule of any sort; the Zealots, indeed, made resistance a permanent religious duty.

Sixty years later, its terrorist offshoot, the *sicarii* ('the dagger men'), would, according to Josephus, be in large part responsible for

the Jewish Revolt of AD 66–73/4 (see chapter 19). Led by Judas' son
Menahem, who may well have had the same Messianic pretensions
as his father,[6] the *sicarii* murdered the high priest and other
conciliatory/moderate Jews for collaborating with Roman rule.
Menahem and most of his followers were in turn killed by the
priesthood – among them was Josephus – in the fighting between
the various revolutionary factions. In AD 70, following the destruction
of the Temple and the fall of Jerusalem, Eleazar (who was probably
Menahem's nephew) led the surviving remnants of his uncle's *sicarii*
army in what would be the final stand of the Jews against the
Romans. From the fortress of Masada, built on a huge isolated rock
at the edge of the Judaean Desert, the *sicarii* held out for four years.
According to Josephus, when defeat seemed inevitable, they
committed mass suicide with their wives and children rather than be
taken captives by the conquering Roman army.

But in the immediate aftermath of the census protest of AD 6,
groups of Jews in Palestine decided neither to fight the Roman world
nor to compromise with it. Instead, they withdrew from the world
and prepared for the coming of the Messiah. Cults sprang up all over
Galilee and Judaea, proclaiming their belief that the kingdom of God
was at hand and that the Messiah would appear in their lifetime.
They included the Morning-Dippers or Hemerobaptists, the cult led
by John the Baptist, and the Essenes, the authors of the Dead Sea
Scrolls found at Qumran over 1,900 years later.

In the desolate wasteland between the Dead Sea and Jerusalem,
where John the Baptist made his home, a group of Essenes had
created a community of the righteous, dedicated to preparing the
way for the Messiah. Yet, although they believed fervently in the
coming of the Messiah, the Essenes and their austere way of life did
not pose much of a threat to Roman rule. Celibacy is not the path to
pursue if a cult wants to gain a significant following. The Essenes
were in fact such extreme separatists that as long as they could live
according to their religious laws, untouched by the Gentiles, they
accepted the political authority of the latter, however irreligious it

might be. In fact, they believed it was their duty to do so. According to Josephus, who implies that he was initiated into the Essene brotherhood, the Essene made a specific vow when he joined the sect that he 'ever show faithfulness to all men and especially to those in authority, because no one obtains the government without God's assistance'.[7]

It was John and his Messianic cult of baptists who were far more dangerous. Like the Essenes, John and his cave-monks held their property in common, endowed baptist practices, that is the act of cleansing by washing, with an important spiritual significance symbolizing inner purification and transformation, and had as their central ritual the eating of a communal meal at which they believed the Messiah was spiritually present. But, unlike the Essenes, the Baptists preached to large crowds.

According to Josephus, Herod Antipas, a loyal client king like his father Herod the Great, 'feared lest the great influence John had over the people might put it into his power and inclination to raise a rebellion'. In about AD 29, soon after he is said to have baptized Jesus, John was executed. His severed head was set on a platter before Antipas' stepdaughter, Salome. Antipas claimed the execution had been at her request.

Jesus and John the Baptist had rival ministries, according to the Gospel of John the Apostle. But the author of Acts, who may also have written the Gospel of Luke, writes that after John the Baptist's death Jesus took over many of John's followers, as he did John's message that the Kingdom of God was at hand. The Jesus that is described in the Gospels was thus from the start associated with sedition, thanks to his relationship with John, his cousin and spiritual father. How much the Gospels provide an accurate account of a real historical figure has been and is bitterly debated, though most scholars agree on a bare minimum: that Jesus existed, was a holy man, and was executed as his cousin had been.

The Gospel writers, of course, make Jesus a far more troublesome character to the authorities than John. John the Baptist only heralded the coming of the Messiah; whereas Jesus in the Gospel of John clearly states that he is the Messiah and his followers are convinced of his claim. The other Gospels are less assertive. They portray Jesus as a holy man who was ambiguous, or perhaps ambivalent, about whether he was indeed the Messiah, but whose failure to deny the claim would prove fatal.

In the words of Josephus, Jesus was 'a wise man, if it be lawful to call him a man; for he was a doer of startling deeds, a teacher of the people who receive the truth with pleasure'.[8] This is the most substantial non-biblical reference to Jesus, though it may be, like Josephus' other Christian references, a later insertion by a Christian editor eager to provide proof of the reality of Jesus the Messiah.

Unlike the Pharisees who taught in the towns and cities, and were far more prominent in Judaea than Galilee,[9] the Jesus of the Gospels mainly confined his preaching to the Jewish peasants of Galilee's luxuriant farmlands and to the fishermen in the villages on the shores of the Sea of Galilee, in reality a heart-shaped lake surrounded by hills with the Golan Heights to the east. Criss-crossing Galilee, he followed the practice of many holy men, preaching, healing and casting out devils. Like other religious masters, he was accompanied by his core of dedicated disciples, some of whom were married, but who lived lives of poverty like Jain and Buddhist monks or Brahmanic *sadhus*.

On the whole, Jesus avoided the larger cities such as Sepphoris, only 4 miles from Nazareth, whose citizens had raided the royal arsenal on the death of Herod, or the new city of Tiberias, built by Herod Antipas on the western shores of Lake Galilee, or the Decapolis, the ten semi-autonomous Greek-run cities to the south-east of Lake Galilee where Greek culture dominated and Gentiles were in the majority. Jesus had, however, left Nazareth for the most important town on the shores of Lake Galilee, the sombre-looking little town of Capernaum, whose stone houses were hewn out of the black lava rock hills rising behind it. Situated on the Via Maris trade route, Capernaum was a more mixed and less conservative place than

323

Nazareth. Travellers passed through, and it was home to merchants as well as fishermen and farmers. A contingent of Roman soldiers was based there whose relations with the Jewish inhabitants were good enough, according to Luke's Gospel, for its centurion commander to build the town a synagogue where Jesus preached, and for the Jews to beg Jesus to heal the centurion's servant, 'For he loveth our nation and has built us a synagogue'.[10]

Jesus did indeed heal the centurion's servant, according to Luke, but his ministry to a Gentile was exceptional. Matthew's Gospel, written, as were the other Gospels, at a time when the Jewish nature of the cult was a central issue, presents a very Jewish Jesus.* 'Go not into the way of the Gentiles, and into any city of the Samaritans enter ye not: But go rather to the lost sheep of Israel [the Jewish population of Palestine],' Matthew has Jesus tell his disciples before sending them out on their mission to preach the coming of the Kingdom and 'heal the sick, cleanse the lepers, raise the dead, cast out devils'.[11] Again, according to Matthew, Jesus told a Canaanite woman who asked him to exorcize her daughter that to preach to Gentiles would be like taking bread from children and throwing it away on dogs.[12] His Jesus nevertheless retains some of the universalism that Paul had several decades earlier injected into the Christian cult: Matthew's Jesus also reaches out to the Gentiles – or at least those who had faith. It was because of the Canaanite woman's faith that immediately after proclaiming the exclusivity of his mission Jesus healed her daughter. Matthew's Gospel never entirely reconciles the Jesus whose mission was exclusively to the Jews and the Jesus whose mission was a universal one to all nations. It stands as a testament of the tension at the heart of the Jesus cult of the time.

About one or two years after he had started preaching, Jesus and some of his followers joined the hundreds of thousands of Jews from all around the empire travelling to Jerusalem for Passover. It was

---

* The Matthew Gospel traces Jesus' genealogy back to Abraham, the father of the Jews, while in the more universalist Luke's Gospel Jesus' genealogy goes back to Adam, the father of all mankind.

springtime; the rainy season was over; crocuses, tulips and narcissi carpeted the hills; the pilgrims sang as they walked past groves of olives, ripening figs, grapes and walnut trees, and through the villages of Galilee. They travelled in large groups for safety. The shortest route to Jerusalem in the south took about eight days and went through the oak forests of the province of Samaria, where the pilgrims were always in danger of being attacked by Samaritans. Hostility between Jews and Samaritans had become more violent after the Samaritans had visited the Temple in the middle of the night and scattered human bones in the porches and the sanctuary, the ultimate desecration. Jews and Samaritans were now sucked into a tit-for-tat cycle of sectarian killing and vengeance. Samaritans murdered Galilean pilgrims travelling through Samaria on the way to Jerusalem: Jews attacked Samaritan villages in return. 'The Jews have no dealings with the Samaritans,' a Samaritan woman had told Jesus when to her amazement he had asked her for water.

In the light of such hatred, Jesus' story of the Samaritan helping a Jewish traveller was particularly telling. The good Samaritan had not just helped a stranger who in all likelihood he would never see again, but his love had triumphed over a deep-rooted national/religious hatred; he had made of the hated stranger a neighbour. Jesus may have confined his preaching to the Jews, but for him 'neighbour' did not just mean your fellow Jews and a few deserving Gentiles, but the rest of the world as well. The injunction in Leviticus to 'love thy neighbour as thyself' had taken on far greater significance. 'Love your enemies,' Matthew records Jesus as saying in what we know as the Sermon on the Mount, though the 'sermon' is most probably a collection of sayings stitched together later by Matthew as a summary of Jesus' spiritual and ethical teachings. These, though firmly rooted in the Old Testament, were in part a radical reworking of aspects of Jewish law, with their universalization of the command to love and their concentration on, and blessing of, those traditionally considered the least blessed, the most needy spiritually as well as physically.[13]

Although the Gospels present Jesus as being in disagreement with

THE DEATH OF JESUS

the Pharisees, they were actually very close. For Jesus, as for the Pharisees, to love God and to love your neighbour were the basic principles of the Torah.[14] Where Jesus is portrayed as fundamentally disagreeing with the Pharisees was in his relaxed attitude to Jewish law. The Gospel writers may have contradicted themselves over some aspects of the Jesus narrative, but when it came to his opposition to the rigid piety of the Pharisees they were unanimous. But of course they were (with the possible exception of Mark) writing after the failed Jewish revolt of AD 66 to 73/4 and were therefore eager to make Christianity more palatable to the Romans by highlighting the divergences between Jesus and Judaism. Admittedly, John, whose Gospel was the last to be written, probably between AD 100 and 110, and whose anti-Semitism has always disquieted biblical scholars, often just blames 'the Jews' collectively for their opposition to Jesus. But even this Gospel has Jesus specifically attacking the Pharisees as children of the devil and singles them out for their involvement in his arrest and execution.[15] Jesus loathed those Pharisees who were more concerned with obeying the letter of the law than with the guiding spirit behind the rules, which was love.[16] Follow what the Pharisees preach, not what they do, Jesus told his disciples in the most violent diatribe against the Pharisees given him by Matthew, where he calls them 'hypocrites', 'blind guides' and a 'generation of vipers'.[17]

The Pharisees were shocked that in Capernaum Jesus sat down to eat with 'publicans and sinners', that is, tax collectors like Matthew, and prostitutes. The prophets had embraced the weak, the poor, the widows and the fatherless, but Jesus was treating as friends the unclean, those shunned by the pious.[18] The Pharisees were appalled that on the Sabbath day Jesus' disciples plucked ears of corn to stave off their hunger as they walked through the fields, thus flouting the law banning agricultural labour on the Sabbath. According to Mark, the Pharisees even consulted the Herodians (the supporters of Herod Antipas and the Herodian dynasty, whose founder Herod the Great the Pharisees had originally supported in their bid for power against the Sadducees; see chapter 6) as to how to suppress Jesus when he broke the law forbidding work on the Sabbath by healing a man with a withered hand.[19]

Yet, according to the biblical historian Geza Vermes, Jesus would probably never have been executed if he had stuck to preaching to the peasants and fishermen of Galilee and not made his religious pilgrimage to Jerusalem. It was only in the already tense city of Jerusalem that his opposition to the Pharisees, his association with John the Bapist, and the claims made by his followers that he was the Messiah became such an incendiary combination to the authorities.

Passover was the most politically sensitive, as well as one of the most important, of all the Jewish festivals. It celebrated the liberation of the Israelites from their bondage in Egypt. It was the time when, according to Jewish tradition, the Messiah would reveal himself – the Messiah who was both holy man and political deliverer from oppression. Thirty-five years earlier, 3,000 pilgrims had been killed for protesting against the deaths of the Pharisees who had smashed Herod's golden eagle. Pilate's soldiers were therefore on the alert for disturbances as hundreds of thousands of Jews from Palestine, Gaul, Rome, Egypt, Syria, Arabia and the Parthian Empire crowded into Jerusalem.

The city echoed to the sound of bleating lambs – about 30,000 were tethered waiting to be sacrificed. The Jews of the Diaspora were reuniting with families and friends. Houses and courtyards were packed with pilgrims. Dressed in striped trousers, brocaded gold tunics, black robes, shining silks, the Galilean Jews amongst them in their white and brown striped cloaks, the women with their daughters and the men with their sons climbed up the great stairway of their vast white and gold Temple and passed into the Court of the Gentiles.

In the marble pillared halls the size of cathedrals that surrounded the court, pilgrims from all over the empire changed their money for the local bronze coinage and bought doves (inflated by as much as 100 times the normal price) or more expensive animals such as oxen and sheep, for their sacrifices. The pilgrim Jesus was outraged by this commercialization of the Temple. According to the Gospel writers, he overturned the money-changers' tables, scattered their money and drove out the shopkeepers and the animals.

Jesus' violent protest antagonized the Sadducees. After losing power to the Pharisees during the reign of Herod the Great, the Sadducees were regaining their position under the Romans who now controlled appointments to the Sanhedrin, the ruling body of Judaea. The Sadducees saw little difficulty in following the dictates of Jewish law, running the Temple and also overseeing the administrative and judicial affairs of Judaea for their Roman rulers, while for the Pharisees relations with Rome were far more difficult. Although the Pharisees had to some extent set themselves up in opposition to the Sadducees, Jesus had united them in antagonism towards him, just as he had, according to Matthew's and Mark's Gospels, united the Pharisees and the Herodians (the supporters of rule by members of the Herod family). At the prompting of the Sadducees, the Pharisees tried to incriminate Jesus. They asked him whether it was right to pay taxes to Rome. If he answered yes, he would prove himself to be both irreligious and a collaborator with Rome. If he answered no, he would prove himself to be seditious. In answering them, Jesus asked for a coin. At that time the inscription on coins in the Roman Empire read *Ti[berivs] Caesar Divi Avg[vsti] F[ilivs] Avgvstvs* (Caesar Augustus Tiberius, son of the Divine Augustus). The coin made what for the Jews was a blasphemous claim, that Augustus was a god. For Jesus, the Pharisees' question was, however, unproblematic. Matthew the tax collector, the publican, was, after all, one of his Apostles. But to 'Render to Caesar the things that are Caesar's, and to God the things that are God's' was no solution for strict religious Jews, especially the Pharisees. It was precisely because God's law applied to every aspect of their lives that they could not separate church and state.

Jesus' answer did not help him. He was seen as a political danger by the Sadducee high priest Caiphas, the Roman-appointed political and religious head of the Jews. Of all the high priests appointed by

Rome, Caiphas was the ablest at managing Jewish–Roman relations, judging by his length of tenure. He lasted seventeen years, longer than any other Roman appointee, and given that ten of those years were served under the insensitive Pontius Pilate, he was clearly particularly attuned to keeping the lid on trouble. But he knew that if he lost control, he would be dismissed. The Romans allowed the Sadducees to rule only for as long as they kept the people compliant.

Jesus, a Messiah-figure, whose cousin had been beheaded for sedition, who opposed the Sadducees and was prepared to use violence to do so, was a potential rallying point for rebellion in a city filled to overflowing with Jews celebrating their ancient liberation and return from exile. Several of his followers made him appear even more dangerous. The affiliation of Simon the Zealot, one of the least known of the Apostles, was clear. But Judas too may have been highly suspect. It is possible that the Gospel writers called him Iscariot after the *sicarii*, the dagger-men assassins opposed to Roman rule. A connection between Judas and the *sicarii* would finally provide a satisfactory explanation as to why he betrayed Jesus: in the eyes of the *sicarii*, Jesus was a collaborator. However, many scholars believe that the *sicarii* post-date Jesus' arrest and Iscariot may just mean that he came from Kerioth in Judaea.

It was clear to Caiphas and the Sanhedrin that Jesus had to be arrested. As the Gospel of John describes it, they argued that if Jesus was not arrested, 'all will believe on him: and the Romans shall come and take away both our place and nation'. The Sadducees saw themselves as protecting Judaea's independence from direct intervention by Rome. 'It is expedient for us,' said Caiphas, 'that one man should die for the people, and that the whole nation perish not.'[20]

Jesus was arrested by the Temple guard, which Paul had already or would soon join, and was charged with blasphemy. But blasphemy was a crime only under Jewish not Roman law and members of the Sanhedrin were keen to involve Rome in determining Jesus' fate. So he was further charged with being a royal pretender, or political agitator, claiming to be the Messiah. This *was* an act of sedition, which was a crime under Roman law. Jesus was taken to Pontius Pilate, who (according to Luke's Gospel) in turn passed him on – this time back to his native Galilee and its ruler Herod Antipas. But though he had beheaded Jesus' cousin and spiritual mentor John the Baptist only about two years previously, Antipas refused to get involved in the trial of Jesus and sent him back to Pilate.

Pilate passed the buck for the final time and let the mob decide Jesus' fate. The crowd's power to decide the life and death of a criminal was not unusual. In Rome, it was one of the few powers left to them. When gladiators fought to 'cut-off point', it was the crowd who decided whether the defeated gladiator should live or die. But why the Roman procurator Pontius Pilate and Caiphas, the Roman-appointed ruler of Jerusalem, and Antipas, Rome's client king, were so keen to escape responsibility for Jesus' execution is unclear. It may well have been because Jesus had come to Jerusalem at a time when tensions between Jews and Romans were riding so high that the need to appease both 'sides' was both particularly important and particularly difficult. It was unlikely to have been fear of Jesus' popularity, since the crowd standing in the courtyard of Pilate's fortress gave the thumbs down to Jesus. Instead, the crowd chose to reprieve the bandit Barabbas (a common name meaning simply 'Father's Son'), who had, according to Mark, committed murder in an insurrection, leading some scholars to think he may have been a Zealot or even a member of the terrorist *sicarii*.

On 30 April (scholars put the year as anywhere between AD 26 and 36, the years of Pontius Pilate's rule as prefect of Judaea), Jesus was crucified between two thieves on Golgotha, a knoll near the Damascus Gate. Crucifixion, the usual method of execution for slaves, rebels and common criminals, was agonizingly painful but perhaps no more so than the alternatives for all non-citizens of low status – being torn apart by animals or being burned alive. Crucifixion was, however, a slow death. The crucified man died by suffocation, though death came more quickly if his legs were broken so that the weight of his body as he hung by his arms increased. Jesus died at 3 p.m., about the same time that the lambs were being slaughtered in the Temple for the Passover feasts that evening. According to John, one wealthy follower, Nicodemus, brought myrrh and aloes with which to anoint Jesus' body, which was then wrapped in a shroud of linen and buried in a grave blocked with a large rock as was the Jewish custom.

Caiphas continued as high priest until AD 36. That same year, Pontius Pilate was recalled to Rome to stand trial, following complaints by the Samaritans at his inordinately heavy-handed suppression of what they called a religious procession that he had interpreted as an uprising. He is thought to have committed suicide. Antipas survived as ruler of Galilee until he was deposed – on the promptings of his nephew – by Caligula.

Around the time that Jesus was crucified, Tiberius executed the former 'partner of his labours', Sejanus, for plotting to overthrow him. Sejanus' body was torn to pieces by the mob. What had been a trickle of executions in the days when Tiberius had ruled with Sejanus now became in Tacitus' words 'a massacre'. As many as twenty people a day, including women and children, were executed, their bodies flung on to the Stairs of Mourning where they were left to rot or dragged to the Tiber with hooks. No one and nowhere was safe; senator informed on senator; a chance remark in the Forum or at a dinner party could lead to prosecution and death. A senator celebrating his birthday was dragged to the Senate-house accused of treason, and instantly condemned and executed. A historian, Aulus Cremutius Cordus, was executed for praising Brutus and describing Cassius as 'the last of the Romans'. Senators committed suicide rather than be taken to the Mamertine Prison in Rome, where according to tradition Peter and Paul would be incarcerated.

Six years after Sejanus' execution, Tiberius lay dying, a lonely, balding old man of seventy-eight, his ulcerous face covered with plasters. On 16 March AD 37, his death was announced. Immediately, Caligula appeared before the fawning, cheering crowds, ready to take up his uncle's throne. But then, according to Tacitus, 'it was suddenly reported that Tiberius had recovered'. Amongst the 'general panic-stricken dispersal', Caligula 'stood in stupefied silence, his soaring hopes dashed'. But Macro, Sejanus' replacement as head of the Praetorian Guard, was 'unperturbed'. He simply 'ordered the old man to be smothered with a heap of bed-clothes and left alone'.[21]

Cheering crowds, chanting 'to the Tiber with Tiberius', bore his body to the river. When Caligula asked the Senate to deify his uncle, they refused, as they would refuse to deify the divine megalomaniac Caligula himself and Nero, the last of the Julio-Claudian line. Of Augustus' four successors, only Claudius briefly made it to divine status at his death, only to have it rescinded by Nero who considered his stepfather to be 'a doddering old idiot'.

In engineering the apotheosis of Augustus, Livia, the mother of Tiberius, grandmother of Claudius, great-grandmother of Caligula, and great-great-grandmother of Nero, had helped ensure the survival of the empire. But, like the Chinese Mandate of Heaven, it was at the cost of conditionality. The apotheosis of the preceding emperor was a politicized process formally in the hands of the Senate. But just as Heaven, interpreted by the Confucian scholar-officials, could withdraw its Mandate from 'bad' Chinese emperors, so the Senate – with or without the prompting of the incoming emperor – could withhold its approval of a request to deify the preceding emperor.

The Senate had passed its posthumous judgement. Tiberius was not going to become a god. Jesus, however, was about to become one.

19

AND PAUL CREATED
CHRIST

The contagion of this superstition [Christianity] has spread not only
to the cities, but also to the villages and even to the farms. It seems
possible, however, that it can be arrested and cured.

Pliny the Younger, Governor of the province of Bithynia-Pontus to the
Emperor Trajan, Letters X.96, 97, c.AD 111

Thou hast conquered, O Galilean!

Apocryphal dying words of Julian 'the Apostate',
Roman Emperor, AD 363

We command that those persons who follow this rule [the decree
that all imperial subjects should practise the Christian religion]
shall embrace the name of Catholic Christians. The rest, however,
whom we adjudge demented and insane... shall be smitten first by
divine vengeance and secondly by the retribution of our own
initiative.

Theodosius I, Roman Emperor, AD 380

Christianity was the vampire of the *imperium Romanum*.

Nietzsche, The Antichrist, 1895

... the Gospel of the 'lowly' *makes* low...

Nietzsche, The Antichrist

Six years after Jesus' crucifixion, one of his followers was
stoned to death outside Jerusalem's city walls on the orders
of the Sanhedrin. Stephen had blasphemously criticized the
Temple and God's Law. Holding the clothes of the men who stoned
Stephen to death was Saul, a Pharisee and member of the Temple
police who zealously persecuted the Jewish heresy of the Jesus cult.

A few years later, Saul was sent by the high priest to arrest members of the Jesus movement in Damascus, which the Emperor Caligula had just 'given' to the Arabian kingdom of Nabataea. On the way he underwent a transformative experience that turned him from Saul the fanatical persecutor to Paul the passionate believer in the Jesus cult, or at least in the cult as he conceived it. Bandy-legged, galvanic, quick to take offence, a brilliant organizer and superb letter writer – his epistles are the earliest Christian writings, predating the first Gospel by about twenty years – Paul would split the cult in two, and turn Jesus the man who died a criminal's death on the cross into Christ the redeemer, whose death and resurrection gave all mankind, Gentile as well as Jew, woman and man, slave and free, the promise of salvation and eternal life.

Paul represented in extreme form the problems of assimilation experienced by every conquered person of the Roman Empire – and particularly by the inhabitants of its cities. Unlike Jesus the villager, who was born and remained in Palestine, Paul was a Diaspora Jew born in the great multicultural port city of Tarsus in southern Turkey. It was 'a city of wags and bullies', whose luxury-loving inhabitants lolled by the banks of the River Cydnus 'like so many waterfowl', according to the holy man Apollonius who had travelled to Parthia and the Kushan Empire in pursuit of spiritual truth, and who was believed to have been resurrected after his death (see chapter 10). Thirty years before Paul was born, Cleopatra had glided down the river from Tarsus in her barge to meet Mark Antony. Strabo said it exceeded Athens and Alexandria as an intellectual city. It was a centre for the linen industry, home to a sizeable Jewish community, and to seafarers and merchants. Every year worshippers paraded through the streets bearing a great statue of Heracles, the man-god and son of Zeus who went down into the underworld to rescue human souls from death and rose to life again in the spring. Tarsus was the archetypical booming Graeco-Roman city of the Near East (what is now Turkey and the Middle East), just as Paul was the quintessential city-dweller struggling to combine old and new identities.

Paul was a strict religious Jew who had studied under the great Pharisee scholar Gamaliel the Elder in Jerusalem, and had rigorously policed religious orthodoxy as a member of the Temple guard. But he was also Greek-speaking, Greek-educated and a Roman citizen by virtue of his father, who had been granted citizenship for being a tent-maker to the Roman army. Paul followed his father's trade and also collected taxes for the Romans. That made him both a contravener of God's law and a collaborator twice over, as far as radical Pharisees were concerned, since he was aiding Rome's military as well as financial oppression of the Jews. The Pharisees' insistence on the strict observance of every element of Jewish law made it increasingly difficult for Jews to live under Roman rule, and to live alongside non-Jews. Paul probably died a few years before the catastrophic Jewish revolt against Rome, which ended with the total destruction of the Temple and of Jerusalem, but he was living in a climate of rapidly deteriorating relations between Jews and Gentiles.

In AD 38, the notoriously anti-Semitic inhabitants of Alexandria turned on its Jewish community. Friction between Alexandrian Greeks and Jews had been growing since the Jews had supported the Roman takeover of Egypt, which the Greeks bitterly resented. The Jews had also benefited from Rome's overt protection of their religious liberties. Unlike the Greek Alexandrians, however, Jews had to pay the Roman head tax and, to the irritation of the Greeks, they had been campaigning for Alexandrian citizenship, rather than just citizenship of the Jewish council, the *politeuma*, so that they too could be exempt from the tax.

Greek mobs burned down synagogues or desecrated them with portraits of the Emperor Caligula. Prompted by the Greek Alexandrians, the Roman prefect Aulus Avillius Flaccus deprived the Jews of the privilege of living in any part of the city they wished and hounded them into one area. Men, women and children were dragged out of their houses and burned to death, their shops looted and destroyed. Those caught trying to escape from what was the first known ghetto in the ancient world[1] were tortured and killed.

Overcrowding caused the outbreak of an epidemic. Half the members of the Jewish council of elders, which ran the affairs of the Jewish community, were arrested. As part of the celebrations for the Emperor Caligula's birthday, they were paraded round the amphitheatre before jeering crowds, stripped naked and flogged – a punishment from which the Jews had been exempted – so severely that several died. Others were hanged, or chained to the rack, after which the audience was entertained with dancing, mime and music.

Two years later, Caligula demanded that the Jews erect a statue to him in the Temple at Jerusalem. Whether his unspeakably blasphemous demand was made out of divine megalomania or as a deliberate test of how far the Jews would submit to his own tyranny is not clear. Only Caligula's assassination pre-empted the mass uprising threatened by the Jews. But riots instigated by Jews and Greeks in Alexandria continued to break out. In AD 41, Caligula's successor Claudius wrote a stern letter that was displayed in the city for all to read. Greek Alexandrians, he wrote, must be

> forgiving and kindly towards the Jews who for many years have lived in the same city, and… allow them to observe their customs as in the time of the Deified Augustus, which I also, having heard both cases, have sanctioned; and I order the Jews not to work for more privileges than they formerly had… while enjoying their own privileges and sharing a great abundance of advantages in another's city, and not to bring or admit Jews who sail from Egypt or from Syria… Otherwise I will by all means take vengeance on them as fomenters of a general plague infecting the whole world.[2]

In the event, Claudius did not need to take his threatened vengeance on the Alexandrian Jews, but eight years after his letter he expelled the Jews from Rome. For Paul, the tensions of trying to juggle Jewish and Roman identities, with all the potential for humiliation that entailed for someone whose pride and touchiness is obvious to every reader of his letters, became unbearable. On the road to Damascus, he underwent the blinding revelation that released him. He was born again, resurrected into a new life. The experience became for Paul the cornerstone of his version of the Jesus cult. To be a good Jew had meant following the law, which would for ever separate him from the non-Jew and make assimilation so tortuous; Paul's revelation was that it was not the law but faith which saved. Salvation, rebirth and resurrection depended on this moment of faith in Jesus, and not on following God's law as revealed in the Torah. 'A man is not justified by the works of the law, but by the faith of Jesus Christ,' Paul told Peter.[3]

The centrality of his conversion experience also enabled Paul to break free of the historical Jesus and remould him according to his own vision. Paul, unlike all the other Apostles, had never heard Jesus talk, had never argued with him, touched him and eaten meals with him. But Paul did not need the historical Jesus; in fact he would hardly ever refer to events in Jesus' life. Paul's Jesus was the Jesus he encountered on the road to Damascus and in subsequent visions, spirit rather than man. His Jesus was very different from the Jesus the other Apostles had known, and that would be a perpetual source of tension between them.

As fervent now for the Jesus cult as he had been opposed to it, convinced of the righteousness of his own vision, Paul did not even consult the Apostles before beginning to preach in Damascus and the rest of the kingdom of Nabataea. As he later proudly wrote to the Galatians, 'I conferred not with flesh and blood: Neither went I up to Jerusalem to them which were apostles before me; but I went into Arabia.'[4] According to his own account, Paul spent three years preaching in 'Arabia', by which he meant the kingdom of Nabataea, whose former chief minister Syllaeus had once contributed to the disaster of Aelius Gallus' Arabian invasion (see chapter 5). Acts, the only other source we have for Paul's life, does not mention this first missionary journey. But Acts is not totally reliable. Luke, who was probably the author and who accompanied Paul on some of his missionary journeys, was writing in the aftermath of the Jewish revolt against Rome. Acts is coloured by his attempt to distance the Christians as far as possible from the Jews in Rome's eyes, so he was keen to highlight the hatred Paul aroused among devout Jews. It may perhaps be that while in Arabia Paul had not yet begun to antagonize the Jews in the way that he would, even in Paul's own account, when he returned to Damascus.

When Paul began preaching, the total number of Jesus' followers probably numbered a little over a hundred. Led by Jesus' brother James, they considered themselves to be good practising Jews and their movement as open only to fellow Jews and proselytes. They did not believe that Jesus was divine – it is not clear whether even Paul did, since it was such a blasphemous idea for monotheists; he describes Christ as being 'sent' by God. The Gospel of John, which was probably not written until the early second century AD, is the first Christian writing to state unambiguously Christ's divinity. But Jesus' followers did believe that God had appointed Jesus as 'the anointed one', Christos, the Messiah, although their Messiah, an ordinary man who suffered a death reserved for criminals, shockingly diverged from the traditional Jewish conception of the Messiah. The Jewish Messiah was royal and triumphant; he did not die and therefore had no need to be resurrected. Like the Pharisees, however, Jesus' followers wanted to purify the Jewish religion and open it up – beyond the confines of the Sadducee aristocrats – to all Jews. But there were far fewer members of the Jesus cult than there were Pharisees, who numbered about 6,000.

Jesus was also competing against a cornucopia of holy men and healers, ascetics and Messiahs, and his following was tiny compared with the most popular of the pagan cults. The supreme goddess Isis, who offered a personal relationship to her devotees and the promise of some kind of life after death, had her temple in most cities of the empire from Gaul to Egypt. Caligula had just become an Isis devotee and it was probably thanks to him that the festivals of Isis were now included in the official Roman calendar. A vast new temple to Isis with sphinxes, portraits of the pharaohs and obelisks was being built in Rome in the Campus Martius where Augustus had his mausoleum. Stoicism, which believed in the brotherhood of man because every man had god within him, had a big following amongst the most powerful men of the empire and the intellectual elite. The imperial cult did not provide the solace of Isis or the autonomy of Stoicism; nor was it a matter of choice. But it was the natural inheritance of every Roman subject and as such involved almost every subject of the empire.

And yet, 300 years after Paul's relentless missionary work, Christians had become the majority in some major cities such as Antioch and Alexandria, and Christianity had become the official religion of the empire. Paul had transformed a small cult into a universal religion that would both reflect and shape the Western world. Jesus, the Jewish man, the potential saviour of the Jewish people, who had been executed as a common criminal, became the resurrected Christ, the saviour of all mankind. Paul built on the Jews' monotheistic religion with its inbuilt advantages of commanding extreme loyalty and commitment, but transformed it from an ethnic-based exclusive religion into a universal one. The Jews' God had chosen them; to be chosen, you had to be or become a Jew. Paul created the religion for a new tribe, the tribe of man. In doing so, Pauline Christianity promised not just the Jews, but everyone living under Roman rule, relief from the burden of assimilation. It was no longer a matter of having to choose how far to be a Roman and how far to retain an older identity. According to Paul, these boundaries had been dissolved by Christ's love.

Such a universalist message had an obvious appeal to the displaced peoples of the vast new multi-ethnic cities. It gave them a new community to replace the old one they had lost. And it gave them a sense of self-worth, though later writers like Gibbon and Nietzsche would consider it to be a devastatingly distorted one, which denigrated rather than elevated mankind. Paul's universalism was also a proclamation of equality. Christ's love for all mankind, even if this mankind was now considered to be sinful and worthless, made everyone equal. They might not be equal in the material world, but the poorer were equal if not superior to the richer in the spiritual world. Paul's Christianity transformed the everyday indignities felt by the powerless in the face of the wealthier neighbour, rich city official or Roman conqueror into badges of virtue. It was a good recipe for creating docile, contented subjects.

In about AD 40, after three years preaching in Arabia (with how much success we do not know), Paul was ready to meet the original followers of Jesus in Jerusalem. Barnabas, one of the earliest members of the group, with whom Paul would suffer the pain of stonings and floggings, and the triumphs of conversions, probably introduced Paul to Peter. As Paul pointedly wrote, however, of all Jesus' followers in Jerusalem, Paul only met Peter, with whom he stayed for fifteen days, and Jesus' brother, James, in effect the leader of the Jesus movement. Acts, like Paul himself, is silent regarding what the three talked about, and how James and Peter viewed their former persecutor and upstart fellow Apostle, who had never even known Jesus physically but was so sure he knew him intimately through his visions. We do not know how much his view of Jesus and theirs had already diverged, but over the next nine years, as he journeyed around the cities of his homeland, it would do so radically.

Paul's missionary work took him on a 10,000-mile journey around his homeland of the Near East and Greece, staying in the houses of sympathizers, preaching amongst small groups, dazzling some and enraging others. As Paul told the Corinthians, 'Thrice was I beaten with rods, once was I stoned, thrice I suffered shipwreck, a night and a day I have been in the deep; In journeyings often, in perils of waters, in perils of robbers.' Unlike Jesus, who had confined his preaching to villages and small fishing towns and rarely visited the great Hellenistic cities of Caesarea or Sepphoris in Galilee, Paul concentrated exclusively on the cities. He preached in synagogues and public places to Jews and Gentiles, and established small groups of followers. There were probably no more than a dozen people in each. They met in each other's houses to pray and submit to the ecstasy of speaking in tongues. And in the most important expression of 'church' membership, Jew and Gentile shared a meal – that great symbol of togetherness and equality – in memory of Christ their saviour's last supper. Once Paul's followers had become an *ekklesia*, the Greek word which originally meant the assembly of citizens in a city-state, but was used by Paul to mean a group who met locally together for a common purpose, Paul could move on to establish the next one. But he kept in contact through his letters, inspiring, criticizing, sometimes furiously asserting his own authority – he called his opponents in Philippi 'dogs' and 'evil workers'.[5] And all the time he constantly worked and reworked his theology of the crucified and resurrected Christ.

'Syrian Antioch' (so called to distinguish it from 'Psidian Antioch' 500 miles to the west), in what is now southern Turkey, was the capital of Rome's province of Syria and became Paul's base in the Near East. Luke is traditionally thought to have been born there. It was one of the most magnificent cities of the empire, the third biggest city after Rome and Alexandria, with a population of 150,000 slaves, Jews, Syrians, Greeks, Romans and ex-legionaries from Gaul and Germany. Lying on the Orontes River, which was spanned by seven bridges, Antioch was both a terminal for overland Eastern trade and a fortress guarding Rome's border with Parthia. There were temples to the Syrian goddess Atargatis (see chapter 8), and to the Roman gods Apollo, Daphne and Jupiter. The city was subject to successive earthquakes and was constantly being destroyed and rebuilt. When Paul arrived, in about AD 44, a vast marble-paved street had just been built; Antiochenes could now stroll for over 2 miles across the city, sheltered from the sun by the roofed colonnades that flanked each side of the street.

Antioch was also recovering from an explosion of violence against the Jews four years earlier. The Jews had outraged some of the Roman or pro-Roman Antiochenes by protesting against Caligula's demand, in AD 40, that a statue of him should be placed in the Temple. At this perceived snub to Rome, organized mobs had burned down the synagogues and murdered a large number of Jews.

How common such outbreaks of ethnic violence were in a city that was divided into eighteen identifiable ethnic quarters we do not know. But such a tense atmosphere would only have enhanced the appeal of Paul's universalist religion. Indeed, Antioch was probably home to the first Christian church with a substantial Gentile membership.[6] It was here that the word 'Christian', that is, 'Messianist', was first coined and where the Gospel of Matthew would be written more than forty years later. Antioch was the heartland of Christianity for three centuries until it, like the rest of the Near East and the Christian lands of Egypt and North Africa, was conquered by a new empire and turned to Islam.

In about AD 48, Paul and Barnabas set off on their first missionary journey together. At 'Psidian Antioch' (confusingly, like 'Syrian Antioch' in modern Turkey), where Augustus had founded a colony of 3,000 retired Roman legionaries, Paul preached his first recorded sermon. He stood up in the synagogue and told his listeners that through Jesus Christ 'all that believe are justified from all things, from which ye could not be justified by the law of Moses'. His words so impressed the Gentiles in the synagogue, presumably the God-fearers who were admirers of the Jewish religion but not converts, that they asked him to preach to them again. Paul did so and, according to Acts, attracted such crowds that the Jews 'were filled with envy'.[7] Of course, this must be read in the light of Acts' desire to emphasize the difference between Christians and Jews by highlighting the antagonism of the latter. Nonetheless, it is equally clear from Paul's letters that he did indeed arouse the loathing of many religious Jews. As he told the Corinthians, he was not just 'in perils by the heathen' but also 'in perils by mine own countrymen'.[8] In reaching out to the Gentiles, Paul was deliberately downplaying the importance of God's law; Pauline Christians did not have to be circumcised, or follow God's other meticulous requirements; all they needed was faith. That was not just blasphemous but undermined the Jews' own uniqueness and unique relationship with God, which was defined by their observance of the law.

Paul, the self-styled 'Apostle of the Gentiles', who had been commissioned by Jesus 'to bear my name before the Gentiles',[9] was expelled from Antioch along with his fellow missionary Barnabas. The two men were nearly stoned to death by Jews and Gentiles in the city of Iconium (also in modern-day Turkey). In Lystra, they were again stoned, on the instigation of the Jews, according to Acts, though some of the inhabitants took the two missionaries for Zeus and Hermes, after Paul had miraculously healed a cripple.

For Paul and for the Jews who opposed him, both within the Jesus movement and without, the whole question of their relationship with the Gentiles had become a far more lethal one since the death of Herod Agrippa I, the client king of Palestine, in AD 43. Agrippa had ruled over his grandfather Herod the Great's kingdom, thanks to the patronage of his friend Caligula and subsequently Claudius, whose succession Agrippa had supported after Caligula's murder. Like his grandfather, Agrippa (named after Augustus' second in command) had been a loyal client king, too loyal for the more radical Jews, who saw his death as divine punishment for his pleasure at being taken for a god when he attended the games to honour the emperor. As a good client king, however, Agrippa had kept a lid on the hotheads – the radical offshoots of the Pharisees, the Zealots and the *sicarii*. Agrippa had also clamped down on the followers of Jesus. He had executed John's brother James, the brother of John, and arrested Peter, though according to Acts this was more to please the Jewish opponents of the cult than to quell any potential political trouble.

After Agrippa's death, the whole of Palestine was returned to direct Roman rule under insensitive procurators who only exacerbated the existing tensions. In AD 49, the Emperor Claudius returned from securing the conquest of Britain and imposed martial law on an increasingly violent Palestine. That same year, Paul travelled to Jerusalem for a conference to try to heal the differences between the 'party of the circumcision', led by James, which believed that 'Except ye be circumcised after the manner of Moses, ye cannot be saved', and the 'party of the uncircumcision', led by Paul, who believed that the boundaries between Jew and Gentile should be dissolved, and that the law had been superseded by faith. The result, according to Paul, was 'that the gospel of the uncircumcision was committed unto me, as the gospel of the circumcision was unto Peter'.[10] Paul and Barnabas were told 'to go unto the heathen'. In a joint letter to the Gentile followers of Christ in Antioch and Cilicia, James and Paul told them that they did not have to be circumcised, but that they must accept some dietary restrictions, including not eating meat that had been offered in sacrifice.[11]

But the split between the two factions was never healed. Soon after the meeting in Jerusalem, Peter was staying in Syrian Antioch with Paul and Barnabas. Together they shared their meals with non-Jews. This was part of Paul's mission to the Gentiles, a sign of their fellowship. But for a Jew it was an extraordinarily radical step to take: it signalled a break from his fellow Jews because the law forbade eating with Gentiles or sharing their unclean food. Paul had advised the Jewish followers of Jesus not to ask about the source of the food they were eating when they were in another person's house; this was probably what some Diaspora Jews had been secretly doing anyway. According to Paul, Peter ate with the Gentiles of Antioch until James' supporters appeared, at which point, 'fearing them which were of the circumcision', he pretended he had never shared a table with his Gentile friends.[12] Even Barnabas, who had shared so many hardships with Paul, followed Peter.

For Paul, this was both a betrayal of himself and of the agreement reached in Jerusalem. Fierce for the truth and the rightness of the Pauline way, Paul 'withstood him [Peter] to the face', as he told the Galatians. 'Why compellest thou the Gentiles to live as do the Jews?' Paul asked Peter. 'Knowing that a man is not justified by the works of the law, but by the faith of Jesus Christ.'[13]

Soon after this confrontation, Paul and Barnabas parted company. Paul was breaking away from the 'false brethren', as he called them.

After about fourteen years preaching in the cities of the Near East, he left his homeland and headed for Greece with Silas, a new Gentile follower, where they would be joined by Timothy (who would become his closest friend and fellow missionary worker) and Luke.

Their first convert, in fact the first recorded 'European' convert, was a woman in Philippi, a city in what is now north-eastern Greece on the Via Egnatia, one of the primary routes for troops and trade travelling between Rome and the East. Lydia was a Gentile, though a God-fearer, and ran a business selling purple dye. She invited the men to live in her house – Paul stayed for a year and a half – and it became the first ever 'house church', marked with a special red cross to show that Christians met together there. Lydia would be one of a number of women who became prominent in Paul's circle as missionaries, helpers and patrons, and who offered hospitality to Paul in the cities that he preached in. Reasonably wealthy women, like Lydia, or Phoebe, one of the leaders of the Christian group in Cenchreae, Corinth's port, or Chloe, who ran a business either in Corinth or Ephesus, could enjoy a position within the Christian community which it was far more difficult, if not impossible, to achieve in the outside world.

Paul's Christianity appealed precisely, in fact, to those moving up in the world but whose status was not recognized by the rest of society. It made its converts among the merchants, traders, artisans, relatively prosperous women and freedmen. As the biblical scholar Wayne Meeks pointed out, the extreme top and bottom of Roman society was missing from the Pauline communities. There were no destitute, no peasants, hired day labourers or agricultural slaves – though there were household slaves: Lydia had requested that hers be baptized with her, along with her relatives. There were no landed aristocrats, senators or equites. 'Not many are powerful, not many are well-born,' Paul said of his Christian converts.[14] The Christian communities had a mix of social levels unusual in such a hierarchical society, but most were of middling wealth and in transit socially, as so many had been physically when they moved to the cities.

Aquila and Priscilla, Paul's beloved 'helpers in Christ... unto whom not only I give thanks, but also all the churches of the Gentiles',[15] were typical. They were part of the influx of refugees swelling the Jewish community in Corinth, capital of Roman Greece and one of the most important trading cities of the Mediterranean world. Perched on an isthmus between the Adriatic and Aegean Seas, Corinth was a relatively new Roman city built by Julius Caesar on the ruins of the old Greek one. Strabo describes looking north from its rocky summit, where there was a temple to Aphrodite, to the 'lofty, snow-clad mountains' of Parnassus and Helicon. A temple to Octavia, Augustus' sister, showed the imperial cult was well established. About 50,000 people lived in Corinth. Their numbers had recently been swelled by Claudius' expulsion of Jews from Rome in AD 49. According to Suetonius, Claudius was concerned that 'the Jews were continually causing disturbances at the instigation of Chrestus'. The disturbances may well have been a reaction to the fact that Christian missionaries like Paul were preaching in the synagogues.[16] But Rome was also becoming increasingly suspicious of the Jews and saw the followers of Christ, that 'dangerous cult' as Tacitus called it in one of his few mentions of them, as yet another Jewish group to watch. Christians were caught up in the general expulsions of the Jewish community – about 30,000 strong – from Rome.

Aquila, who was like Paul a tent-maker, and Priscilla were well off and had been well assimilated into Graeco-Roman culture. Now they had to make a new home for themselves in Corinth. They found it through Paul, as so many displaced persons would do. Whether Aquila and Priscilla had already become followers of Jesus Christ before they were forced to leave Rome is not clear, but in Corinth they became patrons of the Christian group that Paul was building during his eighteen-month stay with them. Paul was creating a new family.

In the Christian initiation ritual, the initiate stripped off his or her clothing, symbolizing, according to Paul, a stripping away of all previous social and religious categories, and was reborn after a purificatory bath into a new family. The initiate cried out 'Abba!' (Father!). He or she had been adopted as God's loved child and now acquired new brothers and sisters in the Christian community. Paul's letters are rich with the language of family love. He calls them 'brother', 'sister', 'children' and sends them 'an holy kiss'. New Christians had become part of a small intimate group of people who were bound together, theoretically anyway, by love and who were made equal by love. God loved and valued each of them. They shared the passionate excitement of believing they knew the truth, they were the 'saints', the 'holy ones', 'the elect', who were privy to miracles and wonders, and could perform them too. They spoke in tongues, and prophesied, though this often degenerated as the communicants vied to outdo each other in a confused babble of unknown, unknowable tongues. 'How is it then, brethren? When ye come together, every one of you hath a psalm, hath a doctrine, hath a tongue, hath a revelation, hath an interpretation?' Paul wrote with some exasperation to the Christians in Corinth.[17]

The immigrant, the *déraciné*, the up-and-coming man or woman who had left one position in society but had not yet found purchase in another, and any inhabitant of the empire trying to come to terms with being a Roman subject, could perhaps find their new family, their new meaning, a sense of worth and position of which they were deprived elsewhere, in their Christian house church.

All men were equally valuable in the sight of God. Corinth's city treasurer, Erastus, met in the same house as Corinth's freedmen; the city was, according to Strabo, colonized 'with people that belonged for the most part to the freedmen class'. Inevitably, that brotherhood was often more of an ideal than a reality. In Corinth, hierarchical divisions still festered, as no doubt they did in other Christian house churches. 'Despise ye the church of God, and shame them that have not?' Paul wrote to the Corinthians when he heard that at the sacramental communal meal the rich were eating first, leaving the less well-off waiting in the atrium getting hungry and drunk.[18]

Paul's religion had, even if more in principle than practice, burst the barriers of tribe, sex and wealth. But it was not unique in this. Stoicism, Isis and the other mystery cults had done the same. Isis in particular had created a new community. It too appealed to the city-dweller, and to all those uneasily hovering between the rungs of the status ladder. The Isis initiation, far more spectacular than the Christian one, also provided the sense of sloughing off the old to take on a new life and become attached to a new community. But it could never give such a sense of belonging and commitment as initiation into a family – that most fundamental of all social relationships – could do. The cult of Isis was based around the temple and its priests, who distinguished themselves from the laity by their extraordinary commitment, including castrating themselves. Paulinism, on the other hand, was based on the family; the house church was in the home; its 'holy ones' were not a caste apart but ordinary people who needed only to have had a conversion experience. Christianity had not yet adopted Isis' organizational model, and was capable of becoming far more embedded in people's lives than Isis and the other mystery cults could ever be.

And Christianity offered more. Isis offered protection to her followers, but Christ had laid down his life for mankind. Isis offered some form of life after death through the death of Osiris who she brought back to life, but from the little we know of the cult's beliefs, her emphasis was more on prolonging *this* life: Paul's Christianity offered life everlasting.

Paul tried to take his message to the Greek elite also. But when he spoke to the Epicureans and the Stoics in Athens he was ridiculed as a 'babbler'. Paul made no attempt to argue for his beliefs in front of the philosophers, but simply asserted his faith in 'God that made the world and all things therein' and in the resurrection, at which, according to Acts, some of his sceptical listeners laughed.[19]

It was the meeting of two incompatible world views: the Graeco-Roman one of analytical reasoning and the Pauline one of faith. But Paul was used to derision. It only strengthened his convictions. His response to his mockers was that they would be deprived of everlasting life. 'For the preaching of the cross is to them that perish foolishness; but unto us which are saved it is the power of God,' he wrote to the Corinthians. Faith, not reason, would triumph.[20]

Of course, Stoicism too preached the brotherhood of man; Seneca urged his fellow Stoics to 'Treat your inferiors as you would be treated by your betters'.[21] In fact 'our Seneca', as Tertullian, the Christian apologist from Carthage in what is now modern Tunisia, called him, was thought to have been converted to Christianity by Paul.

But the Stoic god was *logos*, Reason. The Christian God was *Logos* too, but he was also Love. The Stoic had to distance himself from his emotional experiences in order to achieve his aim of autonomy, an endeavour that could be deeply satisfying for the Roman aristocrat secure in his wealth and his position, but was far less appealing to the insecure. Although Stoicism emphasized the kinship of all men, it certainly did not laud the humble, idealize poverty, or ennoble and give meaning to suffering in the way Christ's death and resurrection did. Stoicism was a religion for the elite. It offered little comfort to the vulnerable.

Paul offered a poorer man's version of Stoicism, where the poor became glorified and charity was a virtue not an irrational act. He in effect created a religion that provided a third way between Jerusalem and Graeco-Rome. It was neither grounded in adherence to traditional Jewish law, nor based on the Greek, Stoic view of accepting that the world was a given, where man's role was to understand it and accord with its workings. 'For the Jews require a sign, and the Greeks seek after wisdom,' Paul wrote to the Corinthians. 'But we preach Christ crucified, unto the Jews a stumbling block, and unto the Greeks foolishness. But unto them which are called, both Jews and Greeks, Christ the power of God, and the wisdom of God.'[22]

Paul's preaching aroused not just the derision of the Graeco-Roman pagan elite, but the fury of the ordinary pagan worshipper. In the great port city of Ephesus (on the western coast of modern Turkey), cult centre of the many-breasted, heavily necklaced Ephesian Artemis, goddess of fertility, her devotees held a mass protest in the theatre against Paul's belittling of their goddess. There were commercial objections too. Demetrius, a silversmith making souvenirs for the thousands of pilgrims who flocked to the city to worship Artemis, warned his fellow craftsmen that Paul might do them out of business. As a result, Paul was probably imprisoned for two years before being released and making his way back to Greece.

But it was amongst the 'unbelieving Jews', as Paul called them, that he aroused the deepest opposition. Certainly, according to the author of Acts, it was invariably the Jews who stirred up the crowds and the magistrates against Paul and his preachers. The Jews were both appalled by his preaching to the Gentiles and concerned that he was stirring up trouble at a time when relations with Rome were already so tense. Paul and his disciples had 'turned the world upside down', the Jews of Thessalonica told the authorities, 'and these all do contrary to the decrees of Caesar, saying that there is another king.'[23]

But Paul had in fact depoliticized his king. His Christ is a purely spiritual figure, as Geza Vermes and many other New Testament scholars have pointed out. The Jewish Messiah was a king who, with God's help, would come to liberate an oppressed Israel, sweep the Romans from power, encourage the return of the Jews from the Diaspora and preside over a world without evil. The Jews' Messiah was part spiritual, part political saviour. Paul's Messiah owed more to Isis and the other mystery deities for whom death and resurrection played a crucial role. Christ was a cosmic saviour only, concerned with another world, not this one. He promised a better life not on earth, but in Heaven.

Paul recreated the Jewish religion in a way that drastically reduced the tensions between Rome and its non-Roman subjects, whether Jew or Gentile. In the Gospel writers' accounts, Jesus had tried to solve the problem of how a Jew could be a good Roman without compromising himself as a Jew by making a distinction between what was owed to Caesar and what to God. It was an attempt to separate the religious from the political world, but it did not solve the problem for religious Jews. Paul's Christianity built a separate spiritual world for the individual, in which Romans as well as Jews were all equally welcome, where it was not obedience to Jewish law, with all its potential for conflict with Rome, but faith in Christ which mattered. Of course, Paul never could effect a strict separation: there would always be a merging if not a struggle for dominance between the two worlds.

But Paul's compromise was for many Jews unacceptable and anyway too late. Jews were killing Jews for 'collaborating' with the Romans. In AD 57, *sicarii* killed the high priest Jonathan. The following year, Paul, probably now in his fifties, finally returned to Jerusalem, where he and James again tried to heal the split between them. James, the brother of Jesus, persuaded Paul to prove that he was still a devout Jew by going to the Temple with four religious Jews. When Paul arrived, the news spread quickly. An angry mob accused him of bringing a Gentile from Ephesus into the Temple, an offence worthy of the death penalty, though Paul had actually only been with him in the city. They dragged Paul outside the Temple walls and beat him, claiming that he 'teacheth all [men] every where against the people, and the law, and this place'. Paul's religion had diverged too far from theirs. He was arrested and taken to the Antonia Fortress beside the Temple, where he paused on the fortress's steps and turned to address the shouting crowd, speaking to them in Aramaic. The Lord, he said, had sent him to the Gentiles. But that only enraged the crowd. 'Away with such a fellow from the earth,' they shouted, according to Acts, 'for it is not fit that he should live.'[24]

Paul was brought before the Sanhedrin. He was, according to their lawyer, a 'pestilent [fellow], and a mover of sedition among all the Jews throughout the world, and a ringleader of the sect of the Nazarenes, who also hath gone about to profane the temple'.[25] After hearings before the Sanhedrin, the Roman procurator and Herod Agrippa II (the son of Herod Agrippa I, who ruled as Rome's client king over parts of Galilee) Paul demanded to be tried as a Roman citizen under Roman law – Roman citizens could not be tortured, flogged or crucified. Escorted by soldiers, he left Jerusalem for Rome.

The last glimpse we have of Paul is of him preaching under house arrest in Rome. He may have continued his missionary work in Spain, as he had intended, or he may have died a martyr's death. Acts, unfortunately, does not tell us.

In AD 64, fire broke out amongst the squalid timber-built shops clustering round the Circus Maximus in Rome. It raged for six days and destroyed the homes of thousands of poor people. The Emperor Nero, called *Kyrios* ('lord' or 'master', as a sign both of his divine and political power) by his devout subjects, found a convenient scapegoat in the followers of Christus. They were, said Tacitus, killed by Nero because of their 'antisocial tendencies'; like the Jews, the Christians would not worship the emperor.

Christians were rounded up. Some were crucified; others were dressed in the skins of wild beasts and put into an arena with hungry dogs who tore their human prey to pieces; yet others were forced into leather jerkins, daubed with pitch and set alight – to serve as illuminations in Nero's gardens in the Vatican (where the bishops of Rome would one day set up residence). This was the first persecution of the Christians, one in fact of surprisingly few. Dreadful though the persecutions of Diocletian were in the early fourth century AD, they did not compare to the savagery that the Christians later inflicted on the pagans, their fellow Christians and any number of faiths subsequently. Of course Christians were often loathed or feared by their pagan neighbours, who accused them of being godless, practising ritual cannibalism, holding orgies, not being loyal Romans, and being, according to Apuleius' caricature of a Christian woman in *The Golden Ass*, 'crabbed, cruel, lascivious, drunken, obstinate, niggish [*sic*], covetous, and... a despiser of all the Gods, whom others did honour'. Polytheists were, however, by definition tolerant in a way that monotheists could not be. Christianity was more ruthless than any pagan cult and more competitive than Judaism in asserting its superiority over what it considered to be every other 'rival'.[26]

But when Paul died, in whatever circumstances, the survival of his brand of the Jesus movement was still uncertain, though no doubt

Paul, convinced of his Heaven-sent mission, did not think so. Paul had planted house churches in cities from Arabia to Rome. But the churches were small. There were almost no Christians in Jesus' own birthplace, Galilee. Christianity had reached Africa, according to Acts, with the conversion of the Candace of Meroe's eunuch minister (see chapter 4). The disciple Thomas had made converts in India before he was murdered by irate Brahmins (see chapter 10). But there were probably fewer than 7,000 Christians in the whole empire – less than 0.1 per cent of its fifty million-strong population.[27]

It was the Jewish revolt or war against the Romans that helped ensure Christianity's survival. Religious nationalism, which had first found its voice with the Zealots and took on more violent form with the *sicarii,* had been exacerbated by the oppressive policies of a series of Roman governors of Judaea who were not only corrupt but insensitive to Jewish religious practice. In AD 66, Temple priests refused to continue the sacrifices for Rome and the emperor. According to Josephus, 'this was the true beginning of our war with the Romans'. It was both a civil war – of Greeks against Jews, anti-Roman Jews against pro-Roman Jews – and a war of the Jews against the Romans. Herod Agrippa II, who ruled part of Galilee, fought on the side of the Romans; the historian Josephus commanded anti-Roman Jewish troops in Galilee, but then changed sides (see chapter 6), although in his *Vita* Josephus claimed that he never in fact supported the war/revolt but had to appear to do so in order to control it. In July AD 70, after besieging Jerusalem for two years, the Emperor Vespasian's son, Titus, and his legions broke through the city walls, ran through the streets slaughtering everyone they could find, and destroyed the Temple. Jerusalem 'was so completely levelled with the ground', wrote Josephus, 'as to leave future visitors to the spot no ground for believing it had ever been inhabited.'[28] The Jews would try but fail to recapture the city in AD 135. Jerusalem had disappeared from the face of the world, to be replaced by the Roman city of Aelia Capitolina. On the site of the Temple, the Romans built a temple to Jupiter and placed a statue of their Emperor Hadrian inside.

The Jews recouped and rebuilt their community around the Pharisees: the Sadducee families had been virtually wiped out with the destruction of the Temple. But the Jews were now indelibly suspect in Roman eyes. Acts and the Gospel writers, particularly the author of the Gospel of John, capitalized on that. They made sure to emphasize the sharp distinction between the 'unbelieving Jews', who had persecuted Paul and his preachers, and the Christians, converted Gentiles as well as Jews, who were loyal Romans. James, the leader of the determinedly Jewish faction of Jesus' followers, had already been executed. Jewish Christians did not disappear but remained as small marginal sects like the Ebionites who practised circumcision, refused to associate with Gentiles and rejected the teachings of Paul. The revolts had finally separated Judaism from Christianity.

Missionary work seems to have almost died with Paul, but through individual contacts, with family, neighbours and friends, the Christian groups slowly expanded and continued to do so as the empire became more and more unstable. The military had become too powerful and were seating and unseating emperors with abandon.[29] Between AD 217 and 253, twelve emperors came and went; not one died a natural death. The Germans were pressing on the northern frontiers of the Danube and Rhine. Successive emperors failed to raise enough revenue to meet the increasing financial burden of the army, and resorted to requisitioning food supplies, resulting in famine and depopulation.

In the face of such chronic instability of empire and emperor, the imperial cult was bound to lose meaning, even more so since it had been tarnished by Caligula's crazed pretensions to divinity and the record of incest, bigamy and murders committed by successive emperors.

Nevertheless, the Roman imperial cult was, and would continue to be for at least another century, an extraordinarily effective state religion. But it was to some extent fatally dependent on the character of the human deified. In that way it was always going to be more precarious than the Confucian alternative in China. The Chinese emperor was legitimate not because he was or would become divine, but because the Mandate of Heaven had been bestowed on him. If he failed, the Mandate was simply taken away from him and bestowed elsewhere. But in the Roman version, legitimacy was born and died with the divine aspirations of each individual ascender or contender for the throne.

The organization of the Roman religion, including its imperial cult, was running down. The senatorial and local elites were becoming increasingly reluctant to finance the civic, including the imperial, festivals. Senatorial families caught up in the merry-go-round of emperors were losing their lives or their fortunes. In uncertain and financially tough times, festivals were just too expensive.

By 286, the empire could no longer be controlled by one man and was split between two *Augusti*, two emperors, ruling over the East and West, each with their deputy, their 'Caesar'. But such a division soon degenerated into civil war. When the emperor of the West, Constantius, died in 306, his son Constantine had to fight to inherit his father's title.

On 28 October 312, Constantine marched on Rome with what he called 'the heavenly sign of God' inscribed on his soldiers' shields and defeated Maxentius, his rival as emperor. Maxentius drowned in the Tiber, driven into the water by his own fleeing troops as they tried to escape across the Milvian Bridge, one of the major routes in and out of the city.

Constantine had experienced his own Pauline conversion. The day before the battle, as he and his troops were marching towards Rome, Constantine had seen a vision. In its earlier incarnation, the vision had been of Constantine's guardian deity Apollo and the goddess of victory, along with the letters XXX, symbolizing the years that Constantine would rule. But by the end of his life Constantine told Eusebius, the bishop of Caesarea in Palestine, that what in fact he and his troops had seen as they had looked up at the sun was a cross etched across the midday sky inscribed with the Greek words ἐν τούτῳ νίκα, usually translated into Latin as *in hoc signo vinces*, meaning 'By this sign, conquer'. That night, Constantine said, Christ had appeared to him in a dream ordering him to inscribe 'the heavenly sign of God' on his soldiers' shields. Constantine, the former devotee of Apollo, who may well have been associated with the Emperor Diocletian's persecution of Christians initiated in 303 (Constantine's father had been promoted by Diocletian), now believed that paganism was 'a false error'.

The year after his victory at Milvian Bridge, work began on the first monumental Christian building in imperial Rome, St John Lateran, which would soon be followed by the Basilica of St Peter's, a building designed to be as imposing and as symbolic of Rome as any in Augustus' Forum.[30]

Constantine acknowledged that he had felt the need of a superior god in his battle with Maxentius, who was relying on the pagan gods for help. But his conversion may well have been out of genuine belief as well. Although the support of the Christians might have been of some help to him against his pagan rivals, the majority of his army, the elite and most of his subjects were still pagan. Christians were a small minority, though admittedly a noticeable one, since they were concentrated in the most important cities of the empire. At this period they probably made up little more than 2 per cent of the empire's total population, according to the historian Robin Lane Fox (Stark puts it considerably higher at 15 per cent, that is, about nine million people), and included almost none of the elite's men though some of the elite's wives.

But no other cult in the empire had grown so rapidly or was run by such a powerful organization as the Christian one. From the beginning, Paul had ensured that the congregations he founded were not left to develop autonomously, but were held together under his firm leadership through his letters and his visits. Christian leaders understood the importance of central control, though they did not always manage to maintain it. By the time of Constantine, Christian devotees were organized under a hierarchy of bishops and their officials, reaching up to the central authority of the bishop of Rome himself.

A centralized religion, bent on uniformity, worshipping a single all-powerful God, was particularly appealing to a man bent on reuniting the two halves of the Roman Empire under his sole rule. And such a religion made good subjects. The Jewish-Christian Ebionites in fact considered Paul's Christianity to be little more than a religion for making Romans.[31] It was pre-eminently quietist and upheld the status quo. The duty of the devout Christian was to obey authority, including that of the Romans, because 'the powers that be are ordained of God. Whosoever therefore resisteth the power, resisteth the ordinance of God.'[32] The Romans, Paul said, were 'God's ministers'.

Though slave and slave-owner were equal in the sight of God, Paul and his Christians made no attempt to abolish slavery. The mistreated slave could seek protection in the Jewish synagogue or the Roman temple, but Paul told him to return to his master. 'Let every man abide in the same calling wherein he was called,' was Paul's non-revolutionary message. 'For he that is called in the Lord, being a servant, is the Lord's freeman: likewise also he that is called, being free, is Christ's servant.'[33]

Every Christian was a servant and that was what made Christianity so appealing to an imperial ruler and so abhorrent to later elitists like Gibbon and Nietzsche. Christ's love made everyone equal, but they were equal as dependents on Christ's grace and they were schooled to love their dependency: to be poor, and of lowly status, rather than noble, to be meek rather than courageous, self-effacing rather than assertive.

'If no man shall think himself wronged, then is there no more any such thing as wrong,' was the Stoic Emperor Marcus Aurelius' version of 'turn the other cheek'.[34] The Stoic solved the problem of humiliation by refusing to feel humiliated; the Christian by celebrating his humiliation.

Paul's Christianity, which made the subject proud to be subject, which urged him or her to love their neighbour, however alien, was a far better glue for an empire than an imperial cult which, pre-Constantine, had been losing credibility thanks to the character and political instability of its emperors.

For Constantine, Christianity may well have seemed to be a glorified form of imperial cult anyway. He certainly maintained the cult, was worshipped as a god in the city that bore his name and at his death was proclaimed *divus*. Christianity, after all, slotted into a tradition of a ruler becoming god, and, like the imperial cult, worshipped a supreme god-ruler.

In AD 391, the Emperor Theodosius banned all pagan cults and established Christianity as the sole religion. Universal monotheism had formally allied itself with the Roman Empire. Theodosius was, however, the last emperor to rule over a united empire. After his death, the Eastern and Western parts were permanently severed.

The religions that this book has analysed have all thrived on a collusive but often unstable alliance between a mighty state and a priestly, bureaucratic organization. Each alliance had its own particularities and accidents that shaped the states that adopted them, and the people who lived with them, whatever the extent of their belief or disbelief. Confucian meritocracy and the inner court developed a paternalistic utilitarianism that hardly touched the private sphere of the ordinary peasant. Brahmins and Kshatriya maintained a caste-based order that withstood the assault of Buddhist and Jainist universalizing religions. Ashoka's Indian Empire, as much as the Kushans', would try to use Buddhism as a unifying religion, but failed. Partly because of its world-denying creed, Buddhism never embedded itself as deeply in the day-to-day lives of the people of India as Brahminism would, although it would do so in the rest of Asia.

Pauline Christianity had its own unique elements. Unlike Confucianism, it was markedly not an elite or a state religion. Nor was it, like Jainism or Theravada Buddhism, divorced from the ordinary lives and concerns of its practitioners. The cult grew in city homes, not in the temple or monastery; the mark of being a Christian was the experience of conversion, of rebirth, and that was open to all. It did not depend on deeds or on wisdom, but on an arbitrary gift from God that knew no boundaries. Unlike Buddhism, it was not, in its formative centuries, imposed by rulers from the top. Indeed, it defined itself in large part *against* the imperial cult that it eventually supplanted. But Christian opposition, unlike the catastrophically oppositional stance of mainstream Judaism, was not political or ultimately threatening to mighty Rome.

Pauline Christianity, quietist though it was, nevertheless contained a contradiction within it that allowed it to make quiescent subjects but also revolutionary ones, both bureaucrats wedded to the state and those antagonistic to it. For the Confucian and the Hindu, the individual's role was to contribute to the perfection of the social group; for them, society was paramount. Similarly, pagan Romans lauded 'pietas' which meant both reverence and devotion to the gods, but also reverence and loyalty to the customs and traditions of Rome; worship of the emperor was a statement of allegiance to Rome.[35] But for the Christian, piety was about a one-to-one relationship with God which took place in a private spiritual realm, one which was different from and better than the physical world.

Christianity, more even than Stoicism and the mystery cults, divided the spiritual from the physical world. Constantine had still controlled both worlds in the way the emperors had in the old pagan days when there had been no distinction between the two – he continued the imperial tradition founded by Augustus, of being *pontifex maximus*, head of the religious affairs of the empire. But the way was open for a separation of church and state. Once church and state were separated, and with them the believer from the subject, the state was always vulnerable to critics who could claim a higher authority than the ruler. Though Christians believed on the whole that their duty was to support the state, ultimately they knew their God was superior.

As a potentially revolutionary creed, Paulinism went even further. Paul's sidestepping of Jewish law, his insistence that the pure experience of Christ was the only fundamental requirement for being a Christian, liberated his followers from the constraints of tradition and offered the possibility of a universal, open and equal relationship between all mankind. From this perspective, Paulinism is one cornerstone of the West's contribution to the great tradition of respect for the flourishing of the individual, for human rights, for egalitarianism.

Paulinism has also been seen by its critics, pre-eminently Nietzsche, as fatally denigrating mankind. Paul may have offered a realm of dignity and fulfilment, but because of Rome's inability to tolerate a political Messiah, that realm had to be in Heaven and not on earth, with the compensation on this earth that powerlessness and weakness were not to be ashamed of but to be lauded. 'I take pleasure in infirmities, in reproaches, in persecutions, in distresses for Christ's sake,' Paul wrote. 'For when I am weak, then am I strong.'[36] The result, according to Nietzsche, was to degrade mankind and make subjects who are less than man can be. Nietzsche's critiques might be dismissed as the rantings of a late Romantic suffering from syphilis, but it is a view he shared with an earlier, far soberer critic, the great eighteenth-century historian of Rome, Edward Gibbon, who believed that 'the decline of the Roman Empire was hastened by the conversion of Constantine'. 'The clergy', Gibbon said, 'successfully preached the doctrines of patience and pusillanimity; the active virtues of society were discouraged; and the last remains of military spirit were buried in the cloister.'[37] Or, as Nietzsche would put it, Christianity was the triumph of a slave morality over the old Roman warrior virtues.

Today's *pax Americana* has created as many, if not more, tensions than those thrown up by the trade-induced mixing in the Mediterranean world of the *pax Augusta*. Paul had tried to solve the tensions of his world by universalism: everyone was the same. But such universalism came at a cost. Hinduism and Judaism concentrated on the group, and made that group distinctive from every other group. Paul created an imperial subject in which such difference did not exist, but in doing so denied something of value. His triumphant assertion that we are 'neither Greek nor Jew' may not, after all, be the best answer. Sometimes we do indeed need to celebrate our common, equal humanity. But in the ideal of the Pauline universe, difference would be eradicated: neither Greeks nor Jews in all the glory of their distinctiveness would exist. We need a way of viewing the world in which we recognize and celebrate the value both of the universal and of the particular. That synthesis still eludes us.

Notes

Introduction

1 Wayne Meeks, *The First Urban Christians* (Yale University Press, 2003).

Chapter 1 The Rebranding of Rome

1 Suetonius, 'Augustus', *The Twelve Caesars*, p. 79 (trans. Robert Graves, revised with an introduction by Michael Grant, Penguin, 1979).
2 All quotes in this paragraph, in the order they appear, are from Virgil, *The Aeneid* (trans. Robert Fitzgerald, Everyman's Library, 1992): VI.1064–5; VII.347; (although Virgil often describes Aeneas as 'duty-bound', see, e.g., I.519); IX.894–5; IV.315.
3 *Oxford History of the Classical World*, see under 'equites' (ed. John Boardman, Jasper Griffin and Oswyn Murray, Oxford University Press, 1986).
4 Suetonius, 'Augustus', *The Twelve Caesars*, p. 44.
5 Scheidel, Walter, 'Slavery in the Roman Economy', p. 5 (Princeton/Stanford Working Papers in Classics, Stanford University, 2010).
6 Virgil, *Aeneid*, I:379.
7 Ronald Syme, *The Roman Revolution*, p. 297 (Oxford University Press, 1939, 2002).
8 Cassius Dio, *The Roman History: The Reign of Augustus*, 52.16 (trans. Ian Scott-Kilvert, Penguin Classics, 1987; available online at: <http://penelope.uchicago.edu/Thayer/E/Roman/Texts/Cassius_Dio/home.html>).
9 Keith Hopkins, 'Taxes and Trade in the Roman Empire (200 BC–AD 400)', *Journal of Roman Studies*, 70 (1980): 101–25.
10 Michael Ivanovich Rostovtzeff, *The Social and Economic History of the Roman Empire*, vol. 1, p. 82 (1926, 2nd edn, revised by P. M. Fraser, Clarendon Press, 1957).
11 Suetonius, 'Augustus', *The Twelve Caesars*, p. 35.
12 Cassius Dio, *Roman History*, 53.15.
13 Hopkins, 'Taxes and Trade in the Roman Empire'.
14 Suetonius, 'Augustus', *The Twelve Caesars*, p. 52.

Chapter 2 Augustus: God and First Citizen

1 Larry Kreitzer, 'Apotheosis of the Roman Emperor', *The Biblical Archaeologist*, 53/4 (December 1990): 210–17.

2 Cassius Dio, *Roman History*, 53.16.

3 Ibid. 52.36.

4 Seneca, 'Against Superstitions', in Augustine, *City of God*, VI.10. (Wm. B. Eerdmans Publishing Company, 1886, University of Virginia Library Electronic Text Center, available at: <http://etext.lib.virginia.edu/modeng/modengA.browse.html>).

5 Paul Veyne, ed., *A History of Private Life*, vol. 1, *From Pagan Rome to Byzantium*, p. 214 (trans. Arthur Goldhammer, Belknap Press, 1987).

6 Marianne Bonz, *Religion in the Roman World*, (WGBH Educational Foundation, 1998; available at: <http://www.pbs.org/wgbh/pages/frontline/shows/religion/portrait/religions.html>).

7 Cassius Dio, *Roman History*, 52.35.

8 John E. Stambaugh, *The Ancient Roman City*, p. 199 (Johns Hopkins University Press, 1988).

9 See, Nietzsche, *On the Genealogy of Morals*, I.13–14, (Oxford World's Classics, 2008) and *The Antichrist* (trans. Thomas Dayne, Algora Publishing, 2004).

10 Plutarch, 'On Talkativeness', *Moralia* (trans. Harold North Fowler, Loeb Classical Library, 1936; available at: <http://penelope.uchicago.edu/Thayer/E/Roman/Texts/Plutarch/Moralia/ Praecepta_gerendae_reipublicae*.html>).

11 All references to Seneca in this chapter are from his *Moral Epistles* (I.xxxi, III.cxiv, III.ci, II.xcii, I.iii).

12 Suetonius, 'Augustus', *The Twelve Caesars*, p. 52; Cassius Dio, *Roman History*, 54.1.

13 Suetonius, 'Augustus', *The Twelve Caesars*, p. 76.

14 Macrobius, II.4.12.

15 Corinthians 6.13

16 Cassius Dio, *Roman History*, 54.6.

17 Michael Ivanovich Rostovtzeff, 'The Near East in the Hellenistic and Roman Times' (Dumbarton Oaks Inaugural Lectures, 1940, *Dumbarton Oaks Papers*, Harvard University Press, 1941).

18 Philo, of Alexandria, *The Legatio ad Gaium* (*On the Embassy to Gaius*), XXXVII (trans. with commentaries by E. Mary Smallwood, Leiden, 1961).

19 One of the anonymous ancient scholiasts (commentators) on Juvenal, cited in Josiah Osgood, *Caesar's Legacy: Civil War and the Emergence of the Roman Empire* (Cambridge University Press, 2006).

20 See Paul Zanker, *The Power of Images in the Age of Augustus*, p. 302 (University of Michigan Press, 1988, 1990), and S. R. F. Price, *Rituals and Power: The Roman Imperial Cult in Asia Minor*, p. 6 (Cambridge University Press, 1985).

21 Cassius Dio, *Roman History*, 51.19.

22 Acts of John, 38 (available at: <http://www.gnosis.org/library/actjohn.htm>).

23 Tacitus, *Annals*, I.2. (*The Annals of Imperial Rome*, trans. Michael Grant, Penguin, 1956, 1996; available at: <http://www.fordham.edu/halsall/ancient/asbook.html>).

24 Veyne, *A History of Private Life*, p. 10.

25 Suetonius, 'Augustus', *The Twelve Caesars*, p. 51.

26 The following quotes are from Ovid's *The Poems of Exile*, 'Tristia' V.

27 Ovid, *The Poems of Exile*, 'Ex Ponto' (From the Black Sea), EII.VIII. 1–36.(Available at: <http://www.tonykline.co.uk/PITBR/Latin/Fastihome. htm>).

Chapter 3 Alexandria: Gods in the City

1 Meeks, *The First Urban Christians*.

2 Strabo, *Geographia*, XV.1 (trans. H. L. Jones, Loeb Classical Library, Harvard University Press, 1917–32; available at: <http://penelope.uchicago.edu/Thayer/E/Roman/Texts/Strabo/home.html>).

3 References to Strabo in the following description of Alexandria are from *Geographia*, XVII.1–2.

4 Hock, *Social Context of Paul's Ministry*; Alan K. Bowman and Dominic Rathbone Bowman, 'Cities and Administration in Roman Egypt', *Journal of Roman Studies*, 82 (1992): 107–27.

5 Strabo, *Geographia*, IV.5.2.

6 Cassius Dio, *Roman History*, 39.58.

7 Strabo, *Geographia*, XVII.38.

8 References to *The Golden Ass* in this chapter are to Apuleius, XI.48.

9 Robin Lane Fox, *Pagans and Christians in the Mediterranean World*, p. 43 (Penguin, 1986, 2006), citing Virgil's *Georgics*.

10 John E. Stambaugh, *The Ancient Roman City*, p. 220.

11 Ovid, *Fasti*, III: 15 March: Idęs (available at: <http://www.poetryintranslation.com/PITBR/Latin/OvidFastiBkThree.htm#_Toc69367772>).

12 Cato, *On Agriculture*, 139 (Loeb Classical Library, 1934; available at: <http://penelope.uchicago.edu/Thayer/E/Roman/Texts/Cato/De_Agricultura/I*.html).

13 Jörg Rupke, *Religion of the Romans*, p.14 (Polity, 2007); Jo-Ann Shelton, *As the Romans Did*, p. 371 (Oxford University Press, 1988).

14 Pliny the Elder, *Natural History*, 28.3 (trans. John Bostock; available at: <http://www.perseus.tufts.edu/cgibin/ptext?doc=Perseus%3Atext%3A1999.02.0137&query=toc&layout=&loc=35.2>).

15 R. E. Witt, *Isis in the Ancient World*, pp. 216–17 (Johns Hopkins University Press, 1971, 1997).

16 Sharon Kelly Heyob, *The Cult of Isis among Women in the Graeco-Roman World*, ch. 6, n.18 (E. J. Brill, 1975).

17 Rodney Stark, *Cities of God: The Real Story of How Christianity became an Urban Movement and Conquered Rome* (HarperSanFrancisco, 2006).

Chapter 4 The African Goddess-Queen

1   All Strabo quotes in this chapter are from Strabo, *Geographia*, XVII.1 and 2.
2   The Book of the Contending of St Tekle Haimanot (*The Contending of St Tekle Haimanot, Geez & Amharic, 1953*, cited in *The Liturgy of the Ethiopian Church*, introduction Abuna Yesehaq, 1959, 2006; available at: <http://www. ethiopianorthodox.org>).
3   Philip Pullman's *The Good Man Jesus and the Scoundrel Christ* (Canongate Books, 2010) is very interesting on this.

Chapter 5 The Mirage of Arabia: Rome's Fiasco

1   Shelagh Jameson, 'Chronology of the Campaigns of Aelius Gallus and C. Petronius', *Journal of Roman Studies*, 58/Parts 1 and 2 (1968): 71–84.
2   Highet, on whom, along with Breton, I have relied heavily for information about Southern Arabian cities (Juliet Highet, *Frankincense: Oman's Gift to the World*, Prestel, 2006; Jean-François Breton, *Arabia Felix from the Time of the Queen of Sheba: Eighth Century BC to First Century AD*, trans. Albert LaFarge, University of Notre Dame Press, 1998).
3   All references to Strabo in this chapter are from *Geographia*, XVI.4; references to Pliny are from *Natural History*, VI.32 and XII.30–35.
4   Gary K. Young disputes this, however, in *Rome's Eastern Trade: International Commerce and Imperial Policy, 31 BC–AD 305*, p. 24 (Routledge, 2001).
5   Diodorus Siculus, *The Library of History*, III.3, (available at: <http://www. penelope.uchicago.edu/Thayer>)
6   According to the sixth-century Christian pilgrim Antoninus Placentinus, cited by Robert G. Hoyland, *Arabia and the Arabs: From the Bronze Age to the Coming of Islam* (Peoples of the Ancient World, Routledge, 2001).
7   Martin Goodman, *Rome and Jerusalem: The Clash of Ancient Civilizations*, p. 338 (Allen Lane, 2007).
8   Breton, *Arabia Felix*, p. 101.
9   Cassius Dio, *Roman History*, 56.33.

Chapter 6 How Herod and the Pharisees Radicalized the Jews

1   Josephus, *Against Apion*, 2.10 (*The New Complete Works of Josephus*, trans. William Whiston, commentary Paul Maier, Kregel Publications, 1999).
2   Theodor Mommsen, *The Provinces of the Roman Empire: From Caesar to Diocletian*, vol. 2, trans. W. P. Dickson, 1906; (Gorgias Press, 2004).
3   Minucius Felix, *Octavius*, VI (available at: <http://www.earlychurchtexts. com/public/minucius_felix_octavius.htm>).
4   Prudentius, *Contra Symmachum* II.347 (ed. T. E. Page, Loeb Classical Library, Heinemann, 1955).
5   See Geza Vermes, *The Changing Faces of Jesus*, pp. 258–9 (Penguin, 2001).
6   See Josephus, *The Life of Flavius Josephus* (*The New Complete Works of Josephus*, trans. William Whiston, commentary by Paul L. Maier, Kregel

Publications, 1999).

7   Rodney Stark, *The Rise of Christianity: How the Obscure, Marginal Jesus Movement became the Dominant Religious Force in the Western World in a Few Centuries*, p. 138 (HarperCollins, 1997).

8   Paul Veyne, *Quand notre monde est devenu chrétien (312–394)*, p. 272 (Editions Albin Michel, 2007).

9   Marcus Aurelius, *Meditations*, VIII.50 (introduction by Diskin Clay, Penguin Classics, 2006).

10 Stark, *The Rise of Christianity*, p. 57.

11 John Stambaugh and David Balch, *The Social World of the First Christians*, p. 26 (SPCK, 1986).

12 *The Letter of Aristeas*, 139 (ed. R. H. Charles, Clarendon Press, 1913).

13 *The Cambridge History of Judaism*, pp. 82–3 (vol. 3, *The Early Roman Period*, ed. William Horbury, W. D. Davies and John Sturdy, Cambridge University Press, 1999).

14 P. Segal, 'The Penalty of the Warning Inscription from the Temple of Jerusalem', *IEJ*, 39 (1989): 79–84.

15 Leviticus 19:18.

16 Deuteronomy 7:3.

17 Martin Goodman, *Mission and Conversion: Proselytizing in the Religious History of the Roman Empire* (Oxford University Press, 1994).

18 *Cambridge History of Judaism*, p. 232.

19 A. Cotterell (ed.), *The Penguin Encyclopedia of Ancient Civilizations* (Penguin, 1990).

20 Pliny, *Natural History*, V.17.

21 2 Maccabees 2:17.

22 A. N. Wilson, *Paul: The Mind of the Apostle* (Sinclair-Stevenson, 1997).

23 *Cambridge History of Judaism*, p. 440.

24 See *Cambridge History of Judaism*, pp. 419–21.

25 Quotes from Josephus in the rest of this chapter are from *Jewish Antiquities*, XV.3, 8–9; XVII.6; XVIII.1.

26 Luke 11:46; Matthew 23:4.

Chapter 7 Galilee: Jesus and the Messiah-Bandits

1   Geza Vermes, *The Changing Faces of Jesus*, p. 3.

2   Josephus, *The Life of Flavius Josephus*, I.11.

3   See Tacitus, *Histories*, IV.81.

4   E. P. Sanders, *Judaism: Practice and Belief 63 BCE–66 CE* (Trinity Press International, 1992).

5   Martin Hengel, *The Zealots: Investigations into the Jewish Freedom Movement in the Period from Herod I until 70 AD* (T. & T. Clark, 1997).

6   Isaiah 51:11, 52:13.

7   Isaiah 56:3–7.

8   Stark, *The Rise of Christianity*.

9   This and all quotes until 'smash the arrogance' in the following paragraph
    are from Psalms of Solomon, XVII.
10 In particular, Psalms 72:10–11: 'The kings of Tarshish and of the isles shall
    bring presents: the kings of Sheba and Seba shall offer gifts. May all kings
    fall down before him.' But see also Psalms 68:29 and Isaiah 60:3.
11 Robin Lane Fox, *The Unauthorized Version: Truth and Fiction in the Bible*
    (Viking, 1991).
12 References to Josephus in the rest of this chapter are from Josephus, *Jewish
    Antiquities*, XVII.9–13.
13 Psalms 118:10.
14 Sanders, *Judaism: Practice and Belief*, p. 118.
15 E. Meyers and J. Strange, *Archaeology, the Rabbis, & Early
    Christianity* (Nashville: Abingdon, 1981); article 'Nazareth', in the *Anchor
    Bible Dictionary* (New York: Doubleday, 1992).

Chapter 8 Castrating Priests and Trading Gods in Palmyra

1   Apuleius, *The Golden Ass*, VIII.36 (trans. William Adlington, John Lehmann,
    1946).
2   All references to Lucian in this chapter are from *De Dea Syria* (*The Works of
    Lucian of Samosata*, trans. H. W. Fowler and F. G. Fowler, Clarendon Press,
    1905; available at: <http://www.sacred-texts.com>).
3   Ramsay MacMullen, *Paganism in the Roman Empire*, p. 12 (Yale University
    Press, 1981, 1983).
4   Lucian, *De Dea Syria*, 51.
5   Juvenal, *Satires*, VI.523–27, (trans. William Gifford, Everyman's Library,
    1954).
6   Franz Cumont, *Oriental Religions in Roman Paganism*, p. 85 (Dover, 1956).
7   Apuleius, *Florides*, I.1 (*The Apology and Florida of Apuleius of Madaura*, trans. H.
    E. Butler, Greenwood Press, 1970).
8   Cumont, *Oriental Religions*. Rives mentions a shrine to Epona in a stable in
    central Greece, and another shrine has been found in Pompeii. But though
    these certainly show that the cult was reasonably prominent, it is no proof
    that the cult spread beyond the Gauls. The shrines could well have been
    erected by the Gauls themselves.
9   *Florus: Epitome of Roman History* (introduction and trans. E. S. Forster,
    Loeb Classical Library, 1929; available at: <http://penelope.uchicago.edu/
    Thayer/E/Roman/Texts/Florus/Epitome/home.html>).
    See also Diodorus Siculus, *The Library of History*, II.34/35.1–48 (at: <http://
    www.fordham.edu/halsall/ancient/3slaverevolttexts.asp>) and Peter Green,
    'The First Sicilian Slave War', *Past & Present*, 20 (November 1961): 10–29.
10 Robert Turcan, *The Cults of the Roman Empire* (Wiley-Blackwell, 1996).
11 Seneca, 'Against Superstitions', as quoted by Augustine, *City of God*, VI.10.
12 Stark, *The Rise of Christianity*, p. 199.

Chapter 9 Political and Religious Chaos in Parthia

1 Plutarch, 'The Life of Crassus' (*Parallel Lives*, trans. Bernadotte Perrin, Loeb Classical Library, 1916; available at: <http://penelope.uchicago.edu/ Thayer/E/Roman/ Texts/Plutarch/Lives/Crassus*.html>).

2 Vesta Sarkhosh Curtis and Sarah Stewart, *The Age of the Parthians*, p. 61 (I. B. Tauris, 2007).

3 The following account of the battle of Carrhae is based on Plutarch; Plutarch, 'The Life of Crassus', *Parallel Livcs*, 21–33.

4 Strabo's account of the Parthians is from *Geographia*, XV.3.

5 *The Cambridge History of Iran*, p. 911.

6 Strabo, *Geographia*, XVI.1.16.

7 Michael Ivanovich Rostovtzeff, *Dura Europos and its Art* (Clarendon Press, 1938).

8 *Cambridge History of Iran*, p. 873; see also Mommsen, *Provinces of the Roman Empire*, p. 5; and Malcolm A. R. Colledge, *The Parthians*, p. 103 (Praeger, 1967).

9 *Vis and Ramin*, pp. 224–5 (trans. from the Persian of Fakhr ud-Din Gurgani by George Morrison, Columbia University Press, 1972).

10 Ibid.

Chapter 10 A 'Pagan Christ' in Babylon

1 Edward Gibbon, *The History of the Decline and Fall of the Roman Empire*, vol.1, p. 328, n.71 (ed. Dero A. Saunders, Penguin Classics, 1952, 1985; available at: <http://www.gutenberg.org>).

2 The account of Apollonius in this chapter is taken from Flavius Philostratus, *Life of Apollonius of Tyana* (trans. F. C. Conybeare, Loeb Classical Library, 1912; available at: <http://www.livius.org/ap-ark/apollonius/life/ va_00.html>).

3 Philostratus, *Life of Apolloniu*, I.16, .

4 The following account of Apollonius' visit to Babylon is from Philostratus, *Life of Apollonius*, I.25–40.

Chapter 11 India: Brahmins versus Monks

1 Philostratus, *Life of Apollonius*, II.3. All other quotes from Philostratus and the account of Apollonius' visit to Taxila in this chapter are from II.23–38 and 40–42.

2 See: <http://www.mongolianculture.com/indomongolian.htm#_edn10> (citing Thomas Watters, trans., *On Yuan Chwang's Travels in India*, 2 vols, London 1904–5, rpt. Delhi, Munshiram Manoharlal, 1961).

3 *Shilappadikaram* (*The Ankle Bracelet*) by Prince Ilangôô Adigal, p. 90 (trans. Alain Daniélou, A New Directions Book, 1965).

4 Philostratus, *Life of Apollonius*, II.23.

5 *Laws of Manu*, VIII.371–80 (trans. George Bühler, available at: <http://www.

sacred-texts.com/hin/manu.htm>).

6 Jeannine Auboyer, *Ancient India: From 200 BC to 700 AD*, p. 85 (Phoenix Press, 1965).

7 Periplus of the Erythraean Sea; available as ancient history sourcebook: <http://www.fordham.edu/halsall/ancient/asbook.html>.

8 Begley, citing Casson, in V. Begley and R. D. De Puma, *Rome and India: The Ancient Sea Trade* (University of Wisconsin Press, 1991).

9 Vatsyayana, *The Kama Sutra of Vatsyayana*, ch. 4, pp. 24–6 (Echo Library, 2009).

10 *Shilappadikaram* (*The Ankle Bracelet*), pp. 28–9.

11 Ibid., p. 16.

12 *Laws of Manu*, I.99.

13 From the *Dhammapada*, a versified Buddhist scripture traditionally ascribed to the Buddha himself.

14 Xinru Liu, *Ancient India and Ancient China: Trade and Religious Exchanges AD 1–600*, pp. 68–9 (Oxford University Press, 1988).

15 *Laws of Manu*, X.43.

16 Max Weber, *The Religion of India: The Sociology of Hinduism and Buddhism* (trans. Hans H. Gerth and Don Martindale, Free Press, 1962).

17 Kautilya, *Arthashastra*, XIII.4 (trans. R. Shamasastry, 1915; available at: <http://www.bharatadesam.com>).

18 Ibid., V.2.

19 Ibid., XIII.1.

20 Philostratus, *Life of Apollonius*, II.25.

Chapter 12 The Buddha in a Toga

1 Burton Watson, trans., *Records of the Grand Historian of China: Han Dynasty II*, p. 245 (translated from the *Shiji* of Sima Qian. ch. 123: 'The Account of Dayuan', Columbia University Press, rev. edn, 1993).

2 Cassius Dio, *Roman History*, 54.9.

3 Strabo, *Geographia*, XV.1.73.

4 From the *Cullavagga*, which sets out the monks' duties. *The Khandhaka Rules*, ch 9 (trans. T. Bhikku, 2007–12; available at: <http://www.accesstoinsight.org/lib/authors/thanissaro/bmc2/bmc2.intro.html>).

5 *Shilappadikaram* (*The Ankle Bracelet*), p. 60.

6 See Stanley Wolpert, *A New History of India* (Oxford University Press, 1993, 2008).

7 Danielou, cited in Avari, p. 131.

8 Kautilya, *Arthashastra*, XIII.5 (trans. R. Shamasastry, 1915; available at: <http://www.bharatadesam.com>).

9 From the Rabatak inscription carved into a rock near Rabatak in Afghanistan.

10 *Laws of Manu*, VII. 20–24.

11 Ibid., VII.133.

12 *Shilappadikaram*, (*The Ankle Bracelet*) p. 23.
13 See *The Khandhaka Rules*.
14 *Bhagavad-Gita*, IX.26 and 30–32.
15 Romila Thapar, *A History of India*, vol. 1, p. 133 (Penguin, 1966, 1990).
16 Strabo, *Geographia*, XV.2.

Chapter 13 Confucius' Religion for Civil Servants

1 My accounts in this and the following chapter are largely based on the *Hanshu*, in particular chapters: X, 'The Annals of Emperor Hsiao-Cheng'; XI, 'The Annals of Emperor Hsiao-Ai'; XII, 'The Annals of Emperor Hsiao-P'ing'; and XCIX, 'The Memoir of Wang Mang' (available at: <http://www.jefferson.village.virginia.edu/xwomen/intro.html>).

2 E. R. Hughes, *Two Chinese Poets: Vignettes of Han Life and Thought* (Princeton University Press, 1960).

3 *Liji (Book of Rites)*, IV (trans. James Legge, The Institute of Advanced Technology in the Humanities, copyright 2003 by Anne Kinney and the University of Virginia; available at: <http://www.jefferson.village.virginia.edu/xwomen/intro.html>).

4 *Guanzi*, IV.8 (trans. T'an Po-fu and Wen Kung-wen; ed. Lewis Maverick, 1954; available at: <http://www.chinaknowledge.de/Literature/Diverse/guanzi.html>).

5 Walter Scheidel, 'From the "Great Convergence" to the "First Great Divergence": Roman and Qin-Han State Formation and its Aftermath' (Princeton/Stanford Working Papers in Classics, Version 2.1, 12-page abstract, Stanford University, 2007).

6 *Liji (Book of Rites)*, Book 10: 2.11

7 *Liji (Book of Rites)*, Book 1: 2.1.1 and 16; Book 1: 2.3.7.

8 Alfred Schinz, *The Magic Square: Cities in Ancient China* (Axel Menges, 1996).

9 *Hanshu*, XCIX, 'The Memoir of Wang Mang'; Appendix II, 'Wang Mang's Economic Reforms'.

10 Ibid., Glossary, chapter X, 'Emperor Cheng' (trans. Homer H. Dubs, available at: http://libweb.uoregon.edu/ec/e-asia/read/CHPXfinal-1.pdf).

11 *Hanshu*, 'The Annals of Emperor Hsiao-Ai', II.6b.

12 James, 1995.

13 *Shanhai Jing (Classic of the Mountains and Lakes)*. The book, which was compiled between the third century BC and the second century AD, was intended as a guide to pilgrims in China, telling them of the strange creatures they might encounter and their spiritual powers.

14 Homer H. Dubs, 'An Ancient Chinese Mystery Cult', *Harvard Theological Review*, 35/4 (October 1942): 221–40.

15 Ibid.

16 *Hanshu*, XCIC, 'The Memoir of Wang Mang', Part B.

Chapter 14 Wang Mang the Pious Usurper

1 *Hanshu*, Glossary, X.404, 'Emperor Cheng' (trans. Homer H. Dubs, at: <http://libweb.uoregon.edu/ec/e-asia/read/CHPXfinal-1.pdf>). For the rest of the chapter I rely on *Hanshu*, XCIX, 'The Memoir of Wang Mang' (available at: <http://www.jefferson.village.virginia.edu/xwomen/intro.html>).

2 *Hanshu*, XCIX, 'Memoir of Wang Mang', Part A.

3 Rudi Thomsen, *Ambition and Confucianism: A Biography of Wang Mang*, p. 63 (Aarhus University Press, 1988).

4 *Hanshu*, XIII, 'The Annals of Emperor Hsiao-P'ing'.

5 Ibid., XCIX, 'Memoir of Wang Mang', Part A.

6 Ibid., Part B.

Chapter 15 The Dragon Who Flew Too High

1 This chapter is based on *Hanshu*, XCIX, 'Memoir of Wang Mang', Parts B and C (available at: <http://www.jefferson.village.virginia.edu/xwomen/intro.html>).

2 Ibid., Part B.

3 Amartya Sen, *Poverty and Famines: An Essay on Entitlements and Deprivation* (Clarendon Press, 1982).

4 Cho-yun Hsu, *Han Agriculture: The Formation of Early Chinese Agrarian Economy (206 B.C.–A.D. 220)*, p. 136 (University of Washington Press, 1980).

5 *The Cambridge History of China*, vol. 1, p. 243 (*The Ch'in and Han Empires, 221 BC–AD 220*, eds Denis Twitchett and Michael Loewe, Cambridge University Press, 1986).

6 Homer H. Dubs, 'Wang Mang and His Economic Reforms', p. 261 (*T'oung Pao*, Second Series, vol. 35, Livr. 4, 1940).

7 Otto B. van der Sprenkel, 'Max Weber on China' (*History and Theory*, 3/3 (1964): 348–70).

8 Thomsen, *Ambition and Confucianism*, p. 147.

9 *Hanshu*, XCIX, 'Memoir of Wang Mang', Part B.

10 *Hanshu*, Glossary, chapter 99c, 370, 'Wang Mang' (trans. Homer H. Dubs, available at: <http://libweb.uoregon.edu/ec/e-asia/read/chp99c.pdf>).

11 *Hanshu*, XCIX, 'Memoir of Wang Mang', Part C.

12 *Hanshu*, XCIX, 'Memoir of Wang Mang', Part C.

13 Ibid. Part B.

14 Ibid. Part C

Chapter 16 Recalcitrant Spirits: The German Resistance

1 Josephus, *The New Complete Works of Josephus*.

2 Duane W. Roller, *The World of Juba II and Kleopatra Selene: Royal Scholarship on Rome's African Frontier*, p. 170 (Routledge, 2003).

3 See F. M. Snowden, *Blacks in Antiquity: Ethiopians in the Greco-Roman Experience* (Harvard University Press, 1970).

4 Cassius Dio, *Roman History*, LV.28.
5 Velleius Paterculus, *Roman History*, II.107 (trans. Frederick W. Shipley, Loeb Classical Library, 1924; available at: <http://penelope.uchicago.edu/Thayer/E/Roman/Texts/Velleius_Paterculus/home.html>).
6 Velleius Paterculus, II.117.
7 Simon Schama, *Landscape and Memory*, p .95 (HarperCollins, 1995).
8 Velleius Paterculus, II.118.
9 The following account is drawn from Cassius Dio, *Roman History*, LVI.18–24.
10 Ibid., LVI.24.
11 All quotes in this paragraph are from Tacitus, *Annals*, II.81–2.

Chapter 17 Rome: The Emperor Becomes God

1 Cassius Dio, *Roman History*, LVI.42.
2 Suetonius, 'Tiberius', *The Twelve Caesars*, p. 24 (trans. Robert Graves, revised with an introduction by Michael Grant, Penguin, 1979).
3 Ibid., p. 58.
4 Strabo, *Geographia*, IV.4.5.

Chapter 18 The Death of Jesus

1 Philo of Alexandria, *Philo: Legatio ad Gaium (On the Embassy to Gaius) Volume X*, (Loeb Classical Library No. 379, trans F. H. Colson, 38 (301), 1962; available at: <http://www.earlyjewishwritings.com/philo.html>).
2 Josephus, *The Jewish War*, II.9.3, *The New Complete Works of Josephus*.
3 Josephus, *Jewish Antiquities*, VIII.3.2.
4 Suetonius, 'Tiberius', *The Twelve Caesars*, pp. 43, 62.
5 Vermes, amongst other notable scholars, believes this.
6 See chapter 6 and *Cambridge History of Judaism*, vol.3, p. 157.
7 Josephus, *Jewish War*, II.8.7, *The New Complete Works of Josephus*.
8 Josephus, Appendix, Dissertation 1, p. 988, *The New Complete Works of Josephus*.
9 Vermes, *The Changing Faces of Jesus*, p. 167.
10 Luke 7:5.
11 Matthew 10:5–6.
12 Matthew 15:26.
13 Vermes, *The Changing Faces of Jesus*, p. 23.
14 Hyam Maccoby, *The Mythmaker: Paul and the Invention of Christianity*, p. 40 (HarperCollins, 1987).
15 John 8:44.
16 Mark 7:7–8; Matthew 15:19–20.
17 Matthew 23:3ff.
18 Vermes, *The Changing Faces of Jesus*, p. 254.
19 Mark 3:6.
20 John 11:50.
21 Tacitus, *The Annals of Imperial Rome*, VI.50.

Chapter 19 And Paul Created Christ

1 *Cambridge History of Judaism*, vol. 3, p. 182.
2 Josephus, *Jewish Antiquities,* XIX.5.2.
3 Galatians 2:16.
4 Galatians 1:16.
5 Philippians 1:15, 3:2.
6 Stark, *Cities of God*, p. 38.
7 Acts 13:45.
8 2 Corinthians 11:26.
9 Acts 9:15.
10 Galatians 2:7
11 Acts 15:28–9.
12 Galatians 2:12.
13 Galatians 2:14,16.
14 1 Corinthians I:26.
15 Romans 16:3–4.
16 *Cambridge History of Judaism,* vol. 3, p. 176.
17 1 Corinthians 14:26.
18 1 Corinthians 11:22.
19 Acts 17:24, 32.
20 1 Corinthians 1:18.
21 Seneca, *Moral Epistles*, 47.
22 1 Corinthians 1:22–4.
23 Acts 17:6–7.
24 Acts 22:22.
25 Acts 24:5.
26 Mary Beard, John North and Simon Price, *Religions of Rome*, p. 309 (vol. 1, *A History*, Cambridge University Press, 1998).
27 Robert Louis Wilken, *The Christians as the Romans Saw Them* (Yale University Press, 1984).
28 Josephus, *Jewish Wars*, 7:1.1.
29 I am indebted to A. H. M. Jones for this gallop through the third century; see his *Constantine and the Conversion of Europe* (University of Toronto Press, 1978).
30 Ibid.
31 A. N. Wilson, *Paul: The Mind of the Apostle*.
32 Romans 13:1–2.
33 1 Corinthians 7:20, 22
34 Marcus Aurelius, *Meditations*, IV.7 (trans. George Long, available at: <http://classics.mit.edu//Antoninus/meditations.html>).
35 Arthur Cushman McGiffert, 'The Influence of Christianity upon the Roman Empire' (*Harvard Theological Review,* 2/1, Jan.1909: 28–49).
36 2 Corinthians 12:10.
37 Gibbon, *The History of the Decline and Fall of the Roman Empire,* vol. II.

Select Bibliography

Adams, William, Y., 'Sacred and Secular Polities in Ancient Nubia', *World Archaeology*, 1974, pp. 39–51.

Apuleius, *The Golden Ass*, trans. William Adlington, John Lehman, 1946.

Auboyer, Jeannine, *Ancient India: From 200 BC to 700 AD*, Phoenix Press, 1965.

Barton, Carlin A., *The Sorrows of the Ancient Romans: The Gladiator and the Monster*, Princeton University Press, 1993.

Beard, Mary, North, John, and Price, Simon, *Religions of Rome*, vol. 1, A History, Cambridge University Press, 1998.

Begley, V., and De Puma, R. D., *Rome and India: The Ancient Sea Trade*, University of Wisconsin Press, 1991.

Bellah, Robert, 1964, 'Religious Evolution', *American Sociological Review*, 29/3 (June 1964): 358–74.

Bellah, Robert, 'Max Weber and World-Denying Love: A Look at the Historical Sociology of Religion', *Journal of the American Academy of Religion*, 67/2 (June 1999): 277–304.

Berger, P., *The Sacred Canopy*, Anchor Books, 1967.

Bielenstein, Hans, 'Wang Mang and the Restoration of the Han Dynasty and Later Han', vol. 4, The Government, *Bulletin of the Museum of Far Eastern Antiquities*, 51 (1979): 1–300.

Bielenstein, Hans, *The Bureaucracy of Han Times*, Cambridge University Press, 1980.

BokSer, B. M., 'Wonder-working and the Rabbinic Tradition: The Case of Hanina ben Dosa', *Journal for the Study of Judaism*, 16 (1985): 42–92.

Bonz, Marianne, *Religion in the Roman World*, WGBH Educational Foundation, 1998; available at: <http://www.pbs.org/wgbh/pages/frontline/shows/religion/portrait/religions.html>.

Bowersock, G. W., *Roman Arabia*, Harvard University Press, 1983.

Bowersock, G. W., *Studies on the Eastern Roman Empire: Social, Economic and Administrative History, Religion, Historiography*, Biblioteca Eruditorum, 1994.

Bowman, Alan K., and Rathbone, Dominic, 'Cities and Administration in Roman Egypt', *Journal of Roman Studies*, 82 (1992): 107–27.

Boyce, Mary, 'Zoroaster the Priest', *Bulletin of the School of Oriental and African Studies*, 33/1 (1970): 22–38.

Boyce, Mary, *A History of Zoroastrianism*, Brill, 1996.

Breton, Jean-François, *Arabia Felix from the Time of the Queen of Sheba: Eighth Century BC to First Century AD*, trans. Albert LaFarge, University of Notre Dame Press, 1998.

Burnell, Peter, 'The Death of Turnus and Roman Morality', *Greece & Rome*, second series, 34/2 (October 1987): 186–200.

The Cambridge Ancient History, vol. 10, *The Augustan Empire, 43 BC–AD 69*, 2nd edn, ed. Alan K. Bowman, Edward Champlin and Andrew Lintott, Cambridge University Press, 1996.

The Cambridge History of China, vol. 1, *The Ch'in and Han Empires, 221 BC–AD 220*, ed. Denis Twitchett and Michael Loewe, Cambridge University Press, 1986.

The Cambridge History of Iran, 7 vols, ed. Harold Bailey, Cambridge University Press, 1993.

The Cambridge History of Judaism, vol. 3, *The Early Roman Period*, ed. William Horbury, W. D. Davies and John Sturdy, Cambridge University Press, 1999.

Carcopino, J., *Daily Life in Ancient Rome*, Pelican Books, 1940, 1956.

Casey, John, *Pagan Virtue: An Essay in Ethics*, Oxford University Press, 1990.

Cassius Dio, *The Roman History: The Reign of Augustus*, trans. Ian Scott-Kilvert, Penguin Classics; available online at: <http://www.penelope.uchicago.edu/Thayer/E/Roman/Texts/Cassius_Dio/home.html>.

Casson, Lionel, *Travel in the Ancient World*, Johns Hopkins University Press, 1974, new edn, 1994.

Ch'ü, T'ung-tsu, *Han Social Structure*, ed. Jack L. Dull, University of Washington Press, 1972.

Cicero, trans. Michael Grant, Penguin Classics, 1960; see also: <http://www.perseus.tufts.edu/cache/perscoll_Greco-Roman.html#secondary1>.

Clarke, Katherine, 'In Search of the Author of Strabo's Geography', *Journal of Roman Studies*, 87 (1997): 92–110.

Colledge, Malcolm A. R., *The Parthians*, Praeger, 1967.

Cotterell, A., ed., *The Penguin Encyclopedia of Ancient Civilizations*, Penguin, 1990.

Cumont, Franz, 'After Life in Roman Paganism', Classical Philology, 20/1 (January 1925): 94–5.

Cumont, Franz, *Oriental Religions in Roman Paganism*, Dover, 1956.

Curtis, Vesta Sarkhosh and Stewart, Sarah, *The Age of the Parthians*, I. B. Tauris, 2007.

Dillon, M., ed., *Handbook of the Sociology of Religion*, Cambridge University Press, 2003.

Diodorus Siculus, *The Library of History*, available at: <http://www.penelope.uchicago.edu/Thayer/E/Roman/Texts/Diodorus_Siculus/home.html>.

Dubs, Homer, 'The Victory of Han Confucianism', *Journal of the American Oriental Society*, 58/3 (September 1938): 435–49.

Dubs, Homer, 'Wang Mang and His Economic Reforms', *T'oung Pao*, second series, vol. 35, Livr. 4, 1940, pp. 219–65.

Dubs, Homer, 'An Ancient Chinese Mystery Cult', *Harvard Theological Review*, 35/4 (October 1942): 221–40.

Dueck, Daniela, *Strabo of Amasia: A Greek Man of Letters in Augustan Rome*, Taylor & Francis, 2007.

Dumont, Louis, 'A Modified View of Our Origins: The Christian Beginnings of Modern Individualism', *Religion* 12 (1982): 1–27.

Durkheim, Émile, Elementary Forms of Religious Life, ed., Mark S. Cladis, trans. Carol Cosman, Oxford World's Classics, 2001.

Edwards, David N., 'Meroe and the Sudanic Kingdoms', Journal of African History, 39/2 (1998): 175–93.

Fishwick, Duncan, 'Dio and Maecenas: The Emperor and the Ruler Cult', Phoenix, Phoenix, 44/3 (autumn, 1990): 267–75.

Gibbon, Edward, The History of the Decline and Fall of the Roman Empire, ed. Dero A. Saunders, Penguin Classics, 1952, 1985; also available at: <http://www.gutenberg.org>.

Goodman, Martin, Rome and Jerusalem: The Clash of Ancient Civilizations, Allen Lane, 2007.

Gradel, Ittai, Emperor Worship and Roman Religion, Oxford University Press, 2002.

Grant, Michael, The Jews in the Roman World, Littlehampton Book Services, 1973.

Grant, Michael, Herod the Great, Macmillan, 1974.

Grant, Michael, The Army of the Caesars, Macmillan, 1974.

Hamburger, Max, 'Aristotle and Confucius: A Comparison', Journal of the History of Ideas, 20/2 (April 1959): 236–49.

Hanshu, The History of the Former Han Dynasty, trans. Homer Dubbs, 1955; available at: <http://www.jefferson.village.virginia.edu/xwomen/intro.html>, and: <http://www.e-asia.uoregon.edu/homer/>.

Haycock, B. G., The Kingship of Cush in the Sudan, Society for Comparative Studies in Society and History, 1965.

Hearn, Maxwell, 'The Arts of Ancient China, Wen Fong', Metropolitan Museum of Art Bulletin (1973), the Metropolitan Museum of Art.

Hengel, Martin, The Zealots: Investigations into the Jewish Freedom Movement in the Period from Herod I until 70 AD, T. & T. Clark, 1997.

Highet, Juliet, Frankincense: Oman's Gift to the World, Prestel, 2006.

Hitti, Philip K., History of Syria: Including Lebanon and Palestine, Macmillan, 1951.

Hock, Ronald F., The Social Context of Paul's Ministry, Augsburg Books, 1995.

Hopkins, Keith, 'Elite Mobility in the Roman Empire', Past and Present, 32 (December 1965): 12–26.

Hopkins, Keith, 'On The Political Economy of the Roman Empire', The Dynamics of Ancient Empires: State Power from Assyria to Byzantium, eds Ian Morris and Walter Scheidel, Oxford University Press, 2009: 178–204.

Hopkins, Keith, 'Taxes and Trade in the Roman Empire (200 BC–AD. 400)', Journal of Roman Studies, 70 (1980): 101–25.

Hopkins, Thomas J., The Hindu Religious Tradition, Wadsworth Publishing Company, 1971.

Horace, The Collected Works of Horace, trans. Lord Dunsany and Michael Oakley, 1961, Everyman's Library, Dent.

Horsley, Richard A., 'The Sicarii: Ancient Jewish "Terrorists" ', Journal of Religion, 52 (1979): 435–58.

Horsley, Richard A., Galilee: History Politics, People, Trinity Press International, 1995.

Horsley, R. A., and Hanson, J. S., Bandits, Prophets, and Messiahs: Popular Movements at the Time of Jesus, Trinity Press International, 1999.

Hsu, Cho-yun, 'The Changing Relationship between Local Society and the Central Political Power in Former Han 206 B.C.–8 A.D', *Comparative Studies in Society and History*, 7/4 (1965): 358–70.

Hsu, Cho-yun, *Han Agriculture: The Formation of Early Chinese Agrarian Economy (206 B.C.–A.D. 220)*, University of Washington Press, 1980.

Hughes, E. R., *Two Chinese Poets: Vignettes of Han Life and Thought*, Princeton University Press, 1960.

Irwin, Lee, 'Divinity and Salvation: The Great Goddesses of China', *Asian Folklore Studies*, 49/1 (1990): 53–68.

Isidore of Charax, *Parthian Stations*, notes by Wilfred H. Schoff, available at: <http://www.parthia.com/doc/parthian_stations.htm>.

Jameson, Shelagh, 'Chronology of the Campaigns of Aelius Gallus and C. Petronius', *Journal of Roman Studies*, 58, Parts 1 and 2 (1968): 71–84.

Jaynes, Julian, *The Origin of Consciousness in the Breakdown of the Bicameral Mind*, Princeton University Press, 1976, 2000.

Johnson, Paul, *A History of the Jews*, Phoenix, 1987, 2001.

Jones, A. H. M., 'Taxation in Antiquity', in P. A. Brunt, ed., *The Roman Economy: Studies in Ancient Economic and Administrative History*, Blackwell, 1974, pp. 151–85.

Jones, A. H. M., *Constantine and the Conversion of Europe*, University of Toronto Press, 1978.

Josephus, *The New Complete Works of Josephus*, trans. William Whiston, commentary by Paul L. Maier, Kregel Publications, 1999.

Kautilya, *Arthashastra*, trans. *R. Shamasastry, 1915, available at:* <http://www.bharatadesam.com>.

Kreitzer, Larry, 'Apotheosis of the Roman Emperor', *Biblical Archaeologist*, 53/4 (December 1990): 210–17.

Lactantius, *The Works of Lactantius,* ed. Alexander Roberts and James Donaldson, trans, William Fletcher, *The Divine Institutes*, 56, Book 1/ 5:23, T. & T. Clark, 1871; available at: <http://www.archive.org/stream/ theworksoflactan02lactuoft/ theworksoflactan02lactuoft_djvu.txt>.

Lane Fox, Robert, *The Unauthorized Version: Truth and Fiction in the Bible*, Viking, 1991.

Lane Fox, Robert, *Pagans and Christians in the Mediterranean World*, Penguin, 1986, 2006.

Laughlin, John C. H., 'Capernaum: From Jesus' Time and After', *Biblical Archaeologist*, 56 (1993): 54–61.

Liji Book of Rites, trans. James Legge, The Institute of Advanced Technology in the Humanities, copyright 2003 by Anne Kinney and the University of Virginia, available at:

<http://www.jefferson.village.virginia.edu/xwomen/intro.html>.

Lind, L. R., 'Concept, Action, and Character: The Reasons for Rome's Greatness', *Transactions and Proceedings of the American Philological Association*, 103 (1972): 235–83.

Liu, Xinru, 'Migration and Settlement of the Yuezhi-Kushan: Interaction and Interdependence of Nomadic and Sedentary Societies', *Journal of World History*,

12/2 (fall, 2001): 261–92.

Livy, *The History of Rome, Vol. I* , ed. Ernest Rhys, trans. Rev. Canon Roberts, Everyman's Library, 1905; available at: <http://www.fordham.edu/halsall/ancient/asbook.html>.

Loewe, Michael, *Everyday Life in Early Imperial China during the Han Period 202 BC–AD 220*, Hackett, 1973.

Loewe, Michael, *Crisis and Conflict in Han China*, Allen & Unwin, 1974.

Loewe, Michael, *Ways to Paradise: The Chinese Quest for Immortality*, George Allen & Unwin, 1979.

Loewe, Michael, *Divination, Mythology and Monarchy in Han China*, Cambridge University Press, 1994.

Loewe, Michael, 'Wang Mang and His Forbears: The Making of the Myth',
T'oung Pao, second series, vol. 80, fasc. 4/5, 1994, pp. 197–222.

Loewe, Michael, *Faith, Myth and Reason Han China*, Hackett, 2005.

Loewe, Michael, *The Government of the Qin and Han Empires 221 BCE–220CE*, Hackett, 2006.

Lohwasser, Angelika, 'Queenship in Kush: Status, Role and Ideology of Royal Women', *Journal of the American Research Center in Egypt*, 38 (2001): 61–76.

Lucian, *The Works of Lucian of Samosata*, trans. H. W. Fowler and F. G. Fowler, Clarendon Press, 1905; available at: <http://www.sacred-texts.com>.

Luttwak, Edward, *The Grand Strategy of the Roman Empire: From the First Century AD to the Third*, Johns Hopkins University Press, 1979.

Maccoby, Hyam, *The Mythmaker: Paul and the Invention of Christianity*, HarperCollins, 1987.

McGiffert, Arthur Cushman, 'The Influence of Christianity upon the Roman Empire', *Harvard Theological Review*, 2/1 (January1909): 28–49.

MacMullen, Ramsay, 'Market-Days in the Roman Empire', *Phoenix*, 24/4 (winter 1970): 333–41.

MacMullen, Ramsay, *Roman Social Relations: 50 BC to AD 284*, Yale University Press, 1974.

MacMullen, Ramsay, 'Romans in Tears', *Classical Philology*, 75 (1980): 254–5.

MacMullen, Ramsay, *Paganism in the Roman Empire*, Yale University Press, 1981, 1983.

MacMullen, Ramsay, *The Enemies of the Roman Order*, Harvard University Press, 1966, 1992.

Macrobius, *The Saturnalia*; available at: <http://www.penelope.uchicago.edu/Thayer/E/Roman/Texts/Macrobius/Saturnalia/home.htm>.

Malandra, William M., 'Zoroastrianism: Historical Review', in *Encyclocpedia Iranica*, 2005; available at: <http://www.iranica.com>.

Mattingly, Harold, 'The Roman "Virtues"', *Harvard Theological Review*, 30/2 (April 1937): 103–17.

Matyszak, Philip, *The Sons of Caesar: Imperial Rome's First Dynasty*, Thames & Hudson, 2006.

Meeks, Wayne A., *The Origins of Christian Morality The First Two Centuries*, Yale University Press, 1995.

Meeks, Wayne A., *The Moral World of the First Christians*, Westminster/John Knox Press, 1999.

Meeks, Wayne A., *The First Urban Christians: The Social World of the Apostle Paul*, Yale University Press, 2003.

Meyers, E., and Strange, J., *Archaeology, the Rabbis, & Early Christianity* Abingdon Press, 1981.

Meyers, E., and Strange, J., Article 'Nazareth', in the *Anchor Bible Dictionary*. Doubleday, 1992.

Millar, Fergus, *The Emperor in the Roman World*, Gerald Duckworth, 1992.

Millar, Fergus, *The Roman Near East: 31 BC–AD 337*, Harvard University Press, 1995.

Millar, Fergus, 'Caravan Cities: The Roman Near East and Long-distance Trade by Land', in *Modus operandi: Essays in Honour of Geoffrey Rickman*, ed. M. Austin, J. Harries and C. Smith, Institute of Classical Studies, 1998.

Miller, Kent D., 'Competitive Strategies of Religious Organizations', *Strategic Management Journal*, 23 (2002): 435–56.

Mommsen, Theodor, *A History of Rome under the Emperors*, ed. Barbara and Alexander Demandt, Routledge, 1996.

Mommsen, Theodor, *The Provinces of the Roman Empire: From Caesar to Diocletian*, vol. 2, trans. W. P. Dickson, 1906, Gorgias Press, 2004.

Nicolaus of Damascus, *Life of Augustus*, trans. Clayton M. Hall, 1923, available at: <http://www.csun.edu/~hcfll004/nicolaus.html>.

Nock, Arthur Darby, *Studies in the Graeco-Roman Beliefs of the Empire*, Society for the Promotion of Hellenic Studies, 1925.

Nock, Arthur Darby, *Essays on Religion and the Ancient World*, Oxford University Press, 1972, 1986.

Nylan, Michael, 'Confucian Piety and Individualism in Han China', *Journal of the American Oriental Society*, 116/1 (January–March 1996): 1–27.

Osgood, Josiah, *Caesar's Legacy: Civil War and the Emergence of the Roman Empire*, Cambridge University Press, 2006.

Overmyer, Daniel L., Keightley, David N., Shaughnessy, Edward L., Cook, Constance A., and Harper, Donald, 'Chinese Religions – The State of the Field – Early Religious Traditions: The Neolithic Period through the Han Dynasty', *Journal of Asian Studies*, 54/1 (February 1995): 124–60.

Ovid, *Fasti, Poems of Exile* © 2004 A.S. Kline, available at: <http://www.tonykline.co.uk/PITBR/Latin/Fastihome.htm>.

The Oxford Classical Dictionary, ed. Simon Hornblower and Antony Spawforth, Oxford University Press, 2003

Oxford History of the Classical World, ed. John Boardman, Jasper Griffin and Oswyn Murray, Oxford University Press, 1986.

Periplus of the Erythraean Sea; available at ancient history sourcebook: <http://www.fordham.edu/halsall/ancient/asbook.html>.

Petronius, *The Satyricon*, trans. J. P. Sullivan, Penguin Classics, 1965.

Phillips, Jacke, 'Punt and Aksum: Egypt and the Horn of Africa', *Journal of African History*, 38 (1997): 423–57.

Philo of Alexandria, *The Legatio ad Gaium*, trans. with commentaries by E. Mary

Smallwood, Leiden, 1961.

Philostratus, *Life of Apollonius of Tyana*, trans. F. C. Conybeare, Loeb Classical Library, 1912; available at: <http://www.livius.org/ap-ark/apollonius/life/va_00.html>.

Pliny the Elder, *Natural History*, trans. John Bostock, available at: <http://www.perseus.tufts.edu/cgibin/ptext?doc=Perseus%3Atext%3A1999.02.0137&query=toc&layout=&loc=35.2>.

Plutarch, *The Life of Augustus*; available at: <http://www.perseus.tufts.edu/cgibin/ptext?doc=Perseus%3Atext%3A1999.03.0078&query=head%3D%235>.

Plutarch, 'The Life of Crassus', *Parallel Lives*, trans. Bernadotte Perrin, Loeb Classical Library, 1916; available at: <http://www.penelope.uchicago.edu/Thayer/E/Roman/Texts/Plutarch/Lives/Crassus*.html>.

Plutarch, 'Precepts of Statecraft', *Moralia*, trans. Harold North Fowler, Loeb Classical Library, 1936; available at: <http://www.penelope.uchicago.edu/Thayer/E/Roman/Texts/Plutarch/Moralia/ Praecepta_gerendae_reipublicae*.html>.

Price, S. R. F., *Rituals and Power: The Roman Imperial Cult in Asia Minor*, Cambridge University Press, 1985.

Purcell, N., 'Livia and the Womanhood of Rome', *Proceedings of the Cambridge Philological Society*, 32 (1986): 78–105.

Raaflaub, Kurt, A., ed., *War and Peace in the Ancient World*, Blackwell, 2007.

Raven, Susan, *Rome in Africa*, Routledge, 1993.

Reinhold, Meyer, *Marcus Agrippa: A Biography*, The W.F. Humphrey Press, 1933.

Rives, James Boykin, 'Imperial Cult and Native Tradition in Roman North Africa', *Classical Journal*, 96 (2000–2001): 425–6.

Roller, Duane W., *The World of Juba II and Kleopatra Selene: Royal Scholarship on Rome's African Frontier*, Routledge, 2003.

Rostovtzeff, Michael Ivanovich, 'The Caravan-Gods of Palmyra', *Journal of Roman Studies*, 22, Part 1: Papers Dedicated to Sir George Macdonald K.C.B. (1932): 107–16.

Rostovtzeff, Michael Ivanovich, 'Hadad and Atargatis at Palmyra', *American Journal of Archaeology*, 37/1 (January–March 1933): 58–63.

Rostovtzeff, Michael Ivanovich, *Dura Europos and its Art*, Clarendon Press, 1938.

Rostovtzeff, Michael Ivanovich, 'The Near East in the Hellenistic and Roman Times',

Dumbarton Oaks Inaugural Lectures, 1940, *Dumbarton Oaks Papers*, Harvard University Press, 1941.

Rostovtzeff, Michael Ivanovich, *The Social and Economic History of the Roman Empire* vol 1, 1926, 2nd edn, revised by P. M. Fraser, Clarendon Press, 1957.

Rostovtzeff, Michael Ivanovich, *Caravan Cities*, Rostovtzeff Press, 1932, 2008.

Runciman, W. G., 'Capitalism without Classes: The Case of Classical Rome', *British Journal of Sociology*, 34/2 (June 1983): 157–81.

Sanders, E. P., *Jesus and Judaism*, SCM Press, 1985.

Sanders, E. P., *Paul: A Very Short Introduction*, Oxford Paperbacks, 1991.

Sanders, E. P., *Judaism: Practice and Belief 63 BCE–66 CE*, Trinity Press International, 1992.

Sanders, E. P., *The Historical Figure of Jesus*, Penguin, 1993, 1995.

Sanders, Jack T., *Charisma, Converts, Competitors: Societal Factors in the Success of Early Christianity*, SCM Press, 2000.

Schafer, Edward H., 'Hunting Parks and Animal Enclosures in Ancient China', *Journal of the Economic and Social History of the Orient* 1968, 11/3 (October 1968): 318–43.

Schama, Simon, *Landscape and Memory*, HarperCollins, 1995.

Scheidel, Walter, 'From the "Great Convergence" to the "First Great Divergence": Roman and Qin-Han State formation and its Aftermath', Princeton/Stanford Working Papers in Classics, Version 2.1, 12-page abstract, Stanford University, 2007.

Scheidel, Walter, 2008, 'State Power and Social Control in Ancient China and Rome', International Conference sponsored by the Chiang Ching-kuo Foundation, Stanford University, March 17–19, 2008.

Scheidel, Walter, 'Slavery in the Roman Economy', Princeton/Stanford Working Papers in Classics, Stanford University, 2010.

Schinz, Alfred, *The Magic Square: Cities in Ancient China*, Axel Menges, 1996.

Schürer, Emil, *The History of the Jewish People in the Age of Jesus Christ (175 BC–AD 135)*, revised and edited by Geza Vermes, Fergus Millar and Martin Goodman, T. & T. Clark, 2000.

Seckel, Dietrich, *The Rise of Portraiture in Chinese Art*, Artibus Asiae, 1993.

Seneca, 'Against Superstitions', in Augustine, *City of God*, VI.10, Wm. B. Eerdmans Publishing Company, 1886; available at University of Virginia Library Electronic Text Center; <http://www.etext.lib.virginia.edu/modeng/modengA.browse.html>.

Seneca, *Moral Epistles*, trans. Richard M. Gummere, Loeb Classical Library, 1917–25; available at: <http://www.stoics.com>.

Shaw, Brent D., 'Bandits in the Roman Empire', *Past and Present*, 105 (1984): 5–52.

Shelton, Jo-Ann, *As the Romans Did*, Oxford University Press, 1988.

Shilappadikaram (The Ankle Bracelet), by Prince Ilangôô Adigal, trans. Alain Daniélou, A New Directions Book, 1965.

Shinnie, P. L., review of *Apedemak, Lion God of Meroe: A Study in Egyptian-Meroitic Syncretism*, by L. V. Zabkar, in *International Journal of African Historical Studies*, 10/3 (1977): 492–4.

Smallwood, Mary E., *The Jews under Roman Rule from Pompey to Diocletian*, vol. 20, *A Study in Political Relations*, Brill, 1976, 2001.

Snowden, F. M., *Blacks in Antiquity: Ethiopians in the Greco-Roman Experience*, Harvard University Press, 1970.

Spawforth, Anthony, ed., *The Court and Court Society in Ancient Monarchies*, Cambridge University Press, 2007.

Stambaugh, John E., *The Ancient Roman City*, Johns Hopkins University Press, 1988.

Stambaugh, John, and Balch, David, *The Social World of the First Christians*, SPCK, 1986.

Stark, Rodney, *The Rise of Christianity: How the Obscure, Marginal Jesus Movement*

Became the Dominant Religious Force in the Western World in a Few Centuries, HarperCollins, 1997.

Stark, Rodney, *Cities of God: The Real Story of How Christianity became an Urban Movement and Cconquered Rome*, HarperSanFrancisco, 2007.

Stark, Rodney, and Bainbridge, William Sims, *A Theory of Religion*, Rutgers University Press, 1987.

Stark, Rodney, and Finke, Roger, *Acts of Faith: Explaining the Human Side of Religion*, University of California Press, 2000.

Strabo, *Geographia*, trans. H. L. Jones, Loeb Classical Library, Harvard University Press, 1917–32; available at: <http://www.penelope.uchicago.edu/Thayer/E/Roman/Texts/Strabo/home.html>.

Suetonius, *The Twelve Caesars*, trans. Robert Graves, revised with an introduction by Michael Grant, Penguin, 1979.

Swanson, Guy, *The Birth of the Gods: The Origin of Primitive Beliefs*, University of Michigan Press, 1960.

Syme, Ronald, *Tacitus*, Clarendon Press, 1963.

Syme, Ronald, *The Roman Revolution*, Oxford University Press, 1939, 2002.

Tacitus, *The Annals of Imperial Rome*, trans. Michael Grant, Penguin, 1956, 1996; available at: <http://www.fordham.edu/halsall/ancient/asbook.html>.

Taylor, Lily Ross, 'The Worship of Augustus in Italy During His Lifetime', *Transactions and Proceedings of the American Philological Association* (1920): 116–33.

Taylor, Lily Ross, *The Divinity of the Roman Emperor*, Oxford University Press, 1931, 1981.

Thapar, Romila, *A History of India*, vol. 1, Penguin, 1966, 1990.

Thomsen, Rudi, *Ambition and Confucianism: A Biography of Wang Mang*, Aarhus University Press, 1988.

Thorley, J., 'The Development of Trade between the Roman Empire and the East under Augustus', *Greece & Rome*, second series, 16/2 (October 1969): 209–23.

Thorley, J., 'The Roman Empire and the Kushans', *Greece & Rome*, second series, 26/2 (October 1979): 181–90.

Turcan, Robert, *The Cults of the Roman Empire*, Wiley-Blackwell, 1996.

van der Sprenkel, Otto B., 'Max Weber on China', *History and Theory*, 3/3 (1964): 348–70.

Velleius Paterculus, Roman history, trans. Frederick W. Shipley, Loeb Classical Library, 1924; available at: <http://penelope.uchicago.edu/Thayer/E/Roman/Texts/Velleius_Paterculus/home.html>.

Vermes, Geza, 'Hanina ben Dosa: A Controversial Galilean Saint from the First Century of the Christian Era', *Journal of Jewish Studies*, 23 (1972): 28–50; 24 (1973): 51–64.

Vermes, Geza, *Jesus the Jew*, SCM Press, 1973, 2001.

Vermes, Geza, *The Changing Faces of Jesus*, Penguin 2001.

Vermes, Geza, *The Nativity: History and Legend*, Penguin, 2006.

Veyne, Paul, ed., trans. Arthur Goldhammer, *A History of Private Life*, vol. 1, *From Pagan Rome to Byzantium*, Belknap Press, 1987.

Veyne, Paul, *Quand notre monde est devenu chrétien (312–394)*, Editions Albin Michel, 2007.

Virgil, *The Aeneid*, trans. Robert Fitzgerald, Everyman's Library, 1992.

Vis and Ramin, trans. from the Persian of Fakhr ud-Din Gurgani by George Morrison, Columbia University Press, 1972.

Walzer, Michael, *On Toleration*, Yale University Press, 1997.

Watt, James C. Y., 'The Arts of Ancient China', *The Metropolitan Museum of Art Bulletin*, 48/1 (summer 1990): 1–72.

Weber, Max, 'The Social Psychology of World Religions', *From Max Weber: Essays in Sociology*, ed. and trans. H. H. Gerth and C. Wright Mills, Oxford University Press, 1946.

Weber, Max, *The Religion of China: Confucianism and Taoism*, trans. Hans H. Gerth, Free Press, 1951, 1968.

Weber, Max, *The Religion of India: The Sociology of Hinduism and Buddhism*, trans. Hans H. Gerth and Don Martindale, Free Press, 1962.

Weber, Max, *The Sociology of Religion*, trans. Ephraim Fischoff, Beacon, 1963.

Wells, Benjamin W., 'Trade and Travel in the Roman Empire', *The Classical Journal* (October 1923): 7–16; (November 1923): 67–78.

Wilken, Robert Louis, *The Christians as the Romans Saw Them*, Yale University Press, 1984.

Williams, Bruce, '*The Kingdom of Kush*, by Laszlo Torok', *Journal of Near Eastern Studies*, 59/4 (October 2000): 306–10.

Williams, Bruce, 'Meroe City, an Ancient African Capital: John Garstang's Excavations in the Sudan', *Journal of Near Eastern Studies*, 60/3 (2001): 197–200.

Wilson, A. N., *Paul: The Mind of the Apostle*, Sinclair-Stevenson, 1997.

Witt, R. E., *Isis in the Ancient World*, Johns Hopkins University Press, 1971, 1997.

Wolpert, Stanley, *A New History of India*, Oxford University Press, 1993, 2008.

Young, Gary K., *Rome's Eastern Trade: International Commerce and Imperial Policy, 31 BC–AD 305*, Routledge, 2001.

Zanker, Paul, *The Power of Images in the Age of Augustus*, University of Michigan Press, 1988, 1990.

Useful Websites

Ancient History Sourcebook, including East Asian History Sourcebook, at: <http://www.fordham.edu/halsall/ancient/asbook.html>.

A great source for Latin texts and English translations is available at: <http://www.penelope.uchicago.edu/Thayer/E/home.html>.

A huge collection of primary and secondary sources for the study of ancient Greece and Rome is available at:

<http://www.perseus.tufts.edu/cgibin/ptext?doc= Perseus%3Atext%3A1999.02.0 137&query=toc&layout=&loc=35.2 ->.

See also: <http://www.sacred-texts.com>.

A very good source for ancient China, with essays and translations of early Chinese histories, including from the *Hanshu*, is available at: <http://www2.iath.virginia.edu/xwomen/intro.html >.

Index